Policy Analysis for Effective Development

Strengthening Transition Economies

Kristin Morse
Raymond J. Struyk

with
Margarita Pinegina
Clare Romanik
Marina Shapiro

LYNNE
RIENNER
PUBLISHERS

BOULDER
LONDON

Published in the United States of America in 2006 by
Lynne Rienner Publishers, Inc.
1800 30th Street, Boulder, Colorado 80301
www.rienner.com

and in the United Kingdom by
Lynne Rienner Publishers, Inc.
3 Henrietta Street, Covent Garden, London WC2E 8LU

Library of Congress Cataloging-in-Publication Data
Morse, Kristin, 1968–
Policy analysis for effective development : strengthening transition economies / by
Kristin Morse, Raymond J. Struyk.
    Includes bibliographical references and index.
    ISBN 1-58826-366-5 (hardcover : alk. paper)
    ISBN 1-58826-391-6 (pbk. : alk. paper)
    1. Europe, Eastern—Economic policy—1989– 2. Former Soviet Republics—
Economic policy. 3. Community development—Europe, Eastern. 4. Community
development—Former Soviet Republics. 5. Policy sciences. I. Struyk, Raymond J.
II. Title. HC244.M625 2005
338.947'009'049—dc22

2005019725

British Cataloguing in Publication Data
A Cataloguing in Publication record for this book
is available from the British Library.

Printed and bound in the United States of America

The paper used in this publication meets the requirements
of the American National Standard for Permanence of
Paper for Printed Library Materials Z39.48-1992.

5   4   3   2   1

Contents

Tables and Figures

Figures

Preface

The responsibilities of governments in transition countries have been utterly transformed over the past decade. The delivery of public services has changed from a responsibility of the central government to one resting with localities. This dramatically alters the responsibilities of both local and federal officials. Government officials increasingly feel the pressure of budget constraints, accountability, and higher public expectations of and needs for public services; they must now develop, implement, and evaluate policies and programs addressing a range of pressing social and economic issues. This book provides professionals and students with the practical skills and information they need to meet today's urban challenges.

Our goal is for this book to be as practical and interactive as possible. Public policy and important current events lend themselves to lively discussion and debate. Although the book includes a certain amount of economic and governmental theory, key concepts are always applied to real world problems. Students, including those who are already accomplished policymakers, should find the topics covered here relevant and useful to careers in public policy or program administration.

The book is intended to equip students "with intellectual tools to aid practitioners in the identification and specification of policy problems and the development of sensible, useful, and politically viable solutions,"[1] all in the context of a basic market-oriented approach to the division of public and private functions. We introduce students to analytical decisionmaking methods and describe how to monitor and evaluate programs. Other topics include key concepts in policymaking, such as considering the distributional aspects of policies (who benefits/pays), developing explicit decisionmaking criteria, balancing political and technical factors, defining public goods and services, and introducing competition into the public sector.

The ultimate objective of the book is critical thinking. Many public officials—throughout the world—tend to operate at what might be termed "the descriptive level." In other words, when discussing a problem, they can describe a situation and outline a proposed policy, often relying heavily on the experience of how they solved similar problems in the past. This approach describes how many people solve problems. However, the demands on policymakers require that they reach a higher "analytic level," where the problem and potential solutions are analyzed in terms of incentives that affect behavior. Hence the task of this book and instructors using it is to constantly challenge students to defend their statements in terms of rigorous analysis of incentives, behavioral relations, and consistency with general principles of good management.

Students of public policy include both traditional university students and professionals. It is our belief that students better integrate new information or skills when given an opportunity to apply them to concrete problems. Best practices in adult education generally emphasize an interactive approach. Those with professional experience are accustomed to expressing their views and can add considerably to a group discussion. Younger students are also more likely to master material in an active environment than when sitting passively in the classroom. Thus, this book is designed to emphasize interaction with students. In addition, the exercises are the most dynamic part of the book, providing students with an opportunity to apply new skills and concepts to practical problems. Many of the exercises offer students a chance to apply concepts to a problem of their own choosing.

The book is based on a public policy course developed by the Urban Institute (Washington, D.C.) and the Institute for Urban Economics (Moscow) to meet the needs of government officials and representatives from nongovernmental organizations (NGOs) in transition countries.[2] Hundreds of professionals and students in Russia, Bosnia, and Kyrgyzstan reported that the course was beneficial to their work, crediting it with helping to "systematize" their approach to public policy issues. Many students offered concrete examples of how our materials had assisted them in developing programs, designing monitoring systems, and facilitating competitive procurement for goods or services. Our purpose here is to make those tools available and useful to a wider audience.

We have prepared a comprehensive Instructor's Manual, available online, that offers ideas for discussion, elaborates on key topics, and provides answers to the exercises. Instructors who would like to access the manual are encouraged to contact Raymond Struyk at rstruyk@ui.urban.org.

* * *

We want to acknowledge the generous support of the US Agency for International Development for the preparation of the original course and the chance to teach it in several countries. Rita Pinegina, Clare Romanik, and Marina Shapiro contributed importantly to the development of the course. Alexander Puzanov provided thoughtful comments in the development of both the course and this book. Marisol Raviz provided valuable comments on one chapter. We are also indebted to the many students who have offered constructive comments over the years. Finally, we thank the Urban Institute for its multifaceted and consistent support for this project. Kathleen Courrier was particularly helpful in guiding us through the publication process.

Why Policy Analysis?

This book aims to improve the quality of public decisionmaking and service delivery. Governments everywhere are under pressure to do better with fewer resources. In transition countries these pressures are even more acute, as they are accompanied by the need to develop the legal and regulatory framework for a market economy, design more efficient ways to conduct the remaining government tasks, and reinvent a social safety net to protect vulnerable citizens from poverty. Added to these overarching tasks is an organizational shift from central planning and management to local government responsibility for the delivery of many public services. Amid these challenges, governments do what they can to maintain current programs, address pressing problems, and implement new initiatives and reforms. Some accomplish this better than others.

This transition is occurring on an uneven playing field. The countries in the region are vastly different in terms of the pace of reform and other attributes. These differences have, in part, affected the countries' reform policies. Table 1.1 groups European transition countries according to their overall transition progress, as assessed by the European Bank for Reconstruction and Development (EBRD).[1] The EBRD defines the main tasks of transition as the following:

- Macroeconomic stabilization.
- Price and trade liberalization.
- Privatization of state assets.
- Institutional reforms to support the development of market finance, to commercialize public infrastructure, and to strengthen public administration.

The literature is divided on whether initial conditions or policy decisions have played a larger role in the shifting economic status of these nations. Influential initial conditions include income, proximity to other markets, natural resources,

Table 1.1   Overall Transition Indicators for European Transition Countries

High Level of Reform	Medium Level of Reform	Low Level of Reform
Croatia	Albania	Azerbaijan
Czech Republic	Armenia	Belarus
Hungary	Bulgaria	Bosnia and Herzegovina
Estonia	FYR Macedonia	Tajikistan
Lithuania	Georgia	Turkmenistan
Latvia	Kazakhstan	Uzbekistan
Poland	Kyrgyzstan	
Slovak Republic	Moldova	
Slovenia	Romania	
	Russia	
	Ukraine	

Source: European Bank for Reconstruction and Development (EBRD), *Transition Impact Retrospective* (London: EBRD, 2001).

industrial concentration, and war. For example, central and southeastern European and Baltic countries benefited from proximity to European markets, market memory, and relatively high incomes (compared to other transition states). Russia benefited from its natural resources, yet struggled with cities concentrated on failing industries and limited public support for reform. Several of the central Asian countries began the transition with weak infrastructure and rampant industrial failure. Bloody conflicts in Armenia, Azerbaijan, Bosnia, Georgia, and Tajikistan absorbed resources, thwarted transition, and blocked economic growth.

A recent World Bank report found that initial conditions explained considerably more of the variation in performance than did policy decisions in the early transition period. These conditions, however, had less of an impact when looked at over the entire decade of transition. Others have found that differences in the pursued policies had a larger impact on outcomes than initial conditions.[2]

East Germany, for example, started the transition with several significant advantages, yet today its feeble growth and rampant unemployment put it in a class with some of the most disadvantaged and least reformed nations in the region.[3] It quickly solved the challenge of developing a legal framework by adopting the laws and government structures of West Germany. It had ample resources to fund private sector investment, generous social protection programs, and other public expenditures through transfers from West Germany. From 1991 to 1997, these transfers amounted to 40 to 60 percent of East Germany's gross domestic product (GDP) and dwarfed Western governments' aid to the entire region. Finally, with German unification, East Germany became an instant member of the European Union (EU), gaining favorable access to European markets years before the central European and Baltic states.

East Germany made a bad turn at the outset, however. Two economic policy choices set a course for disaster. First, in response to political pressures, East German marks were grossly overvalued in the conversion to a single currency, making East Germans quickly—but temporarily—flush. Second, because of a policy to create wage parity between the East and West, East German wages grew unrelated to workers' productivity. This rendered many East German firms unable to compete and workers were knocked out of jobs that might otherwise have been retained as the economy restructured. These policies resulted in high unemployment and obstructed new enterprise growth. This dismal economic scene is somewhat mitigated by massive social protection spending supported by West Germany, which itself suffers from low growth and a rising deficit.

It is easy to imagine the political pressures that contributed to these policy decisions. German policymakers may have also miscalculated that the advantages enjoyed by East Germany at the start of the process would offset some of the economic and political compromises made along the way. After the fact, it is easy to identify poor decisions. But the complexity of these issues makes formulating effective public policy a challenge even for those with the best intentions and training.

Public policy has the potential to dramatically improve people's lives and to achieve multiple social, economic, and political objectives. For example, in fall 1992, Russia needed to quickly relocate and retire about 5,000 military officers stationed in the Baltics. These countries had just won their independence and were less than welcoming toward Russia's continued military presence. At the same time, the officers had served with merit and deserved appropriate housing in Russia. However, Russia suffered from its own housing shortage and hard budget constraints. Waiting lists for newly constructed housing were already many years long—and even a new program to build necessary units for the officers would take years to complete.

The US government stepped in to fund housing for these officers and relieve the tense situation. While the first impulse was to construct new units, a team of US and Russian policymakers developed a different scheme that granted eligible officers and their families vouchers to purchase housing in several Russian cities. Vouchers were set at local market prices and users could contribute their own funds if they wanted larger accommodations or particular amenities. Officers could use the vouchers to purchase new units from the government or private builders or units in the secondary market (existing housing). In addition to relocating the officers in a timely manner to housing that met their needs, the vouchers also served a secondary objective of helping to stimulate private construction and the market for existing housing.

When the program was implemented, Russia's housing market was still in its infancy and it was unclear whether the officers would find enough public or private owners to accept their vouchers. The program proved a success, with 2,700 officers relocated in 1993–1994 using vouchers (the others waited longer, some much longer, for newly constructed units to be completed).[4]

The voucher program is a good example of the creativity involved in policy-making. Because speed was such an important criterion in this case, policymakers were willing to risk a new approach that, if successful, would lead to quicker relocations.

There is a desperate need for creative and effective policymakers. Decentralization from central planning has dramatically expanded the number of policy players in regional and local government. These players, along with NGOs, contribute to defining public problems and pursuing more efficient solutions. Effective policymakers and analysts are those who approach each new problem with critical thinking—that is, they are able to conduct rigorous analyses, generate creative solutions, and bring experience as well as good judgment to decisionmaking. This book encourages critical thinking, teaches effective analytical techniques, and offers practical examples to help readers apply new ideas and skills to real world problems.

Organization of the Book

This book is written for policymakers and students interested in transition countries and development issues. We selected topics based on their immediacy to the policy challenges and political context of transition countries. These topics arise frequently in actual policy development and are those where officials and analysts often lack a solid grounding. The book is in keeping with the basic discipline of policy training as taught in North American universities (see Box 1.1), with a heavy emphasis on international best practices and case studies from the region.[5]

We focus on key policy skills, including analytical decisionmaking and how to monitor and evaluate programs. The book also covers major concepts in policymaking such as the following:

- Considering the distributional aspects of policies (who benefits/pays).
- Developing explicit decisionmaking criteria.
- Balancing political and technical factors.
- Defining public goods and services.
- Improving public services by fostering competition and utilizing the private sector.

Box 1.1 The Study of Public Policy

The field of public policy includes the ideas and actions of government and other players in response to societal problems. A wide variety of actors put problems on the agenda and undertake actions both within and outside government. Furthermore, policy studies address not only laws and regulations, but also how they are implemented and what effect their results have on the population and on the perception of the problem.

The formal study of public policy emerged over the past century as an outgrowth of US political science and an evolution of public management programs. Early in the twentieth century, political science was a discipline focused on how the state and formal government institutions were organized. As early as the 1920s, critics advocated that the discipline expand its study to include the dynamic processes of government actions. It was not until the 1950s, however, that several movements in political science advanced the study of policy. The first such movement to emerge was behavioralism, which sought to establish scientific methods of quantifying the development of laws and predicting or describing political behavior. Another significant movement called for a more multidisciplinary approach to policy studies that would draw from legal studies, economics, sociology, and problem solving, with an emphasis on rational decisionmaking. By the 1960s and 1970s the field further expanded to include more analysis on how groups of citizens and other external factors influence policymaking.[a]

Public administration programs trained public servants to implement and administer government programs. These programs eventually expanded their scope to include public policy, and many universities began to offer public affairs programs. By the 1960s and 1970s, economists and others had developed techniques for analyzing public problems, which prompted more formal policy programs to become popular. Today, public policy is taught in countless universities throughout the world and programs vary from those with a heavy emphasis on public administration to those with a more analytical approach.[b]

Notes: a. The description of the evolution of policy studies from political science is drawn largely from Jessica R. Adolino and Charles H. Blake, *Comparing Public Policies: Issues and Choices in Six Industrialized Countries* (Washington, D.C.: Congressional Quarterly Press, 2002), pp. 10–11.

b. Association of Public Policy Analysis and Management website, http://www.appam.org.

The book draws on examples of policies, social and economic problems, and current practice to make the material practical and engaging.

In each chapter, students have the opportunity to use exercises or assignments to apply the concepts and skills from the text to practical policy problems. For example, after a description of how to conduct policy analysis, there is an exercise on how a city might reduce its traffic congestion problems. Similarly, following the text on using the private sector to improve the delivery of public services, there is an exercise on how to contract out social services on a competitive basis. These and other exercises are based on contemporary economic and social problems and make the study of public policy a lively and relevant process. The exercises are fully described at the end of each chapter, and the opportunity for an exercise is called out at the relevant location in the text. If you are using this book as part of a class, your instructor may assign these exercises as group activities to be completed and presented during the class period.

At the end of many of the chapters is a reference to a supplemental reading that provides additional information or a new viewpoint on a particular topic. These readings ensure that interested students have an opportunity to expand their understanding of a topic in some depth. Many of these readings are available online. Examples of readings include an assessment of social safety net programs in the region, experiences with contracting out for public services in India and Ghana, and an evaluation of administrative reforms in Russia.

Part 1: The Basic Tools. Chapter 2 presents an analytical decisionmaking method that is the cornerstone of public policy teaching.[6] This method, sometimes called the rational model, describes the policy process as a series of steps that range from defining the problem, to weighing policy options against established criteria, to selecting the best alternative. This method encourages policymakers and students to move beyond rote methods of problem solving to using real analytical decisionmaking methods. This chapter introduces some key concepts that are important themes throughout the book. Many of the other chapters present tools, such as stakeholder analysis, data analysis, monitoring and evaluation, and benefit-cost evaluation, that can be used to enrich the basic policy model.

Chapter 3 focuses on understanding the interests and influence of various parties on public policy. In defining a problem, the first step in policy analysis, it is crucial to identify who is affected by it and who stands to gain or lose by implementing a proposed solution. Identifying and taking proper account of incentives to stakeholders is a key determinant of success in policy and program design. This chapter provides instructions for how to conduct an analysis that identifies key stakeholders, quantifies their interests/influence, and maps strategies of how to properly engage them.

Chapter 4 focuses on using data to inform decisionmaking and monitor program performance. Often public managers fail to consult data that would help them to better understand the problems they face or evaluate the impact of public policies and programs. This chapter discusses how to use data, including how to critically examine data in tables, how to organize effective data collection, and how to analyze data using quantitative and qualitative methods.

Part 2: Designing and Implementing Policies and Programs. Chapter 5 discusses how government resources are allocated, using the strategies of targeting and subsidies. Targeting assistance to those most in need has emerged in transition economies as a critical strategy for better meeting public needs and making more efficient use of limited resources. The chapter focuses primarily on strategies to target assistance to poor households. The subsidy and benefits sections present various types of subsidies and different designs for structuring public benefits.

Chapter 6 presents the roles and responsibilities of different levels of government, focusing on the assignment of expenditure responsibility and revenue authority among federal, regional, and local governments. The chapter presents some basic economic theory and provides examples of how various countries have divided these responsibilities.

Chapter 7 describes how competition and the private sector can be used to improve the delivery of public services. Specific strategies for carrying out government functions include direct provision, contracting out, leasing, concessions, and privatization. The chapter outlines conditions under which each approach is most likely to be successful.

Chapter 8 provides a hands-on description of how to design and implement competitions for contracting out public services. Special attention is given to this topic because of the need throughout the region to improve efficiency in service delivery; contracting out is an attractive approach.

Part 3: Monitoring and Evaluating Programs. Monitoring is the routine measurement and reporting of important indicators of program operations and results. Chapter 9 provides the rationale for monitoring public programs and presents examples of monitoring programs as well as instructions for developing a monitoring system.

Performance measurement, discussed in Chapter 10, is a type of monitoring that assesses public programs based on the results gained by the customers or citizens served. Traditional measurements of government programs often track expenditures (inputs) and number of persons served (outputs). Performance measurement focuses outcomes (results) and uses performance indicators that are directly connected to specific government goals. Performance measurement can provide decisionmakers with useful information to improve public services, to improve resource allocation and justify agency budgets, and finally to encourage accountability. Performance management is the practice of using performance measurement to improve service delivery. Basic concepts and techniques are presented and readers have the opportunity to develop performance indicators for specific social and economic programs.

Chapter 11 presents the early history of program evaluation and defines the different types of evaluation discussed in this book. The chapter then describes process evaluations, which assess the extent to which a program has been implemented as intended. Readers learn how to conduct evaluations and participate in an exercise to design their own evaluations.

Chapter 12 introduces students to impact evaluation. This type of evaluation attempts to better understand how much of the program's outcome is due to program activities (program impact) and how much may be the result of other factors. The standard practice of impact evaluations is to contrast the outcomes for an experimental group that receives a service with a control group that does not. This chapter presents basic concepts and examples of impact evaluations.

Chapter 13 reviews the procedures used to identify and place monetary values on costs and benefits of a program. The uses and limitations of benefit-cost evaluation are explained. Also included are descriptions of cost-effectiveness analysis for program benefits when specific monetary values cannot be determined.

Part 4: Preparing Policy Recommendations.   Policy analysts must be able to write clear and well-reasoned policy statements to convey their ideas to policymakers. Chapter 14 outlines strategies for writing effective policy statements. Readers review examples of effective policy briefs and complete exercises and case studies involving drafting policy memoranda on social and economic policy issues.

Appendix: Policy Case Studies.   This section includes the case studies used for policy analysis and writing recommendations. Cases include, for example, proposals to reform inefficient social assistance departments, strategies for combating the spread of AIDS, and the challenge to improve municipal heating systems at reasonable costs. The range of cases allows readers and instructors to select cases based on their interest in the topics or the particular policy skills required for each case.

PART 1

THE BASIC TOOLS

CHAPTER 2

The Policy Analysis Model

Public policy matters because it affects people's lives. There is always a risk that a proposed solution will not solve the problem, or worse, that it may have unintended negative consequences for the population. For example, will imposing hard budget constraints on inefficient state enterprises free resources for the development of private enterprise, or merely result in mass unemployment? What other factors need to be in place for this strategy to work, to minimize economic hardship? What can be done given the current political climate and resources available? The objective of policy analysis is to reduce some of the uncertainty inherent in policymaking.

There are opportunity costs to nearly every public action, and policymakers confront difficult decisions such as whether to fund programs to fight deadly diseases, feed hungry children, or invest in economic development. Few would argue against any of these initiatives, yet limited resources (such as time, money, and capacity) constrain public commitments.

Policymakers must weigh political and technical factors, as the "best" solution in economic terms may not be politically feasible. Certain policy decisions may challenge vested interests, benefiting one group of citizens while costing others. Also, the best solution is rarely the cheapest, and policymakers often have to compromise with a lesser solution that falls within budget constraints.

Finally, the policy environment is often chaotic, with numerous players, competing agendas, and unpredictable time frames. Although issues can brew for a long time, the window of opportunity for a policy intervention can arrive suddenly and important decisions can be made "on the fly." Other policy decisions are drawn out, the result of lengthy negotiations with various stakeholders where specific wording of legislation or an agreement may be debated in detail. Rarely does policymaking follow the classic textbook model. However, the basic model presented below is one that can be quickly applied to an immediate decision or used to carefully research and analyze a long-term concern. It is often referred to as the policymaker's tool-box, and using it can help ensure that important factors are not overlooked, whether you are a new policy analyst completing an assignment or a high-level policymaker evaluating proposals.

The subsequent chapters all build on the basic policy analysis method. For example, data analysis and stakeholder analysis are important aspects of defining a policy problem, benefit-cost evaluation is used to help evaluate policy options, and evaluation techniques are used to assess whether a policy is successful.

The Policy Analysis Method

The policy analysis method is an analytical approach to solving complex societal problems. This systematic method is a quick and effective way to develop rational public policy solutions. There are six basic steps in policy analysis:

1. Verify, define, and detail the problem.
2. Establish evaluation criteria.
3. Identify alternative policies.
4. Evaluate and compare alternative policies.
5. Select the best policy among the alternatives considered.
6. Monitor and evaluate the proposed policy.

Each step is described below and specific examples are given.

• Step 1: Verify, Define, and Detail the Problem

Defining the problem sounds like a simple step, but in practice it requires good research and judgment, and the definition may be revised throughout the policy process as more information comes to light. For example, a city may seek to address its problem with high unemployment. However, after looking into the nature of its unemployment, the city may find that the problem is tied to a national decline in industry, or that it affects mainly older workers or women, or that the city has had less new business development than neighboring towns.

How the problem is defined will influence the policy alternatives considered. A certain level of specificity will likely lead to better results. Returning to the unemployment example above, if the problem were simply identified as high unemployment, a broad array of policy options could be offered as a solution. The danger of this approach is that overly ambitious plans, such as a ten-point plan to end unemployment, often end up as no more than lofty and unfulfilled goals. Alternatively, a broad problem definition can lead to interventions that really do not fit the problem. For example, if manufacturing has declined throughout the country, yet a city decides to subsidize a new factory, it may not garner the same number of new jobs as would investments in growing industries or other strategies.

Collecting good information and determining who is most affected by the problem is key to effectively framing the issue.

Basic Data Collection. Examples of types of information or data needed include:

- Who is affected by this problem?
- Is the problem growing?
- What is currently being done to address the problem?
- Is it working?
- How does the city (or other relevant jurisdiction) compare to others?

Table 2.1 is an example of some basic unemployment data that the city of Scengin might consider in trying to understand recent unemployment trends. What do the data suggest?

- Unemployment is clearly a growing problem in Scengin.
- Unemployment is growing at a greater rate in Scengin than in other similar cities (nearby and similar size shown in the table).

Table 2.1   Unemployment Data for Selected Cities

	Scengin			Pozna			Wroblin		
	1999	2000	2001	1999	2000	2001	1999	2000	2001
Population	420,500	418,200	410,900	527,500	524,900	524,900	735,800	738,600	740,900
Number of unemployed	10,008	11,000	13,140	5,700	5,636	5,934	9,898	6,422	3,897
Unemployment rate (per 1,000)	23.8	26.3	32.0	10.8	10.7	11.3	13.5	8.7	5.3
Percentage change in employment rate (from previous year)	11.8	9.5	17.4	−67.0	−0.6	5.0	−29.9	−54.7	−65.3

Note: City names have been fictionalized.

- Other cities have generally had a decrease in the unemployment rate.
- The population in Scengin is declining.
- Wroblin had such dramatic declines in unemployment that it may not be a good comparison city. There may be factors unique to the city that are driving the change in unemployment.

The data answer many questions, but raise others. What additional information might be helpful?

- Who are the unemployed?
- What is the structure of the city's labor market (i.e., service, manufacturing, public sector, etc.)? How has this changed in recent years?
- How vibrant is the city's private sector? How many small and medium enterprises are there? How many people do they employ?
- What is the city doing to support job creation? Are its tax rates competitive?
- How do these factors compare to other cities? Are there other cities that might be better comparison cities?
- What happened to reduce unemployment in Wroblin? (Employment in Wroblin is dominated by auto manufacturing—the unemployment reduction may indicate the opening of a new plant—something Scengin could not replicate.)

Good sources of information include government statistics, reports from universities, policy organizations, or business associations, recent media coverage, and interviews with experts and others. The data collected do not need to be exhaustive, but should reflect a solid understanding of the issue. (Chapter 4 presents data issues in greater detail.)

As you collect information and work through the policy process, the problem definition can be changed or refined. Keep coming back to this definition and make certain that it reflects the growing understanding of the problem.

Is the "problem" part of a larger problem? What part of the problem is appropriate for your level of government or department to solve? Define the problem based on your department or level of government's sphere of influence and options available. Many social and economic problems are multifaceted and affect a number of different sectors, regions, or groups of people. In defining the problem it is important to identify the part of the problem that could be effectively addressed by your organization or level of government. The more specific you can be in the definition of the problem, the more likely it is that your policy will have a meaningful impact.

Who is concerned about the problem? Most public problems affect a number of persons in a variety of different ways. Rarely are there solutions or resources to satisfy all stakeholders or interested parties. For example, citizens have an interest in cleaner air and water, while industry is likely to oppose efforts to restrict or tax their pollution output. Policymakers need to find a balance that protects citizens yet does not squeeze industry to the point that its net revenues decline, workers are laid off, or factories move to regions or countries with more liberal policies.

Understanding who is affected by the problem or any proposed policy change is a critical part of defining the problem. This is because a problem can have many dimensions that can only be fully understood from the perspective of different stakeholders. Important questions to ask are: Will a proposed solution hurt the vested interests of some group? Will it change the behavior (positively or negatively) of some other group?

Chapter 3 describes how to conduct a stakeholder analysis. This analysis helps to identify the interests and influence of all stakeholders and develop a strategy of how to productively engage the various stakeholders in implementing a proposed solution.

• *Step 2: Establish Evaluation Criteria*

Evaluation criteria help to clarify the program's goals and objectives and are the basis on which the proposed solutions will be judged. Criteria are often established by the major decisionmakers and may be explicit or implicit. For example, the mayor may state that he expects a solution that can be implemented within three months and within a certain budget. In other instances, the criteria may not be defined and the policy analyst may draw from a set of commonly employed criteria. Examples of evaluation criteria are listed in Table 2.2. Select which evaluation criteria are most appropriate for the particular problem and which are most relevant for its major stakeholders. Use them to evaluate the policy options (Step 4).

• *Step 3: Identify Alternative Policies*

Often there is a limited number of truly applicable policy options. However, in developing a short-list of potential solutions, it is worth considering the full range of options. Brainstorming, talking to experts, and consulting other agencies or regions that may have faced similar problems are good ways to generate policy ideas. Different policy options will often tackle different aspects of the problem. (As you work through the policy options it may be worth revisiting the definition of the problem.) Sometimes the final policy will actually be a combination of approaches.

Governments have a number of different ways that they can accomplish their

Table 2.2　Evaluation Criteria

Cost	What is the cost of the program to taxpayers (e.g., the cost of implementing the program in terms of staff, equipment, operating expenses, benefits paid, etc.)?
Net benefit	What is the net benefit from the perspective of the beneficiary? Participants should receive some benefit, but how do these relate to the costs involved? For example, housing developers may be eligible for tax incentives if they allocate a certain number of units to low-income households at reduced rents. For the developer, the net benefit is the tax incentive less the reduced revenue from the low-income units, and indirect costs, such as time spent applying for the tax incentive, documenting household income, and other compliance burdens.
Efficiency	What is the program's efficiency? Is it the least costly way to produce the desired good or service?
Equity	Most social programs redistribute money from taxpayers to the unemployed or poor with the goal of creating more equity. Another important equity consideration is the distribution of benefits among program participants and between program participants and other poor families. For example, a program serving the unemployed may exclude the working poor—who may be as needy and certainly deserving.
Administrative ease	How easily can the solutions be implemented? Will the solution require a new structure, staff, or other resources?
Legal issues	Does the proposed solution require a new law or approval from other departments or levels of government? Does your client or agency have the legal authority to implement the proposed solution?
Political acceptability	Will the proposed solution be acceptable to political leaders or popular among general citizens?
Extent of uncertainty	How much uncertainty is there in implementing the policy (especially if it is a new program)?

goals. The most obvious is to provide particular goods or services. Other interventions use the market to achieve policy goals by providing private sector players with certain incentives, such as subsidizing real estate development to foster the creation of new housing or commercial space. Governments can also use their "police authority," for example, to pass laws to prohibit the sale of drugs or to require the use of safety belts. And governments or community groups can use moral persuasion to achieve objectives, such as mounting campaigns to educate the public about the dangers of smoking or inform the public about an upcoming election.

Table 2.3 presents the basic types of public policy options in a way that highlights the level of intervention and resources required. Some examples help to explain the terms in the table:

- *Direct/monetary.* Direct government action using public funds to provide police force and protection or to purchase utility services from a private contractor.
- *Direct/nonmonetary.* Direct government action that does not require direct budget outlays (though enforcing laws and regulations do have real costs), such as prohibiting driving under the influence of alcohol or requiring licenses for emitting pollutants.
- *Indirect/monetary.* The use of government funds to encourage others to act in a specific manner by, for example, taxing corporate profits or subsidizing hospitals to provide health care.
- *Indirect/nonmonetary.* The use of information to encourage others to act in a specific manner by, for example, informing small business owners about services tailored to their needs, or by using a public relations campaign to encourage citizens not to litter.

Not all problems lend themselves to all of these approaches. For example, a new tax would not be introduced simply to fund an after-school program for youth, nor would it be appropriate to merely implore citizens not to murder one another. However, in addressing a policy problem it is a good exercise to consider these various types of policy actions. Too often policymakers or analysts become accustomed to approaching all problems with the same basic tool—such as always providing new services—at the cost of possibly missing more effective interventions.

Table 2.3   Types of Policy Actions

	Direct	Indirect
Monetary	Provide	Tax
	Purchase	Subsidize
Nonmonetary	Prohibit	Inform
	Require	Implore

Source: Carl V. Patton and David S. Sawicki, *Basic Methods of Policy Analysis and Planning,* 2nd ed. (Englewood Cliffs, N.J.: Prentice Hall, 1993), p. 10.

See Exercise 2.1: Types of Policy Actions on page 32.

This exercise is an opportunity for you to provide your own examples of the different types of policy actions. Your examples can address a single policy problem (such as lack of affordable housing) or a number of unrelated policy areas.

• Step 4: Evaluate and Compare Alternative Policies

After generating as many policy ideas as possible, it is necessary to narrow the options to a few key strategies. It is always good to consider the option of no action. Sometimes the options are likely to be so ineffective, and resources or stakeholder interest so limited, that doing nothing (at least for the time being) is the best option.

Once the main policy options have been selected, the next step is to distinguish among the options based on the evaluation criteria established for this particular policy problem (Step 2). It is also important to note any important constraints. Constraints are generally related to the weighting of the criteria. If budget constraints are very severe, then the program cost will be a critical factor. The involvement of different actors (participants, various parts of the government, NGOs, private firms, interest groups) may also be discussed in the evaluation criteria as either a constraint or an opportunity.

A table or matrix is an effective way to compare the alternative policies. Table 2.4 provides an example of a scenario table. This example is based on an initiative to find jobs for unemployed workers in Perm, Russia. The city leadership of Perm was interested in providing support to those not traditionally receiving assistance and stimulating unemployed members of poor households to find work. Perm initially had a poorly targeted, semiannual poverty benefit available to all low-income families citywide. However, there was no program that encouraged low-income families to find work. The table shows the current status (Policy Option 1) and two alternative interventions considered by the Perm social assistance department: providing enriched benefits for those actively searching for jobs (Policy Option 2) and retraining (Policy Option 3). The table reveals the differences among the approaches and compares their performance on each of the criteria. Note that the options perform differently on many of the criteria. This is true with most policy problems, and rarely does a solution fully satisfy all evaluation criteria. If, for example, cost were the decisive criterion for the Perm decisionmakers, Option 1 or Option 3 would be the leading contender. If the main criterion were efficiency, Option 2 might be the strongest.

Table 2.4   Scenario Table for the Perm Jobs Program

	Policy Option 1	Policy Option 2	Policy Option 3
	Status quo (current poverty benefit).	Provide a benefit targeted to low-income families; require that beneficiaries actively search for employment.	Maintain current poverty benefit; offer retraining for industrial workers who have been laid off.
Attributes	a. This is a cash benefit. b. Program is targeted to families with income below the subsistence minimum. c. This is a targeted flat benefit because the same cash benefit is offered to all eligible beneficiaries.	a. This will be a cash benefit. b. Would serve families with low incomes who also have an able-bodied adult who is interested in seeking employment. c. This will be a modified gap benefit, with poorer families receiving a larger benefit, and beneficiaries able to retain a portion of their earned income.	a. Training will be an in-kind subsidy. b. Would serve families with low incomes who have an able-bodied adult who is interested in participating in retraining. c. This is a targeted flat benefit because the same cash benefit and training will be offered to all eligible beneficiaries.
Evaluation criteria			
Cost	Families receive 215 rubles two times per year. Approximately 26,000 families participate and annual benefit costs are estimated at 11.2 million rubles. Caseloads are high and administrative costs are fairly low. Note: Due to budget shortfalls families do not always receive full benefits and actual expenditures may be lower.	Cost per beneficiary is higher than the current poverty benefit because of higher benefits and greater administration costs. Participants receive an average of 690 rubles per quarter (2,760 per year). Total annual cost of benefits for the 100 participant households is approximately 276,000 rubles (this does not include administrative costs).	Cost per beneficiary is higher than the current poverty benefit because of the cost of providing the training (whether provided by staff or contracted out). The federal employment center provides job search assistance and counseling, and private, for-profit providers offer placement services. There were no other training programs operating in the city. Costs for such programs would vary depending on the intensity of training provided, but it is likely that costs would be less than the jobs pilot (Option 2).

(continues)

Table 2.4 Continued

	Policy Option 1	Policy Option 2	Policy Option 3
Net benefit	Beneficiaries receive a cash benefit of 430 rubles per year with little cost on their part. They must initially apply for the benefit and provide income information.	Beneficiaries can receive a greater cash benefit than with the current poverty benefit, but they also must invest time in applying for the new program and in seeking jobs.	Beneficiaries will receive the same cash benefit as with the current poverty benefit. In addition they receive training. The value of the training (relative to the time invested by the beneficiaries) will depend on its usefulness in obtaining a new job.
Efficiency	Political leadership unhappy that the program does not motivate family members to find work.	Beneficiaries are motivated to find work. (Penalty for noncompliance is termination of benefits and possible loss of other social assistance for up to six months.)	Beneficiaries are not given monetary incentive to find work. However, the training might encourage them in their job search and make them more attractive to employers.
Equity	All program participants receive the same benefit, regardless of the depth of their poverty, their work effort, or family size.	Some poor beneficiaries receive a greater cash benefit. As beneficiaries earn money, their benefit decreases, but they always have greater total income than if they didn't work.	All program participants receive the same cash benefit. Only those selected to participate and who are willing to attend training will benefit from it.
Administrative ease	Household income must be verified to determine eligibility. Calculation of benefit is simple because it is the same for all.	Staff must calculate benefits, which may be different for each beneficiary and which should also change for a particular beneficiary. Staff time is also required to verify that the beneficiaries were actively seeking employment.	For distribution of cash benefit, same as the current poverty benefit. Staff must devote time to developing good training programs (or training can be contracted out to a separate firm) and to monitor participation.

(continues)

Table 2.4 Continued

	Policy Option 1	Policy Option 2	Policy Option 3
Legal issues	None.	Participants who do not comply with program requirements can be sanctioned with the loss of benefits. There is an appeals process that involves the supervisor and, if requested, an independent appeals commission.	None.
Political acceptability	Already in place, so not an issue.	Possibly controversial because it is a new program with different eligibility requirements and certain penalties, and some poor families now receive more cash than others. Participants of the current poverty benefit who are ineligible for this program may complain that their benefit is too small. Political leadership supports the idea.	Unlikely to be controversial.
Extent of uncertainty	Already in place, so not an issue.	Uncertainty because of acceptability by population and participants, and effectiveness in stimulating beneficiaries to find (permanent) work.	Uncertainty because of the effectiveness of the training in preparing beneficiaries for the job market.

Evaluating the alternatives is the real meat of the analysis. After constructing such a table, most analysts write a narrative that describes how the options compare, highlights the most important criteria, and explains any conclusions that might be drawn. This analysis should be well structured and as objective as possible. A policymaker reading such a report should be able to see how each option measures against the relevant criteria. The policymaker may question the analyst on some of the assumptions made in the analysis. For example, costs may assume an unreasonable construction schedule, too high an interest rate, or too few students requiring a service.

A strong analysis incorporates good research, a thorough assessment, and sound judgment. Take the example of Russia's housing crisis for retiring military officers, presented in Chapter 1. The research required determining:

- Number of officers affected.
- Cost of constructing new housing.
- Time required to construct new housing.
- Location and other specific housing needs of the officers should new construction be undertaken.
- Availability of existing housing.
- Cost of purchasing existing housing.

Assessment would outline the following factors:

- Approximately 5,000 officers and their families needed to relocate.
- The cost of each publicly produced unit of housing would be approximately $25,000.
- New construction would require nearly five years to complete, from initial planning to occupancy.
- Officers would return to their home towns throughout Russia, but housing would be built only at selected sites throughout the country. (Vouchers could facilitate greater geographic choice.)
- The availability and costs of existing housing were generally unknown—though limited data suggested that existing housing could be had for less than $25,000 per unit in most urban areas.

Finally, judgment:

- Speed was the primary criterion and argued against new construction.
- Vouchers to purchase existing housing had the potential to speed relocation, meet the location and other specific housing needs of the officers, and reduce housing costs.

- The availability of existing housing was an uncertainty. This uncertainty was worth the risk, because vouchers could be tested relatively easily and at a low cost (vouchers could be issued to a limited number of officers for a limited amount of time and if housing were not secured there would be no direct costs). New construction would remain an option and would be only slightly delayed by pursuing vouchers.
- Vouchers would serve the secondary goal of stimulating the housing market for existing housing.

There is no single approach for evaluating policy options. Some analyses may require a more thorough assessment of benefits and costs or may involve equity issues where there are no easy answers. The style and focus of the analysis should be tailored to fit the problem and any demands articulated by the decisionmakers. Several of the subsequent chapters provide additional tools to help evaluate policy options, including stakeholder analysis, data analysis, benefit-cost evaluation, and preparing policy recommendations.

At the end of this chapter is an example of a policy analysis developed for the US housing allowance program. It provides another variation on how to evaluate policy options.

• Step 5: Select the Best Policy Among the Alternatives Considered

This is the time for a reality check. Although a certain option may look good on paper, it may not be feasible given the present constraints (such as limited time, budget, political will, etc.). Keep in mind that a technically superior alternative may not be a politically viable one.

Policy recommendations must be justified. A strong analysis (Step 4) will likely point toward a particular policy recommendation, but it is important that a policy recommendation be accompanied by a clear justification. The justification can be a conclusion of sorts. See Box 2.1 for a policy recommendation and justification based on the Perm Jobs example used in the scenario table in Step 4.

Analysts often encounter the problem that no option is clearly superior on all criteria. How to proceed? Sometimes the negative points are quite minor and therefore a superior option can be identified. Where options are more competitive, it may be tempting to assign greater weight to some criteria than to others and thereby have the basis for declaring one option as comprehensively superior. Generally, however, it is not the analyst's task to assign weights to the criteria. Rather, this is the policymaker's job. After an analyst has worked for a particular policymaker for some time, he or she will know how the policymaker generally weights different criteria. But even then the best practice is still to provide full information in the first policy memo. After a discussion, it can be

---

Box 2.1   Perm Unemployment and Poverty Problem

Recommendation

Option 2. Provide a more generous income support benefit to low-income families with an adult member who will actively seek employment.

Justification

The city is interested in assisting low-income persons with children to obtain employment. Current programs provide no assistance to help such families find employment, and the necessarily low-benefit levels leave families barely able to meet their basic needs.

Programs that help poor persons look for work have a successful track record. Job search assistance combined with the motiva-tion instilled by higher benefits and frequent monitoring of search effort should lead to increased job search activities and, ultimately, employment. Families who do not comply with the work rules will lose their benefits, so there is little risk of the program being abused by those who are not actually motivated to seek work. This option was selected over the option of retraining because retraining pro-grams do not have the same successful track record.

The program will require a substantial budget outlay. It is recommended that the project be tested with a small pilot and then expanded if it results in real employment gains and reductions in poverty.

---

amended on the basis of the weights explicitly or implicitly assigned to different factors.

• *Step 6: Monitor and Evaluate the Implemented Policy*

Policy implementation is a dynamic process where ideas are put into action. Many good policies have been foiled by weak implementation, just as good implementation has further developed and tested policy notions. Policymakers must avoid the temptation of considering a problem solved once they have selected a policy and then move on to the next, exciting issue. Monitoring the implementation of a policy and evaluating its impact are critical to affecting pos-itive social change.

Chapters 9 and 10 describe monitoring and evaluation in greater detail, but a few major points are worth mentioning here. The objective of monitoring is to determine what is and is not working. Policymakers or program managers should develop a plan for regular monitoring, as well as formal evaluation at critical junc-tures. Monitoring is an ongoing process that is an important part of basic program management. Some policies or programs may establish strict monitoring require-ments that describe what data are to be reported and how frequently. Most monitor-ing data can be collected by staff as they perform their regular functions and reported to supervisors and other stakeholders on a periodic basis. Programs with poor results may be required to develop improvement plans or risk losing a portion of their funding or even being discontinued.

Requesting feedback from program participants is very important. Most of the data collected by staff members will be *quantitative* in nature (how many beneficiaries, benefit levels, family size and composition, etc.). While these data are very useful, they do not tell whether the participants are satisfied with how the program is being implemented. Such *qualitative* data can be collected from anonymous comments, focus groups, and surveys of the participant population.

Evaluations are generally conducted when monitoring reveals a problem or some other program change motivates a closer look into the operations or results of a policy/program.

Example of Policy Analysis

The following example is a policy analysis that was requested by the Millennium Housing Commission, a commission established by the US Congress to recommend improvements in national housing policy. The commission contracted for studies on options for making improvements. The analysis in this example addresses the housing allowance program.

Abt Associates, a private policy research organization, completed the analysis on the issue of whether to change the housing quality standards in the national housing allowance program. Because the analysis was written for individuals familiar with the program, several notes have been added here in brackets to provide background on the program and related issues. In addition, the original did not label all of the sections of the report (problem, background, criteria, analysis, etc.), so these labels have been added to make the organization of the document more clear. The example does not follow the policy analysis steps in the same order as does this book; the basic ingredients, however, are all here.

• *Problem Statement*

[Should the commission recommend the continuation of housing quality standards?[1] Note that additional information about the problem is included in the Background and other sections. In your own policy analyses you may wish to include more information here.]

• *Background*

[The housing allowance program in the United States provides eligible low-income families with vouchers that they can use to rent apartments. This is a federal program, and the rules and regulations are the same in every jurisdiction. However, the program is administered by local government agencies. Only renter households are eligible to participate. The housing allowances are called vouchers. The program has a Housing Quality Standard, which requires that as a condition of receiving the subsidy payment the family must live in a dwelling unit that meets certain minimum quality standards. To enforce this provision, the local agency inspects each unit proposed by a family as the unit it will live in with the assistance of the housing allowance payment.]

The current Housing Quality Standards (HQS) promulgated by HUD [US Department of Housing and Urban Development] for tenant-based programs developed out of lessons learned from experiments conducted under the Experimental Housing Allowance Program (EHAP) of the 1970s. The Housing Allowance Demand Experiment examined how housing quality standards affect household participation in the program. The experiment concluded that more stringent standards lower household participation in the program by reducing the number of landlords willing to participate. The experiment also found, however, that many units did not meet the standards for health and safety developed by a national public health group. This is not surprising given the range of local and state housing and inspection codes that exist nationally and their uneven enforcement. The experiment also found that housing subsidies helped to preserve and upgrade the supply of existing housing by stimulating repairs and continuing maintenance of units that were minimally substandard. More recently, researchers have found that the overall physical adequacy of units for households with housing allowances is higher than for comparable unassisted households.

- *Criteria*

  - Maintain landlord participation (do not add to time or cost of program participation).
  - Do not make housing even less affordable or accessible to voucher holders (by raising costs of HQS).
  - Protect housing quality.

Since at least the early 1990s, affordability rather than housing quality has been recognized as the dominant housing problem in the United States. HUD's 2000 report on "Worst Case Housing Needs" found that severe rent burden was the only housing problem for over three quarters of very low income families [families with incomes under 50 percent of the median income in the metropolitan area] with severe housing needs. As a result, attention has shifted from the role of HQS in improving housing quality to how to make housing more affordable and accessible to low-income families. There is a perception that the quality standards and inspection process may act as a disincentive to landlord participation in the voucher program, particularly in low-vacancy markets where voucher holders are in strong competition with unassisted renters for particular units. For example, the National Association of Realtors (NAR) has identified the length of time that it takes for PHAs [public housing agencies—the local agencies administering the program] to inspect a unit while the unit is vacant as a major disincentive to landlord participation in the program.[2]

• Analysis

The 1994 HUD-sponsored study of voucher success rates provides some evidence that landlord unwillingness to have an inspection may contribute to low per-unit success rates among voucher holders looking for units to lease. Landlords agreed to an inspection for only 37 percent of the units that voucher holders said they wanted to rent. However, where inspections were completed, the voucher holder was successful in leasing the unit in 89 percent of the cases, even though 48 percent of the units required some repairs. This suggests that once a unit is inspected, it is highly likely that the lease will be approved, even though many units require repairs.

A new study of voucher success rates recently completed for HUD provides support for this finding. Among voucher holders who were successful in leasing units, 68 percent of the units passed the initial HQS inspection. However, 28 percent of the units required multiple inspections before the unit passed HQS. For successful voucher holders who leased their unit after one inspection, the initial inspections were completed within an average of two weeks, and only one week passed on average between the inspection and the effective date of the lease. These results suggest that among a significant portion of voucher holders, landlords have a strong enough incentive to participate in the program to make repairs to their units, if they agree to have an inspection. The 2001 study does not provide information on how many voucher holders were unsuccessful in leasing because the landlord did not agree to the initial inspection. In HUD's 1995 Property Owners and Managers Survey, owners who reported that they would not accept tenants who wanted to use their housing allowance to pay rents most often cited three reasons: problems with tenants, too many regulations, and too much paperwork. However, further analysis of these data would be needed to identify which aspects of the paperwork and regulations were most problematic.

Thus, recent studies of voucher success rates do not offer overwhelming evidence that HQS discourage landlords from participating in the program over and above other factors such as negative attitudes toward voucher holders and program restrictions on rent levels. At a recent HUD training conference for housing allowance administrators, however, it was apparent that many administrators believe that HUD's lead-based paint standards [standards not permitting the presence of lead-based paint in units rented by families with small children because of fear of the children ingesting paint chips], included as part of HQS, will discourage landlords from participating in the program and/or provide them with an excuse not to serve voucher families.[3]

• Options

A. Continue to require all units in the voucher program to pass every element of the HQS before subsidy payments can begin. Use the current HQS, including the lead-based paint requirements.
B. Maintain the current HQS, but weaken the clearance requirement of the current lead-based paint legislation for the tenant-based program.
C. Make the application of HQS more flexible in order to attract additional owners to the program, while continuing to apply the current lead-based paint standard for units occupied by families with children under six years of age. Options for greater local flexibility include:
  • Require tenants to inspect units for critical health and safety violations and to certify that the housing unit is free of such violations before housing allowance payments begin. Inspect the units within the first month of occupancy to enforce HQS.
  • Qualify multifamily rental properties on the basis of inspection of a sample of units.
  • Allow PHAs to sign agreements with landlords quickly as part of efforts to expand the range of owners and neighborhoods participating in the program, with inspections within the first month of occupancy to enforce HQS.
D. Eliminate the HQS requirement.

• Recommended Option: C

Early studies of the housing allowance program found enforcement of local housing codes to be uneven, other than for new construction and alterations or in response to community complaints. Moreover, housing codes, where they exist, do not always include lead standards, and these may be only sporadically enforced. The current HQS provide a national floor for the quality of housing acceptable for tenant-based housing subsidies. HUD allows PHAs to upgrade the HQS, but they may not approve housing that fails to meet the HQS minimum

See Exercise 2.2: Policy Analysis on page 33.

This exercise provides an opportunity to apply the six-step policy analysis method to a contemporary policy problem.

standards. The argument for maintaining HQS in the tenant-based program begins with the premise that housing quality is an important goal of the program, even if it compromises the goal of housing affordability. Further, the federal government has responsibility for ensuring that subsidized units minimize the health hazards to children from lead dust and lead-based paint in the home. Current research does not allow us to quantify fully the possible negative effect of HQS enforcement on owner participation in the program and success rates among voucher holders. We also do not know whether particular elements of the HQS discourage owner participation or whether the problem, where it exists, is the delay in beginning rental income associated with the timing of the inspection. Sufficient anecdotal evidence exists, however, to warrant experimenting with streamlining the HQS process and other ways to encourage landlord participation in tight housing markets.

Chapter Summary

Policy analysis is a rational decisionmaking approach to social and economic problems. The policy analysis method is a flexible process that helps policymakers and analysts work through complicated issues. The process can be conducted formally and result in a well-researched policy brief, or can be used as a mental checklist when evaluating policies or making quick decisions. The basic policy analysis consists of six steps:

> *Step 1: Verify, define, and detail the problem.* What data are needed to define the problem? Are additional data needed? Does this problem fit into a larger problem? What part(s) of the problem can your level of government address? Consider stakeholder interests and influence: Who is affected by the problem? Who can influence the success of an intervention? Who will be opposed to an intervention and what resources do they have to support their opposition?
>
> *Step 2: Establish evaluation criteria.* Which of the following evaluation criteria are applicable and how should they be weighted (according to their relevance to influential and/or important stakeholders)?

Efficiency	Equity (distribution)
Cost	Extent of uncertainty
Political acceptability	Administrative ease
Net benefit	Legal issues

Step 3: Identify alternative policies. Which types of policy actions (direct/indirect or monetary/nonmonetary) will you consider?

Provide	Prohibit
Purchase	Require
Tax	Inform
Subsidize	Implore

Step 4: Evaluate and compare the alternative policies. Select the most promising policy options (one of the options can be the no-action scenario). Evaluate and compare the options based on the criteria. A scenario table can be used to compare the attributes of the proposed policies and evaluate each according to the established criteria.

Write an objective analysis that compares the strengths and weaknesses of the options (much of this information can be taken from a scenario table). This analysis should be a concise and well-structured narrative that outlines the arguments for and against each of the selected options.

Step 5: Select the best policy among the alternatives considered. Select the main policy or policies that you are recommending and provide a justification. The justification can be a short summary of the problem and why your solution best meets the criteria.

Step 6: Monitor and evaluate the implemented policy. In the policy development stage it is important to describe how the policy will be monitored and evaluated. What are the basic reporting requirements and procedures? What information needs to be collected on a regular basis?

Recommended Reading

Gail Vittori, John Ruston, Virginia Jones Smith, and Sally Lewis. *Reducing Houston's Solid Waste: A Plan for the City's Environment and Economy.* Austin, Tex.: Environmental Defense Fund, November 1993.

This reading is a policy analysis written by an environmental organization. It recommends that Houston, Texas, diversify its solid waste program to include recycling. The city has already set modest recycling goals, and the report makes the case that as much as half of the city's solid waste could be recycled.

The report describes the costs of the current waste disposal programs and the costs and benefits of waste reduction and recycling (benefits: conserving scarce natural resources, avoiding damages created by landfilling and incineration, and economic development). The costs of implementing a recycling collection program are significant and outlined in Section II of the report. Recycling requires the establishment of material recovery facilities to sort and prepare the materials for sale and reuse. Section IV describes these facilities and their development and operating costs, and outlines options for public and private models of facility ownership and operation. The report compares the various public and private options, clearly stating the advantages and disadvantages of each option. The report concludes with the recommendation that Houston initiate the project and contract with private firms to construct and operate the facilities.

Exercise 2.1: Types of Policy Actions

In the table below, provide additional examples of each type of policy action. Your examples can be for a number of different sectors, as in the examples below, or for a particular policy issue, such as small business development.

	Direct	**Indirect**
Monetary	**Provide** police force and protection	**Tax** charge fee for use of market space
	Purchase communal services from a private contractor	**Subsidize** health care
Nonmonetary	**Prohibit** driving under the influence of alcohol	**Inform** about services for small business owners
	Require licenses for architects	**Implore** citizens not to litter

Exercise 2.2: Policy Analysis

Complete a policy analysis for each of the policy problems described below. The first problem deals with the poor quality of school lunches and the second addresses traffic congestion problems in a medium-sized city. Each of these cases describes the problem and lists the important criteria. Students are expected to generate ideas for policy options, evaluate the options based on the criteria, and recommend and justify a policy intervention.

The chapter summary provides a review of how to conduct a policy analysis. It outlines each of the steps and highlights the key questions that you will need to answer. There is a blank scenario table following the exercise that can be used to help organize your analysis.

Your final product should be a completed scenario table and a two- to three-page policy memorandum.

- *1. Arzamas School Lunch Program*

The Perceived Policy Problem.   The city of Arzamas, Russia, is interested in providing affordable, quality lunches to students attending municipal schools. Currently all children receive free meals provided by the city. However, due to limited resources, low-quality school meals often result, sometimes as little as a cup of tea. Parents and school administrators are dissatisfied with the current lunch program.

The mayor has asked you to present alternatives to the current program. You are asked to provide new strategies that will not require additional expenditures. Key objectives (criteria) to keep in mind are as follows:

- Poor children must be able to afford lunch.
- Quality of lunches must improve.

Additional Information

- Approximately 14,000 students are enrolled in municipal schools.
- Nearly half of the students are from families with incomes below the poverty level.
- The cost per meal is 4 rubles. Free lunch for all students costs the city approximately 1.2 million rubles per month, although this amount is not always available and contributes to the low quality of the meals.

- *2. Policy Problem: Traffic Congestion in Riboch*

Background.   The city of Riboch in the Czech Republic, population 400,000, suffers from severe traffic congestion in its core downtown area—a region consisting of about fifty square blocks. This zone is the economic heart of the city, where the city and regional administrations are located, along with numerous banks, insurance companies, and other white-collar employers. Additionally, this zone houses the main shopping opportunities in the region.

Traffic congestion has been building for the past five to six years, as more families have been able to afford to purchase a car and nothing has been done to increase the capacity of downtown streets. Actually, capacity has fallen thanks to the combination of motorists illegally parking their cars on the street in what should be traffic lanes, and the lax enforcement of parking violations by the militia. There are no parking lots in the city center and the only place to park cars is on the streets.

The congestion affects not only automobile occupants but also the passengers of the city's bus and trolley systems. The low quality of bus and trolley service—infrequent service, overcrowding, and unreliable schedules—has pushed a significant number of former patrons into using automobiles, particularly for their journeys to work.

Trolley and bus services have deteriorated over the past several years, because of the huge losses the companies experience due to low fare collection, the high number of riders who have privileges, and the unwillingness of the previous mayor to press the city legislature for fare increases. ("Privileges" is the term used in many transition countries for in-kind subsidies provided to certain populations or occupation groups—for example, the elderly, the disabled, or police officers. In this case, the privilege is the right to use public transportation free of charge.) There has been no fare increase since summer 1997, so in constant Czech crowns, fares today are only a fraction of what they were in 1997.

The new mayor was elected six weeks ago mainly on his promise to do something to reduce the congestion problem and to improve public transportation. In his campaign he was able to be vague about what he intended to do. But now he is rushing to develop a set of recommendations to place before the people and city legislature while he still has the momentum of his victory. The mayor, understanding the city's financial problems, has ruled out any significant increases in spending on transportation services.

Criteria. The policy recommendations at a minimum should contain at least one initiative to address congestion and one to improve public transportation and make a case as to how they complement each other. Other criteria for judging the recommended program:

- It meets all of the mayor's constraints (especially cost).
- It is likely to have a significant impact on congestion. For example, improved enforcement of parking regulations is unlikely to dramatically reduce congestion, because of problems with the local militia and because the number of cars on city streets would not diminish significantly.
- It addresses administrative feasibility and indicates how to overcome any challenges associated with the recommended actions.

Scenario Table		
	Policy Option 1	**Policy Option 2**	**Policy Option 3**
Attributes			
Evaluation Criteria			
Cost			
Net Benefit			

Scenario Table			
	Policy Option 1	**Policy Option 2**	**Policy Option 3**
Equity			
Administrative ease			
Legal issues			
Political acceptability			
Extent of uncertainty			

Stakeholder Analysis

When the city of Moscow decided to improve the quality of housing maintenance by contracting with private firms, the tenants took to the streets, fearing that their apartments were being sold out from under them. The city agencies responsible for basic maintenance and repair were inefficient public monopolies complacent to provide generally poor services at relatively high costs. The city's plan to use competition from the private sector to improve the quality of services and, potentially, reduce costs, threatened the entrenched interests of the public maintenance agencies.

In response to the threat, the maintenance agencies mounted a public misinformation campaign, whipping tenants into a frenzy that they would soon be living in the streets, their homes sold to wealthy foreigners. Tenants protested to the city district government that had agreed to the experiment and the project—to improve the living conditions of tenants and demonstrate how competition could benefit public service delivery—was soon in jeopardy.

The district staff and a team of policy advisers developed the project. And although the project was well designed in terms of its objectives and plans for introducing competition and structuring some of the first public-private contracts in the country, it failed to adequately account for stakeholder interests and influence.

The threat to existing maintenance agencies could certainly have been predicted. These agencies stood to lose a good deal of money and perhaps even their very existence. But how could their opposition have been better planned for? A stakeholder analysis is a method of identifying the interests and influence of the various groups affected, modifying the project to meet the groups' needs (if possible or desirable), and planning strategies of how to engage or placate the various groups. If a stakeholder analysis had been completed for the housing maintenance project, its implementation may have been smoother. The housing maintenance agencies would still be threatened—that was actually an important part of the reform—but some of their weapons may have been taken away. Tenants could have been informed of the initiative and easily enlisted to support, rather than oppose, the project.

This chapter describes how to conduct a stakeholder analysis. Understanding the impact on stakeholders is an essential part of policy analysis, critical to defining the problem and weighing the proposed solutions. A stakeholder analysis can be an ongoing and participatory process or it can be an assessment conducted by a single party, such as an analyst or planner of a ministry or organization. A stakeholder analysis as a participatory strategy is designed to solicit ideas and feedback from the various stakeholders. It is conducted with the belief that participants will help to design better policy and that their participation will contribute to successful implementation. Interactions with the main stakeholder groups are planned to take place throughout the project design and implementation. Although final decisionmaking and responsibility generally remain with the lead agency, this type of participation strategy requires a commitment to certain level of openness and process.

Alternatively, a stakeholder analysis can be an exercise undertaken by an analyst or other party to understand and plan for the interests of various stakeholders. This analysis can be based on previous knowledge of the stakeholders or can involve formal or informal contacts with stakeholder groups. In this type of stakeholder analysis the process or participation are not inherently as important as the insights that the analysis brings to policy planning or evaluation. Examples of both types of stakeholder analyses are presented at the end of the chapter.

The basic steps of a stakeholder analysis include:[1]

Step 1: Identify key stakeholders.
Step 2: Assess stakeholder interests and the potential impact of the project on these interests.
Step 3: Assess stakeholder influence and importance.
Step 4: Outline a stakeholder participation strategy.

- *Step 1: Identify Key Stakeholders*

  - Who are potential beneficiaries?
  - Who might be adversely impacted?
  - Have vulnerable groups been identified?
  - Have supporters and opponents been identified?
  - What are the relationships among the stakeholders?

A stakeholder analysis is a critical part of policy analysis and is often used to help define the problem. Stakeholder analysis can also be used to plan for program implementation. It is a way of identifying who is affected by the problem or the proposed solution and understanding their interests. By identifying likely supporters or critics of a policy, policymakers can make better decisions and try to mitigate opposition. This is the political part of policy analysis.

Who will be affected (positively and negatively)?

- Potential beneficiaries
- Former beneficiaries of a previous program (could be adversely impacted if no longer eligible)
- Staff members implementing the program (could be adversely affected if their responsibilities increase without additional resources)
- Vulnerable groups (some could be left out)

This first stage requires identifying the various parties affected by the problem and noting whether they stand to gain or lose.

Who can influence the program?

- Politicians
- Nonelected government officials (such as agency directors)
- Interest groups, including NGOs

Among these, who supports or opposes the program? Among the various stakeholders are those with the power to influence the outcome of the policy or program. Government officials often hold the authority to approve new policies, determine funding levels, and make other key decisions. Donor agencies, interest groups, business associations, and others may also wield significant influence. For example, the International Monetary Fund (IMF) is able to alter national policies as a condition for financial assistance.

Who needs to be involved in program implementation?

- Staff members of the implementing agency
- Coordinating agencies
- NGOs for outreach and/or implementation
- Private sector (may compete to receive contracts for implementation)
- Clients, who have to be sufficiently convinced of the merits of a program to participate

Do these groups work well together and respect each other or do competing interests prevent cooperation? The stakeholders involved in implementation are not always powerful in the sense of having political or business influence. Rather they are the staff members or participants who are responsible for the day-to-day implementation. Without their cooperation the policy cannot be successfully implemented.

- *Step 2: Assess Stakeholder Interests and the
Potential Impact of the Project on These Interests*

  - What are the stakeholders' expectations of the program?
  - What benefits or costs are there likely to be for the stakeholders?
  - What resources might the stakeholders be able and willing to mobilize?
  - What stakeholder interests conflict with project goals?

Expectations. Expectations may vary based on information available and on how the individual or group defines the problem. For example: closing a mine. Is the problem the loss of jobs for individuals or the loss of economic production and tax revenues for the city? A policy proposal to extend unemployment benefits to former miners would, at least in the short term, meet the needs of the displaced workers—but do nothing to replace the lost jobs and only minimally restore city tax revenues.

Benefits/costs. In the first step, stakeholders are identified and classified according to whether they will be positively or negatively affected. The second step takes the analysis further by describing the specific ways that stakeholders may gain or lose. For example, the city education department may save money from consolidating some of its neighborhood child care centers. However, for parents who would then have to travel farther to bring their children to the centers, the costs would include lost time and possibly higher transportation expenses. Or, using the Moscow housing example from the beginning of this chapter, the city government stood to save money and improve housing maintenance, the private sector to benefit from new business, but the public maintenance agencies were clearly going to lose revenue and turf.

Resources. Stakeholders can bring a variety of resources to bear upon the issue. Some of the resources from various stakeholders include:

Government

- Personnel with expertise in implementing similar programs
- Computer networks, office space, other necessary equipment
- Ability to lobby internally

NGOs

- Access to potential beneficiaries
- Ability to deliver services
- Access to the media

Private Sector

- Ability to deliver services
- Political influence

These players can apply their resources either in support or opposition of a particular policy or program.

Conflict. Some conflict among stakeholders may be inevitable, as a new program or policy is likely to change how things are done or grant new benefits to a particular group. But policymakers can mitigate or at least predict conflict by considering the interests of different groups.

- *Step 3: Assess Stakeholder Influence and Importance*
  - Political, social, and economic power and status
  - Degree of organization
  - Control of strategic resources
  - Informal influence
  - Power relations with other stakeholders
  - Importance to the success of the project

Influence refers to the power that stakeholders have over a project being accepted. Some stakeholders have direct decisionmaking power over a project, whereas others lack formal authority but may have access to leaders or the ability to shape public opinion or otherwise influence policy outcomes.
  Examples of individuals/groups who may be able to influence the program:

- Politicians—controlling political and financial power.
- Nonelected government officials—including directors of the agency in charge of the program and directors of other agencies that might need to support the program either formally or informally. These persons have decisionmaking power, control of strategic resources, and informal influence.
- Interest groups—representing business groups, certain segments of the population, or people concerned with particular issues. These groups wield social power, voting blocs, and informal influence.

Importance relates to the degree to which the achievement of project objectives depends on the active involvement of a given stakeholder group. Who is important for successful program implementation? For example, agency intake workers usually cannot formulate and institute a new policy, but they can sabotage its implementation if they disagree with the policy. They do not have influence over program design, but they are important to the success of the project. Other important players are the persons whom the project seeks to benefit. When staff, participants, community groups, or other groups have the ability to affect program outcomes, policymakers need to develop strategies to foster their involvement. Often something as simple as sharing information can go a long way toward winning the support of important, though not necessarily powerful, stakeholders.

Both influence and importance of stakeholders should be assessed. The process up to this point yields information critical to policy development—that is, to assessing alternative solutions to a problem. The remaining steps are action-oriented and seek to ensure the acceptability of a selected policy alternative. Step 4 involves developing different strategies for involving the various stakeholders.

• Step 4: Outline a Stakeholder Participation Strategy

The stakeholder participation strategy should be outlined according to the following:

- Interests, importance, and influence of each stakeholder group
- Particular efforts needed to involve important stakeholders who lack influence
- Appropriate forms of participation

Government administrations and organizations have varying levels of openness toward the involvement of other parties. In some administrations, a narrow group of policymakers makes decisions and outlines the implementation specifications. This top-down structure generally allows only limited roles for other stakeholders. Other administrations are more open to broader participation. The stakeholder strategy should generally align with the basic culture or decisionmaking process of the implementing organization. However, if the problem or policy is likely to spark controversy, some organizations may need to alter their practices to respond to the needs and interests of key stakeholders.

Following are some general strategies or best practices of how to involve stakeholders.

Stakeholders of high influence and high importance. Should be closely involved during all stages. These are the major decisionmakers and they or their designees will likely lead the project.

Stakeholders of high influence and low importance (e.g., politicians not directly involved). Should be kept informed and their views acknowledged. These persons will generally not be involved with the actual planning and implementation—but should be consulted or informed of most major decisions.

Stakeholders of low influence and high importance (e.g., agency staff, participants). Should not be overlooked. They should be engaged to make sure their needs are met and their participation is meaningful. Staff or clients can be provided with information and opportunities to offer feedback.

Examples of Stakeholder Analysis

The following examples present two very different types of stakeholder analyses. The first is a stakeholder analysis that was conducted in the planning stages of a watershed development project in India. Stakeholder participation is a central part of this project and beneficiaries, NGOs, and others will be consulted during the planning, implementation, and monitoring phases of the project. The second stakeholder analysis was written by the director of an emergency food program to question how international emergency food aid is allocated. It questions the motives and actions of various stakeholders and charges that emergency food aid does not necessarily go to those most in need. The second example is an analysis of the politics affecting public policy rather than a participatory analysis.

The two examples present very different styles of stakeholder analysis and different ways that stakeholder analyses can be used to develop programs or to evaluate current policies and advocate for new approaches.

• 1. Karnataka Watershed Development Project

Background. The government of Karnataka, a large state in southern India, is proposing a watershed development project with the goal of alleviating poverty in rural areas, and involving local communities in increasing agricultural productivity.[2] The region suffers from poor land management practices that contribute to deteriorating soil fertility, declining crop yield, depletion of water resources, deforestation, destruction of natural pastures, and other problems. The project includes five districts that encompass roughly 1,400 small villages. The districts were selected based on percentage of poverty, small and marginal farmers, and rain-fed arable land.

Stakeholder Analysis and Participation Strategy. According to the government's proposal, participation of local communities is an essential component of the project. In its environmental and social assessment, the government has identified several watershed programs that failed or had poor results due to the lack of local involvement and highlights several programs for which such involvement was integral to appropriate project design, effective implementation and operation of local water facilities, and other improvements. Specifically, the project will include participatory watershed treatment, agricultural improvements, income-generating activities, and strengthening local institutions.

Table 3.1 identifies roles for all participants in the planning, coordination, and physical/financial monitoring. The state retains sole responsibility for making policy and, with a district committee, is the final arbiter of the success of the project. Plan approval rests with the state, districts, and watershed committees. The clear logic behind these decisions is to limit the number of policymakers, to establish clear accountability, and to ensure some consistency (and perhaps timeliness) of key decisions. Social mobilization and implementation are shifted downward and the districts and villages are responsible for those activities. Beneficiary committees and NGOs are given opportunities to participate actively throughout the process but are not decisionmakers.

As part of the stakeholder analysis, district residents were also asked to rank what they perceived as the most important environmental issues in their area. Fifteen percent of the population in a sample of 63 villages were interviewed and contributed to this preliminary assessment. (Proposal authors stated that all 1,400 villages would be polled when the project got under way.) Table 3.2 presents the range of residents' concerns (1 = major problem, 10 = no problem) about problem areas, from specific land use issues, to the quality of health and education services, to the level of community participation. The table reflects a significant range in priorities for each district—suggesting that to respond to residents' needs the project may need to vary its approach, activities, or expectations for each district.

Conclusion. Tables 3.1 and 3.2 provide a basic sense of the priorities of local communities and the proposed roles of stakeholders in the watershed project. The proposal outlines an ambitious participation strategy—one that it describes as essential to the program's success. Such a strategy may be pragmatic or may be based on a commitment to the notion of local participation. The costs associated with this type of process include outreach, staff time, field visits, meetings, and conferences; local participants may also incur costs such as transportation, lost work time, child care needs, and more.

Table 3.1 Proposed Roles of Stakeholders for the Karnataka Watershed Development Project

Level	Stake-holder	Policy-making	Plan Preparation				Plan Implementation			Monitoring/Evaluation		
			Social Mobili-zation Facilitator	Technical Advice	Planning	Approval	Facili-tators	Coordi-nation	Imple-mentation	Physical/Financial	Process	Success
State	Project Advisory Committee	X		X	X	X	X	X		X	X	X
District	Zilla Panchayat Standing Committee				X	X	X	X		X	X	X
	District Watershed Development Office		X	X	X	X	X	X	X	X	X	
Watershed	Micro Watershed Development Committee		X	X	X	X	X	X	X	X	X	
Village	Village Watershed Development Committee		X	X	X		X	X	X	X		
	Beneficiary Committees		X	X	X		X	X	X	X		
	NGOs		X	X	X		X	X	X	X		

Source: Tata Energy Research Institute, "Report on Regional Environmental Assessment and Social Assessment," Bangalore, India, March 2001, p. xxi.

Table 3.2   Residents' Ranking of Problems

Problem	Tumkur	Kolar	Chitradurga	Haveri	Dharwad
Land use					
Depleting groundwater	3	6	1	5	5
Soil erosion	1	8	3	1	2
Reduction in soil productivity	5	3	3	4	3
Reduction in vegetative cover	2	1	5	2	1
Lack of pastureland	3	4	2	5	5
Mono-cropping	7	7	5	4	5
Scarcity of fodder	6	5	7	3	7
Scarcity of fuel	8	2	7	3	3
Basic amenities					
Lack of roads	2	7	6	6	6
Drinking water problem	2	6	1	4	3
Lack of health facilities	1	2	3	3	2
Lack of education	2	1	4	1	1
Lack of market facilities	5	3	6	2	3
Electricity problem	4	4	2	7	6
Lack of financial institutions	6	4	5	5	7
Community concerns					
Management of tanks	1	2	1	2	1
Misuse of forestland	3	3	2	1	2
Encroachment of community land	2	1	3	3	3
Institutional arrangement					
Lack of interest in village development activities	5	3	3	4	4
Lack of unity	3	2	3	3	3
Lack of unity among users	3	4		1	1
Community participation levels	2	5	2	2	2
Low representation of women	1	1	1	5	5
Environmental issues					
Lack of drainage	2	1	3	1	1
Misuse of water bodies (ponds, kalyani, etc.)	4	2	1	2	2
Contamination at water sources	3		4	3	3
Solid waste management/improper disposal of garbage	1	3	2	4	4

Source: Tata Energy Research Institute, "Report on Regional Environmental Assessment and Social Assessment," Bangalore, India, March 2001," p. 6.2.
Note: Rating scale: 1 = major problem, 10 = marginal or no problem.

- *2. Emergency Food Aid in Southern Africa*

Background. The author of the stakeholder analysis is the head of operations for the Food Aid Program of Médecins sans Frontières (MSF), an international humanitarian aid program.[3] The author argues that international organizations often define famine as the result of natural disasters, such as drought or HIV, rather than recognizing that political situations are often the trigger. The result, she argues, is that too often aid does not go to where it is most needed. The author makes her case by describing the international response to famines in Angola and southern Africa in 2002. It is important to note that the author, or her organization, is a stakeholder and that this analysis may reflect a certain perspective.[4]

Angola. The war in Angola was Africa's longest and most brutal civil war. The end of nearly forty years of conflict in April 2002 allowed international aid organizations to safely expand their assistance to the long-suffering Angolans. MSF reported that as much as 15 percent of the population suffered from severe acute malnutrition, the most serious type of hunger, and that 30 to 35 percent of the population suffered from acute global malnutrition. Mortality rates were far above emergency thresholds and MSF quickly expanded its efforts throughout much of the country and assisted an estimated 1.5 million.

Angola's political leaders declared their support for the new peace with a demobilization and food aid program. The government and international aid organizations targeted assistance to rebel fighter camps and served 85,000 former fighters and 300,000 of their relatives. Thousands of Angolans not associated with the fighters were left without desperately needed food relief.

The World Food Programme (WFP), the UN's major hunger program, did not call for emergency operations; rather it expanded its ongoing operations. These efforts fed an additional 200,000 or more people during the summer and fall, yet the US Agency for International Development (USAID) identified approximately 800,000 people as needing assistance. Other emergency relief agencies (with the exception of MSF) did nothing.

The WFP collected $86 million for efforts in Angola (from April 2002 to March 2003). International assistance may have been dampened by the belief that Angola's oil resources would be redirected from funding the war to supporting its people. Although Angola is rich in natural resources, the humanitarian crisis is expected to last for years.

Southern Africa. The World Food Programme did issue an emergency appeal on behalf of southern Africa in July 2002. This $507 million initiative aimed to provide food assistance to more than 10 million people in Malawi, Zambia,

Zimbabwe, Mozambique, Swaziland, and Lesotho. According to MSF, need in Zimbabwe was indeed acute; however, in Malawi and Zambia, MSF reported no increase in need.

Predictions of famine led to a generous international response and the World Food Programme raised $362.7 million for southern Africa. The early warning system used by the WFP is based on meteorological and agricultural factors. Agricultural data are provided by the country governments and can be manipulated to increase aid. The author provides an example of a 20 percent reduction in official crop estimates in Malawi in a three-week period, during which time the agricultural ministry could not have completed the necessary studies. This information was used by international agencies to allocate food aid.

Stakeholder Analysis

National governments. National governments that are finding it difficult to obtain economic aid have an incentive to use emergency aid to generate quick resources for their countries. National policies have enormous impacts on the ability of nations to minimize poverty and ensure food for the population. The author points to Zimbabwe's recent agricultural policy changes that have devastated that country and Malawi's sale of strategic grain reserves as evidence of national governments whose priorities run counter to the well-being of their citizens.

Donor governments. Donor governments have a number of interests and may be more generous when strategic as well as humanitarian issues are at stake. Aid to countries surrounding Zimbabwe may help to stabilize that troubled region and the political situation may have contributed to the generosity of some nations.

International organizations. International NGOs and UN agencies depend on governments and other donors to support their operations. The declaration of a famine can help to galvanize their funding base and strengthen those organizations.

Conclusion. The author advocates that emergency needs should be independently evaluated from evidence collected in the field and that aid be allocated according to the greatest need. From a humanitarian standpoint this is probably the correct position. However, as the analysis makes clear, the particular interests of major stakeholders mean that a purely humanitarian allocation of aid is extremely unlikely. Political interests will remain important to donor governments. However, more accurate information, more input from those working in the field, and changes to the early warning system would enable donor governments and international agencies to make better decisions and limit the ability of national governments to manipulate aid formulas.

This stakeholder analysis was written by a stakeholder to advocate a change in

See Exercise 3.1: Stakeholder Analysis on page 50.

This exercise involves completing a stakeholder analysis for a proposed educational reform. The task involves identifying stakeholders, rating their influence and importance, and developing an engagement strategy.

policy. Her group is clearly an important player in emergency relief efforts, but one that is struggling to have a greater influence on policy decisions. This analysis, posted on an international development website, is itself an advocacy tool.

Chapter Summary

A stakeholder analysis is a process of identifying who is affected by a problem, assessing their interests, influence and importance, and developing appropriate strategies to involve stakeholders. A stakeholder analysis is an important part of policy analysis, as described in Chapter 2. It is also employed in program planning and implementation.

The basic steps of a stakeholder analysis include:

Step 1: Identify key stakeholders.
Step 2: Assess stakeholder interests and the potential impact of the project on these interests.
Step 3: Assess stakeholder influence and importance.
Step 4: Outline a stakeholder participation strategy.

A stakeholder analysis can be conducted as a onetime analytical exercise to inform policy decisions or as part of a participation strategy that spans project development, implementation, and evaluation. The issue, the goals, and the culture of the decisionmakers will likely govern the approach to stakeholders.

Recommended Reading

Jennifer Rietbergen-McCracken and Deepa Narayan, "Case Study: Ukraine Coal Pilot Project." In Jennifer Rietbergen-McCracken and Deepa Narayan, *Participation and Social Assessment: Tools and Techniques.* Washington, D.C.: International Bank for Reconstruction and Development/World Bank, 1998, pp. 108–110.

Chapter 3 draws heavily from the presentation of stakeholder analysis in this report. The report also contains several case studies that are good examples of stakeholder interests. For instance, one case study describes a stakeholder analysis conducted in anticipation of mine closures in Ukraine. The analysis concluded that the social costs of mine closures would be much greater than originally anticipated, with as much as 80 percent of redundant workers unable to find new employment for as long as two years. The workers at greatest risk were low-skilled women heads of household working in ancillary services. Only skilled mine workers were expected to find work in other mines.

This case study describes time and other constraints that limited the scope of the stakeholder analysis and the powerful interests of the Ukrainian government and the World Bank to move ahead with the mine closures as soon as possible. This description of the context makes this case study a good example of a real world application of stakeholder analysis. Unfortunately, the study does not describe what assistance was eventually offered to the displaced workers.

Exercise 3.1: Stakeholder Analysis

Complete a stakeholder analysis based on the case described below. You are an analyst working for the governor and he has asked you to recommend strategies for ensuring that his education proposal is adopted and successfully implemented. The governor has the authority to issue an executive order. However, he would like to win support from the regional legislature.

Background.   The regional government is considering changing its education funding to a formula that allocates aid to cities on a per capita basis. The current financing system is based on a number of factors, including need, local tax base, population, and political factors. Critics have charged that the current system is not transparent and that favoritism and other political concerns exacerbate inequality. Moreover, there are significant fluctuations in funding from year to year, so that many education departments have difficulty planning and meeting their financial commitments.

The governor and regional budget authorities are strongly in favor of the proposed change. The governor was recently elected on a platform of ending corruption and improving transparency and efficiency in the public sector.

The regional education department is opposed to the plan because it will constrain its ability to allocate funds as it sees fit. Department officials argue that the per capita formula will disregard high needs—such as cities with high poverty, those in the northern area that have higher expenses, and cities with short-term emergency needs. They also say that the current system allows them to reward cities that are pursuing reforms that improve academic achievement and school facilities.

Regional legislators and cities are divided on the proposal. Cities that receive a disproportionate share of resources are obviously threatened by the proposed changes. Some cities have experienced recent declines in population and are concerned that this policy will be an excuse to reduce the already low education budget. Many poor cities do not actually receive the added funds that their need status may suggest; however, several poor cities, encouraged by the education department, are advocating for continuing the system that includes need as a factor.

The opinions of school personnel and parents generally align with the positions taken by their cities and the local media.

In the table below, imagine and describe the interests, influence, and importance of each group based on the case description.

Part I: Identification of Stakeholder Groups and Their Interests, Importance, and Influence

Stakeholder Groups	Interest(s) at Stake in Relation to Program	Effect of Project on Interest(s)	Degree of Influence of Stakeholder over Project	Importance of Stakeholder for Success of Project
+ (positive)		U = unknown 0 (neutral) – (negative)	U = unknown 1 = little/no importance 2 = some importance 3 = moderate importance 4 = very important 5 = critical player	1 = little/no influence 2 = some influence 3 = moderate influence 4 = significant influence 5 = very influential

Source: For all tables in this exercise, Jennifer Rietbergen-McCracken and Deepa Narayan, *Participation and Assessment: Tools and Techniques* (Washington, D.C.: World Bank, 1998). Permission to reprint granted by the Copyright Clearance Center.

Using the stakeholder information generated in the first part of the exercise, map their interests in the table below. This part of the exercise does not provide new information but is a helpful and visual way to prioritize the interests/influence of stakeholders.

Part II: Mapping Key Stakeholders' Relative Influence and Importance

Influence of Stakeholder	Importance of Activity to Stakeholder					
	Unknown	Little/No Importance	Some Importance	Moderate Importance	Much Importance	Critical Player
Unknown						
Little/no influence						
Some influence						
Moderate influence						
Significant influence						
Very influential						

In the table below, using either of the previous two tables as a basis, outline ideas about how and when to engage the various stakeholders. Insert specific participation strategies for key stakeholders (such as an information campaign for the general public, meetings with poor cities, etc.).

Part III: Formulation of Stakeholder Participation Strategy

Stage in Project Process	Type of Participation			
	Information Sharing (one-way flow)	Consultation (two-way flow)	Collaboration (increasing control over decisionmaking)	Empowerment (transfer of control over decisions and resources)
Project proposal/ identification				
Project development				
Implementation, supervision, monitoring				
Evaluation				

CHAPTER 4

Data Collection and Analysis

Policymakers must be well informed in order to make effective decisions and to monitor policy implementation. Policymakers collect data in a number of ways: informal conversations with colleagues, experts, beneficiaries, or other affected persons; official government statistics and reports; policy memoranda from institutes or universities; and information from the media and other sources. Data may reflect the numbers of people affected by a problem, the results of recent government interventions, the resources used by those interventions, and changes in these indicators over time or jurisdictions.

This chapter describes how data can be used to help understand social and economic problems. It provides an overview of different types of data and reviews basic data analysis and presentation techniques.

Bringing data to bear on an issue is a critical part of the policy analysis process. Data is collected to define and understand the problem, and data analysis techniques are frequently used to evaluate and compare policy options.

Reading Data for Meaning

The first major problem with data presented in tables is that too many managers fail to even look at them. Collecting the right data can illuminate what a program has or has not accomplished, the costs of services provided, or how one city compares to another. For routine policymaking and monitoring, most data are presented and analyzed in a very straightforward way, requiring no special knowledge of statistics. Benefiting from data requires taking the time to read simple data tables and draw conclusions about how the figures can be used to inform policy or strengthen program performance.

Below, Tables 4.1 and 4.2 provide two cases that challenge the reader to carefully assess the contents of a table. The first is an example of how data are used to plan programs and develop policy; the second illustrates how data are used to improve existing programs.

• Using Data for Program Planning and Policy Development

An important part of developing effective programs and policies is defining the problem and conducting a needs assessment. This includes gathering basic facts about the problem, such as the number of residents affected, whether the problem is increasing or decreasing, how the city compares to others, the characteristics of the problem or persons affected, an inventory of programs/policies addressing the problem, and interviews with local experts or other cities with successful interventions.

Table 4.1 provides data on the poverty rates of various types of households in Russia. If the national government were interested in developing a new program to aid households living in extreme poverty, what are the facts it needs to know? Study the entries in the table for a few minutes and write down a couple of conclusions. Compare yours with the findings listed below the table. (You can find the table entry supporting each conclusion using the superscript letters in the body of the table.)

Table 4.1   Distribution of Poverty by Household and Age

	12/94[d]	10/95[d]	10/96[d]	11/98[d]	10/00[d]
Household-level poverty					
Under 50% of poverty line	6.9	11.5	20.0	16.6	9.9
50– < 100% of poverty line	10.3	18.0	16.3	22.4	18.9
Total under poverty line	17.2	29.5	36.3	39.0	28.8[a]
Children aged 0–6					
Under 50% of poverty line[b,c]	12	16.1	23.7	25.7	14.6
50– < 100% of poverty line[b]	13.3	22.1	20.8	29.8	24.9
Total under poverty line[b]	26.3	38.2	44.5	55.5	39.5
Persons of pension age					
Under 50% of poverty line	2.4	6.7	19.0	9.5	3.1[e]
50– < 100% of poverty line	6.5	14.4	11.6	16.0	12.0
Total under poverty line	8.9	21.1	30.6	25.5	15.1

Source: Tomas A. Mroz, Laura Henderson, and Barry M. Popkin, "Monitoring Economic Conditions in the Russian Federation: The Russia Longitudinal Monitoring Survey, 1992–2000," report submitted to the US Agency for International Development (Chapel Hill: Carolina Population Center, University of North Carolina at Chapel Hill, March 2001), p. 17.

Findings

a. Nearly 30 percent of all households are poor (2000).
b. Young children are the largest segment of the poor. This is true for all years.
c. Young children are the largest segment of the very poor.
d. For all groups, poverty increased from 1994 to 1998—and then decreased in 2000. In 2000, poverty was still higher than in 1994 but the downward trend is promising.
e. Pensioners make up an extremely small percentage of the very poor (3.1 percent in 2000).

These data can be used to address specific questions related to program design. Two examples follow.

How have poverty rates changed over the years and what factors could explain these changes? Possible explanation: Poverty rates increased during the 1990s as the Soviet economy collapsed, social protections deteriorated, and households struggled through the transition. The particularly high poverty rates in 1998 can probably be attributed to the financial crisis, when the country defaulted on its international debt. The decline of poverty in 2000 could reflect improvements in the overall economy. More recent data would be helpful to understand whether poverty has continued to decline.

If the program's architects were interested in serving only the poorest of the poor, how should they define the target population? The program should target its assistance to all households with incomes under 50 percent of the poverty line—or to families with young children living under 50 percent of the poverty line, because they represent most of the very poor. Table 4.1 does not provide the actual number of households in each category, which policymakers would need in order to assess the cost of a program, set allowance rates, and determine how narrowly they may need to define eligibility if cost is an issue. Pensioners are often thought of as being very poor, and it is surprising to see that they actually account for a small segment of the very poor population.

• Using Monitoring Data to Improve Programs

Table 4.2 uses data to track program performance. It is a short annual report that describes the main program activities and accomplishments for a child placement and adoption program. What does this table say about this program? Where might services be breaking down and how could the program be improved?

Table 4.2   Placement and Adoption Services for
Abused Children and Orphans, Annual Report 2003

The goal of the program is to secure permanent homes for orphans and children whose parents have forfeited their parental rights. In 2003 the program sought homes for 100 children, many of whom had special needs and the majority of whom were over the age of six. The program solicits and attracts potential adoptive families, assesses the interests and capacity of the interested families, and matches families with children who need homes. The program also assists with trial visits, preparing legal documents, and conducting follow-up visits.

Number of families screened for adoption	45
Number of families accepted	40
Number of families matched with a child	17
(includes assessment, psychological screening, and short-term visits with child)	
Number of placements	12
Number of permanent placements	9
(permanent legal adoption with six-month follow-up visit)	

Findings

- The program accepts nearly all the families it screens.
- Less than half the families accepted are matched with a child.
- It seems that a reasonable number of matches result in placements (12 out of 17).
- The vast majority of placements become permanent placements.

Possible Conclusions

- At the current placement rate, most children served by the agency will wait years before being placed with a family.
- The high percentage of interested families accepted into the program and then the small number of matches suggests that the program may need to improve its screening practices. It may be that the program needs to better assess whether the families are interested and able to care for children with special needs. It may also be that the program simply is not attracting enough families and needs to increase its outreach efforts so that it has a larger pool to select from. Given the special needs of many of the agency's children, maybe its outreach efforts need to be better targeted toward the families it seeks (e.g., teachers, medical workers, churches, and other

groups may have members who are more sympathetic and capable of caring for these children than would the general population).

- The attrition from match to placement to permanent placement seems reasonable—though administrators may want to compare this to the previous year or to other similar programs.

Table 4.2 is a good example of how data can be used to inform program changes. The data show that the agency had more children than prospective families for adoption and that many families were not successfully matched with children. The director of the agency can conclude that he or she needs to attract additional families or seek alternative placements for children.

Data Collection

Collecting data can be time-consuming and costly. So it is important that data collection efforts focus on gathering the information needed to understand the problem or assess the impact of a program. Collecting data can become an activity unto itself and policymakers or program managers need to keep the collection effort limited to gathering data that inform action. Too much data can be distracting, or worse, can lead to the data being completely ignored.

• *Identify Existing Data Sources*

Before organizing original data collection, it is sensible to identify existing data sources and the usefulness of these data for the purposes of analysis. The most obvious and probably the most useful existing data sources are administrative records. Most government and private agencies maintain information about the persons they serve, services provided, resources consumed, and less often, results attained.

• *Identify Additional Data Needs and Their Sources*

The next step is to identify other necessary data that are not part of the program's administrative records or other existing data sources. Collecting new data is a big

See Exercise 4.1: Drawing Conclusions from Data on page 78.

This exercise asks you to answer questions based on a table of data provided. It provides practice in reading data and drawing conclusions.

job, so the analyst should propose new data collection only for answering questions that are essential to running or assessing the program.

Potential sources for additional data include:

- Program staff and staff of other programs, agencies, or organizations whose mission or operations are related to the program.
- Program beneficiaries (when programs have specific beneficiaries). Besides actual participants, it may be useful to contact those who interact with them. For example, parents and teachers (if participants are children) or employers (if participants are adults).
- Universities or think tanks, which often produce reports or articles on current topics. Some institutions will be more objective than others.
- The general public (when programs do not have specific beneficiaries). An example is a neighborhood improvement program or a public education and awareness campaign. This can be focused based on geography (such as neighborhood or community residents) or demographic groups (such as teenagers, parents, pensioners, single mothers, or homeless families).

• Determine Methods for Obtaining New Data

Data are classified into two major types, quantitative or qualitative. *Quantitative* data are numerical and lend themselves to statistical analysis or simple arithmetic. Data on costs, prevalence, and persons served are examples of quantitative data. *Qualitative* data are often in narrative form and are useful in understanding why a program is not performing as expected, or collecting the opinions of stakeholders. Examples of these types of data follow.

Quantitative Methods
- A questionnaire self-administered by beneficiaries can provide information on their satisfaction with the program
- Administrative records of the number of services provided or resources spent
- A formal survey of beneficiaries

Qualitative Methods
- Case studies that provide in-depth information about selective cases
- Focus groups with beneficiaries, staff, and other stakeholders
- Interviews with staff members and others

Sampling. It is often not feasible to collect data for an entire population, and analysts frequently use samples. While questionnaires or surveys generally employ either random sampling or try to cover all beneficiaries, qualitative methods typically employ purposeful sampling. For example, for a random sample, an evaluator may select one out of every ten case files, following a random start within the first ten cases. For a purposeful sample, an evaluator performing case studies may select cases based on their record of excellent or poor performance. Or an evaluator will attempt to interview particularly knowledgeable staff members who are able to supplement or clarify the data found in the administrative records.

Administrative Records. Administrative records, including service and client records, financial records, and other basic program information, are a primary source for good data. Administrative records are discussed in Chapter 9.

Surveys and Questionnaires. Because the annex to Chapter 10 includes additional information on surveys and there are many useful publications and websites that provide instructions on how to prepare effective questionnaires or survey instruments, we will not delve too deeply into that topic here. A few basic tips: Focus questions on factors that will be useful in understanding and improving program services. Each question should pass the test that it may contribute toward taking some specific action step; this may include information on client attributes, such as age and household composition, needed to interpret more direct program information. Other basic considerations are that questions be clearly worded and not lead respondents toward a particular answer. It is always a good idea to pretest a survey instrument before administering it to the study population, by asking a sample of staff and clients to fill out the questionnaire.

Focus Groups. Focus groups bring together a group of people to solicit their opinions on a particular topic. The facilitator of the group should come to the meeting with a set of prepared questions. Several of the questions should be general enough that participants have an opportunity to raise their own concerns. Other questions should seek specific feedback on the main research questions. Separate focus groups should be planned for each major stakeholder group, so that, for example, staff are free to speak without their supervisors in the room, or parents can speak without the school principal present.

Factors to consider in determining which data collection methods to use include:

- Cost.
- Amount of training required for data collectors.
- Completion time.
- Expected response rate.
- (Perceived) objectivity.

For example, in selecting an interviewing method, self-administered question-naires can be relatively low-cost and generally do not require training. However, if you need to ask complex questions or if you are trying to interview former program beneficiaries, it may be helpful to have a professional administer the survey. Likewise, using a professional facilitator for a focus group can help participants understand complex issues.

Although focus groups can be organized relatively quickly and inexpensively and provide almost instant results, the focus group facilitator must also be well trained to elicit discussion from the group and yet not impose his or her opinions on the groups.

Perceived objectivity is also included as a factor. Usually, quantitative methods are perceived as more objective, because they often include a larger sample than used in qualitative research. The analysis of quantitative data is numerical and can be easily checked by another analyst, whereas the analysis of qualitative data can be a subjective process.

Qualitative data are analyzed using a technique called content analysis. A primary activity in content analysis is coding and categorizing the data after collection. Although the data collection process is directed, the responses are generally open-ended and thus the answers cannot be precoded. For example, the analyst may compile a representative sample of comments from participants on a particular topic, or group comments into categories, such as "very positive," "positive," "somewhat positive," "negative," "very negative," and "other." Another strategy is to highlight comments that may not be representative but that seem particularly insightful or help to answer key research questions.

Typical Problems with Data

Policymakers and managers can make better decisions, direct staff, monitor programs, and manage resources more efficiently if they understand how to work with data. An essential first step is to assess the quality of the data. There are a number of typical problems associated with data.

• Missing or Incomplete Data

When data are missing or incomplete, it is best to go back to the original source to fill in the gaps. When data cannot be retrieved, in some cases it is possible to fill in a best estimate. (It should be indicated that filler data are estimates and not reported data.) When a best estimate cannot be made for missing data, exclude these cases in tabulations regarding the missing data. (In the notes to tables presenting the data or analysis based on it, state how many cases were excluded for this reason.)

- *Data Available Only in an Overly Aggregated Form*

For example, there is only a record of how many beneficiaries were served per month, but the records do not indicate how many of the beneficiaries were new to the program. If possible it is best to go back to the original data source and to re-create the data with the groupings that you need.

- *Unknown, Different, or Changing Definitions of Data Elements*

This can happen when data are collected from different sources or at different times. Sometimes a solution is to compare percentage changes instead of absolute values. For example, different districts of a city define crimes slightly different. Instead of comparing number of crimes across city districts, a solution is to look at the percentage change over time in each district and compare these.

- *Data That Are Linked Across Time and Clients*

When data are collected from different sources or at different times, sometimes it is not clear if Ivan Ivanov from Dataset X is the same as Ivan Ivanov from Dataset Y. One person can seem like two people if his or her name is spelled differently. Two people can seem like one person if they have identical names. Therefore, it is often useful to look at two identifiers (such as birth date and name) to ensure that data are appropriately matched.

Data Checks for Reasonableness

Several simple tests can be performed to check the broad accuracy of data.

- *Outliers*

In "eyeballing" the data, some numbers may "jump out" because they don't fit a pattern. These are called outliers. An outlier may or may not be a valid value. If it is a valid value, there is usually a good explanation why it is so different from the other data.

- *Range Checks*

Assign ranges of possible values to see if any of the data fall outside those ranges. For example, an entry of 110 for a person's age would be outside the expected range.

• *Missing Data*

Missing data is different from the valid responses of "0," "none," "not applicable," or "don't know." Expect to see these different responses and make sure that you can distinguish the difference. The coding of each of these types of responses should be unique and explained in a data dictionary (list of data terms and definitions).

• *Logic Checks*

Perform logic checks on the data to make sure that there is consistency across data elements. For example, if the beneficiary says he or she has no children, there should be no information in later fields about the children's ages. Another example of performing a logic check is comparing the trends over time. Finally, when the data includes a total (e.g., total household income) and various elements that should sum to this total (such as income of each household member), make sure these match. This is called computing *control totals*.

• *Confusion over Definitions*

It is also important to be alert to questions that might have two possible responses, depending on the person's interpretation of the question. For example, a beneficiary's age could be noted as his or her birth date instead of age (or vice versa). Clearly one should try to avoid questions that can yield ambiguous results.

Practical Data Analysis

This section describes different types of data and useful methods for analyzing data, including measures of central tendency, distribution, and variation.

• *Types of Data*

Ratio/Numerical Data. These are called ratio data because you can form quotients and perform other mathematical operations on them. Put simply, these are

---

See Exercise 4.2: Checking Data for Reasonableness on page 81.

This exercise presents a table of housing data with several common errors. The task is to find the errors.

true numbers. Another name for this type of data is numerical data. For example, the number of families participating in a program or the amount of benefits awarded per month.

Nominal Data. This means that qualitative data have been coded into numbers, but the numbers have no meaning in themselves. The numbers merely serve as a convenient abbreviation of information. For example, 1 = married, 2 = single, 3 = divorced, 4 = widowed.

Ordinal Data. In this case, qualitative data have been coded into numbers and the numbers do have meaning, but cannot be used for calculations. For example, 1 = very pleased with efficiency/politeness of intake worker, 2 = satisfied, 3 = somewhat unsatisfied, 4 = very unsatisfied.

• *Data Methods*

The most useful methods for summarizing data, along with practical examples, are presented below.

- Central tendency:
    Mean
    Median
    Mode
    Ratios
- Distribution:
    Percent distribution
    Frequency distribution
- Variation:
    Range
    Interquartile range
    Standard deviation
    Coefficient of variation

Central Tendency

Mean. The mean is the average, or the sum of *n* numbers divided by *n*. A mean is a useful statistic because it is relatively reliable in the sense that means of many samples drawn from the same population usually do not fluctuate very much. A weighted mean should be used when calculating an overall mean for a combination of samples or populations with different sizes.

Median. The median is the midpoint of a set of observations on something. To find the median, data must be arranged from lowest to highest value; the midpoint is then determined by dividing the number of observations by 2 (when there is an even number of observations the median is the average of the two adjoining numbers). For example, the median of a data set of 100 observations is the average of the values of the 50th and 51st observations.

It can be useful to measure the median when data include very small or large values that could distort the picture. Income data often have highs or lows that can skew an average, whereas the midpoint will generally balance those extremes.

Table 4.3 presents an example of mean and median. Note that average incomes in Murmansk are significantly higher than average incomes in all other cities. The Murmansk data inflate the mean to 2,918, whereas the median is 2,424—nearly 20 percent lower.

Mode. The mode is defined simply as the value that occurs with the highest frequency and more than once. For many data, the mode is not terribly meaningful. However, if you were interested in the marital status of clients, the mode would be a useful measure.

Ratios. Analysts and program managers often combine raw data to form useful information, such as comparing the ratio of total family income to the poverty line, or the ratio of staff to clients. Ratios are usually expressed in a form such as "24

Table 4.3   Average Family Income for Selected Cities, 2002

City	Average Monthly Family Income (rubles)
Murmansk	6,668
Cherepovets	3,652
Novgorod Veliki	3,378
Tihvin	2,714
Ul'yanovsk	2,424
Dimitrigrad	2,424
Kaluga	2,424
Ryazan	2,400
Vladimir	2,254
Cheboksary	2,032
Yoshkar-Ola	1,728
Mean	2,918
Median	2,424

staff : 4,507 clients," or "500 rubles income : poverty line of 800 rubles." These figures can easily be transformed into percentages or averages. So that, using the examples above, the average caseload is 188 clients per case worker (4,507 ÷ 24); and a family's 500 ruble income is equal to 62.5 percent of the poverty line (500 ÷ 800).

Distribution. Distributions provide a good overall picture of a large number of observations on a single phenomenon or variable. Whereas the mean or median identifies the middle of the data, a distribution enables one to better understand the range of responses. Examples of distribution are the number of households in each income quintile or the percentage of citizens who rated public transportation poor, good, and excellent.

Percentage distribution. The percentage distribution presented in Table 4.4 is based on the length of time that participants of a job training program retained employment. The table shows that the majority of program participants kept their jobs for one year or less. The program would need additional information to understand why only a third of their participants kept jobs for longer than a year, but this basic data clearly reveal a potential problem. Possible explanations are that program participants may need additional services once they are employed or that many participants receive seasonal or other short-term positions. Additional data or follow-up interviews with clients and staff would help to explain these trends.

When creating a table like this, keep three points in mind:

1. The intervals you select should generally be uniform to make it easier for a person to interpret the table (such as similar periods of time or intervals of 200 euros).

Table 4.4   Percentage Distribution

Length of Job Retention	Number of Participants	Percentage
Less than three months	87	27.3
Three months to one year	121	37.9
More than one year to two years	63	19.7
Two years or more	48	15.0
Total	319	100.0

2. If there are logical breakpoints (e.g., poverty level, eligibility level), include them as an interval boundary.
3. The intervals selected should show a distribution of the data. In other words, you do not want most of the data falling within one interval.

Frequency distribution. Distribution by category is a useful way to present nominal or ordinal data. Table 4.5 is an example of client survey results from a housing allowance program. Eighty-five program clients were interviewed regarding their satisfaction with intake workers. The frequency distribution represents the number of clients in each of the four response categories.

• *How to Decide Which Techniques to Use*

For basic policy analysis and program management, computing totals, averages, percentages, and distributions will allow you to sufficiently analyze routine data. These simple procedures explain a lot about a problem or program performance and are easily understood by most stakeholders. So long as the data are of reasonable quality and are clearly reported, more advanced techniques may not be required. More important is that programs produce reports on a timely basis and use the reports to better understand their performance. Larger programs or major policy initiatives, such as a regional monitoring initiative or programs with many observations and disparate values, may benefit from the techniques described below.

Measures of Variation. Measures of variation describe the dispersion of the data; in other words, they determine how scattered or closely bunched the observa-

Table 4.5   Frequency Distribution

Satisfaction of Applicant with Efficiency/Politeness of Intake Worker	Number of Applicants
Very pleased	23
Satisfied	34
Somewhat unsatisfied	20
Very unsatisfied	8
Total	85

tions are. For example, the average student math scores for a city might be 62 (out of a potential 100). However, educators may also be interested in knowing whether the scores are clustered around the average or whether there are many low- or high-performing students. One school may have a high average because of the special attention it devotes to a few gifted students—whereas the majority of students may not be learning as they should. The range, standard deviation, and coefficient of variation are methods for understanding the variation of data.

This section describes what each measure says about data and how to calculate it. We focus on understanding what each measure means, as many analysts rely on computer programs (such as Excel) to perform the actual calculations. Consult a standard math or statistics textbook for additional information.

Determining variation of the data requires arranging the data by size, as is done to calculate the median.

Range. The range of a set of data is the largest value minus the smallest. For example, a program that serves children from 3 to 18 years of age, has a range of 15 years.

Interquartile range. The interquartile range tells us about the middle 50 percent. Interquartile ranges are typically used when it is important to avoid distortions caused by extreme values at the opposite ends of a data series. The data, value-ranked, are divided into four quarters (each representing 25 percent of the observations) with three breakpoints, referred to as Q1, Q2, and Q3. Q2 is the same as the median. The interquartile range is Q3 – Q1, which by definition covers the middle half of the data.

For example, suppose annual incomes in a region range from 0 to 123,000 rubles. Table 4.6 divides residents' incomes into quarters. Note that the quartiles are based on the number of observations, not on 25 percent of the income range.

Table 4.6   Interquartile Range

Quartile	Range	Breakpoints
Q1	0–3,000	Q1 = 3,000
Q2	3,001–40,000	Q2 = 40,000
Q3	40,001–80,000	Q3 = 80,000
Q4	80,001–123,000	

Median: 40,000
Interquartile range: 80,000 − 3,000 = 77,000

The normal curve. In most data sets, the observations are concentrated around the mean, with fewer observations at the two extremes. This is also referred to as a bell-shaped distribution, because when it is graphed it looks like a cross section of a bell. If data form a bell curve, this indicates that more of the cases are closer to the mean and fewer cases are far away from the mean. Most data distributions follow the bell or normal curve, as Figure 4.1 illustrates. Figure 4.2 represents the average incomes for a sample of cities. The data fall into a fairly normal curve.

The variance and standard deviation specifically describe the dispersion of the sample in relation to the mean. The *standard deviation* measures how widely the values are dispersed from the mean. (One standard deviation in either direction of the mean accounts for 68 percent of the data; two standard deviations from the mean account for 95 percent of the data.)

In the example of average income for selected cities (graphed in Figure 4.2 and listed in Table 4.3), the standard deviation is quite significant—1,360 rubles—indicating that the data are fairly widely distributed from the mean. We can see that this is true by looking at the data: the mean is 2,918 rubles and incomes range from 1,728 to 6,668 rubles. A high standard deviation generally tells us that it is important to look beyond the mean to understand the dynamics of the data. In the exam-

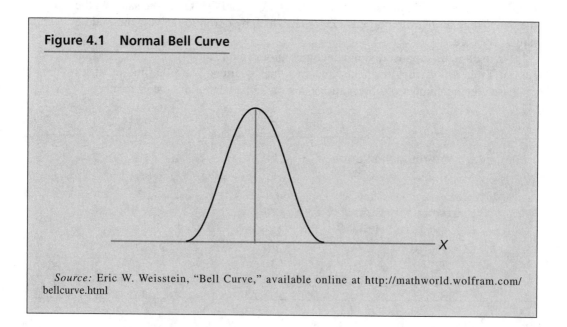

Figure 4.1   Normal Bell Curve

Source: Eric W. Weisstein, "Bell Curve," available online at http://mathworld.wolfram.com/bellcurve.html

Figure 4.2   Example of a Normal Bell Curve

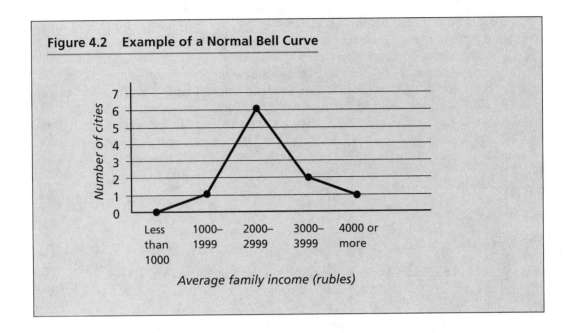

Average family income (rubles)

ple, high incomes in a single city mask the lower incomes in the majority of cities. This same pattern holds when we look at the coefficient of variation.

The *coefficient of variation* is a measure of relative variation. It expresses the standard deviation as a percentage of what is being measured. (It is the standard deviation divided by the mean and is expressed as a percentage.) By standardizing a standard deviation of a variable by its mean, it is possible to compare the variation in variables of different orders of magnitude—for example, the relative variation on incomes in Hungary and in Bosnia and Herzegovina.

Returning to the example of income in selected Russian cities (Table 4.3), the coefficient of variation in total household income is 47 percent. This can be expected for the same reason that the mean is greater than the median: there are people/cities with very high incomes.

*   *   *

The formulas for these methods are listed below. Excel and other computer programs can calculate the variance or standard deviation, so learning the formulas is less important than understanding what these measures say about the data. Beyond being able to compute the summary measures covered here, there will be many instances where you will want to determine whether there are significant differences between the mean of one group and that of another, or between distributions. For example, if there is a mean difference of 0.6 years achievement in the reading scores of 300 third-grade students from one school and 150 students from another, is it a statistically significant difference? Or, one may ask a similar question about the share of households with incomes below the poverty line in different municipalities. There are standard parametric tests for determining if such differences are statistically significant, and they can be found in standard elementary statistics texts.

To repeat, a high standard deviation or coefficient of variance suggests that the data are widely dispersed from the mean. The distribution techniques described in the previous section can help in understanding large variations in data.

Variance

$$s^2 = \frac{\Sigma(x^1 - \bar{x})^2}{n - 1}$$

The sample variance is calculated by squaring the difference between each value and the mean, and summing these squares of differences (or *deviations*). This is then divided by the sample size minus 1.

Example

Using the income data for selected cities in Table 4.3, the variance is calculated as follows:

$$\frac{(6{,}668 - 2{,}918)^2 + (3{,}652 - 2{,}918)^2 + \dots \text{[data for 9 other cities} - \text{mean]}}{11 - 1}$$

$$= \frac{18{,}496{,}896}{10} = 1{,}849{,}689.6$$

Standard Deviation

$$s = \sqrt{\frac{\Sigma(x^1 - \bar{x})^2}{n - 1}}$$

The standard deviation is the square root of the variance. How do we interpret the standard deviation? If the standard deviation of a set of data is small, the values are concentrated near the mean, and if the standard deviation is large, the values are scattered widely about the mean.

Example

Using the income data for selected cities in Table 4.3, the standard deviation is calculated as follows:

$$\frac{(6{,}668 - 2{,}918)^2 + (3{,}652 - 2{,}918)^2 + \ldots \text{[data for 9 other cities} - \text{mean]}}{11 - 1}$$

$$= \frac{18{,}496{,}896}{10} = 1{,}849{,}689.6$$

$$\sqrt{1{,}849{,}689.6} = 1{,}360$$

The standard deviation for this data is rather high, telling us that the data are widely distributed from the mean.

Coefficient of Variation

$$V = (s \div x) \times 100$$

Where

    s = the standard deviation of the sample
    x = the mean of the sample

The coefficient of variation is a measure of relative variation. It expresses the standard deviation as a percentage of what is being measured, at least on average.

Example

Using the income data for selected cities in Table 4.3, the coefficient of variation is calculated as follows:

$$\frac{1{,}360}{2{,}918} \times 100 = 0.466 \times 100 = 46.6\%$$

A 46.6 percent coefficient of variation in total household income can be expected for the same reason that the mean is greater than the median: there are people/cities with very high incomes.

Data Interpretation

The focus of this section is how to divide data into useful subcategories, such as according to demographic characteristics, and compare changes in data.[1]

• Analyze the Data Broken Out by Key Characteristics

Disaggregating the data by groups of clients, geographic region, or other factors permits comparisons among groups and distinguishes groups that may have substantially different outcomes from others. Breakouts can be used for purposes such as the following:

- To help pinpoint where problems exist as a first step toward identifying corrective action(s).
- To help identify positive outcomes that can be highlighted as "best practices" and disseminated to other programs.
- To assess the equity with which services are allocated to specific population groups.

Data are often divided into the following categories:

- *Geographical location.* Data sorted by region, district, or neighborhood. The presentation of data by geographical area gives users information about where service outcomes are positive and negative.
- *Organizational unit/project.* Distinct outcome information on individual supervisory units is a much more useful management tool than information on several projects lumped together. For example, it is useful to have separate performance information on each public works department. Another example of the use of breakouts is to track the performance information on the different units within a police department, so that response times can be examined for individual units that specialize in particular crimes or other emergencies.
- *Demographic characteristics.* Breakouts by demographic characteristics (e.g., age, gender, and education) can be very useful in policy development or highlighting the outcomes of public services. For example, if unemployment were concentrated among young men with little formal education, the policy implications would be different than if, say, most of the unemployed were single, female heads of household. For another example, park staff may find that they have put too much effort into satisfying parents with children and that their parks lack facilities that the elderly or young adults can enjoy.
- *Degree of difficulty* (in carrying out the task in question). All programs have tasks that vary in difficulty. A more difficult program or task will have a harder time achieving performance goals, and distinguishing the degree of difficulty of a task will change the perception of its outcomes. To show good performance an organization may be tempted to attract easier-to-help customers, while discouraging service to more difficult (and more expensive) customers. Reporting breakouts by workload difficulty can eliminate this temptation.
- *Type of process or procedure used to deliver the service.* Presenting per-

formance data by the type and magnitude of activities is useful. For example, a street-cleaning program can comprise sweepers, garbage cans and dumpsters, and garbage trucks. Data presented on each specific activity and its outcomes help to pinpoint areas of effectiveness.

• Compare Findings to Benchmarks or Program Goals

Once data for a particular time period are available, it is important to decide if the level of performance is good or bad. For example, a region reports an unemployment rate of 6.5 percent; judging whether this is good or bad requires comparing the region's unemployment rate to that of the previous time period or to that of other regions. Comparing current data with a baseline or other referent (benchmark) is highly useful. Major types of benchmarks include:

- *Previous performance.* Compare current performance to that of previous time periods to better understand the change in performance over time.
- *Preselected targets.* Governments or agencies may establish expectations and set performance targets at the beginning of the year, such as announcing the goal to ensure that 90 percent of school children receive immunizations. Performance results can then be compared to the targets. Preset targets should be challenging but doable.
- *Comparison to other regions.* It is useful to compare data to those of other regions. In making such comparisons it is important that regions be similar, such as similar-sized cities, nearby countries, or countries with similar gross domestic products. For example, comparing Hungary's growth rate to Poland's is much more relevant than comparing it to that of the United States or Ghana.
- *Performance of similar programs.* This involves comparisons with programs that provide essentially the same service to approximately the same type of customers. For meaningful comparisons, the goals of the programs should also be similar. For example, a recent survey conducted in four Albanian cities has demonstrated that one municipality is performing significantly better in targeting its social allowances. Poor-performing municipalities can look to the activity of the successful municipality and identify practices they may be lacking.
- *Different service delivery practices.* Programs periodically consider new, alternative methods of delivering services. Data can be used to assess the results of the new practices, such as new operating procedures, technologies, staffing arrangements, policies, providers (e.g., private contractors), or changes in the level of service provided to individual customers.

Data Presentation

In policy analysis, data are used to understand an issue, make an argument for a particular strategy, or evaluate the efficacy of government interventions. Knowing what analytical techniques to use, interpreting the data, and presenting the findings in a compelling manner are essential to using data effectively. This section provides several suggestions on how to analyze and present data to inform policy or program decisions.

• Presentation Formats

Data analyses or performance reports can be formatted any number of ways, depending on the needs of the audience or characteristics of the data or programs:[2]

- *Changes over time.* Comparing this year's performance to last year's performance is a simple and powerful way to present change.
- *Actual outcomes versus targets.* This format compares actual outcomes to targets for the current and previous reporting periods. For example, citywide elementary school math scores have increased this year by 3 percent, missing the target goal of a 5 percent increase (and compared to a prior-year citywide increase in math scores of 7 percent). Chapter 10 discusses targets in greater detail.
- *Comparisons across geographical locations.* For example, reduction in armed robberies in various city neighborhoods, or changes in police response time by neighborhood.
- *Demographic characteristics.* Analyzing data by demographic characteristics helps to understand how problems or programs affect different segments of the population. For example, job placement data according to the educational level of program participants, or case management outcomes sorted according to the clients' degree of mental illness, can help one to better understand program results.
- *Graphs.* Graphs are particularly useful for showing changes in data over time. Several different indicators can be charted on the same graph, such as changes in the incidence of various violent crimes, or a single indicator presented for various demographic characteristics or geographic breakdowns, such as the change in poverty by age or region.
- *Bar charts.* Bar charts are useful for presenting findings that are broken out by different demographic characteristics of respondents or by different service delivery characteristics (e.g., citizen satisfaction with trash collection, disaggregated by trash collection route). Bar charts are effective for illustrating frequency distributions.

- *Pie charts.* Pie charts are useful for presenting distributions or percentages. Figure 4.3 below presents residents' satisfaction with local street-cleaning services.
- *Maps.* Maps are a dramatic way to present geographic data, and to compare one region to another.
- *Color-coding.* Some agencies color-code data on program performance as red, yellow, or green. Red denotes a problem area that requires immediate attention, yellow that the program needs further evaluation, and green that the program is on track and achieving its goals.

Chapter Summary

Policymakers and analysts depend on data to understand complex social and economic problems, to plan new initiatives, and to monitor program performance. Data may come from program records, official government reports, analyses by independent policy organizations, surveys of citizens or program beneficiaries, the media, and countless other sources. Data are categorized as quantitative or qualitative.

The basic analytical techniques summarized in this chapter, including measures of central tendency (mean, median, and mode), distribution, and variation (standard deviation and coefficient of variation), should be used to convey how a

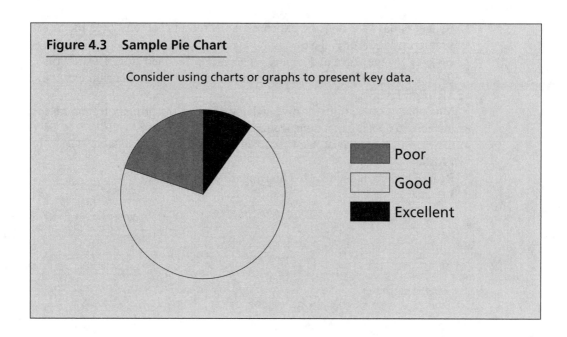

Figure 4.3   Sample Pie Chart

Consider using charts or graphs to present key data.

Poor
Good
Excellent

program/policy is working, and to inform improvement strategies. Ideas for how to disaggregate data into meaningful subcategories and presentation strategies are also discussed.

Recommended Reading

US Department of Housing and Urban Development. "Manufactured Housing: An Adequate and Affordable Alternative." Washington, D.C.: Department of Housing and Urban Development, Office of Policy Development and Research, Fall 2002. Available online at http://www.huduser.org/periodicals/ushmc/fall02/summary_2.html (more recent versions of the report may be accessible).

This HUD report is an example of how data can be used. In very clear language and tables, the report describes the attributes of manufactured housing in the United States. Data from the US Census and the annual American Housing Survey document the prevalence of manufactured housing, its location, building conditions, costs, demographic characteristics of residents, and more.

Exercise 4.1: Drawing Conclusions from Data

Examine the table on pages 79–80 and determine which of the following statements can be supported by the data. Indicate whether each statement is true or false.

1. Budget outlays for housing expenses increased in each city over the three-year term. TRUE or FALSE
2. Housing maintenance and capital repair needs declined from 1994 to 1995, resulting in a corresponding reduction in maintenance and capital expenses. TRUE or FALSE
3. Municipal responsibility of divested housing was the primary reason for the increase in housing maintenance/repair costs. TRUE or FALSE
4. Cities with the greatest need received the most federal transfers. TRUE or FALSE
5. Ryazan had the most divested housing. TRUE or FALSE

Municipal Budget Outlays for Housing Stock and Sources of Funds in Vladimir, Ryazan, and Petrozavodsk (millions of rubles)

	Petrozavodsk			Ryazan			Vladimir		
	1993	1994	1995	1993	1994	1995	1993	1994	1995
Budget outlays for housing maintenance, heating, capital repair, housing allowances, of which:	7,413.1	21,392.9	57,135.4	3,945.5	26,022.7	71,849.0	4,022.0	31,788.3	54,670.0
Housing maintenance (%)	19.7	21.5	5.2	59.1	61.1	26.8	9.6	61.7	35.0
Heating (%)	76.1	74.0	92.4	3.4	21.8	58.2	28.7	22.2	57.3
Capital repair (%)	4.1	4.3	1.6	37.5	17.2	14.9	41.7	16.0	7.6
Housing allowances (%)	NA	0.1	0.4	NA	NA	0.2	NA	0.1	NA
Budget outlays for housing maintenance, heating, capital repair, housing allowances for divested housing	541.2	2,053.7	5,599.3	7.9	4,840.2	27,302.6	12.1	826.5	5,685.7
As percentage of total budget outlays for housing	7.3	9.6	9.8	0.2	18.5	19.9	0.3	2.6	10.4
Revenue sources in principle available to cover housing outlays	1,519.0	7,870.0	14,543.9	7,686.9	37,667.0	59,929.0	1,725.0	19,170.0	7,619.0
1.5% tax (70% by city decree in Petrozavodsk)	1,440.2	6,727.2	14,170.7	7,686.9	7,686.9	55,432.9	1,725.0	4,735.0	6,483.8
Transfers from federal budget	78.9[a]	1,142.7[b]	373.2[c]	0.0	0.0	4,496.1[d]	0.0	14,435.0[e]	1,135.2[f]

(continues)

Continued

	Petrozavodsk			Ryazan			Vladimir		
	1993	1994	1995	1993	1994	1995	1993	1994	1995
Difference between sources of funds and outlays for divested housing	977.8	5,816.3	8,944.6	7,679.0	32,826.8	32,626.4	1,712.9	18,343.5	1,933.3
Budget outlays for housing maintenance, heating, capital repair, housing allowances of divested housing, as a percentage of total city budget	1.6	1.7	3.7	0.02	2.6	13.2	0.04	0.8	5.2

Source: Raymond J. Struyk, ed., "Restructuring Russia's Housing Sector: 1991–1997" (Washington, D.C.: Urban Institute, 1997), p. 102.
Notes: a. Federal transfer received from Ministry of Finance in October 1993.
b. Federal transfers received from Ministry of Finance in May 1994 and October-November 1994.
c. Funds received through Mutual Settlement Account.
d. Federal transfer for 1994 funds received from Ministry of Finance in January 1995.
e. Federal transfer received from Ministry of Finance in August 1994.
f. Federal transfer for 1994 funds received from Ministry of Finance in September 1995.

Exercise 4.2: Checking Data for Reasonableness

Identify mistakes in the following table. Look for missing or incomplete data, as well as inconsistencies. Do the numbers make sense? Are they what you would expect given other facts? There are six errors.

Oblast or City	1996 District Heat Tariff per Square Meter	1996 Hot Water Tariff per Person	1996 Water-Sewerage Tariff per Person	1996 Kvarplata Tariff per Square Meter	1996 Maintenance Tariff per Square Meter	1996 Total Communal Services Tariff for Family of 4 with 65-Square-Meter Apartment	1996 Bottled Gas Price per Liter	1996 Electricity Tariff per Kilowatt Hour	Electricity Cost Recovery Level (%)
St Petersburg	335	3,012	9,860	400	368	123,183	40,000	10,000	43
Moscow City	492	9,138	6,968	310	310	136,704	0	13,000	49
Moscow oblast	650	7,579	7,776	404	404	156,190	21,000	13,000	49
Syktyvkar	777	14,625	5,175	542	375	189,310	12,495	18,400	61
Leningrad oblast	600	8,000	5,000	373	373	139,490	40,000	10,000	43
Tula	291	4,254	2,768	139	139	65,073	15,225	5,000	27
Kaluga	350	4,000	3,000	150	107	325,728	31,500	10,000	35
Nizhniy Novgorod	480	5,064	3,496	543	543	136,030	30,000	8,000	49
Cheboksary	350	4,500	400	77	77	52,360	27,300	7,000	56
Penza	450	2,079	1,594	103	100	57,137	29,400	9,000	50
Lipetsk	276	6,905	5,263	369	336	112,437	26,000	3,700	85
Tambov	300	3,500	2,000	168	96	58,660	48,300	6,000	30
Kazan	300	1,200	2,084	990	900	155,486	25,200	12,000	38
Saratov	305	3,185	2,934	45	45	50,151	21,000	9,000	38
Pskov	305	3,185	2,934	45	45	50,151	21,000	9,000	38
Volgograd	300	4,000	1,500	197	176	65,745	21,000	9,000	45
Rostov-na-Donu	450	6,500	6,000	202	200	105,380	22,000	8,000	50
Krasnodar	550	9,075	6,090	300	300	135,410	20,000	12,000	50
Stavropol	500	5,000	6,000	276	276	112,380	20,000	100	45
Orsk	763	4,881	6,337	420	400	147,767	25,000	8,000	41
Perm	397	4,500	0	252	156	70,325	6,300	10,000	38
Miass	831	10,983	10,085	322	315	179,692	50,000	8,000	32
Tomsk	700	4,320	5,050	300	154	112,490	40,000	10,000	43

Note: Figures are in 1996 rubles.

PART 2

DESIGNING AND IMPLEMENTING POLICIES AND PROGRAMS

CHAPTER 5

Allocating Government Resources

The change from central planning to market economies created tremendous social and economic hardship in all Eastern European transition countries. Poverty increased dramatically as industry collapsed, jobs disappeared, and Soviet-era protections and welfare programs became unaffordable. Poverty rates in the region increased from 2 percent in 1988 to 28 percent in 1998.[1] In many countries poverty rates were significantly higher.

Traditional Soviet-era benefits and privileges included guaranteed employment, pensions, subsidized housing and communal services, and other consumer subsidies—in addition to more general public services such as education and health care, often provided by state enterprises. Based on assumptions of full employment, relative equality, and enterprise-based welfare programs, Soviet social policies no longer functioned in the new economic environment. Enterprises began to focus on profit-producing activities and divested their social welfare programs to local governments. Local governments often strained under new responsibilities, increased local needs, and declining revenues. Federal and local governments have had to adapt to this wildly altered economic landscape with new social programs and new divisions of responsibilities.

Social assistance programs in transition countries now include unemployment benefits, pensions, subsidies for housing/utilities, child allowances, social services, and various welfare payments. Expenditures are highest for general public services such as health care, education, and communal services, followed by pensions and unemployment, with lower allocations for welfare services.[2] That is, most government expenditures benefit the general population, with a smaller portion of spending dedicated specifically to the poor.

In reforms throughout the region, governments seeking to save money and make better use of their resources have begun to target some of their programs.

Some countries have progressed quite far, although programs targeted by income remain a small portion of social spending.

Programs may be targeted based on any number of criteria, such as pensions for the elderly, scholarships for gifted students, technical assistance for small businesses, or monetary support for low-income families.

Certain services or public goods do not lend themselves readily to targeting and are often referred to as "universal" goods or services. Something like a police force probably does not have a target group, because it is supposed to serve the whole community. Police protection is a service that is usually not procured from the market, though wealthy persons may enhance their security with private guards and other measures. For goods or services such as public parks or roads, there is little to gain from targeting, as each person's consumption of these services does not have a direct budget impact. Another type of example is childhood immunizations against deadly diseases, where nonimmunized children pose a public health risk and it is in society's interest to encourage or subsidize vaccines for much of the population.

This chapter presents the rationale for targeting benefits, describes how to define a target group, and explains specific methodologies for targeting programs. Much of the chapter focuses on targeting programs to assist the poor.[3] The chapter also explores different types of government assistance, from supply-side public subsidies covering consumption of services from an entire sector of the economy, such as those that reduce the costs of transportation or energy, to demand-side cash or in-kind subsidies granted to individuals or families. The chapter concludes with some principles of allocating benefits and specific methodologies for structuring or calculating benefits.[4]

Step 3 of the policy analysis method described in Chapter 2 is to identify alternative policies. Targeting and different ways of structuring public interventions are useful strategies that are particularly timely for governments looking to improve the quality of services and maximize scarce resources.

Targeting

• Why Do We Target Programs?

Targeting the allocation of a benefit to a defined set of persons reinforces societal values. This may include not letting the elderly be put out on the streets or ensuring that newborn infants receive health care and proper nutrition. In Russia, for example, programs or benefits reward individuals for their special past service to the state (e.g., labor heroes and veterans) or current service (benefits to military personnel and judges). Programs also target families in need, such as those with disabilities, children, or low incomes. Other programs target based on merit, such as scholarship programs for talented young musicians or scientists.

Governments target programs because there is simply not enough money to provide all services for all people. For example, many societies believe that it is in the public's interest that children receive a decent, basic education to enable them to grow into productive members of the community. At the same time, most societies provide only limited assistance to help individuals attend university.

Generally programs are targeted because some people can afford to pay for services, while others cannot. The expectation is that richer families will pay for their children to attend university, while the public may subsidize the tuition of bright poor children. This concept is called *vertical equity*—government redistributes resources to people with lower incomes so that they too have access to basic or important goods and services. Another important concept of equity is *horizontal equity*—when a benefit is offered to a certain group, all members of that group should have equal access. For example, all poor families are entitled to child allowances, not just some.

Overview: Basic Conceptual Steps in Targeting

• Step 1: Define the Target Group

Targeting can be based on virtually any criteria or policy goal and is simply a way of rationing scarce resources. The chapter discusses different strategies for targeting:

- *Self-targeting*. Persons elect to receive a service or benefit themselves that higher-income families tend not to consume.
- *Category*. Groups of people, such as persons with disabilities or public employees.
- *Income or means testing*. Prospective recipients must provide information on their household income.
- *Income and assets*. In addition to income data, persons must present information on any assets that they own, such as a house, car, business, and the like.
- *Proxy-means testing*. Uses a number of indicators that are associated with poverty.
- *Community-based systems*. Community leaders determine who should receive benefits based on a locally defined criteria.

• Step 2: Develop Methods for Identifying the Target Group

Once the target group has been determined, policies and practices need to be implemented to evaluate whether persons meet the eligibility criteria. Administrators of a program providing free meals to the poor could simply decide to serve all persons who seek its assistance, reasoning that the cost of screening recipients could be higher than the cost of the meal or that standing in line and identifying oneself as needy in exchange for a simple meal is a sufficient deterrent to those who do not truly need assistance. A program providing cash benefits will be more likely to require applicants to document their resources or needs. Money provides an incentive for persons to take advantage of the program, because it can be spent on many things, not just a basic meal, for example.

Targeting methods should be based on the goals of the program, the type of assistance provided, and local administrative capacity. No single method is best. Program planners should consider the costs of applying allocation tests and effectiveness of the various methods. The simplest approach is often the most effective if it is well implemented.

• Step 3: Create the Administrative Structure

An administrative structure is needed to implement the targeting requirements. Major programs with national or other significant funding sources may require very specific implementation procedures. For example, a family assistance program may require identification and income documentation for all family members living in the household; a small business support program may require copies of tax receipts and documentation on the number of employees. Administrators will likely have some discretion in designing the structure of locally initiated or smaller programs. Planners should take into account the costs of program administration and design the best structure given the resources available and goals of the program. Key issues to consider include:

- What are the staffing needs to implement the targeting requirements?
- How will potential participants learn about the program?
- Is there discretion in the targeting criteria or does staff follow specific rules or formulas?
- Is the necessary documentation of eligibility available to would-be applicants at a reasonable cost?
- How will the program guard against excluding needy persons or granting assistance to those who do not really meet the criteria?

Alternative Targeting Methods

• Self-Targeting

With self-targeting, participants themselves decide whether to participate in programs, which are often designed to deter the nonpoor. Self-targeting often works best when the value of the goods or services is low and/or the transaction costs high. Transaction costs may include the stigma of identifying oneself as poor, standing in line and overcoming other logistical hurdles, or having to work in exchange for benefits. For example, Argentina's Trabajar program provides very low wages (equal to the earnings of the lowest 10 percent of the population) in exchange for construction work. Persons with jobs or other economic opportunities have little incentive to participate and the targeting is quite effective in this and similar public works programs.[5]

Other common self-targeted programs include food price subsidies and free or reduced-price goods. Some programs deter the nonpoor by providing inferior goods to those found in the market (such as broken rice or surplus cheese) or requiring recipients to travel to a pickup location, stand in line, and so forth.

Programs using the stigma of identifying oneself as poor (or as having AIDS, a mental disability, or other potentially vulnerable condition) may also deter their intended population. Using stigma as a targeting device can be a blunt instrument and should be used with care. Similarly, the transaction costs should not be so high that potential beneficiaries are deterred.

• Categorical

Categorical targeting can be based on a range of characteristics:

- Socially vulnerable demographic characteristics:
  - Children
  - Disabled
  - Pregnant mothers
  - Single parents
  - Elderly
- Rewards to public servants
- Rewards for honorable service in the past (such as veterans benefits)
- Rewards to victimized groups

Table 5.1 provides examples of types of programs or benefits for these categories of persons.

Often when income information is not reliable, program directors find it more realistic to use categorical or proxy-means targeting. In most countries of the former Soviet Union, there are three types of categorical targeting: targeting benefits to "socially vulnerable" people; targeting rewards to those who performed meritorious service in the past; and targeting rewards to public servants. The last two categories have little correlation with poverty. Therefore, benefits given to these categories of persons help more nonpoor than poor people.

The socially vulnerable categories used in Russia, for example, include several

Table 5.1   Categorical Program Examples

Category	Program Examples
Socially vulnerable	
Children	Child allowances
	Primary education
	Health care
Disabled	Social pensions
	Monthly allowance for nonworking person caring for disabled child
Pregnant women	Maternity benefit
	Birth allowances
Single mothers	Child allowances
Elderly persons	Pensions
	Home care for pensioners
Other categories	
Meritorious service	Subsidies for:
Public servants	Housing and utilities
Victimized groups	Health care
	Public transportation
	Education
	Telecommunications services

important segments of the country's poor population. However, these categories include many nonpoor and exclude many poor people. Approximately half of all poor persons in Russia do not fit into any of the socially vulnerable categories— the main groups excluded are two-parent families, single adults, and the working poor.

An example of a group that is often viewed as socially vulnerable is the elderly. Yet because most transition countries maintain relatively high pensions, the elderly represent only a small portion of the poor. In Russia, typical of the region in this respect, the elderly accounted for 15.1 percent of the poor in 2000, whereas young children represented 39.5 percent of the poor.[6] A program categorically targeting the elderly would not necessarily aid the poor.

The government can reward people for their service, but it should recognize that this is separate from the goal of helping people in need. Benefits to public servants are often a way of supplementing their income. In reality, however, it is more efficient to pay public servants an appropriate income than to give them extra benefits. This is because recipients generally value in-kind benefits less than the cost of providing the benefits or granting the recipient the higher wage. The Russian government has begun to limit soldiers' benefits and has instead increased their salaries.

• Targeting Based on Income/Means Testing

Targeting based on income generally limits program participation to those with incomes below a certain level, such as 50 percent of the poverty line or subsistence level. Means-tested programs measure the income or means of applicants and usually require some documentation from the applicant or third party (such as a wage statement from an employer or tax receipt).

Persons may receive income from a variety of sources and informal income is often difficult to measure. Programs operating where only limited income documentation is available may also require interviews or home visits to further assess household means.

Sources of income may include:

- Wages from primary and secondary jobs
- Self-employment income (such as doing odd jobs or income from garden plots)
- Benefits received from the government (pensions and child allowances)
- Unofficial or "gray economy" income
- Interest income/rents
- Money from relatives or friends

Means Testing and the Informal Economy.   Although countries in the region suffer from poor income reporting, many have experimented with means-tested programs. European Union accession countries implemented means-tested social protection programs early in the transition period, though coverage and spending in these programs has been low.[7] Means-tested social assistance programs remain a low proportion of social spending.

Means testing can be done even with imperfect information and implementing such programs can help to build transparency. For example, when the Russian housing allowance program was implemented in 1994 many people believed that it would be impossible to adequately assess income. However, the program was implemented with the belief that in time the economy would become less gray. In fact, over time this has occurred. A major factor was the introduction of a flat 13 percent income tax rate in 2001 that lowered the tax burden and encouraged more accurate income reporting. Moreover, benefits were relatively modest, so the incentive for the nonpoor to lie about their incomes was limited. Now the housing allowance program is considered quite successful and income reporting has become more reliable. It is important, however, especially when incomes cannot be verified, to design subsidy programs that minimize the incentives for people to lie about their earnings.

By 1999, Russian federal legislation recommended means-testing social assistance programs and described procedures for developing a minimum subsistence level for use in targeting. In addition to implementing the federal targeting policies, many local governments introduced their own programs that specifically target the poor. Eligibility for many local social assistance programs relies on a *double-filter* method, wherein recipients must meet both categorical and means tests (such as those targeting low-income families with children). These programs are often a mix of cash, subsidies, and in-kind benefits.

Including the Short-Term Poor. Targeting based on income without consideration of assets will include many persons who are transitionally poor, such as persons who are temporarily unemployed who may have savings or other assets that cushion their poverty. The administrative costs of programs that include the short-term poor are higher, as recipients quickly cycle in and out of the program. So program designers must decide whether to serve all persons who are poor at a point in time or those poor for a minimum period, perhaps six months—the so-called permanently poor. A rationale for assisting the short-term poor is to help prevent them from becoming chronically poor.

• Targeting Based on Income and Assets

Targeting based on income and assets is a way of further defining the population and tends to benefit the long-term poor, as the long-term poor are likely to possess few or very limited assets.

Assets usually considered include a house or apartment, new consumer durables, car, business, savings account, investments, or farmland (dacha or garden plot). There are three typical ways for assets to be included in an income test:

- An *asset screen* limits eligibility to those who do not possess a particular asset, such as a second home. In Armenia, eligibility for social benefits is based on a formula to estimate the family's means. The formula is called a proxy means test because it uses certain characteristics (including reported income) to estimate the family's means. In addition to the formula, eligibility is denied to certain families based on an asset screen. For example, if a family owns a car, has a registered trade or private enterprise, or has a child in a paid higher education facility, then they are not eligible for the benefit. An asset screen can be a blunt targeting instrument, as a car may be essential to a family's ability to generate some income yet may be worth very little as a capital asset.

- An *asset cap* sets a limit on the value of a particular asset—an eligible household may own the asset, but the value of the asset may not exceed the cap. Commonly a family can own its own housing unit and be eligible, but not own a second home.
- An *asset adjustment* involves determining the value of a particular asset owned by an applicant family and adding the value, or a portion of the value to income. For example, the value of a car could be amortized over its expected life and the equivalent imputed income added to the monthly income of the family.

Examples of means-testing and asset-measuring programs are highlighted in Box 5.1.

• Proxy-Means Testing

Proxy-means testing collects data on factors associated with poverty, such as social and demographic characteristics, and income and assets. These various indicators are given weights and used to construct a score for each household. The score determines if a family is eligible for assistance.

Box 5.1   Examples of Means-Testing and Asset-Measuring Programs

Income Testing Only
The housing allowance program in Russia provides a subsidy for low-income households. Eligibility is based only on household income and there are no categorical or asset requirements. Beneficiaries receive a subsidy that is the difference between the maximum social rent (maintenance and communal services for a standard apartment unit for a family of their size and composition) and what they can afford to pay (a percentage of their income). Local governments determine what types of income are counted and the portion of income contributed (usually 10 to 22 percent; Moscow sets its rate at 13 percent).

Income with Categorical Screen
The child allowance program in Russia provides poor families a grant of 70 rubles

(approximately $2.10) per month, per child. Eligibility is granted if the family includes a child under sixteen and if the monthly per capita income is below the subsistence level.

Income Test, Asset Cap, and Categorical Screen
The family allowance program in Ukraine uses household demographics, income, and assets to determine eligibility. First, applicants must pass a categorical screen—only families with no working adult are eligible. Eligible families must have low incomes. Families are permitted to have assets, but only up to a certain level. For example, a family could own an apartment and a car, but ownership of a second car or apartment or more than 0.05 hectares of land would make them ineligible.

Proxy-means tests are generally used when reported income is not considered a reliable indicator of poverty and when other characteristics, such as location, gender, education, disability, and family size, are strongly correlated with poverty, particularly long-term poverty. Sophisticated proxy-means tests use data gathered through a household survey to assess family need and define the relation between need and a series of indicators. The indicators are then assigned weights so that a needs score can be computed for each applicant household. Applicants with scores above a critical value are eligible for the benefit.

Proxy-means tests have generally not performed very well in transition economies, as with Armenia's Paros program, described in Box 5.2. One problem with such tests is somewhat specific to transition economies: because of economic

---

Box 5.2   Early Proxy-Means Testing in Armenia

Armenia's Paros program was the first proxy-means program in Eastern Europe and Central Asia. The program was introduced in 1994 to allocate humanitarian aid in response to the devastation caused by the 1988 earthquake and the ongoing war with Azerbaijan. More than 70 percent of the population registered for the program. The record registration was surprising because in most countries a much greater portion of higher-income households opt out. The program based eligibility on housing status, location (with preference given to those in the earthquake zone), household size, income, and various social conditions. The social conditions, such as child of single mother, unemployed person, pensioner, disability, orphan, and others, were given weights and contributed to an overall score that assessed family need.

The program failed to target the poor and was widely criticized. Many of the social conditions measured and subjective weights assigned to those conditions did not accurately reflect family need. For example, of those in the poorest Paros-estimated quintile, only one-third were in the lowest consumption quintile—that is, the Paros measure gave high-need rankings to many households that were relatively well-off. There was no eligibility limit and each aid shipment was distributed according to rank (Paros score) until it was gone. Moreover, the program required frequent reranking and scores were adjusted to reflect each aid disbursement. Thus eligibility was redefined for each shipment and families had no way to predict their eligibility status. Participation of poor households was further diminished by lack of information about the program, inability to pay fees to collect documentation and travel to program offices, and disabilities, pregnancies, or other factors that prevented them from waiting in lengthy lines.

The program has been somewhat reformed; scores are now based on statistical analyses of household survey data and eligibility status is no longer constantly reassessed. The revised Paros methodology is now used to target poverty allowance benefits in Armenia.

Source: World Bank, "Improving Social Assistance in Armenia," Report no. 19385-AM (Washington, D.C.: World Bank, Human Development Unit, Country Department III, Europe and Central Asia Region, June 8, 1999).

dislocations in the transition, there is not a high correlation between typical social indicators such as the amount of formal education and years of experience with earnings or income. For example, a middle-aged analyst who worked at a research institute under the old system will have a high education and many years of experience, but his or her skills will not necessarily be well paid in the new system. With many cases like this it is very hard for statistical models to accurately account for variations in family income.

• Community-Based Targeting Systems

In community-based targeting systems, respected members of the community determine who receives benefits and the size of the benefit. A community leader or group of community members may be charged with allocating benefits based on criteria that reflect local needs. This system has the advantage of being flexible, utilizing various sources of information to determine family needs, and costing little to implement. Community-based systems work best where local communities are clearly defined and cohesive, and where programs serve a small segment of the population and benefit levels are relatively low. There is some risk with this model that community decisionmakers may have interests that are not always in keeping with effective program administration and that community leaders may replicate any existing patterns of social exclusion.[8]

At least two countries in Eastern Europe—Albania and Uzbekistan—have had success with systems in which local committees make decisions about who receives social assistance and how much they receive. Uzbekistan's Mahalla system relies on leaders of local community groups to allocate social assistance benefits. The program has general guidelines but no strict formula for eligibility, and the Mahallas (community leaders) also have discretion on the amount of assistance given. The program appears to favor typically needy households, such as families with children, female-headed households, and the unemployed.[9] A 2000 study of the Mahalla system gives it a favorable rating: 26 percent of households in the lowest income quintile received benefits, against 6 percent in the richest; 54 percent of benefits went to the poorest 40 percent of households. (But applications from the poorest households appear to be discouraged by the complex application process.) A general study of targeting in the Eastern Europe–Commonwealth of Independent States (CIS) region found this to be a comparatively good targeting record.[10]

Which Targeting Method Is Best?

Different targeting methodologies exist because some work better in certain situations. There are two main criteria for evaluating targeting methodologies:

1. *Does the methodology effectively focus resources on the intended benefici-aries?* Methodologies that unintentionally exclude people in the target group or include nontarget people are not effective methodologies.

   For example, income testing alone will allow the nonpoor to partici-pate if they can hide their income. An asset test or a categorical screen helps to keep out the nonpoor, especially when the informal economy is large. The advantage of an income test alone is that it usually includes all the poor in your target group. With a categorical screen, some of the poor (particularly the working poor) are likely to be left out of the target group.

   Policymakers are often more concerned about the number of house-holds who are erroneously excluded than those who are included, as pro-grams that exclude too many of their intended recipients are not achieving their basic goal of improving social welfare. See Box 5.3 for techniques policymakers use to measure targeting performance.

2. *Is the methodology feasible to implement?* The local administration must be able to practically implement the targeting method. Combining asset and income testing can be helpful in targeting, because it is often easier to observe or verify ownership of an asset than money. However, adding an asset requirement to the eligibility test may add to the burden of implement-ing the verification procedures. Cost, staff time, and technical expertise should be considered.

Box 5.3   Measuring Targeting Performance

Errors

In measuring targeting performance, inclu-sion and exclusion errors can be calculated based on the percentage of households that are misclassified. For example, a program serving 3,000 households wrongly excluded 150 families and included 100 families. The program has an exclusion error rate of 5 per-cent and an inclusion error rate of 3.3 percent.

Size of Error

To assess the severity of the errors, the size of the error is calculated based on the percentage difference from the eligibility limit and the true income value. For example, a family with a monthly income of $50 that was excluded from a program with an eligibility limit of $75 would have an error size of 33 percent. A program could calculate the severity of its exclusion errors by averaging the size of the errors for all households excluded.

- *Capacity Issues in Targeting*

The following administrative and financial issues can affect the effectiveness of various targeting approaches.

Administrative and financial resources. The quality of implementation will depend on the administrative and financial resources available. Are staff already trained in verifying income information and/or other documents? Is there a procedure manual for staff? Are computer systems ready to maintain a database of eligible households? Are there other offices (such as the local tax office or pension administration) where staff can verify applicant data? Will potential participants find it difficult to apply? If the answers to some of these questions are no, then simpler targeting methods should be considered. Box 5.4 provides an example of administrative reforms that reduced transaction costs for participants and administrative overhead.

What is the targeting accuracy? The accuracy of each targeting method depends on the context in which it is employed. The use of categorical targeting does not ensure that the poor are served. In some cases, more nonpoor than poor people are helped. Means testing can be more accurate, but requires decent income data and an administrative structure to collect information and assess eligibility. (Box 5.3 describes ways to measure targeting errors.)

What is the administrative cost effectiveness of the approach? Administrative costs to consider include how much time it will take for a staff member to qualify an eligible beneficiary. For example, a program that conducts home visits to test for assets will require significant staff time to evaluate the eligibility of each applicant. Beneficiaries also shoulder some costs for participating in the program, such as the amount of time and money required to gather documents to prove eligibility. Onerous requirements deter participation and diminish the effectiveness of the program. And finally, if the targeting criteria are very general or only partly implemented, there may be significant costs associated with serving a larger population.

Will the program target the long-term poor or the currently poor? Different targeting methods tend to favor either the long- or the short-term poor. Categorical targeting, proxy-means testing, and income and asset tests, correctly defined and implemented, will favor the long-term poor, since these indicators are fairly stable over time, as in families with children. Targeting based on income will include the currently poor. One reason to assist the currently poor is to prevent them from becoming long-term poor. For example, if a person loses their job, he or she may

Box 5.4 The One-Window Approach Improves Social Assistance Program Efficiency

In 2002 the city of Arzamas, Russia, implemented a reform project designed to ease client burden and improve access to benefits. The "one-window" project introduced a unified application form for all major social assistance programs in the city so that applicants visit only one office and supply one set of documents verifying their eligibility. Benefit processing was also consolidated.

The Old System

Before the introduction of the one-window system, the administration of social benefits was split among three separate municipal agencies, each under the authority of a different department or committee. Each of the three benefit agencies performed all the functions necessary for administration of the benefits they provided, including client intake, eligibility verification, benefit determination, case record management, client database development and maintenance, payment accounting, and appeals hearings. The social protection system also included a network of neighborhood centers that provided emergency assistance to families; however, those offices referred their clients to the main municipal agencies for social benefits.

The old system included a number of disadvantages for clients. Families applying for multiple benefits were required to visit multiple offices and to obtain multiple copies of documents needed by those agencies. Additionally, because of the lack of integration and coordination among the three offices, a client applying for one benefit may not have been advised about other benefits or services available in other agencies.

The Reform

The one-window system involved two major changes to the administration of social benefits. First, the functions of eligibility screening and client intake were separated from the agencies that process the benefits and decentralized. Social workers in the neighborhood centers were trained to interview applicants for all social benefits and to collect application and verification documents. When implementation was complete it was possible to apply for up to ten different federal and municipal benefits, including the housing and child allowance programs at neighborhood one-window offices. In addition, a new application form was created by the three benefit agencies that could be used for all benefits. Thus, applicants need to fill out only one application form at a single nearby office, regardless of the number of benefits for which they are applying.

The second major reform was the creation of the Department of Social Payments, a single agency tasked with eligibility and benefit determination, payment processing, and other functions of benefit administration.

Results

- Consolidation of benefit applications into one single unified application, resulting in a 40 percent decrease in the number of applications that needed to be processed (168 benefits for each 100 applications filed).
- Reduction in processing time, of 31 percent (reduction from 98 to 67.5 hours to process 100 benefits).
- Increase in productivity of benefit workers, of 49 percent (increase from 85 to 127 benefits processed per worker per month).
- Decrease in administrative costs per benefit application, of 32 percent (decrease from 66 rubles to 45 rubles per application).
- Reduction in the time it takes clients to collect the documents needed to complete applications (for a household applying for both the child and housing allowance programs, the time was reduced from about 4 to 2.5 hours).

Source: L. Jerome Gallagher, Raymond J. Struyk, and Ludmila Nikonova, "Savings from Integrating Administrative Systems for Social Assistance Programs in Russia," *Public Administration and Development* no. 23 (2003): 177–195. Copyright © 2003 John Wiley & Sons, Ltd. Reproduced with permission.

See Exercise 5.1: Targeting on page 115.

This exercise provides an opportunity to apply the concepts presented in this chapter to developing targeting strategies for child allowance and transportation subsidy programs.

become currently poor; however, if this person cannot pay their minimal expenses, he or she may risk losing their housing, which could lead to long-term poverty.

Targeting Conclusion: Implementation Matters. A recent study of 100 targeted programs in forty-one countries found that implementation was the most important factor in the effectiveness of targeted programs.[11] No particular method ensures success and administrators should select a targeting approach that is suited to its administrative capacities and the type of assistance provided. The study found that targeting provided more resources to the poor than would random allocations. Table 5.2 summarizes the advantages and disadvantages of the various targeting approaches.

Forms of Government Assistance

Government assistance includes goods (such as food) and services (such as health care). In some cases government provides the good or service outright; in other instances it subsidizes the cost of an item or service. For example, many countries subsidize their agricultural sectors, public transportation systems, health care and other services, or industries. Subsidies can also be directed to specific groups of people, such as low-cost health care for the elderly or heating subsidies for low-income households. Different types of assistance include in-kind assistance, price discounts, tax relief, certificates, and cash.

- *Forms of Assistance: Definitions*
  - *In-kind.* Beneficiaries receive free goods or services, such as housing, energy, health care, education, or food.
  - *Price discounts.* Beneficiaries are allowed to purchase goods at a discounted price; subsidies are provided to suppliers to cover the losses associated with the low prices.
  - *Certificate.* Beneficiaries receive a certificate or voucher that can be used to purchase a particular good or set of goods.
  - *Cash.* Beneficiaries receive cash, which they can spend as they choose.

Table 5.2   Targeting Summary

Method	Advantages	Disadvantages
Self-targeting	• No administrative burden for implementation • Does not exclude needy persons • Especially effective when the value of benefits is low or some effort is required in exchange for benefits	• Can include persons that are not in need • If the self-targeting mechanism is not very strong the program may serve a larger population that would likely add to program expenses
Categorical targeting	• Good strategy when income documentation is scarce • Targets long-term poor • Relatively easy to administer	• Categories may not accurately reflect those in need
Means testing	• Targeting based on income is more accurate than categorical testing—more likely to serve the poor	• Requires some administrative effort (staff to collect documentation and certify eligibility) • Can be difficult to implement if income is not accurately reported
Means and asset testing	• Has same advantages as means testing • Targets the long-term poor	• Asset screens can exclude needy persons • Requires verification of assets—adds to cost of implementation
Proxy-means testing	• By using a combination of factors—proxy-means testing can overcome weak income data	• If indicators are not closely associated with poverty—can lead to significant inclusion/exclusion errors
Community-based targeting	• Can be effective where income data are weak • Allows for local flexibility and local definition of need • Uses local knowledge of households' needs • Moderate implementation costs	• Can reinforce social exclusion • Community decisionmakers may have multiple agendas that impair the effectiveness and fairness of targeting • Can diminish (or tarnish) the effectiveness of community leaders in their original capacities

Table 5.3 offers examples of different types of programs.

- *Targeting Assistance*

Each type of assistance can be allocated to the public based on the various targeting approaches discussed earlier in the chapter. Table 5.4 shows examples of government interventions using each of the targeting approaches.

- *How to Evaluate the Type of Intervention*

Governments use different types of assistance to attain different political or policy goals. From an economist's point of view, cash is often the best type of intervention, because it is the most efficient—that is, it allows consumers to purchase the types of goods or services in the quantity and quality that they most need or value. However, policymakers must respond to a number of practical and political concerns, such as whether the public will support the subsidy program, whether the government will be able to effectively implement the program, and whether the program benefits society.

Criteria used to evaluate government interventions include consumer choice, production efficiency, consumer incentives, administrative simplicity and cost, and political support.

Consumer Choice. Is the household allowed to allocate its resources as it sees fit, or is it forced to consume more (or less) of a good than it would if given greater

---

Table 5.3 Forms of Government Assistance

In-kind	Police protection
	Home visitation for the elderly and disabled that provides housekeeping, medical services, etc.
	Shelter for orphans, abandoned or neglected children, homeless persons, victims of domestic violence, and others in need
	Baby formula for infants of poor families
Price discounts	Discounts on bills paid by consumers for heat, transportation, kindergarten, personal services, etc.
Certificates	Certificates for earthquake victims to purchase housing
	Food vouchers for poor families
Cash	Monthly child allowance benefits for low-income families with children
	Pensions
	Unemployment payments

Table 5.4   Targeting Approaches Applied to Various Forms of Assistance

Targeting Approach	Intervention
No targeting	Fire protection
	Police
Self-targeting	Food program providing only limited types of basic food
Categorical targeting	Birth allowances
	Transportation privileges for municipal workers
Means testing	Housing allowance
	Child allowance
	Poverty allowance

choice? For example, a program providing basic food baskets to poor people rather than money limits their choices in a variety of ways. The family cannot spend the money on other needs or vices (such as vodka). The family also has no say in what food they eat—as everyone receives the same regardless of preferences or dietary requirements. From a government standpoint the assurance that poor people will not go hungry and political support for this form of assistance may be considered more important than consumer choice.

Production Efficiency. Is the proposed solution the most efficient way to address the problem? How much it costs the government to provide the subsidy may depend on how the goods or services are produced or delivered. For example, compare two approaches to feeding poor people: a city-operated store versus food stamps (certificates that people can use in any store to purchase food). The city-operated store is likely to be less efficient, because there is no competition to produce or sell quality food at low prices, whereas with food stamps consumers can seek out the best products. In addition, food stamps have the added benefit of being more convenient to beneficiaries, as they can purchase food when and where they choose.

Another important concept in production efficiency is economy of scale. There are many goods or services that are efficient to produce only if there are a sufficient number of consumers. Public utilities are a classic example of services that are most efficient to provide for a mass of consumers.

Opportunities for corruption or waste can also affect the efficiency or cost of an intervention.

Consumer Incentive: Consumption and Work. How does the assistance affect behavior? The major concerns are that program designs will either promote dependency or encourage beneficiaries to consume more of the subsidy than they need because it is "free" or discounted.

For example, the major program providing financial assistance to poor families in the United States was reformed in 1996 because it was seen as promoting dependency. The old program was called Aid to Families with Dependent Children (AFDC) and offered families income support for many years (until the youngest child reached age eighteen) and penalized them for working (for each dollar earned the subsidy was reduced by a dollar). The reformed program, Temporary Assistance to Needy Families, encourages parents to work by disregarding some of their earnings (so that they can keep more of both their earnings and the subsidy) and limits benefits to a maximum of five years.

An example of a program that might encourage increased consumption is a flat rate for water service, as households that pay the same rate regardless of their usage have little incentive to conserve or value the water they use. Metered rates, on the other hand, force consumers to acknowledge and pay for the real costs of the water.

Administrative Simplicity and Cost. How costly is it to the government to provide and how much effort do beneficiaries need to make to receive the subsidy? Does it require special staff and equipment to qualify participants? What do the participants have to do? In an Armenian assistance program it was found that many of the poorest families did not participate because of (1) insufficient understanding of the program; (2) inability to pay for bus fare to get to the program office; (3) fees (and under-the-table payments) for the documentation required; and (4) difficulty standing in line due to child care duties, disability, or pregnancy.

Political Support. Is there support for the project? Political support can make or break policy initiatives. The political context, that is, what is acceptable or desirable in a particular place and time, influences decisions of what problems to tackle and what strategies to pursue. Seldom is the "best solution" or "worst problem" the main factor that guides intervention. For example, countries in Europe are currently facing a crisis with their pension systems—they all know that their systems are unaffordable and must be reformed, but the necessary changes are unpopular and will likely lead to a reduction in benefits for a growing segment of the population.

Certain types of programs or issues tend to garner political support. Merit goods, such as housing, education, or health care, are often popular, as the benefits are tangible to politicians and taxpayers. Funds that are earmarked for a particular purpose help assure supporters that the government or designated beneficiaries will

*See Exercise 5.2: Analyzing Types of
Subsidies and Targeting Methods on page 116.*

This exercise focuses on the different types of interventions and targeting
methods. The task is to list programs for each targeting/assistance method and
to evaluate each program based on the evaluation criteria used above.

use the resource as intended. Moreover, certain segments of the population are often
viewed as being more or less deserving. Children are often viewed as the innocent
victims of poverty or disease—whereas adults do not always gain sympathy and are
sometimes viewed as bringing their problems upon themselves. Thus, programs for
drug addicts can be a harder political sell than child nutrition programs. However,
an increase in concern about drug-related crime or the spread of AIDS may alter the
political climate, such that drug rehabilitation programs become a new priority.

Table 5.5 summarizes how the different forms of assistance compare on the
evaluation criteria.

Benefit Calculation

This section describes options for designing social assistance benefit programs. It
includes basic principles and examples of different types of program design.

• *Principles of Benefit Calculation*

There are a few basic principles that govern how most public benefit programs are
constructed:

- *A larger family should receive a greater benefit.* If two families have the
  same income, but one family is larger than the other, the larger family is
  likely to have greater needs and thus should be entitled to a greater benefit.
  Note that depending on the program, total family size may be important.
  For other programs, the composition (how many working-age adults, how
  many children, and how many pensioners) may be important in determining
  need.
- *A poorer family should receive a greater benefit.* If two families have the
  same composition, but one family is poorer than the other, then it is generally assumed that the poorer family has fewer resources and thus should be
  entitled to a greater benefit.

Table 5.5   Summary Evaluation of Forms of Assistance

	Consumer Choice	Production Efficiency	Consumer Incentive	Administrative Simplicity and Cost	Political Support
In-kind	No choice	May be government-produced goods—may suffer from lack of competition	May consume more of the good than needed—unlikely to affect work participation	Not complicated, but requires distribution system	Often politically popular
Price discounts	Limited choice	Uses existing products/markets for supply	Will steer consumers toward particular goods	Supply-side payments easy to administer	Can be seen as subsidizing particular products or sectors of the economy
Vouchers	Ability to choose among specific products (e.g., housing vouchers can be used for any apartment—but not other needs)	Likely to be efficient provided vouchers are at a level that allows consumers to meet their needs	Unlikely to lead to overconsumption or dependency	Requires some administrative capacity (to screen recipients and pay sellers)	Political acceptability probably depends on the group served or product purchased; efficiency of this approach may add to political appeal
Cash	Maximum choice	Efficient if money is used for intended need	May reduce work participation—may be used to consume nonintended goods	Will likely require eligibility screening	Can be unpopular if politicians/taxpayers do not favor the recipient group

- *Families who have working members should have higher total income than nonworking families.* If a family will receive less total income (that is, earnings plus benefits) if one or more of its members gets a job or gets a better job, then the program will discourage them from being productive members of society. Calculating the (total or partial) loss of benefit to the family because of new or increased earnings is known as calculating the cumulative tax rate on the working family. "Taxes" include income and social taxes as well as reductions in all social benefits associated with earnings.
- *A family should not be given a strong incentive to lie about its means.* For example, eligibility should not be determined such that a family with slightly more income than another family is rejected for any benefit, while the family with the slightly less income receives a large benefit.

These principles assume that all other factors are held constant.

• Benefit Calculation Methodologies

The basic principles described above can be used with any of the benefit calculation methodologies. Methodologies include flat benefit, tiered benefit, and gap benefit. These methodologies are ways of structuring benefits and are described in order from the simplest to the most sophisticated. The more sophisticated methods will require greater administrative capacity.

Flat Benefit Without Eligibility Limit. With a flat benefit, everybody receives the same assistance regardless of their level of need. A benefit without an eligibility limit provides assistance to all persons regardless of their income level. However, the program is not necessarily a universal entitlement and participation may be limited to a certain number of persons. Examples of flat benefits include birth allowances or pensions.

Table 5.6 compares this simple grant mechanism's impact on the income of households with different incomes.

The advantages to this approach are that there is no complication in determining eligibility or the benefit received. Also, the benefit is not considered a disincentive to work, since total income rises directly with earnings. Subsidies without eligibility limits can be extremely popular, as by definition they have large constituencies.

The disadvantages are that either the benefit is too small to make an impact on the poor or the government is giving away a lot of money to people who do not need it. Thus benefit levels may be quite low, while overall program costs are high. Such programs may require significant resources without really contributing to the social welfare.

Table 5.6   Flat Benefit Example (rubles)

Family	Income	Benefit	Total
A	500	500	1,000
B	700	500	1,200
C	1,000	500	1,500

Figure 5.1 illustrates the flat benefit and how the benefit shifts all incomes upward. The distance between earnings (line *cd*) and total income (line *ab*) represents the benefit. The benefit (line B_1B_2) remains constant for all recipients regardless of earnings.

Targeted Flat Benefit. The same benefit is provided to all eligible individuals or families and eligibility is limited to those with incomes below a certain level. Examples include child or poverty allowances.

The targeted flat benefit has some of the advantages of the flat benefit without

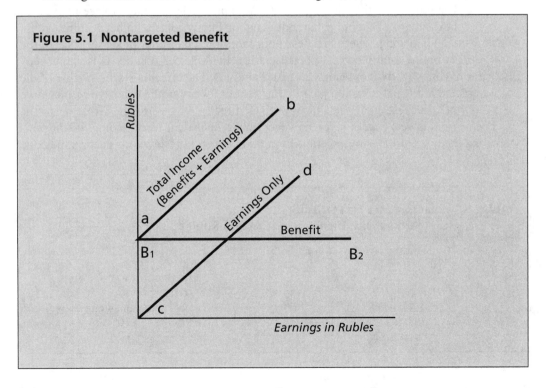

Figure 5.1 Nontargeted Benefit

an eligibility limit. Determining the benefit level is easy, because everyone who is eligible receives the same benefit. Within the eligibility limit, there is no disincentive to work, because total income rises directly with earnings.

The major flaw in the targeted flat benefit is that families who earn a little more than the eligibility limit receive no benefit and thus have less total income than families slightly below the eligibility limit (see Family C in Table 5.7). This provides an almost inexorable motivation for the family with earnings slightly above the eligibility limit to lie about their income. It also strongly discourages the family with earnings slightly below the eligibility limit to improve their lot by seeking employment or a higher-paying job.

Figure 5.2 illustrates the impact of the eligibility limit in the targeted flat benefit. This figure is similar to Figure 5.1 except for the addition of an eligibility limit (line *fb*). The effect of the eligibility limit can be seen where total income (benefits and earnings) is reduced to earnings only (the drop from *b* to *d*).

Tiered Benefit.   Benefits are differentiated according to the income of eligible individuals or families. A tiered benefit recognizes that the poorest families need the largest benefit. With a tiered benefit, the poorest group of families receives the largest benefit, and then the next poorest group receives a somewhat smaller benefit, and so on. Figure 5.3 depicts a three-tiered benefit.

The problem is that earning a little more money in the marketplace may result in a large drop in benefits if the individual or family joins a higher income group. Although reducing benefits for less poor families makes a lot of sense, observe the impact on the total income of beneficiaries. In Table 5.8, Family C is "punished" for having slightly more earnings than Family B. The effect is similar to that of the targeted flat benefit. Within a particular benefit level, families do have an incentive to work, because their total income rises directly with earnings. Crossing to the next (and lower) benefit level, however, will reduce their total income. When nearing the edge of the earnings limit for a particular benefit level (or nearing the edge

Table 5.7   Example of a Flat Subsidy of 300 Rubles with Income Limit of 500 Rubles

Family	Income	Benefit	Total
A	300	300	600
B	499	300	799 (maximum with subsidy)
C	599	0	599

Figure 5.2   Targeted Flat Benefit

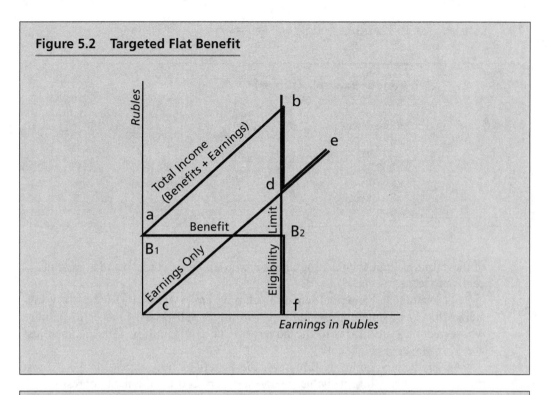

Figure 5.3   Tiered Benefit

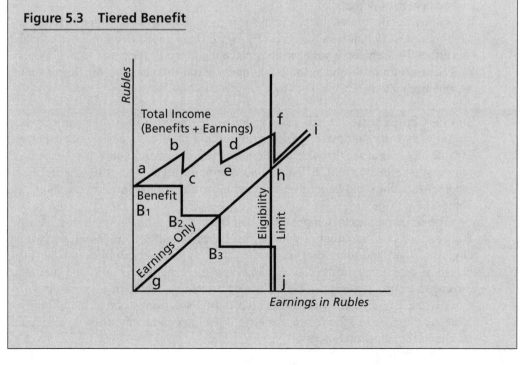

Table 5.8   Tiered Benefit Example (rubles)

Family	Income	Benefit	Total
A	50	600	650
B	250	400	650
C	260	200	460
D	700	0	700

of the earnings limit for the program as a whole), beneficiaries have a great disincentive to work.

For example, a municipal school lunch program in Arzamas, Russia, fully subsidizes lunches to the poorest families and offers half-priced lunches to families whose incomes are closer to the poverty level. But families with incomes just above this level get no benefit.

As another example, in Table 5.8. the benefit is 600 rubles for the poorest group of families, 400 for the next poorest group, 200 for the next poorest group, and no benefit after that.

Figure 5.3 illustrates the potential for jagged income drops with a tiered benefit. The three different benefit levels (B_1, B_2, B_3) are added to earnings to produce this effect. Households whose earnings place them in a lower benefit category may experience a drop in total income (as indicated on the chart by the drop in total income from b to c).

Simple Gap Benefit.   In this case, benefits are designed to fill the gap between earnings and the income eligibility limit. This type of benefit establishes an income floor, that is, through the combination of earnings and the benefit all families have incomes of at least some minimum level. The result is that total income—earnings and benefit—is the same for all eligible families, as shown in Table 5.9.

The advantage to this approach is that there is no disincentive to work as the family approaches the eligibility limit. This is because after their earnings cross the eligibility limit and they lose the benefit, their total income will be greater than before. Figure 5.4 shows that as earnings rise the benefit decreases and that total income is capped at a certain level. The disadvantage is that there is no incentive to work if the employment will not raise a family's earnings above the eligibility limit. As illustrated in the figure, the benefit declines as income rises, to ensure all recipients the same total income.

Table 5.9   Simple Gap Benefit Example (rubles)

Family	Income	Benefit	Total
A	0	1,000	1,000
B	200	800	1,000
C	600	400	1,000
D	1,000	0	1,000

Gap Benefit with Earnings Disregard. The gap benefit with an earnings disregard is a way of encouraging or rewarding families for their work effort. In this model, as total family income (earnings and benefit) exceeds the eligibility limit, families are allowed to continue working with only a partial reduction in their benefits. This is the most progressive benefit model. Its calculation is slightly more complicated than that of the other models and requires some level of administrative capacity.

Figure 5.4   Simple Gap Benefit

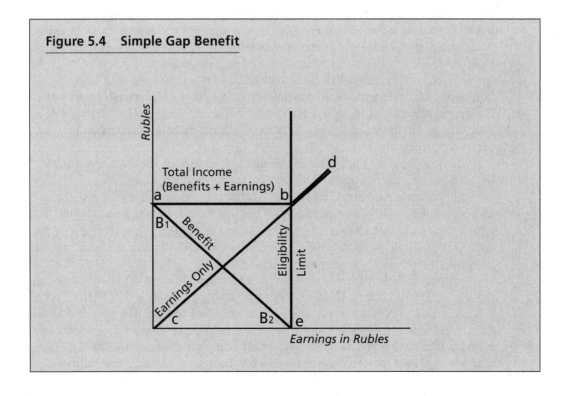

The formula for calculating a gap benefit is:

$$B = P - (t \times Y)$$

Where

B = the actual benefit provided to the household
P = the payment standard or basic benefit
Y = income
t = percentage of income contributed

So that for a program with a payment standard of 300 rubles, the benefit for a family earning 200 rubles per month is:

$$B = 300 - (25\% \times 200)$$
$$B = 300 - 50$$
$$B = 250$$

The payment standard is the generic benefit. Depending on the goal of the program it may represent a minimum level of income (such as a percentage of the poverty line) or the expected cost of some necessary service (such as housing, health care, or education). Payment standards for necessary services should be based on market prices and can be calculated on a per capita or household basis. In some cases, it is expected that there will be economies of scale with larger families, as in the occupancy of an apartment; so a family twice as large as another family might not need twice as much of the same service. In other cases, such as education, it might be appropriate to determine a payment standard based on number of school-age children.

The household's contribution is the share of its income that is counted toward the standard. As the household's income increases, it keeps a percentage $(1 - t)$ of the additional income. For example, an income support program may require that 25 percent of earnings be counted toward the benefit calculation, or a housing program may expect that 15 percent of earnings be contributed toward the cost of the apartment. In these cases, a family would retain 75 and 85 percent of any income increase, respectively.

In Figure 5.5, the payment standard is where benefit and total income meet on the Y-axis. This is because if a family has no earnings, then they should receive the full benefit in order to cover the costs of the specified service. The line at the bottom of the figure is the household's contribution. A percentage of the household's earnings is used to purchase the service or offset a portion of the benefit. If all families are expected to contribute the same percentage of earnings toward the pay-

Figure 5.5   Gap Benefit with Earnings Disregard

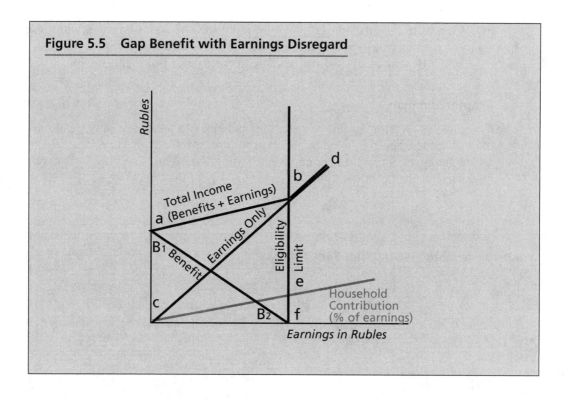

ment standard, then the larger the earnings, the smaller the benefit needed to pay the remaining cost of the service or reach the guaranteed income level. With this formula, the benefit gradually decreases, so there is no strong disincentive to work. Total income rises with earnings (although not as fast). Finally, note that the maximum income of eligible households is the income at which B becomes zero (i.e., $B = 0 = P \div t$).

Figure 5.5 shows how total income is shifted upward for families with higher earnings. Line *ce* indicates the portion of earnings that is disregarded—that is, the amount by which total income increases without a corresponding decrease in bene-

See Exercise 5.3: Benefit Calculation on page 119.

This exercise provides the opportunity to calculate the benefits for three families using each of the benefit calculation methodologies. The exercise illustrates the strengths and weaknesses of each approach.

fits. Whereas in the other models total income (line *ab*) was a flat line, with this approach total income increases at the same rate as the earnings disregard (line *ce*).

Table 5.10 summarizes the various benefit types described in this section.

Chapter Summary

Governments target programs to specific populations to promote equity, reinforce societal values, and minimize public expenditures. Methods of targeting include self-targeting, categorical targeting, means testing, means and asset testing, proxy-means testing, and community-based targeting. Any of these methods can be effec-

---

Table 5.10 Benefit Structure Summary

Benefit Type	Advantages	Disadvantages
Flat benefit	• Easy to administer • No disincentive to work	• Allocates benefits to nonpoor • Benefit levels may be set low to accommodate large number of recipients—little poverty impact • High cost
Flat benefit with eligibility limit	• Easy to administer • No disincentive to work	• Incentive to lie about income or reduce work participation to remain within eligibility limit
Tiered benefit	• Greater equity than flat benefits, as poorest families receive largest benefit	• Incentives to lie about income or reduce work participation if near eligibility limit of tier (or program)
Simple gap benefit	• Benefits tailored to each eligible family's need • No sudden dip in benefits as earnings rise; no disincentive to work as total income does not drop when family crosses eligibility line (instead benefit is tapered off)	• No incentive to work if employment will not raise earnings above the eligibility limit (it is easier to collect benefit than work unless earning higher wages)
Gap benefit with earnings disregard	• Rewards families for work effort • Benefits tailored to family need	• Requires administrative capacity to calculate benefits • Requires documentation of earnings and periodic income reassessments

tive; the important factor is that the targeting approach is effectively implemented. It should be selected based on the goals of the program, the implementation resources, and the local context (i.e., can income be measured?). Methodologies or practices that unintentionally exclude large numbers of the target group or include nonmembers are ineffective.

Public assistance can be provided for either goods or services and can be directed toward economic sectors or individual households. Subsidies to individuals and families include in-kind, price discounts, certificates, and cash. Interventions are evaluated based on consumer choice, production efficiency, consumer incentives (consumption and work), administrative simplicity and cost, and political support.

Government programs that grant benefits to individuals and families need to be structured in ways that are fair and equitable, and that can be easily understood by program administrators and recipients. A few basic principles include that, holding other factors constant: a larger family should receive a larger benefit, a poorer family should receive a greater benefit; families who have working members should have higher total income than nonworking families; and families should not be given incentives to lie about their means. Benefit calculation methodologies include nontargeted benefit, flat benefit, tiered benefit, simple gap benefit, and gap benefit with an earnings disregard.

Recommended Reading

Louise Fox. "Safety Nets in Transition Economies: A Primer." Washington, D.C.: World Bank, March 2003. Available online at http://www.worldbank.org.

Fox compares social assistance programs in the region and assesses the impact of targeting approaches. The report provides additional information on many of the themes discussed in the chapter, and is a good resource for policymakers seeking to implement targeting initiatives. Excellent data tables on poverty and social programs throughout the region make this source a good reference on these topics.

Exercise 5.1: Targeting

Answer the following questions for one or both of the program examples (transportation discounts and child allowances). Recommend a targeting approach for the program, describe how it will be implemented, and explain your reasons for selecting this approach. Your responses should reflect the basic concepts of targeting and an understanding of the strengths and weaknesses of each approach. Remember that the two main criteria for evaluating targeting methods are *effectiveness* in reaching the target group and *administrative feasibility*.

A. Transportation discount. Subsidizes public transportation services for all students in a city.

B. Child allowance. Provides a monthly cash allowance to families with children.

1. Should the program be targeted? Why or why not?
2. If targeted, how should the program be targeted (categorical, means-tested, etc.)?
3. How should eligibility be determined?
4. What socioeconomic conditions are addressed by your approach?
5. Does the approach focus on the long-term or currently poor? Why?
6. Are there any negative incentive effects? How can they be minimized?
7. What are the administrative and financial resources required to implement the targeting strategy?

Exercise 5.2: Analyzing Types of Subsidies and Targeting Methods

In the table that follows, do the following:

1. Provide a program example (in column 3) for each of the different types of subsidies (column 1) and targeting methods (column 2). For some of these types of programs it will be very difficult to come up with an example, such as for a nontargeted cash program.
2. Rate each program example based on the evaluation criteria, consumer choice, administrative simplicity and cost, consumer incentive, production efficiency, and political support, from 1 (lowest) to 5 (highest).

An example is given for an in-kind subsidy with categorical targeting. The statements in parentheses justify the scores awarded.

Evaluation Criteria

(1) Types of Assistance	(2) Targeting Method	(3) Program Examples	(4) Consumer Choice	(5) Administrative Simplicity and Cost	(6) Consumer Incentive and Work	(7) Production Efficiency	(8) Political Support
In-kind	None						
	Self						
	Category	Example: Baby formula	1 (No choice.)	4 (Fairly easy to administer, target group obvious, low-cost benefit.)	5 (No negative incentives.)	3-5 (Depends on how formula is distributed. Formula kitchens are inefficient and may be inconvenient to consumers.)	5 (Program to nourish infants likely to have high political support.)
	Means test						
	None						
	Self						
	Category						
	Means test						
	None						

(continues)

Continued

Evaluation Criteria

(1) Types of Assistance	(2) Targeting Method	(3) Program Examples	(4) Consumer Choice	(5) Administrative Simplicity and Cost	(6) Consumer Incentive and Work	(7) Production Efficiency	(8) Political Support
	Self						
	Category						
	Means test						
	None						
	Self						
	Category						
	Means test	Example: Poverty	5	3	2	4	4

Exercise 5.3: Benefit Calculation

In the table below, calculate the benefits and total income for each of the three families under each of the benefit scenarios.

Calculation of Benefit and Total Income for Three Different Families Under Various Methodologies for Benefit Calculation

	Family A: Monthly Income from Earnings = 2,500 Rubles		Family B: Monthly Income from Earnings = 3,100 Rubles		Family C: Monthly Income from Earnings = 3,600 Rubles	
	Benefit	Total Income	Benefit	Total Income	Benefit	Total Income
Nontargeted benefit of 1,000 rubles						
Targeted flat benefit of 1,000 rubles (eligibility limit is 3,000 rubles income from earnings)						
Tiered benefit: 1,000 rubles for families with earnings from 0 to 2,500 rubles						
750 rubles for families with earnings from 2,501 to 3,000 rubles						
500 rubles for families with earnings from 3,001 to 3,500 rubles						

(continues)

Continued

	Family A: Monthly Income from Earnings = 2,500 Rubles		Family B: Monthly Income from Earnings = 3,100 Rubles		Family C: Monthly Income from Earnings = 3,600 Rubles	
	Benefit	**Total Income**	**Benefit**	**Total Income**	**Benefit**	**Total Income**
No benefit for families with earnings more than 3,500 rubles						
Simple gap benefit: Families are guaranteed total income of 3,000 rubles (families with earnings above 3,000 rubles receive no benefit)						
Gap benefit Benefit = payment standard − ($t \times$ income from earnings) Where: If payment standard = 1,500 rubles, $t = 20\%$						
If payment standard = 1,500 rubles $t = 30\%$						
If payment standard = 1,000 rubles $t = 20\%$						
If payment standard = 1,000 rubles $t = 30\%$						

CHAPTER 6

Assigning Government Responsibilities

The role of government in a market economy is markedly different from that in a centrally planned economy. When most goods and services can be bought and sold in the market, the role of government is diminished. Its primary functions are to set market conditions and to intervene when the market fails—that is, to regulate the market, provide basic public services, and provide social protection for those who cannot compete in the market. Compared with planned economies, this is a radical reorganization of how government works. In making way for the private market, transition governments have had to privatize state assets and remove price controls. Governments have also had to become more service oriented with policies to support the market and protect investments, and efforts to improve the delivery of services. These processes are ongoing and remain vital areas of public policy.

Another important change is the shift from central command to more decentralized and democratic governance systems. Over the past twenty-five years throughout the world there has been a profound decentralization of expenditure responsibility, as higher levels of government devolve functions to lower levels of government. Throughout the Eastern European region, local and subnational governments have assumed additional responsibilities.

The apportionment of responsibility is a fluid process that may or may not be accompanied by added resources. For example, education in the United States has historically been the responsibility of state and local governments. However, over the past several decades the federal government has played an increasingly large role through its funding for low-income and special needs children. Because it controls these funds, the federal government now has greater influence over education policy. The general trend, however, is for national governments to shift responsibility to lower levels of government.

Public services should be delivered at the lowest feasible level of government, according to the principle of *subsidiarity*. The theory behind subsidiarity is that

121

local government has the greatest ability to meet the needs and interests of its constituency. However, there are several situations when subsidiarity is not efficient. Lower levels of government do not always have adequate resources and must rely on transfers from the national government. Some functions have economies of scale or minimum service requirements that are best fulfilled by the national government.

The division of functions ought to be clearly defined for each level of government. The specific assignment of responsibilities and revenue is unique to most countries, though this chapter will offer some basic theory and examples of how various countries have addressed these issues.

Policymakers need to understand the division of responsibility. In defining a problem and considering solutions, it is important to know whether or what aspects of an issue fall under the jurisdiction of the relevant government body. For example, enforcing drunk-driving laws may be a local responsibility, but changing the driving age may require legislation from the regional government. Whether you are a policy analyst working in the governor's office or an NGO, understanding these concepts is an essential part of policy analysis.

The Role of Government in Setting Market Conditions

Government plays a critical role in setting the conditions under which market-based operations can work efficiently. A key element is the enforcement of contracts and consumer rights, and more generally, rule of law. For example, in order for a real estate market to function, transfers of sale must be reliably recorded. Another key element is providing dependable services—such as transportation, heat, and electricity—to permit efficient production. A company producing goods must know that its factories will have power to function. In addition to providing a stable business environment, some governments go a step further by establishing conditions that will make their area a more favorable business environment than others—this often includes incentives such as tax reductions.

• *Should Government Provide This Service?*

In a market economy, most goods and services can be priced and sold in the marketplace and the transactions can be carried out between individuals and/or individual companies with little or no involvement by the government. There are times, however, when the market does not provide a service at all or does not provide it at an adequate level.

Public Goods.   Public goods are generally nonrival in consumption, which means that one person's consumption of the good does not reduce the consumption of another person. Classic examples include public safety, clean air, or even a simple traffic light. With a service that has nonrival consumption, the private market is not interested in providing the service because "free-riders" would benefit from the service without paying for it. There is no practical way to charge for the use of clean air or a traffic light.

Externalities. Externalities are when the activity of one institution or company creates costs or benefits for others that are outside the working of the market mechanism. An example of a negative externality is pollution. If pollution is released into the water or air as part of a production process, then this is a cost associated with production. Who pays this cost? If the market worked perfectly, then the consumers of the product would pay the cost. But usually the market fails and the manufacturer dumps the waste in a water source or the ground. The costs are borne by people who use the surface or ground water, because they must clean the water before using it. Government intervention (i.e., regulation) can correct the market by forcing the company (and ultimately the consumers of the company's product) to pay the cost of reducing this pollution.

Government often provides education and health care services because it believes that there are positive external benefits to providing them. In other words, the community benefits from having healthy and educated members.

Monopolies. Monopolies are sole providers of a good or service. Governments limit the power or existence of monopolies, because monopolies do not provide an adequate supply of a service at a fair price. Monopolies will try to charge a higher price and produce less than companies in a competitive environment. Because of their unique position, monopolies can be inefficient and unresponsive to their customers—this is true of both public and private sector monopolies. For example, prior to recent reforms in Russia, monopolist municipal housing maintenance companies in many cities provided poor maintenance services at costs higher than those charged after competition was introduced.

There are so-called natural monopolies, when the nature of the service calls for one provider. In general, we think of utilities as natural monopolies, because there are economies of scale in production and/or the large fixed costs in creating a distribution network make it inefficient for multiple companies to operate in the same environment. These natural monopolies are either government-owned or heavily regulated.

Expenditure Assignment

We have answered the question of whether government should provide a service (only in the case when the private sector cannot provide this service adequately).

The next question is, if government should provide the service, then what level of government should be the service provider? This section presents criteria and examples of how functions are divided among different levels of government.[1]

• Subsidiarity

The principle of subsidiarity is that responsibility for a public service should be assigned to the lowest level of government consistent with allocative efficiency. The reasoning behind the principle is that local decisions will lead to the quantity, quality, cost, and mix of services that most closely match local needs and preferences. Local provision also increases the accountability of government for the services, because citizens have more direct interaction with elected officials at this level. Subsidiarity can be undermined if the local government has little control over its revenues or lacks administrative capacity. In such cases, local voters are unable to judge the performance of elected officials, who can claim that they are doing what they can with the resources provided. Subsidiarity is an important concept in the European Union Charter on Local Self-Government.

• Situations Where Local Decisions Will Not Lead to an Appropriate Quantity, Quality, Cost, and Mix of Services

When There Are Negative or Positive Externalities. Just as the activity of a private firm can create costs or benefits for others outside the working of the market, the activity of a local government can create costs or benefits for others outside its jurisdiction. A fundamental question is the extent to which the geographic boundaries of local governments coincide with the area of service costs and benefits. If there is greater coincidence or overlap of the two, it is argued that the service be decentralized. If there is less coincidence or overlap, it is argued that greater regional or national policy authority and financing responsibility be maintained. Wastewater treatment is an example of a service that extends beyond the jurisdiction of a local government and has negative externalities for neighboring regions.

With wastewater treatment or solid waste disposal, often the costs will "spill over" the boundaries of individual local governments. If a local government treats wastewater inadequately or not at all, but dumps it into a river, the population downriver, including areas served by different local governments, will be adversely affected. The first local government has no reason to fix the problem suffered by the residents of another area. In this case, a higher level of government regulates the activity of the individual local governments to prevent the problem from occurring.

An example of a positive externality is education. A well-educated person from Town A moves to Town B and starts a very successful business that produces revenues for Town B. This is an argument for a higher level of government to pay for some or all of the costs of educating the population.

Type of Function.   Economic theory attributes certain functions to the public sector. This includes the production of public or quasi-public goods, such as streets, education, and health services. Another function attributed to the public sector includes that of *redistribution*. This includes activities, such as social assistance, that distribute wealth from one part of the population to another.

Not all functions attributed to the public sector are equally well suited for decentralization. In general, the assignment of responsibility for the function of producing public goods follows the principle of subsidiarity, that is, that the best results occur when these functions are assigned to the lowest level of government capable of performing it. This is not an absolute rule. Other criteria discussed below have an impact on the allocation of the production function. The redistribution functions generally are seen as national, but this too is subject to different views.

Economy of Scale.   The question here is one of efficiency. The issue is the extent to which the provision of a service at a smaller or larger scale affects the cost of the service. Economies of scale are often tied to the choice of production technology and may vary over time. Evaluating the economy of scale can be challenging in an environment where data are poor and costs are difficult to allocate, such as with social service delivery. Issues of scale often affect the assignment of responsibility for infrastructure services, such as water. Hospitals are another good example, where the fixed costs of maintaining a hospital (building, beds, equipment, and minimum staff) may be too high for the level of demand for such services in a medium-sized town.

Administrative Capacity.   Local or subnational governments must have the administrative capacity to effectively deliver public services. Poor policy skills, overstaffing, weak training, corruption, and other factors may offset any potential efficiency gains in local service administration.

Other Assignment Criteria.   There are other issues, perhaps less objective but equally important, that affect the choice of what functions to assign to local governments.

Cultural values.   These issues have to do with subjective considerations of what is fair or just. Countries that place a high value on ensuring universal access to and uniform quality of certain services, such as education, may be less inclined to decentralize those services than other countries that place higher value on local choice or control.

Size and diversity. The size of the country and the variety of local conditions, such as population density or fiscal capacity of local governments, also come into play. The assignment of service responsibilities in a larger country with a dispersed population may be different from that in a smaller, more compact country. For example, this may affect the assignment of responsibility for services that rely on a physical network, such as water systems. In a small, compact country there may an argument for maintaining more centralized control over such services than in a larger country where the population is more dispersed or where there is greater distance between population centers.

- ### The Importance of Clear Delineation and Definition of Functions

The legal definition of the functions and responsibilities assigned to local governments determines the extent to which they are explicit, clear, and stable. A clear, legal definition of expenditures is central to intergovernmental relations. The lack of a clear definition can become a source of conflict between central and local governments.

Treatment in the Legislation. The first issue is whether the legislation addresses the question of local functions in general, by specific function, or not at all. Equally important is whether the legislation addresses the nature and extent of the authority of local governments over the functions assigned to them. This includes policy, administrative, and regulatory authority, as discussed later in the chapter. Issues of clarity regarding local functions often concern the relationship between local government laws and laws dealing with specific services or sectors, such as education or urban planning. They also have to do with whether the legislation uses unambiguous terminology or whether it relies on catchall phrases, such as "in accordance with the law." In many countries the roles and responsibilities of local governments are not clearly defined. For example, in Bosnia-Herzegovina, legal expenditure assignments are unclear and nearly silent regarding municipalities. In a recent Organization for Economic Cooperation and Development (OECD) survey, Hungary and Latvia had several outstanding problems in the definition of expenditure assignments, whereas Denmark had no problems.

Stability of Assignment of Responsibilities. A separate issue is how easy it may be to redefine local functions and responsibilities. This applies whether or not the legislation is clear and explicit about the nature and extent of local authority over services. The question here is what the legislation states or established practice shows about how and how often they can change. A related issue is where the authority to make these changes resides and whether or not it is customary or obligatory to consult with local governments in the process.

• *Decentralization and Devolution of Responsibility to Local Governments*

In recent years expenditure responsibilities have been pushed downward. In addition to traditional local functions, municipal governments have had to respond to the need for new social assistance programs (many mandated by the federal government and others simply required by the needs of the local population). Many local governments also inherited the expense of social assets and responsibilities divested by enterprises.

There has been a trend toward decentralizing responsibility to the local level in all regions of the world. Each country must come to its own conclusion about how much decentralization it wants. In other words, it must decide which functions will remain national functions and which functions will become regional or local.

Decentralization vs. Devolution.   Central governments can decentralize functions and allow local governments discretion in how they administer programs. For example, Russia's housing allowance program allows local governments to set the eligibility criteria and benefit levels. Alternatively, functions can be devolved with strict mandates where local governments have little or no discretion and merely implement the federal program. For example, local governments in Russia implement the national child allowance program without discretion and simply administer the program locally according to federal regulations.

Policy control often remains with the entity originating the delegation. Local discretion to manage delegated services is often limited to determining the best way to produce the goods or services, that is, to make choices about the inputs of production—people, technology, or methodology.

Who Finances the Cost of Delegated Functions.   This is a primary concern. If local governments are expected to finance these costs from their own revenues, then this is more a case of an "unfunded mandate" than a delegation of functions. This would be the case, for example, for a subsidy authorized by the national government but paid from the local budget.

• *Elements of Responsibility*

Responsibility can include the following tasks:

- Regulation
- Administration
- Operations
- Maintenance
- Funding
- Capital investment

What does it mean to say that some level of government has responsibility for a particular function? Responsibility has several elements, and different elements may be assigned to different levels of government.

The authority to perform public functions covers a wide range of issues that determine the nature and extent of control assigned to each level of government. The answers to specific issues may differ in a given country by type of service. For example, local governments may have more discretion over certain basic infra- structure services than they do over local social services.

Regulation.   The highest level of authority is the power to make rules—to pass regulations, set policy, and prepare program regulations. National governments fre- quently retain some regulatory authority over major public services, such as setting national standards for education or clean water. Local governments are often required to implement national or regional policies, and enact their own legislation or regulations regarding local issues, such as teacher salaries, water tariffs, or assistance to the poor. Specific aspects of regulatory authority are discussed below.

Authority to determine whether or not a service is required.   One aspect of authori- ty is who decides what services to provide in a given community. Who decides that there is a local problem or a need that requires a public response? Who decides what the appropriate response should be? An important issue for local governments is whether they have the authority to initiate new public services to address a local need or to discontinue or curtail a service that is not a local priority. Conversely, the notion of mandatory or obligatory services represents a lack of authority, where national legislation takes away local discretion not to provide a given service.

Legal basis for local regulatory authority.   Another related issue is whether local governments have a general authority to regulate matters of local interest. This is more than the responsibility to prepare plans, such as urban plans, and extends to the authority to regulate related activities, such as land development and new con- struction.

Other issues to consider are to whom local regulatory authority applies and the methods of enforcement available to local governments. That is, what is the extent of local authority to regulate the activities of citizens, private firms, and non- governmental organizations (e.g., sports or cultural clubs)? The methods of enforcement concern the extent of local discretion in determining penalties or in having recourse in the courts.

Authority to determine service policy and standards.   An important power is the ability to determine the quantity, quality, and cost of the service. Authority may also include the ability to establish eligibility criteria (if not universal) or select the form of financing (direct charge through fees or indirect through general revenues). For example, if local governments are responsible for heating and transportation services, can they also decide that they will sacrifice the quality of transportation services by having fewer buses in order to improve the quality of heating services by making capital investments? Local governments may appear to have policy authority only to find that it is undermined by national service standards.

The impact of national standards on local service delivery is a common and often contentious issue. The issue in this case is not just who sets the standards, but what the standards cover, how clear and objective they are, and how much local discretion they allow. For example, national standards for water systems might detail technical specifications for the water treatment facility (inputs) or they might specify certain minimum standards for residential water quality to ensure public health (outcomes). In the first case, the standards tell the local governments how to do their job. In the second, the standards describe a minimum condition local governments must achieve that is clearly of national interest (health) but leave it up to them to decide how.

Administration. Administration, including operations, maintenance, and funding, is what usually comes to mind when we think of government functions. Examples include administering pensions, operating prisons, maintaining local roads, or funding services for the mentally ill. In the former Soviet Union, large enterprises were often responsible for delivering social services, such as kindergartens. Usually, the operation and maintenance of kindergartens are thought of as a function of a local government.

Authority to organize service delivery. Earlier in this chapter we discussed the concepts of devolution and decentralization. Administrative responsibility may or may not be accompanied with the authority to define the content and scope of services. Even when legislation or regulation limits administrative discretion, implementation carries considerable ability to fulfill, improve, or undermine a policy objective. For example, program staff may disregard eligibility criteria and undermine program targeting, or a city may combine initiatives such as a child care program and a job training program to dramatically improve results.

Separate from issues regarding the content and scope of services, there are questions that concern how the service is organized and who the service providers will be. The general question concerns the authority to decide whether to provide the service directly or to make arrangements to have others produce the service. The next chapter focuses on the options for carrying out government functions, including direct provision, contracting out, leasing, concessions, and privatization. If government involves the private sector in service delivery, its role shifts from direct provision to funding and monitoring program results.

Investment. Investment is a critical but often-overlooked responsibility. Where does the money come from when a new gas line should be put in or when the district heating system needs major repairs?

Ownership of assets. In the transition from a centralized to a decentralized form of government, a number of issues arise about the ownership over the assets associated with the responsibilities assigned to local governments. If ownership of these assets does not follow automatically with the assignment of functions and responsibilities to local governments, it can become an obstacle to the full exercise of their service authority. For example, if local governments are responsible for school investments and major repairs, who owns the school buildings? In the case of services provided by separate corporate entities, such as utilities, does the local government or the corporate entity own the assets? This has important implications for the joint production or privatization of services.

Table 6.1 lists the assignment of expenditure functions for selected countries in the region. Some basic patterns are consistent across countries—such as national government responsibility for defense and foreign economic relations. Local or subnational governments are often involved in the provision of housing, education, local transportation, and some social welfare programs. An equal number of functions, however, are assigned with no cross-country pattern.

• Core Local Government Functions

Although there are differences from country to country on how to delineate functions among the various levels of government, there is some consistency in what constitutes core local government functions. They include the following:

- Provision of drinking water.
- Wastewater collection and treatment.
- Passenger transportation services.
- Operation of homes for the aged and infirm.
- Local road investment and maintenance.
- City development, including land use planning.
- Fire fighting and public safety.
- Management of public (social) housing.
- Local health clinics.
- Administration of social protection programs.
- Cultural and recreational programs.
- Schools.

Table 6.2 summarizes the allocation of administration of social functions to

Table 6.1 Expenditure Assignment to Subnational Authorities

	Bulgaria	CSFR	Hungary	Poland	Romania	Russia
Defense	No	No	No local responsibility	No	No	Military housing
Justice/internal security	Security of farming estates	—	Enforcement of rights of national and ethnic minorities	No	Public security is provided by local branches of the Ministry of Interior	—
Foreign economic relations	No	—	—	—	—	—
Education	All expenditures (capital and current) of primary and secondary schools; some kindergartens; some technical and vocational schools	Partial responsibility in the Czech Republic	Primary and secondary only, including day care and high schools	Kindergarten and preelementary schools only	None	Several special vocational schools; wages, operation construction, and maintenance of all primary and secondary schools; local enterprises build some facilities
Culture and parks	No	—	Supporting cultural activities	—	Overlapping responsibility for cultural activities	Some museums with oblast significance; all recurrent expenditures of all sport and park facilities and all other cultural facilities

(continues)

Table 6.1 Continued

	Bulgaria	CSFR	Hungary	Poland	Romania	Russia
Health	Tertiary care and psychiatric hospitals; polyclinics; some primary care and drugs	No	Basic health and social service	No	None	Paramedics, medicine, primary health clinics, secondary and tertiary hospitals, veteran hospitals, diagnostic centers, and special service hospitals
Roads	Improve traffic safety; maintenance of class-III and class-IV roads and urban streets	No	Maintenance of local public roads	Only local or urban roads/streets	Maintenance	Maintenance of oblast, rayon, and city and commercial roads
Public transportation	All modes of city transport	Urban transport only	Local mass transport	Construction and maintenance of bridges	Public transport investment	Most public transportation facilities, including subway
Fire protection	Most fire protection services	No	Local fire protection	—	None	Most fire protection services
Libraries	Local libraries	No	—	Partial responsibility	No (books purchased through the budget of the Ministry of Culture)	Special library services at the oblast level and most local library services at the rayon level

(continues)

Table 6.1 Continued

	Bulgaria	CSFR	Hungary	Poland	Romania	Russia
Police services	Sofia has a signed contract with the national militia; other municipalities get the service free	No	—	—	—	Road (traffic) police
Sanitation (garbage collection)	Garbage collection and sanitation	—	Garbage collection	—	—	Part of garbage collection at both oblast and rayon levels
Public utilities (gas, electricity, and water)	Water supply infrastructure	—	Water management and maintenance of public cemeteries	Ownership and provision of cold water at all levels; supply street lighting	District heating and water	Subsidies to households (not enterprises) at the rayon level
Housing	Management of common pastures and other municipal property; financing, building, and subsidizing for residential housing	—	Housing management	Shared responsibility	Housing services	Maintenance is the responsibility of the level of government or enterprises owning the housing; capital expenditures are included unless otherwise noted

(continues)

Table 6.1 Continued

	Bulgaria	CSFR	Hungary	Poland	Romania	Russia
Price and other subsidies	Mass transport and drugs; subsidy to intervillage bus service within municipalities; heating subsidy since 1992	Direct subsidies to agricultural cooperatives, and subsidies to enterprises that are not involved in the production of local public goods	Rent subsidies	Rents	Energy subsidies to households and public transport subsidies	For fuels, mass transport, food such as bread and milk, and medicines at the rayon level; also rent subsidies
Social welfare	Homeless, disabled, and orphans	—	Social care facilities such as old-age and handicapped homes		—	Part oblast government responsibility, and the rayon-level management of programs funded by upper-level governments
New public enterprises (productive sectors)	Can establish new domestic joint ventures	Can establish new domestic joint ventures	Can establish new domestic joint ventures	Can establish new domestic joint ventures	Can establish new domestic joint ventures	Capacity to invest in joint ventures (keeps 50 percent of privatization proceeds if rayon subordination); at the rayon level this also includes 10 percent of any other subordination

(continues)

Table 6.1 Continued

	Bulgaria	CSFR	Hungary	Poland	Romania	Russia
Environment	Measures to improve and rehabilitate the environment	—	Protection of the environment	—	—	Responsible for local environmental problems (e.g., preservation of forests)
State-owned enterprises	—	Major local ownership responsibilities	Major local ownership responsibilities	Local ownership responsibilities	Local ownership responsibilities	"Group C" enterprises (e.g., local light industry, housing construction, and food industry); rayon responsibility exists only if the enterprise is transferred to the local level

Source: Jorge Martinez-Vazquez, "The Assignment of Revenue Authority," International Fiscal Relations and Local Financial Management Course, Georgia State University.
Note: — indicates that the information for the entry was unavailable in the source document.

Table 6.2 Allocation of Social Functions to Subnational Governments In Selected Countries

	Austria	Belgium	Denmark	France	Germany	Ireland	Italy	Luxembourg	Netherlands	Norway	Sweden	Switzerland	Turkey	United Kingdom
Preschool education	R, L	L	L	L	L		R, L							L
Primary and secondary education	R, L	R, L	R, L	L	R, L		R, L	L	L	L	L	R, L		L
Vocational and technical training	R	R, L		R, L			R, L	L		R, L	L	R, L	R	L
Higher education	R, L	R, L			R		R, L					R		L
Adult education	L	L	L	L	R, L		R		L	R, L	R, L	R, L		L
Hospitals	R, L	R, L	R	L, D	R, L		R, P, L	L	R, L	R, L	R	R, L	R, L	
Personal health	R, L	L	R, L	L	R, L		R, P, L	L	L	L	R	R	R	
Family welfare services	R, L	R, L	L	L, D	R, L		R, L	L	L	L	L	R, L		L
Welfare homes	R, L	L	L	L	L		R, L	L	L	L	L	R, L		L
Housing	R, L	L	L	L	R, L	L	R, L	R, L	R, L	L	L	L		L
Refuse collection and disposal	L	L	L	L	L	L	L	L	L	L	L	R, L		L
District heating	L	L	L	L	L						L	R, L	R, L	L
Water supply	L	L	L	L	L	L	R, P, L	L	R, L	L	L	R, L	R, L	L

Source: Francis J. Conway, Brian Desilets, Peter Epstein, and Juliana H. Pigey, *Sourcebook on Intergovernmental Fiscal Relations in Eastern Europe* (Washington, D.C.: Urban Institute, August 2001).

Note: R = state, regional government; L = local government; D = departments in France; P = provinces in Italy.

> *See Exercise 6.1: Government Functions and Responsibilities on page 150.*
>
> The task here is to consider the most effective way to assign various responsibilities for each level of government in relation to each of the public services listed. This exercise is an opportunity to apply the concepts from this section to determine the most efficient allocation of responsibility. Key concepts: subsidiarity, efficiency of federal revenue generation/distribution, economies of scale, and externalities.

local and regional governments in selected European countries. The United Kingdom, for example, delegates all social functions to the local level, whereas Austria, Italy, and Switzerland maintain a regional role in most social programs.

Revenue Authority

Although it may be efficient to deliver many services at the lowest possible level of government, subnational governments tend to have limited financial resources. This mismatch of expenditure responsibilities and revenue authority creates many problems for regional or local governments, for whom the lack of adequate resources limits their ability to deliver services efficiently and undermines accountability. National governments tend to have absolute revenue authority and assign taxes and other revenues to lower levels. National governments also assign grants and transfers to lower levels of government to ensure a minimum level of service and to redistribute resources to communities with low fiscal capacity.

• Objectives of Intergovernmental Transfers

Usually national governments have the greatest potential for revenue generation and revenue distribution. The primary reasons for a central government advantage in revenue generation are efficiency in tax administration and collection. Since individuals move and companies operate across jurisdictions, it is often more efficient for a higher level of government to keep track of the income produced.

There are several motivations for revenue redistribution from the national government to lower levels of government.

To Address a Fiscal Gap. Although it may be more efficient for the national government to generate most tax revenues, the principle of subsidiarity encourages functions to be carried out at the lowest appropriate level. This means that there must be a transfer of revenues from the national level to lower levels of government to cover this fiscal gap. This is also sometimes referred to as creating a vertical balance. Two appropriate ways to distribute revenues for this purpose are general transfers and revenue sharing (local governments receive a portion of a national tax).

To Address Horizontal Imbalances. To address horizontal imbalances, or differences among regions, national governments distribute equalization grants. This is important because the poorest regions often have the greatest need for social protection programs, yet have the weakest ability to pay for these services. It is most effective if national governments target these equalization grants to "vulnerable" local governments with low *fiscal capacity* (see box below). In reality, equalization grants (e.g., the Federal Fund for Support of the Regions [FFSR] in Russia) are often allocated based on a combination of need and politics.

To Ensure Minimum Standard of Service. To ensure a minimum standard of service, national and subnational governments distribute transfers. These funds are based on the estimated cost of providing services and are earmarked for expenditure in a specific sector, and sometimes for a specific expenditure within that sector (such as teachers' salaries).

To Correct for Externalities. To correct for externalities national governments distribute conditional matching transfers. With some functions, such as education or pollution control, benefits are enjoyed by the jurisdiction itself and additional benefits or costs accrue to other jurisdictions. To encourage a jurisdiction to provide the appropriate amount of a service, the national government may provide transfers that are directly related to the amount of resources that the jurisdiction itself is willing to provide.

• *Revenue Authority and Expenditure Responsibility*

In principle, the assignment of tasks to a lower level should be accompanied by the transfer of the corresponding financial resources as well. For example, if local gov-

---

Fiscal capacity is the ability of government to raise taxes from the tax bases assigned to it. Higher levels of government want local governments to cover as much of the cost of services they can afford before offering assistance. So in computing equalization grants it is common for national governments to apply standard tax rates to each local government's tax bases to determine what the local government should pay itself.

ernments are assigned responsibility for water treatment, then it is appropriate for local governments to be able to set the water tariffs charged by the water utility.

When local authorities are given greater revenue authority, they become more accountable to their citizens for the quality and mix of services they deliver; accountability is not functional when the link between responsibility and revenue authority is broken (i.e., a local authority can say that it performs a function badly because a higher level of government does not provide the resources).

In general, national governments have complete revenue authority and local governments have somewhat limited revenue authority. Determining the "right" level of revenue centralization is a policy decision that balances macroeconomic stability and administrative efficiency (generally best addressed at a national or subnational level), with the desire to provide subnational and local governments with their own revenue and transfers to fund the local provision of public goods.

• Tax Authority

How much revenue a level of government can generate will depend partly on its revenue authority. There are several aspects of tax and fee authority:

- The general authority to introduce new taxes and fees.
- The specific authority to set the rate for existing taxes and fees (possibly limited within a certain range).
- The authority to enforce collection of taxes and fees. (Can the regional or local government punish a nonpayer?)
- The ability to borrow funds.

• Tax Assignment and Specific Taxes

Tax assignment refers to the level of government that is responsible for determining the level and rate structure of various taxes, collecting the tax, and deciding how the tax will be allocated among different levels of government. Although there is considerable difference in how various countries assign taxes, some taxes have attributes that make them more or less appropriate for various levels of government.

Table 6.3 outlines various types of tax designs and describes them according to the level of autonomy they provide for local governments.

Some basic principles of tax assignment include the following:[2]

National Level

- The tax is aimed at or suitable for economic stabilization or income redistribution.

Table 6.3   Types of Taxes and Intergovernmental Assistance

Own taxes	Base and rate under local control
Overlapping taxes	Nationwide tax base, but rates under local control
Nontax revenues	Fees and charges; generally, the national government specifies where such charges can be levied and the provisions that govern their calculation
Shared taxes	Nationwide base and rates, but with a fixed proportion of the tax revenue (on a tax-by-tax basis or on the basis of a "pool" of different tax sources) being allocated to the subcentral government in question, based on (1) the revenue accruing within each jurisdiction (also called the derivation principle) or (2) other criteria, typically population, expenditure needs, and/or tax capacity
General purpose grant	Subnational government share is fixed by central government (usually with a redistributive element), but the former is free to determine how the grant should be spent; the amounts received by individual authorities may depend on their tax efforts
Specific grants	The national government specifies the expenditure programs for which grants should be spent; the absolute amount of the grant may be determined by central government or it may be "open-ended" (that is, depend on the expenditure levels decided by lower levels of government)

Source: Anwar Shah, "The Reform of Intergovernmental Fiscal Relations in Developing and Emerging Market Economies," Policy and Research Series no. 23 (Washington, D.C.: World Bank, 1994).

- The tax base is highly mobile (such as general consumption taxes that would not be very effective if assigned to local governments).
- The tax bases are unevenly distributed among jurisdictions—for example, those associated with the presence of valuable natural resources like gas and oil.

Local

- Taxes should be visible to encourage local government accountability.
- Taxes should generate sufficient revenue to avoid large vertical fiscal imbalances, and should not be subject to large fluctuations.
- Taxes should be fairly easy to administer (taxes with significant economies of scale should be assigned to higher levels).
- Taxes based on user charges and fees are particularly suitable for local governments.

Table 6.4 lists various taxes, such as property and income taxes, and describes how they can be used most efficiently by local or national governments.

• *Typical Local Government Self-Generated Revenues*

The following is a list of tax and other revenues often utilized by local governments.

Tax Revenues

> Property tax
> Land tax
> Vehicle tax

Nontax Revenues

> Income from leasing or selling land or property
> Share of income from municipal enterprises
> Revenue generated from budget organizations (sports, health care, etc.)
> Local fees (licenses, patents, etc.)
> Fines

In general, local governments in transition countries mostly charge benefit-based taxes or fees. These are applied in direct correspondence to a local service provided. An obvious example is a fee that a vendor pays to rent a place in the municipally owned town market. In industrialized countries, property taxes are often the most important source of locally generated revenues.

• *Ongoing Transition and Reforms*

The process of establishing a viable system of finances for subnational governments in the region occurs amid a set of specific conditions.[3] The political and economic transition, the accompanying economic and fiscal problems, and for some countries, European Union accession, provide the overall context for the policy dialogue on intergovernmental fiscal relations in the region.

First, the very notion of a transition means that established ways of doing things must change. The transition is an evolutionary process that progresses unevenly across a wide range of issues. What does not change probably will remain largely as it was before the transition began. This means that the policy debate on intergovernmental fiscal relations cannot focus exclusively on what is new. Policymakers must focus on changing the system that is in place and adapting to new circumstances. Otherwise, the combination of the new and old may have unintended consequences and produce results different than anticipated.

Table 6.4   Different Types of Taxes and Their Attributes

Tax	Attributes
Property tax	• Often used by subnational and local governments • Administrative costs are generally lower than income taxes • No free-rider problems—as all residents generally pay direct or indirect (renters) property taxes • The main disadvantage of property taxes is that they generate lower amounts than needed; this is partly due to the fact that it is a very visible tax, and therefore unpopular. It can also be perceived as having unwanted distributional consequences in that the tax is borne by renters and not the owners of property • Property values need to be regularly assessed and updated
Personal income tax	• Most countries assign a large portion of income taxes to the national government • Personal income taxes have the capacity to generate significant revenue • A disadvantage to using personal income taxes as a local tax is that many poor persons requiring public services are below the tax threshold • Sometimes used as an overlapping tax to generate income for subnational or local governments • Generally best collected by national or subnational governments due to economy of scale involved in administering these taxes
Sales tax/ Value-added tax	• Sales taxes can be levied at a local level—so long as rates are similar across jurisdictions • Variations in rates can lead to consumers crossing borders for cheaper rates • VATs are generally best assigned to the national government; requires significant administrative capacity and the national government is best able to adjust for varying spatial allocation of production and consumption
Corporate profit tax	• Taxation of large businesses should be left to the national government, as the economic activities of corporations are typically diversified and complex—with various activities located in a number of jurisdictions • Local governments seeking to tax corporate profits may have informational problems • Many countries allocate a share of corporate profit taxes to the locality or region from which those activities originated

Source: John Norregaard, *Tax Assignment: Fiscal Federalism in Theory and Practice,* edited by Teresa Ter-Minassian (Washington, D.C.: International Monetary Fund, 1997), pp. 55–67.

Second, economic instability increased in many countries during the shift to a market economy. Policies that imposed hard budget constraints on previously subsidized enterprises, lifted price controls, and chipped away at social protections caused extreme hardship for many citizens. Some nations emerged from this process better off than others. For some, increasing poverty has diminished the appetite for reform. And in some countries poor policy decisions and weak or corrupt governments have exacerbated fiscal problems.

Third, for Eastern European countries, the devolution of greater fiscal authority to local governments acquires special significance when considered in the context of the complex and difficult decisions that the national authorities pursued to join the European Union. National authorities and the donors that support them may be reluctant to surrender fiscal authority to local governments if they perceive this as leaving them without the tools they need to address the broader national reforms. This means that the policy dialogue on intergovernmental fiscal relations must focus carefully on the timing and sequence of reforms. Otherwise, the process of decentralization may fall into conflict with the larger process of change and lose support.

• Economic and Fiscal Policy Reform Issues

Key reforms taking place in the former Soviet Union and Eastern Europe as part of the overall transition from a centrally planned to a market economy, and from an autocratic to a democratic system of governance, influence decisions regarding the financial resources of governments in the region. Eight especially important aspects of reforms for local governments follow.

1. Fiscal Stabilization. Transition countries face continuing fiscal and economic problems as they strive to reduce and redefine the role of government and adjust to the new market economy. The fiscal stabilization programs adopted in response to these problems have a direct impact on governmental financial resources and policies.

Budget deficit targets. Fiscal stabilization in the region has involved some combination of increases in public revenues and reductions in public expenditures to decrease the overall budget deficit to some target, usually expressed as a share of GDP. It also has included limits on overall debt exposure and debt service targets. These stabilization measures can affect the revenues and expenditures of local governments—in particular, limiting the ability of local governments to borrow or raise capital to finance investments, thereby restricting local decision-making.

Financial administration. Fiscal stabilization also includes measures to maintain tight control over public expenditures and manage the overall cash position of the government. A common measure involves the implementation of a single treasury with jurisdiction over all public funds. While the nature and extent of the controls over local revenues and expenditures exercised by the treasury may vary, this measure will certainly limit local authority over their own finances.

2. Tax Reform. In general, countries in the region implemented broad tax reforms to reduce high tax rates, broaden the tax base, and modernize and strengthen tax administration.

Impact on local revenues. A key question is whether and how these reforms affect the specific taxes assigned to local governments either as local or shared taxes. Some of these taxes may be eliminated as part of the reforms. Others may be restructured completely. For example, the wage tax may be folded into a general income tax. Such reforms may alter the revenues that local governments receive from these taxes, and other local sources of revenues, such as transfers, may need to be adjusted to restore "vertical" balance among the levels of government.

Impact on local tax administration. Reforms in tax administration may diminish or increase local authority to administer taxes. This may also change the necessity and timeliness of information to local governments on taxes administered by the national government on their behalf.

3. Public Administration Reform. Civil service reform is an important part of the changes taking place in public administration. How these reforms are structured can have a significant impact on government finances.

Cost of staff. A key question is the extent to which the new civil service system rules apply to local governments and how they affect personnel costs. Will there be a single national personnel classification and compensation system that applies to all governments? Are the sizes and levels of local government staffs subject to national review and/or approval?

Transfers of functions. When national functions are transferred to local governments, the rules regarding civil servants may or may not be clearly delineated. If they are fully delineated, such rules may not take into account the interests of local governments. For example, when functions are overstaffed, local governments may not have the authority to set their own staffing levels at the time of the transfer of responsibility.

4. Capital Markets Reform. In many respects the use of debt as a financial resource for government is intertwined with the development of the overall capital market. The broad policy and legal framework for capital markets has a direct impact on the ability of subnational governments to access these markets and to compete on equal terms with other borrowers.

Legal framework. Are tax laws neutral as they affect local borrowing (as opposed to other forms of borrowing), or as they affect the sale of local government bonds versus direct bank lending to local government? Do regulations of securities markets and of financial institutions (banks, pension funds, insurance companies) discriminate against the local government sector? To what extent does the legal framework facilitate equity versus debt financing (favoring equity may induce subnational governments to corporatize some operations and to sell shares while retaining a controlling interest)? What is the relative role of commercial lending versus bonds?

Role of government. Do the national government's grant and loan programs that fund local government investments operate in ways that strengthen or compete with development of a private market for local government credit? Beyond ensuring a level playing field, should the national government intervene in a more active way to support local government credit market development by authorizing state transfer intercepts or other forms of credit enhancement? Should there be a municipal development bank and other forms of credit intermediaries?

5. Social Sector Reform. In most transition countries there are ongoing or planned reforms in the financing of health services, social assistance, and consumer subsidies that have significant implications for intergovernmental finances.

Local functions. The first question is whether and how social sector reforms affect the assignment of functions to local governments. In many cases, local governments are already responsible for some part of the existing social service programs; often they are the local administrators of national programs. In all likelihood social sector reforms will increase the local role in providing social services. A critical question is the degree of local authority associated with these additional responsibilities—in other words, is this decentralization or devolution?

Cost of subsidies. Subsidies of consumption of public services, such as heating or transport, and income support programs can have a big impact on local budgets. These subsidies can become a bigger burden as a result of measures to increase prices of such services or as a result of measures to address the social impact of economic and other reforms. What is the nature and extent of local authority and involvement in this area? Is the impact on local budgets of price increases and/or changes in subsidy policies being considered? Are local governments authorized to implement their own subsidy programs for those services assigned to them?

6. State Enterprise Reform.   Many services typically assigned to local governments were previously performed by state enterprises. In all countries in Eastern Europe these enterprises have gone or are going through a profound transformation. This process has a significant impact on intergovernmental finances. Key questions regarding the privatization or restructuring of state enterprises include the short-term impact on local expenditures, and the longer-term issues of who controls the enterprises and how this affects the ability of local governments to execute certain local services through privatization or other means. Who is responsible for subsidizing the enterprises if they do not operate on a break-even or profit basis? What is the legal relationship of the enterprise to the local government? What is the nature and extent of the authority of local governments over the enterprises? In the case of infrastructure enterprises, who owns the assets required to provide the services?

The relationship between local governments and service-providing enterprises varies across the countries of the region. For example, in Bulgaria the transformation of utility enterprises into municipally owned companies or private companies operating at a municipal level has proceeded slowly. The extent of municipal control and involvement in that country varies by sector, with a significant role in garbage collection, a mixed role in water, and relatively less involvement in heating and transport.

In Macedonia, local public enterprises played a crucial role in providing public services to communities during the former government system. They continue to play the same role today, but their relationship to the municipalities has not been fully resolved. Based on the various enabling acts now in effect, the municipalities should be able to exercise oversight and control over the affairs and the finances of the enterprises. However, the lack of clarity on ownership of assets and limited staff capacity in the municipalities constrain their ability to provide adequate oversight.

In Russia, social asset divestiture to municipalities, including divesture of enterprise housing, occurred quickly and thoroughly in a few years beginning in 1995. Enterprises were strongly motivated to free themselves of these substantial expenditures as they struggled to survive during the transition.

7. Landownership and Property Market Reforms.   The legal status of public property is an important issue in transition economies, where it has been necessary to establish a legal regime of public ownership of property. A number of issues surround the new local public property legislation, including the process and the timing of the transfer of ownership to local governments. For example, is the process of allocating property among national, regional, and local governments transparent, and are local interests considered? The general question is whether the implementation of the law results in the transfer to local governments of the public property they need to perform the functions assigned to them.

8. Decisionmaking Process. Intergovernmental relations and reforms are often determined by national, and to a lesser degree, subnational governments. Local governments may be considered in the reform process, though rarely are they full partners in the decisionmaking. Too often the impact of reforms on local governments is not considered and local governments may not even learn about changes until late in the game. When such policies have an adverse impact on local governments, compensating measures or changes to the reforms can mitigate hardship.

For countries seeking to join the European Union, its requirements have driven many fiscal policy decisions. Box 6.1 summarizes some of these issues.

Chapter Summary

The basic principle of a market economy is that goods and services can be most efficiently produced and sold without the intervention of government, and that buyers and sellers will naturally seek out the optimal mix of production and price.

Government plays a critical role in setting the conditions under which market-based operations can work efficiently. Government enforces contracts, consumer rights, and the rule of law. It also provides basic public services and infrastructure to permit efficient production, and offers social protection services to its citizens when the market fails or when certain individuals cannot compete in the market. Governments must also be more active when the market fails, such as when a new mobile telephone monopoly abuses its powers. Public goods, positive or negative externalities, and monopolies are the primary examples of market failure and motivations for government regulation or service provision.

Once a function has been determined to be in the public realm, it must then be assigned to a level of government. Important concepts in assigning tasks to various levels of government include subsidiarity, economies of scale, and externalities. There has been an increasing trend throughout the world toward decentralization, and local governments are assuming many additional tasks. Sometimes these responsibilities are *decentralized,* such that local governments have autonomy in how they perform them; other times these responsibilities are *devolved,* such that local governments have strict mandates and little discretion.

Although local governments may find their responsibilities increasing, these demands may or may not be associated with the funds necessary to fulfill these

Box 6.1   European Union Accession Issues

For Eastern European countries the require-ments to join the European Union have domi-nated many policy decisions. Several of these requirements affect intergovernmental rela-tions and the financial resources dedicated to subnational governments.

Financing Through Regions

Much of the assistance that the EU provides to the countries of Eastern Europe as part of the accession process is disbursed through a regional structure. Although most Eastern European nations already have regional gov-ernments, the EU does not view the system of government as properly structured and gener-ally advocates restructuring aimed at stream-lining and building accountability throughout the governance structure.

For example, in Poland the EU strongly encouraged the national government to (a) cut the number of voivodships (regional entities) from about 50 to 16; and (b) introduce a new system of 375 powiats (counties)—a process that led to a wholesale reallocation of func-tions up from towns to counties (most munic-ipalities were given powiat status) and down-ward from regional entities in order to better balance subsidiarity with economies of scale in service provision.

The provision of financing through a regional structure raises a number of impor-tant questions on the relation between these new regional structures and intergovernmen-tal finances in Eastern Europe.

Nature of the Regions

What is the nature of the new regions? Are they administrative bodies or will they become a new tier of local government? If the new regional bodies are only administrative in nature (appointed, not elected), what is their role in the flow of funds from the national to the local budgets? What is the role of local elected officials in these regional administrative bodies?

In preparation for receiving EU accession funds, Hungary enacted its Act on Regional Development and Regional Planning in 1996. This generated an intense debate over the nature of the region as an administrative unit or as a new tier of elected local government. It also has raised questions about the financing of the new regional structures. This same debate took place in the Czech Republic.

Flow of Funds Through the Regions

Will the EU grants follow the same process as transfers from the national budget or will there be separate mechanisms and proce-dures? What will be the impact on local authority to make spending decisions?

New Standards

The process of accession brings other require-ments that may have an impact on intergov-ernmental finances in Eastern Europe. Many of these requirements concern new standards in areas where local governments have the primary responsibility, such as for air or water quality.

Impact on Local Finances

How these standards are managed may affect the level of authority and resources of local governments. For example, extensive new investments may be required to bring local facilities and equipment up to the new stan-dards. Regular service expenditures may also be affected by higher standards, and it is unclear whether higher levels of government or the EU will support these new expenses.

Nature and Extent of Local Participation

How EU accession is managed within each country may determine the extent to which
(*continues*)

Box 6.1 Continued

the impact on intergovernmental finance is considered at the time that decisions and commitments are made. The key issue is what role, if any, local governments will have in this process.

Maastricht Criteria
The Maastricht criteria require that all countries seeking accession to the European Monetary Union must maintain limits on overall public deficits and debt. Maastricht criteria do not make a distinction between national, municipal, or regional debts or those of national funds and institutions. This will bring local government debt under greater scrutiny and may lead to additional reporting requirements.

The recent experience of the Czech Republic, Hungary, and Poland shows that compliance with the Maastricht criteria will lead to expanded reporting on local debt and perhaps additional limits on the extent of that debt.

Source: Francis J. Conway, Brian Desilets, Peter Epstein, and Juliana H. Pigey, *Sourcebook on Intergovernmental Fiscal Relations in Eastern Europe* (Washington, D.C.: Urban Institute, August 2001).

---

functions. In general, national governments have complete revenue authority and subnational governments have somewhat limited revenue authority. Central governments are in the best position to manage macroeconomic stability and have administrative advantages in collecting revenue. However, subnational and local governments need their own revenues and transfers to fund the local provision of public goods and to form the basis of accountability for local conditions. National governments redistribute revenue to lower levels of government to address the fiscal gap, mitigate horizontal imbalances, ensure minimum service standards, and correct for externalities. Typical sources of revenue for local government includes grants and transfers, self-generated tax revenues (often from property taxes, land taxes, and vehicle taxes), and various user charges, fees, and fines.

Transition countries are still resolving the division of public and private functions. In too many countries, governments still control or participate in profit-making activities. Paring back government involvement, maximizing the public benefit from the sale of assets, and facilitating economic development are vital areas of public policy.

Policy analysts must also have a command of the issues of intergovernmental relations—whether their interests are tax policy or knowing what level of government is responsible for improving higher education standards. The functions of each level of government and the resources available continue to evolve in many nations.

Recommended Reading

Charles E. McLure and Jorge Martinez-Vazquez. *The Assignment of Revenues and Expenditures in Intergovernmental Fiscal Relations.* Washington, D.C., n.d. Available online at http://www.worldbank.org/wbiep/decentralization.

This reading explores expenditure responsibility and revenue authority in greater detail. Its tables provide useful examples of expenditure assignment for transition and other countries. The references at the end of the report are an excellent source of additional materials on the topic.

Teresa Ter-Minassian, ed. *Fiscal Federalism in Theory and Practice.* Washington, D.C.: International Monetary Fund, 1997.

The first several chapters of this reading provide an excellent overview of expenditure responsibility and revenue authority. Tables detail the intergovernmental fiscal relations of many countries.

Exercise 6.1: Government Functions and Responsibilities

This exercise involves assigning various expenditure responsibilities in health, education, pension administration, and other public services to national, regional, and local governments. Responsibilities should be assigned according to the key concepts covered in this chapter, including subsidiarity, efficiency of federal revenue generation/distribution, economies of scale, and externalities (problems that affect several jurisdictions). Do not assign responsibilities as they are currently divided in your country—rather use this as an opportunity to consider what might be the most efficient assignment. Government responsibilities may include: regulatory/policymaking, funding, capital funding/investment, administration/operation, oversight/monitoring. The row for water/wastewater has been filled in as an example.

Public Service	Federal	Regional	Local
Water/wastewater	• Sets clean water standards • May contribute to major capital investments—if project benefits broader groups or introduces new technologies, etc. • Enforces clean water standards	• May contribute to capital or operating expenses • May be delegated to enforce standards	• Sets tariffs • Funds operations through tariffs or local funds • Provides water services and maintains water/sewage systems (and/or contracts with private company) • Identifies investment needs and may seek additional funds from federal or regional government
Education			
Health care			
Pensions			
Unemployment benefits			

(continues)

Public Service	Federal	Regional	Local
Housing/housing allowances			
Fire/police protection			
Sanitation (garbage collection and disposal)			
Courts			
Registering real estate transactions			
Others:			

CHAPTER 7

Implementing Government Programs

Just as the responsibilities involved in performing a function can be distributed among different levels of government, they can also be distributed between the public and private sectors. Some tasks are more appropriate for delegation than others, and governments make decisions about how to involve the private sector based on a range of practical and political considerations. Government generally retains full regulatory responsibility, but may involve the private sector in operations, maintenance, and investment. The primary types of private sector arrangement include contracting out, leases, concessions, and privatization or divestiture.[1]

The private sector is increasingly a partner to government, at times helping to improve service quality and/or lower costs. For example, government contracts with NGOs to provide services to the elderly or legal representation for the indigent. Private firms operate under contracts to provide countless services, manage water utilities, and purchase privatized enterprises and other assets. The private or nonprofit sector often has technical or other expertise that aids service delivery. For example, an NGO working with a previously underserved segment of the population, such as battered women, has insights into effective service and safety strategies. A private concessionaire running a water utility offers management and technical expertise, as well as capital investment.

Another argument for private sector involvement in the delivery of public services is competition. Government monopolies are generally inefficient and the introduction of competition can result in improved services at lower costs. Competition among public agencies can also control expenditures and improve services. However, public agencies are often beholden to strict regulations, collective bargaining agreements, fixed capital costs, and disincentives to reduce spending that limit their ability or willingness to maximize efficiency. Private firms have strong incentives (the profit motive) to provide quality services at the lowest possible price. In addition, private firms and NGOs have greater flexibility in how they structure their capital or human costs and employ new technologies. The ability to pay workers less than their public service counterparts is often a major source of savings for contracted services.[2] Private firms may also be able to rely on cheaper equipment, such as smaller vehicles—whereas public entities may be tied to large buses, trucks, and public maintenance facilities. Smaller vehicles, for example, may not only save money but also facilitate more frequent service—whether passenger transportation or garbage collection—and thereby improve service quality.

This chapter provides an overview of each of these implementation options and outlines criteria to determine which option is appropriate. These strategies may be important to consider when conducting the policy analysis model described in Chapter 2.

Options for Carrying Out Government Functions

Figure 7.1 depicts the various options based on the amount of public and private investment required and the duration of the arrangement. Direct provision by government requires zero investment by the private sector and 100 percent investment by the public sector. The duration of the option is also correlated with the level of delegation to the private sector and the risk involved. Privatization is the ultimate in delegation, where the private sector assumes the rights and responsibilities of ownership. Although government may have some regulatory control over the privatized asset—such as protecting customers from monopolistic pricing or enforcing health and environmental regulations—it has essentially given (sold) all authority to the private sector. A short-term contract, on the other hand, holds little risk for the public or private sector, as the contract can be revoked and services restored to public sector management.

• Provision vs. Production

When is it appropriate for the government to "produce" the service and when is it appropriate to assign it to another entity (NGO or private company)? Clearly, if a function can be adequately executed by the market, the government should not participate or interfere. For example, a city may own commercial office space that it rents to businesses. This is generally not considered a public good nor is it regulating or correcting a market failure—it is simply a business operation. This principle would suggest that the city consider selling the office space to a private company and using the revenue from that sale for public purposes.

In general, governments perform regulatory services directly and do not ask other entities to take on this responsibility. That said, associations often self-regulate their members (e.g., doctors), which reduces the need for government regulation.

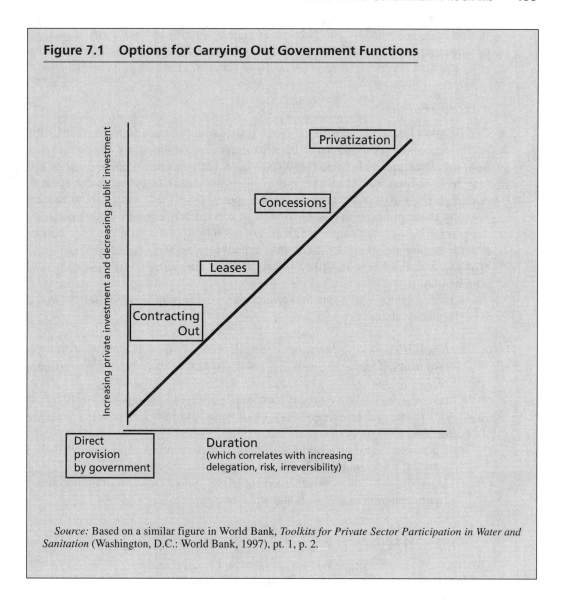

Figure 7.1   Options for Carrying Out Government Functions

Source: Based on a similar figure in World Bank, *Toolkits for Private Sector Participation in Water and Sanitation* (Washington, D.C.: World Bank, 1997), pt. 1, p. 2.

Operations and maintenance services can generally be better performed at lower costs when governments request other entities to compete for this work. This chapter and the next will discuss competitive procurement.

Although it is appropriate for government to determine priority investments in public services, it does not always have the means to carry out these investments.

In this case, government can make an arrangement with another entity (usually a private company) to make the necessary investment. In return, the company delivers the related services and receives tariffs to recapture the cost of its investment.

• Direct Provision

Certain tasks frequently remain the direct responsibility of government, such as the administration of taxes and major benefits programs, public safety and fire protection, infrastructure, and more. These tasks are widely considered public goods and may have economies of scale or externalities that argue for government control. Although most governments consider it important for these functions to remain squarely in the public realm, some aspects of service delivery may be contracted to the private sector, such as private firms contracting to maintain public vehicles or provide computer support for large government offices. With direct provision government maintains responsibility for regulation, financing and investment, and administration.

A classic example of a function retained by government is public safety, which is performed by the local police force:

- *Regulation.* The government (usually the head of the police force) is responsible for making sure that the individual officers behave appropriately.
- *Investment.* The government purchases police cars, computers, traffic control radar, and other necessary equipment and provides officers with the necessary training.
- *Operations.* The government recruits sufficient police officers and makes sure that a set number of police officers patrol the city's streets.
- *Maintenance.* The government ensures that police cars and other necessary equipment are running well and at a low cost.

• Contracting Out

Contracting out opens the door for competition because instead of providing the service directly (and as a monopoly provider), the government signs a contract with one or more other entities to perform the service. These other entities may be a private firm, an NGO, or even a government agency. The focus is not on *who* provides the service, but on *competitive bidding* among potential service providers.

Contracts are generally for short periods of time (from a few months to a maximum of three years). Contracting is most effective when the tasks can be clearly specified and their completion measured.[3] Monitoring the quality and completion of the work is a critical aspect of managing contracts. Without adequate monitoring, contracting out is unlikely to generate the savings or service improvements sought by engaging the private sector in a competitive process.[4]

A performance or management contract is another type of contract that focuses not on outputs (tasks or activities), but on outcomes produced. The contractor is paid according to the results achieved. For example, a traditional contract might pay the contractor a fixed sum for providing job training to 500 participants (or a certain fee per participant), whereas a performance contract would pay a specified amount only for those placed in jobs. All incentives are weighted on the results and the contractor is encouraged to find the most efficient way to fulfill the program goals. This means the government must think seriously about performance targets and how they can be monitored. (Chapter 10 discusses outcomes and performance-based management strategies.)

Examples of contracting out government services in Russia:

- Communal services (maintenance) for residential buildings.
- Provision of school lunches.
- NGOs performing some social assistance functions.
- Private firms providing public transportation services with small vans/buses.

Because of the usefulness of contracting out, Chapter 8 fully describes the process of how to competitively procure public services. For an example of how contracting out can improve public services, see Box 7.1.

• Leasing

There are two broad leasing models. Under the first model, the government leases an asset *to* a private company to deliver a service. The key elements are:

- The private firm leases government assets and has responsibility for operating and maintaining the assets.
- The government (as lessor) retains investment responsibility.

For example, a local government leases its water plant and sewage treatment facilities to a private firm for the latter to operate and provide water and sanitation services to the city.

Under the second model, the government leases an asset, such as an office building, *from* a private firm (lessor). The city's motivation is often to avoid paying the full purchase cost at one time; leasing distributes the payments over a period of years.

Leasing can be an effective mechanism for government or private industry to

Box 7.1   Private Buses in Calcutta

Calcutta is one of the largest, most densely populated, and poorest cities in the world.[a] It supports a population of some 10 million in an area that covers less than 600 square miles. Private buses first appeared in the city toward the end of the nineteenth century but were banned in 1960, when all bus services were vested in the Calcutta State Transport Corporation (CSTC). The CSTC suffered from managerial and financial problems and in 1966 was paralyzed by strikes. In response to public demands before the 1966 elections and to its need for ready cash, the government of West Bengal sold permits that allowed 300 private buses to be put into operations. These vehicles made a profit, even though they charged the same fare (equivalent to about US 5¢ per mile) as the money-losing CSTC and had inferior routes. By the late 1970s, some 1,500 full-sized private buses were operating in Calcutta in addition to about 500 private minibuses. Today, unsubsidized private buses account for about two-thirds of all bus trips in Calcutta. Meanwhile, the CSTC, which operates similar routes at the same fares, has to be subsidized to the equivalent of US$1 million a month by a government that is desperately short of funds for other purposes.

The success of the private bus operators has been attributed to three factors:

- *Keeping vehicles on the road.* As soon as a private bus breaks down, it is repaired, often on the road, and the parts, if necessary, are bought on the black market. The CSTC, in contrast, has to go through formal channels to obtain spare parts, and only half of its buses are generally on the road.
- *Fare collection.* The private bus crews (who are paid a percentage of the revenues) make greater efforts to collect the fares than do CSTC employees. Fare evasion is estimated to be 25 percent on CSTC buses, whereas it is negligible on private buses.
- *Higher labor productivity.* The private buses use fewer staff than the CSTC, which employs fifty employees per bus (1980) and thus has among the highest staffing levels in the world.

Another factor in the success of the private buses in Calcutta is the route association. These associations—in general there is one for each route—were formed voluntarily and spontaneously by the private owners. Each owner retains control over the operation and maintenance of his own vehicle and receives the fares collected on it. The associations have rules to govern relationships between the members; for example, vehicles have to run on-time. This is important because a bus running late tends to pick up more than its fair share of passengers, at the expense of the route's successive bus. Owners of buses that do not run on-time are fined. The fine money is distributed among the other members. It has been reported that the fines are, in some instances, proportional to the delay (at a specified rate per minute) and are paid directly to the owner of the route's successive bus.

Source: Gabriel Roth, *The Private Provision of Public Services in Developing Countries,* World Bank report (Washington, D.C.: Oxford University Press, 1987), pp. 204–205. Reprinted with permission of the World Bank.

attain a particular good or service without the investment expense of ownership. Equipment, vehicles, buildings, land, or particular services, such as operating a utility, are examples of typical goods or services that might be leased. Leases for water utilities have been used in France, Spain, the Czech Republic, Guinea, and Senegal.[5] Municipalities in Russia typically lease out some of their buildings. The lessee, often a private firm, usually pays for maintenance and current repairs, while capital repairs remain the obligation of the municipality/lessor. Another Russian example of government as the lessor is Rosagroleasing—a company specializing in providing cash and equipment to the agriculture industry.

Many private leasing firms specialize in leasing equipment to other companies or government. The term of a lease agreement does not exceed the life of the equipment and is usually close to the time of formal tax depreciation. After the expiration of the term the lessee may continue to use the equipment for a discounted price or buy it at residual value. For example, in Perm, Russia, the municipal transportation company, Gorpassazhitrans, recently signed a preliminary lease-to-own agreement for 100 buses. The buses have a minimum service life of twenty years and at the end of the five-year lease the municipality will own the buses. This arrangement enables the city to quickly increase its bus fleet and spreads the investment expense over the five-year lease period. Leasing can be a particularly useful tool for governments that lack budget funds, as well as small and medium-sized companies that cannot secure bank loans for capital investment.

• Concessions

These public-private partnerships have the following characteristics:

- Private partner is responsible for operations, maintenance and investment.
- Ownership remains with the government.
- Usually a long-term contract (twenty or more years).
- Requires good regulation by government.

With a concession, the private partner becomes responsible for investment as well as for operations and maintenance. Although the government maintains ownership of the asset, the concessionaire has use of the asset for a specified period of time. To encourage the concessionaire to invest in the asset, the period of time must be lengthy. In return, the concessionaire expects a reasonable return over the course of the agreement, such as a guarantee from the government that tariffs will remain stable or increase at a reasonable rate. This means that concessions are not appropriate when the government function does not involve income-generating assets.

The main advantage is that concessions delegate full responsibility for operations and investment to the private firms, creating significant incentives for efficiency in all activities.[6] Concessions are also an effective way to generate investments for cash-strapped governments.

Typically, concessions are used for utilities, such as water. Concession agreements often stipulate that the concessionaire will make physical improvements to the system, such as replacing part of the distribution system or extending water service to underserved communities.

Concessions require strong government regulation and oversight in order to protect the public asset and defend customers from monopoly prices or poor service.[7] Unlike contracting, in which multiple firms frequently compete for short-term contracts, major concessions are generally awarded to a single provider and few firms may have the capacity to even compete for such work. Effective government regulation requires understanding the costs of major capital repairs, expanding or improving service, and ongoing maintenance, so that government can approve appropriate tariff increases to pay for investments.

Concessions are successfully used for water utilities in Hungary, Poland, France, Spain, Côte d'Ivoire, Macao, and Malaysia. Russian cities are using concessions to a limited extent to attract investment, as in a program to install mini-boilers in Samara oblast. Two firms under contracts for ten and fifteen years installed the boilers. The program gives priority to kindergartens and hospitals and is designed to ensure adequate heating services while avoiding the costly rehabilitation of a thirty-eight-kilometer pipeline that is in hazardous condition. The cost of the boilers is significantly less than repairing the pipeline and the oblast deems the project a success.

• *Privatization*

Because privatization is the most difficult option to reverse, governments must be careful before taking this step. There are two basic types of privatization:

- The first type divests assets, such as water utilities, that are essentially public in nature. As with concessions, privatization of assets of a public nature creates a monopoly service. Therefore it is critical that government have a good system for regulating the service provider.
- The second type privatizes assets, such as enterprises or office buildings that are essentially commercial in nature. Generally it is in the interest of governments to divest commercial assets so the private sector can manage them. There is no continuing government regulatory responsibility, and this allows government to focus on its core functions.

All countries in Eastern Europe began the transition needing to diminish the state's role in enterprises and build a private sector. Some countries privatized quickly, while others have taken a more cautious approach. The results have been decidedly mixed, and in many countries privatizations remain controversial.

When the Soviet Union teetered on the brink of collapse, weak governments could no longer effectively control the enterprises, and asset stripping and spontaneous privatizations were eroding the public value of enterprises while enriching their directors. In addition, many enterprises were inefficient and relied heavily on government subsidies and soft budget constraints.

Privatization was seen as a way for enterprises to restructure and increase their productivity to compete in the new economy. Privatization was also an important strategy for reformers in some countries who wanted to quickly create a private sector to counter any threats to revive the communist system.

The faults of those early privatizations are well known: valuable assets were sold off to insiders at fire sale prices, competition was thwarted, the population were granted shares (vouchers or ownership shares) that had little or no value, ill-prepared new owners lacked the incentives or skills to restructure, and enterprises closed and workers were laid off across the region.

There are also success stories. Hungary, East Germany, and Estonia adopted strategies to divest assets to individual investors or concentrated groups of strategic investors through fair and transparent competitions.[8] These individuals or firms had incentives to maximize long-term profits, which led to restructuring and reduced the risk of asset stripping. Openness to foreign ownership expanded the pool of firms with the expertise and capital to transform enterprises into successful businesses. Poland and Hungary were quick to impose hard budget constraints on most state enterprises—forcing them to restructure. Poland's reforms of the banking sector and other reforms helped ensure successful privatizations and strong economic growth.

Throughout the region, privatization of the housing stock is generally considered successful. Housing privatization transferred ownership to residents, providing significant assets to a large portion of the population and paving the way for the development of vibrant housing markets. A limitation, however, in countries like Hungary and Lithuania, was the virtual disappearance of the rental sector, a development that has made it hard for new households and poor families to find accommodation.

- *Evaluating the Options for Carrying Out Government Functions*

Each implementation strategy has its strengths and weaknesses. With direct provision, for example, government maintains full control, which can be particularly important for essential or sensitive service needs. However, as the sole provider government may not provide the best quality of service. Concessions and privatization capitalize on private sector investments, yet governments lose control of the asset. Table 7.1 outlines some of the main strengths and weaknesses of each option.

Table 7.1   Strengths and Weaknesses of Service Delivery Options

Option	Strengths	Weaknesses
Direct provision	With this option, the government maintains the most control; this can be particularly important if the service involves confidential information or is too important or sensitive for nongovernment employees; some examples might be the courts or police	Government is the monopoly provider; there is no outside regulation
Contracting	Contracting out opens the door for competition, which promises to generate efficiency gains in the performance of the service; in some cases, a government agency finds it can do a much better job when confronted with the possibility of a private firm taking over its work This option is flexible and not very risky because of the relatively short-term contracts involved; government can improve the terms of agreement for the next round of contracts, or stop altogether if it believes this is not an appropriate option; also, by limiting the scope, the government can employ this approach in an experimental fashion and compare how well the private firm works to how its own agencies work	Government must shoulder an administrative burden (conducting tenders, monitoring performance)
Concessions/ privatization	Concessions or privatization are attractive when there are large investment needs that government does not believe it can fund; privatization is also the vehicle that permits governments to exit areas where there is no justification for their being a direct service provider	May establish a private, monopoly provider; little opportunity to change strategy once locked into long-term agreement or privatization decision

Evaluation Criteria. Evaluating implementation strategies requires a careful examination of the task at hand, the political context, costs, and other factors. The evaluation criteria introduced in Chapter 2 as part of the policy analysis process are useful here. The basic criteria include:

- *Cost.* How much of the cost will be covered by user fees and how much by taxpayers? Will there be an increase or decrease in the cost to taxpayers?
- *Net benefit.* If recipients pay a fee for this service, what quality and quantity of service will they be receiving in return? Are there other "costs" to recipients (including, say, time spent making a complaint)?
- *Efficiency.* Is this the least costly way to produce the desired service?
- *Equity.* What is the distribution of benefits among service recipients and also those not currently served? Will more people be able to receive the service? Will some people pay more for the service?
- *Administrative ease.* Is there the capacity to establish performance targets and monitor separate institutions in their delivery of service? Is it necessary to train the service providers?
- *Legal issues.* Is there a level playing field among competing providers? For example, are there tax laws that make it difficult for the private sector to compete with government? Do local governments have sufficient regulatory authority to oversee a firm under a concession agreement?
- *Political acceptability.* Will the population have confidence in the service provider due to the nature of the function? (That is, is it particularly sensitive or vulnerable to corruption/abuse?)
- *Extent of uncertainty.* Has the option been tried by other agencies under similar circumstances?

Impact on Stakeholders. The various delivery options should be evaluated in a broad context that goes beyond technical efficiency. In addition to determining which functions are appropriate to various forms of competitive assignment, the views of stakeholders are a critical factor. Questions concerning stakeholders include the following:

- What is the performance record of the government agencies currently responsible?
- What is the capacity of potential private sector players?
- How does changing the delivery mechanism affect the interests/profits of various stakeholders? (For example, will there be major job losses under a concession agreement?)
- Are the current beneficiaries satisfied with the level of service? How much

> *See Exercise 7.1: Options for Carrying Out*
> *Local Government Functions on page 165.*
>
> The task in this exercise is to identify the best option for providing several public services, including education, sanitation, preventive health care, and others.

are they currently paying and how much will they be paying under the various options? Are they willing to pay more for better services?
- Are there populations not currently served, but who should be served? How will the various options affect them?

Chapter Summary

The options for carrying out government functions include direct provision, contracting out, leases and concessions, and privatization. Direct provision is usually reserved for regulatory functions, and tasks that are decidedly public in nature. Contracting out is an effective strategy when activities can be quantified and completion monitored. Concessions can generate needed investments in public infrastructure. Privatization can get government out of essentially commercial ventures and foster economic growth.

Determining the best method of fulfilling government functions depends on the tasks at hand, stakeholder interests, competitive environment, and government capacity to monitor or regulate transactions with the private sector.

Generally, competition is a useful strategy to reduce costs and improve the efficiency of public services. Competition can involve government agencies or departments and the private sector.

The public-private implementation strategies outlined in this chapter are important options to consider when developing new policies or planning new programs.

Recommended Reading

Johan Post, Jaap Broekema, and Nelson Obirih-Opareh. "Trial and Error in Privatisation: Experiences in Urban Solid Waste Collection in Accra (Ghana) and Hyderabad (India)." *Urban Studies* 40, no. 4 (2003): 835–852.

This article compares the experiences of contracting out for garbage collection in two cities in Ghana and India, and draws several general conclusions. In both cases the private sector contributed to improved services, though the governments also increased funding to extend services to underserved populations. General conclusions include the need for government monitoring and funding. The ability of governments to enforce contracts and monitor performance influenced the quality of services delivered by contractors. The poverty of local residents limited the ability to charge user fees, and so financing solid waste removal remained a public responsibility. The public-private arrangements were tailored to the specific local context—and the authors recommend no single, best method of involving the private sector.

Exercise 7.1: Options for Carrying Out Local Government Functions

Consider how to best allocate responsibilities among the various delivery options for each local government function listed in the table that follows. Do not fill out the table based on how services are currently provided in your city. Apply the concepts from the chapter:

- Direct provision works best when tasks cannot be well defined.
- Use direct provision when goods or services are absolutely essential/public in nature.
- Use contracting out for specific tasks, short to medium term in duration, with potential benefits from competition.
- Use concession for long-term contracts with private investment.
- Privatization works best for commercial assets; it is permanent and the value of a future need for the asset should be carefully considered.

Options for Carrying Out Local Government Functions
(Be specific about the reasons you would give for allocating responsibilities among the various delivery options for each function.)

Local Government Function	Direct Provision	Contracting Out	Leasing/Concession	Privatization
Sanitation	Regulatory authority. Investments in landfills. Provides sanitation services.	Operations and maintenance could be contracted out to single or multiple firms (individual firms responsible for investing in their own equipment—e.g., trucks).	Could lease equipment. Concession possible (private firms develop and operate landfills).	Possible, but unlikely.
Provision of drinking water				
Local roads				
Public (social) housing				

Government Function	Direct Provision	Contracting Out	Leasing/Concession	Privatization
Fire fighting and public safety				
Homes for the aged and infirm				
Preschool and kindergarten activities				
Preventative health care				
Social assistance programs				

CHAPTER 8

Outsourcing Public Services

This chapter provides additional information on outsourcing because it is a primary management tool of modern governments. Contracting out for public goods and services is a relatively new strategy with much to offer transition governments. Outsourcing has the potential to reduce costs or improve public service delivery. We present this option in detail so that policy analysts can decide whether to consider contracting in response to particular problems, such as providing shelter to battered women or improving the conditions of streets or parks.

Outsourcing is not a panacea, nor does it always result in cheaper or better services. Effective contracting requires an adequate level of competition and contract monitoring. The tasks must be well defined and results measurable in order to enforce contract requirements.

Some governments or agencies may resist contracting, as it stands to reduce their direct responsibilities. When tasks are contracted to private firms or NGOs, government units formerly performing those tasks are often cut or eliminated. Contracting can also be an added burden in that government must conduct the competitions and monitor contracts. Without high-level support for competitive procurement and fair and transparent competitions, contracting will fail to yield its promised gains in efficiency or effectiveness. Poor implementation or outright corruption undermines many contracting initiatives.

This chapter discusses how to determine what services may be appropriate for outsourcing, describes specific steps for contracting out, and summarizes lessons learned from contracting in the region.

When Is Contracting Out Appropriate?

The federal, state, and local governments of the United States have been experimenting with contracting out on a competitive basis since the 1980s. Australia,

New Zealand, and the United Kingdom have probably gone further in this direction than other countries. Other countries, including transition countries, have been successfully contracting for several years. The experience to date shows that contracting out works best under certain circumstances:

- *When requirements can be specified in advance* (and do not require frequent redefinition). The reason for this is that a contract is a legal document that binds both parties. It is only fair that both parties understand the details of the commitment they are making.
- *When results can be easily measured.* Government must have the ability to enforce the requirements described in the contract. If it is not clear whether the contractor has performed the work, or performed the work adequately, how can the government enforce the contract?
- *When competition exists to discipline suppliers and ensure a fair price.* For an initial competition for a specific service, the level of interest/competition may be unknown and government will need to generate interest through advertising, visiting potential bidders, and other actions. For example, after appropriate outreach, competitions for housing maintenance and social assistance contracts in Russia generated many more bids than some cities anticipated. Do not assume that there will not be enough qualified firms willing to participate. In the long term, competition must be sufficient to ensure that the organizations competing for the work will not collude (i.e., agree among themselves to propose artificially high prices). When government proves a contractor is incompetent, other firms should be available to replace the initial contractor.
- *When the ends are more important than the means.* If the government cares very much about the details of how the work will be performed, as opposed to the results of the work, then it might make sense for the government to do the work itself. The reason why contracting out is efficient and saves the government money is that different organizations will be creative in how to accomplish a task (sometimes employing new technologies or methods or altering staffing patterns and salaries). If contractors are not given this freedom, it is unlikely that contracting out will be more efficient.
- *When external factors beyond the supplier's control are minimal.* Most suppliers will not take the risk of legally committing themselves to a task that may become much more difficult than originally envisioned because of factors beyond their control. If suppliers are willing to take this risk, they will likely charge the government a premium, thus squeezing out any cost savings associated with competing for the work.

Does Contracting Work?
Research Findings from Garbage Collection Contracting
in the United States, Canada, and the United Kingdom

A number of studies have examined the efficiency of private versus public garbage collection. John D. Donahue, in his book *The Privatization Decision,* summarizes the findings of research from the United States, Canada, and the United Kingdom.[1] Garbage collection is a task that is well suited to contracting out, and hence has been widely studied. It involves clearly defined tasks, is easy to monitor, and does not require significant knowledge or equipment investment for firms to compete. For these reasons, we summarize the research on garbage collection to further illustrate the potential benefits and pitfalls of contracting.

The various options examined for garbage collection include public sanitation departments, private contractors (government contracts with firms), private franchises (government grants exclusive rights to serve an area), and open competition (unrestricted competition; households purchase directly from firms).

Garbage collection meets all of the critical criteria for outsourcing:

- The particular goods or services contracted are well defined.
- The terms of the contract clearly define the tasks, yet are flexible enough to allow for cost-saving innovation.
- The environment is competitive, because the cost of new firms entering the market is low.
- It is possible to hold firms accountable, because results can be measured and monitored, and firms can be replaced if performance is unsatisfactory.

• Findings: Costs

Type of Collection. Key factors affecting costs included the type of collection, such as the frequency of pickups and whether service was at the curbside or from the backyard. Backyard pickup cost one-third more than curbside pickup; twice-weekly pickups cost about one-quarter more than weekly pickup. Economy of scale: firms that served less than 20,000 people or used fewer than four trucks operated somewhat less efficiently.[2]

Public vs. Private. The studies found that private contractors were generally the cheapest, followed by public agencies, with open competition (private firms sign up individual customers) the most expensive. In cities where public agencies faced private competition their costs were significantly lower than unchallenged bureaucracies and roughly equal to private firms. Specific findings:

1,378 American Cities

Contractors were the most efficient; private franchise and public collection both cost 12 percent more; open competition cost 50 percent more.[3]

126 Canadian Cities

Public collection cost 41 percent more than contractors; public agencies in "mixed" systems cost 8 percent more than contractors.[4]

317 UK Cities

Public monopolies were 20 percent less efficient than contracting; public bid winners were nearly as efficient as the average private contractor.[5]

Open competition was the most expensive. Possible explanations include (a) poor information—households are ill informed about costs of garbage collection and do not have the ability or inclination to negotiate for lowest cost; (b) added expense of billing individual customers; and (c) collusion.

Why Contractors Had the Capacity to Be Cheaper Than Public Agencies. Private firms generally paid wages 10 percent lower than public agencies. Private firms also had a technical advantage: larger trucks, smaller crews, and flexible scheduling. Public sanitation departments, especially those in noncompetitive environments, were plagued by inefficient size (overstaffed) and work rules that increased costs.

Importance of Competition. Competition was more important than the organizational form (public or private), and competition improved both public and private operations. Unregulated private firms were often corrupt or inefficient, underscoring the importance of contract monitoring. Open competition and monopolistic private franchises were often inefficient and engaged in illicit collusion. Contractors chosen by competitive bidding process were generally the most efficient. In a competitive environment, public departments improved their performance. (Similar results were found in Russian cities when public and private firms competed for housing maintenance contracts—see Box 8.1.)

How to Successfully Contract Out

This section describes how to manage a competition to procure goods and services. The major steps in competitive procurement for services are:

Step 1: Asking "What do you want for your money?"
Step 2: Balancing tasks with available budget funds.

**Box 8.1   Housing Maintenance: An Early
Russian Experiment with Contracting Out**

With assistance from the Washington, D.C.–based Urban Institute, Moscow city officials began a demonstration project for private maintenance of municipal housing units in 1993. The demonstration project included two competitions: the first competition resulted in contracts with three private firms to maintain approximately 650 units each of typical housing; the second competition resulted in government contracts with two other private firms to maintain an additional 5,000 elite units.

A formal evaluation was performed that gathered data on maintenance quality before and after the private firms began maintaining the buildings. Maintenance services were better for the typical buildings and no worse for elite buildings. The evaluations showed that the private firms did better than the municipal maintenance departments in setting a concrete schedule for repairs and fulfilling their promises. The private firms did not cost more than the municipal maintenance departments in performing equivalent tasks.

The most serious problem was that the customer—usually the Housing Committee of the local government—delayed paying the private firms, which greatly decreased the value of the payments because of Russia's high inflation at the time.[a]

After that, many Russian cities set out to bid housing that was divested by enterprises. In other words, municipalities outsourced new obligations but were generally unwilling to displace existing departments and workers through competition. In addition, the divested

housing stock was typically in worse condition than the housing maintained by the municipalities, so that when private contractors took on this stock their tasks were often greater than those of the municipal departments.

Russian government agencies now contract out for many public services. As of February 2002, in numerous Russian cities, much of the housing stock was competitively maintained:

Moscow	100%	Volhov	50%
Cherepovetz	21%	Orenburg	43%
Petrozavodsk	57%	Ryazan	34%

This is the good news. The bad news is that municipalities still find it politically difficult to transfer stock already assigned to the municipal department and much of the privately maintained housing is housing that was transferred from enterprises to municipalities.

The Moscow-based Institute for Urban Economics recently conducted an analysis of the situation and identified a slowdown in new competitions. Reasons cited include municipal management practices that obstruct free market pricing and competition, create defective contractual relations with the contractor, and allow the municipal departments to charge higher rates with no incentive to improve efficiency.[b] The high rates paid to the municipal maintenance departments are a burden on the municipal budget, which in turn makes it difficult for the city to pay the private companies on a timely basis.

Notes: a. K. Angelici, R. Struyk, and M. Tikhomirova, "Private Maintenance for Moscow's Municipal Stock: Does It Work?" *Journal of Housing Economics* 4 (March 1995): 50–70.

b. Sergei Sivaev and Municipal Economics Division, *Analytical Overview: Practice of Reforms of the Housing and Communal Service Sector* (Moscow: Institute for Urban Economics, 2003).

Step 3: The information campaign.
Step 4: The selection process.
Step 5: Concluding a contract.
Step 6: Monitoring the work.

- ### Step 1: Asking, "What Do You Want for Your Money?"

Contracting out for services (or goods) on a competitive basis can save the government a lot of money. But saving money only makes sense when the government is spending money on something it really needs. So if the government proposes to test outsourcing with new services or services offered to new populations, then it is important from the start to have broad agreement that these are needed.

Having established broad agreement that the services are needed, the next step is to specify the technical tasks to be performed. Identify the volume, type, and value of the work to be performed. For example, if purchasing social services, who will be the beneficiaries, what services will they receive, how often, and according to what standard?

If purchasing housing maintenance services, which buildings will be served and what are their specifications (size, location, number of units, entrances, courtyards etc.)? What are the conditions of the buildings? For which tasks will the contractor be responsible? Is there clear delineation between maintenance and current repair?

The tasks must be clear, but not overspecified, because efficiency comes from the ingenuity of the private firms. For example, if the residents are satisfied that garbage collection points and common areas are free of debris (the results), then it is not important what equipment or staffing the contractor uses to achieve this (the means). Another example of overspecifying the contract is to state the wages that the contractor must pay its workers.

- ### Step 2: Balancing Tasks with Available Budget Funds

Financial instability can be a huge obstacle to successful outsourcing. Contracted tasks cannot exceed available budget funds and contractors must be paid regularly. It is not the fault of municipalities and their agencies/departments when the economy is unstable and therefore their revenues are unstable. But it is important to compensate for this instability. Some solutions to this problem include starting with a smaller package of work for which funding is certain. In addition, contracts can be amended to include additional work, as funding becomes available.

To do this, however, it is important for the customer to prioritize tasks so the most important tasks are performed first and less important tasks performed when money is available. When prioritizing tasks, the customer should take into consideration all applicable normative standards.

• Step 3: The Information Campaign

The goals of an information campaign are to attract as many potential bidders as possible, communicate the specifications of the work to be performed, and provide instructions for submitting a proposal. An information campaign is critical to competitive procurement, because for competition to be effective, enough organizations must be aware of the opportunity. In fact, it is a good idea for the government to publish a schedule of upcoming competitions.

The formal announcement of the competition must include:

- Name and address of the organization holding the competition.
- Time and place of the competition.
- Conditions of the contract (types of services, location of the buildings, or which beneficiaries will be served).
- Requirements for the applicants. For example, staff may be required to have formal training (e.g., qualifications of the persons performing certain work such as psychological analysis).
- Evaluation criteria.
- When, how, and where applicants can obtain more detailed information on the competition. (For example, detailed instructions on how to submit a bid may be obtained at the municipal office. Also, there may be a bidders' conference where potential participants can have their questions answered.)
- Application fee (and possibly a deposit to show serious intent) and how payment should be made.
- Deadline for submitting a bid.
- The approximate date when the contract will be concluded and work commence.
- Most countries require that the formal announcement be published some specific amount of time before the deadline.[6]

• Step 4: The Selection Process

Participants should also be informed of how the applications will be evaluated. The application should contain enough information to judge their past performance with similar assignments and their ability to perform the task at hand. However, the selection team might find it necessary to conduct interviews to obtain additional information. If interviews are conducted, they should be offered to all participants that meet the basic requirements or all finalists.

For example, in Moscow, the criteria used to evaluate housing maintenance proposals included: housing maintenance experience, personnel qualifications, references, proposed methods, productive capacity, bid price per square meter of housing, the applicant's financial situation (e.g., debts), and the interview results.

The criteria used by the assessment committee to decide the winner should be the same criteria published in the information campaign.

• Step 5: Concluding a Contract

The relationship between the customer and contractor must be based on the contract, not on exercising administrative control beyond the contract provisions. Also, risk must be equitably shared. If the contractor assumes all the risk and the customer does not fulfill its obligations, the system will eventually break down.

International experience shows that a good contract and conducting proper contractual relations are key to successful contracting out. The contract should specify the following:

- Types of services.
- Beneficiaries and how they will be selected.
- Payment size and schedule.
- Rights and obligations of each side.
- How the government will monitor the work.
- Reporting requirements for work performed and associated costs.
- Responsibilities of each side.
- Duration of the agreement.
- Conditions for canceling the agreement.
- How disputes will be settled.
- Making changes or amendments to the agreement.
- Requisites of both sides.

A contract is only effective if both sides take seriously their various commitments indicated in the contract. Problems arise when the customer delays payments, but expects the contractor to continue work, or when the customer expects the contractor to act as if it were an employee. As discussed earlier, the efficiency from contracting out comes from the fact that private firms have incentives to discover more efficient means of completing the work, and have greater flexibility than government, which is often beholden to strict staffing requirements, collective bargaining agreements, and fixed capital costs. If the customer tries to control the contractor through administrative command, this efficiency will be lost. Finally, if external factors (such as new normative standards) make the work more difficult, the contract should be amended. It is not fair for the contractor to bear the burden of all the risk from changes in the work environment.

Box 8.2 (on page 180) is a sample of a city contract for social assistance services. This contract follows a fairly standard format and appendices include information detailing the specific services provided, work plan and measurable outcomes, sample reporting form, client record forms, and a description of monitoring activities.

• Step 6: Monitoring the Work

Although the customer should not try to control the contractor in how it conducts its work, it is appropriate and indeed essential for the customer to monitor the contractor's work to ensure adequate performance. Regular monitoring is part of proper contractual relations. Effective monitoring often has many different elements and relies on various information sources.

The first level of monitoring is self-reporting by the contractor. The contract should specify what to include in the reports and when they are due. Usually, delivery of these reports corresponds with submission of invoices so the contractor can be paid for the work performed.

The second level of monitoring is analysis of complaints against the contractor. The customer should have access to these complaints. It is important not only what complaints are made, but also how the contractor addresses the problems after it receives complaints.

The third level of monitoring is on-site inspections and interviews. For housing maintenance, the customer visits the buildings to ensure that the contractor is performing the required tasks and that the work is of adequate quality. The customer inspects randomly selected buildings with a representative of the contractor following a clear protocol. Good practices include having the contractor representative also sign the inspection report, not announcing the location of the visit in advance, inspecting approximately 10 percent of the stock each month (more if serious problems are detected), and interviewing contractor employees or recipients of the goods/services.

Chapter 9 describes monitoring in greater detail.

Lessons Learned

This section provides helpful strategies for improving the effectiveness of competitive procurement based on recent experience of contracting out in the region.[7]

• 1. Is There Adequate Competition?

The first lesson is to ensure adequate competition. This partially depends on the local market. Are there enough private firms with the required assets to ensure adequate competition? For example, the Moscow-based Institute for Urban Economics worked with smaller cities such as Arzamas, Bor, and Kstovo on competitive procurement of housing maintenance services. These cities have achieved admirable levels of competitively maintained housing: 66, 100, and 76 percent of municipal housing, respectively. However, one of the challenges of organizing competitions in smaller cities is a limited number of local firms.

Ensuring adequate competition also depends on how many private firms participate in the competition. A well-thought-out information campaign and a published schedule of future competitions help to attract more competitors.

Economy of scale can be an important consideration. For example, the Institute for Urban Economics learned that in the sphere of housing maintenance it is efficient for contractors to work on housing stock that is at least 100,000 square meters (about 1,700 average-sized apartments). In small cities in particular, it might be difficult for companies to maintain such capacity if there are few alternative, similar work assignments.

• 2. Money: When and How?

The second lesson is that contractors must be paid on time and in cash. To continue operating, companies must pay their employees, and fulfill other financial obligations such as paying taxes. Payment in the form of mutual offsets or local government securities is not easily transformed into cash to meet these financial obligations. Private companies face hard budget constraints, that is, they have limited ability to spend or obligate more than they bring in. Some governments often do not appreciate this point, because they can either suspend payments or can be "rescued" by a higher level of government when they overspend their budget. Private companies do not have "rescuers," and if they suspend payments on their obligations, they may face serious legal repercussions.

Recommendations for dealing with difficult financial situations:

- Create contracts for either limited tasks or for shorter periods of time. Contracts can be amended later to extend the time or to add tasks. (If limiting the tasks, be sure to prioritize tasks so that the most important tasks will be completed.)
- Create contracts that list various items (prepriced) from which the customer may select items as funding becomes available and the need arises for such work.
- Long-term contracts may need to be adjusted annually to reflect the realities of the current economy.

• 3. Creating a Level Playing Field

Again, a well-thought-out information campaign plays a key role. A good information campaign should make available documents that contain all details about the work to be performed and other relevant information. Following this with a bidders' conference also helps to ensure that all competitors have equal knowledge, at least in regard to the work to be performed and the application process.

The competition is not fair if some assignments are more difficult than others and this difficulty is not made explicit, with commensurate price adjustments. For example, in Moscow, municipalities found it easier to transfer "new" municipal housing than housing already assigned to municipal maintenance departments (see Box 8.1). However, the former enterprise-owned housing is typically in much worse condition than the average municipal housing. Therefore, it is inappropriate to expect private companies to achieve the same level of maintenance in these buildings at the same cost as the municipal maintenance agencies do in the other municipal housing. If a company takes responsibility for buildings that are in worse condition, it should either be compensated at a higher rate or it should not be asked to meet the same standards.

Another issue of the level playing field is taxation. For example, in Russia, a city agency providing services is not subject to the value-added tax (VAT) for the work it does. But if the same work is contracted by the city, then the VAT is applicable. This makes it more expensive for private companies to perform that same work and is a powerful factor in favoring a public agency in a competition.

• *4. Financial Incentives*

The fourth lesson is that the system must create financial incentives for both the contractor and the customer. Contractors have obvious incentives to provide services efficiently—as their profit is directly linked to lowering expenses while delivering quality services. For the government customer the incentives may be few and may result in resistance to contracting initiatives.

It is appropriate to reward both the customer and contractor for saving the government money when the award price is lower than what it usually costs to perform the same services.

Customers needs some motivation for holding competitions. Competitions represent more work for them because they must organize the competitions and monitor contracts. Moreover, they likely have established relationships with the government agencies currently performing the work and may be disinclined to damage those ties (particularly when political or financial interests are involved). It is easier for them to continue working as they always did.

Ways to build in incentives for the customer include allowing it to retain a portion of the money saved for other projects or programs, or employees may be offered bonuses, public recognition, or some other reward for conducting competitions and effectively managing departmental resources.

Box 8.2   Sample Social Assistance Contract

CONTRACT No. _____

City of Perm   April 30, 2002

Committee for Labor and Welfare of Administration of the City of Perm, represented by NAME, Chairman, acting by its Regulations, hereinafter referred to as "the Customer," being one party, and Public Organization of the Kirovsky District of the City of Perm "Kirovtchanka," represented by NAME, Chairman, acting by its Charter, hereinafter referred to as "the Provider," have concluded the present Contract concerning the following:

1. Subject of the Contract

1.1   For the purpose of fulfilling the Program of Social Support and Rehabilitation of Physically Disabled People in the City of Perm in 2002 and by the decision of the Competition Committee of the Fourth City Competition of Socially Important Projects dated March 25, 2002, the Provider shall render the services as required by the Program of Social Rehabilitation of Physically Disabled Children/Teenagers with Cerebral Paralysis, hereinafter referred to as "the Program" (Appendix 1 to the Contract).

1.2   The Customer allocates 48,000.00 (forty-eight thousand) rubles to the Provider for realization of the Program.

2. Recipients of Services

2.1   Individual recipients of the services of the Provider can be only people of categories specified in Appendix 1 to the present Contract. Some recipients of the services can be identified personally by the Provider in agreement with the Customer.[a]

3. Payments

3.1   Transfer of payments in accordance with Item 1.2 of the Contract shall be made in installments to the settlement account of the Provider.

3.2   Procedure and dates of payments are stipulated in Appendix 2 to the Contract.

4. Rights and Liabilities of the Parties

4.1   Rights and Liabilities of the Customer:

4.1.1   The Customer has the right to supervise the Provider's actions for fulfillment of Provider's obligations without interfering in its current activities. Such supervision is executed by monitoring in accordance with Item 5 of the Contract.

4.1.2   The Customer has the right not to transfer the payment to the Provider before approving the work reports made in accordance with the form stipulated by Appendix 3 to the Contract and financial report in accordance with the form stipulated by Appendix 6 to the Contract, submitted by the Provider.

4.1.3   The Customer shall consider and approve the work reports and financial reports of the Provider within 3 days from the date of receiving the report. In case of discrepancies between the reports of the Provider and monitoring of the Customer, or in case the report does not correspond to the forms stipulated by Appendices 3 and 6 to the Contract, the Customer shall immediately inform the Provider

(continues)

Note: a. If an appropriate number of clients do not enroll in the program, the Provider is responsible for taking measures to attract additional eligible clients.

Box 8.2   Continued

about it. The Customer has the right not to approve the Provider's report until all discrepancies are eliminated.

4.1.4   The Customer shall transfer the corresponding share of the sum in accordance with the Contract within 10 banking days from the date of the approval of Financial Reports of the Provider in compliance with the procedure established in Appendix 2 to the Contract.

4.2   Rights and Liabilities of the Provider:

4.2.1   The Provider shall fulfill the Program in accordance with Appendix 2 to the Contract.

4.2.2   The Provider shall submit a work report to the Customer prior to the fifth day of every month following the reported month. The Provider shall submit the Summary Report on Realization of the Program to the Customer prior to November 15, 2002.

4.2.3   The Provider shall submit financial reports for the period until July 15, 2002, to the Customer prior to July 25, 2002, for the period until September 15, 2002, to the Customer prior to September 25, 2002, and for the period until October 31, 2002, to the Customer prior to November 15, 2002.

4.2.4   The Provider has no right to use any third parties to fulfill the Program without the consent of the Customer.

4.2.5   The Provider shall notify the Program recipients in writing about all available services in accordance with Appendix 1 to the Contract. The Provider shall also inform the recipients about location and contact information of the Customer. The Provider

shall inform the recipients about their right to complain to the Customer about any drawbacks of the Provider's fulfillment of the program.

4.2.6   The Provider shall render services by signed applications of the service recipients, confirming their awareness of the Program and wish to participate in the Program.

4.2.7   The Provider shall keep personal records of the recipients in accordance with the form from Appendix 4 to the Contract.

4.2.8   The Provider shall use its best endeavors to assist the Customer in monitoring the service results as specified in Item 5 of the Contract.

5. Monitoring the Fulfillment of the Program and Contract Terms

5.1   Monitoring the fulfillment of the Program or Contract terms by the Provider is performed by the Customer or by any entity or person designated by the Customer. The Customer notifies the Provider in writing about the authorized entity (person) and the scope of its competence.

5.2   Specification of the monitoring is stipulated by Appendix 5 to the Contract.

6. Responsibility of the Parties

6.1   The parties bear responsibility for partial or total nonfulfillment of the Contract as required by the Civil Legislation of the Russian Federation.

6.2   Unilateral refusal to fulfill the Contract obligations is not allowed except the cases stipulated by the Civil Code of the Russian Federation.

(*continues*)

Box 8.2   Continued

6.3   The Provider has the right to refuse to fulfill the Contract obligations in case the Customer has delayed the transfer of the payment for more than 30 days without any reason. The Customer does not bear any responsibility for the payment delay if there is not state financing provided from the budget to pay for the Program of Social Support and Rehabilitation of Physically Disabled People in the City of Perm in 2002.

6.4   The Customer has the right to cancel the Contract unilaterally if the Provider has delayed the fulfillment of the services for more than 30 days.

6.5   The Party that initiates the cancellation of the Contract in accordance with Items 6.3 and 6.4 of the Contract shall notify the other Party of its intention to cancel the Contract as required by the Civil Legislation of the Russian Federation.

6.6   In case of premature termination of the Contract by mutual agreement of the Parties the Provider shall return the unused moneys to the Customer within 10 banking days from the date of the termination of the Contract.

7. Period of Validity of the Contract

7.1   The present Contract comes into force from the date of its signing by the Parties and shall be valid until complete fulfillment of Contract responsibilities by the Parties.

8. Other Terms

8.1   All disputes in connection with the present Contract shall be settled by the Parties via negotiations.

8.2   In case the Parties cannot come to an agreement via negotiations, they have the right to apply to the Competition Committee of the Annual City Competition of the Socially Important Projects (in accordance with the Regulations for the Annual City Competition of the Socially Important Projects). The decision of the Competition Committee shall be taken within 15 days from the date of such application.

8.3   Any Party to the present Contract can dispute the decision of the Competition Committee in court as required by the Law of the Russian Federation.

8.4   All amendments and additions to the Contract shall be done in writing and come into force from the date of signing by the Parties.

8.5   The Contract is done in two copies, one copy for each side, both copies having equal legal force.

9. Information About the Parties

CUSTOMER

_____

NAME, Chairman

PROVIDER

_____

NAME, Director

> *See Exercise 8.1: Contracting Out Public Services below.*
>
> In this group exercise, teams complete all major steps for contracting out, including planning the competition, submitting proposals, evaluating applications, concluding the contract, and monitoring. The competitions are for social services for the elderly and housing maintenance.

Chapter Summary

Competitive procurement can be an effective means to improve public services or reduce costs. The main strength of contracting out is that it introduces competition into service delivery. With competition both public and private entities perform better.

Contracting out works best when tasks are well defined and completion can be easily monitored, such as in garbage collection, employment services, or housing maintenance. The basic steps to facilitate a competition include: determining what services to contract out and defining the tasks, matching the tasks to available funding, conducting an information campaign to ensure adequate competition, selecting a winner based on well-defined criteria, concluding the contract, and monitoring contract compliance.

Exercise 8.1: Contracting Out Public Services

The exercise includes all of the steps required to contract out, including drafting the guidelines, submitting proposals, evaluating proposals, concluding a contract, and defining a monitoring strategy. The exercise is intended as a group activity requiring several small teams. The groups who submit the proposals should be different from the groups who draft the competition guidelines and select the winners.

The four tasks discussed should be completed for two competitions: outsourcing social services for the elderly, and housing maintenance services. The following table illustrates how four groups (identified as A, B, C, and D) work through each task:

Summary of Tasks

1. Planning the competition. One or more groups can be assigned to plan each of the competitions. In addition to drafting the terms of the competition, the group should define its evaluation criteria. An outline for these tasks follows. Each group should present its work to the full cast of participants.

Task	Social Services for the Elderly	Housing Maintenance
	Group (or individual student)	Group (or student)
1. Planning the competition	A, B (working together)	C, D (together)
2. Preparing the proposal	C, D (working separately so that there are two applications)	A, B (separately)
3. Evaluating the proposal	A, B	C, D
4. Concluding the contract/monitoring	A, B	C, D

2. Preparing a proposal/bid. After the competition guidelines have been defined, the groups should switch, so that those who drafted the housing competition are applying to provide services for the elderly, and vice versa. This ensures that all participants have an opportunity to fulfill each step. Participants can present proposals orally or in written form.

3. Evaluating the proposals. The groups should carefully consider each of the proposals submitted. If presentations are made orally, groups may ask questions to clarify the proposals. The group should then evaluate the submissions according to the evaluation criteria and make a decision.

4. Concluding the contract and monitoring. The customer and contractor should outline and agree to the basic contract terms and any particular concerns. The customer should outline a strategy for how it will monitor the contract.

Instructions for Completing the Tasks
1. Planning the competition. Draft the terms of competition/request for proposals. On a separate piece of paper, provide answers for each of the items below.

a. Contract Terms
- Types of services to be delivered and cost.
- List major areas of work.

- Payments for services provided (e.g. price per client or per service provided).
- Period of service delivery.

b. Background Information

- Information on clients (number, age, special needs, location of service [in their homes or at center], etc.); *or* information on housing stock (square meters/number of units, type of housing/construction, condition, etc.).
- What (if any) assets/services will the city provide (office space, etc.)?

c. Applicant Requirements

- Experience working with elderly or similar populations; *or* experience in housing maintenance and repair.
- Types of entities eligible to participate (private firm, NGO, municipal enterprise).
- Qualifications of employees (years of experience, specialization [e.g., medical training, engineer], etc.), and/or higher education requirements.
- Full description of costs included in bid (i.e., must fully account for all costs—municipal agencies that compete cannot shift costs to other departments).
- Evidence of past performance (positive ratings from previous customers/clients). What documents or assurances will be required?
- Evidence of financial stability (absence of debts and salary arrears). What documents or assurances will be required?

d. Competition Information

- Name of competition initiator (department/individual).
- Deadline and procedure for submitting applications.
- Time and place of competition.
- Contact or procedure for obtaining additional information (including site visits).
- Application fee (if any).
- Deposit fee (if any). Specify whether municipal firms will be required to pay deposit.
- Outreach strategy (how will people learn about the competition?). Assume you have a modest budget.
- Other requirements and information (if any).

Evaluation Criteria for Task 1. Criteria can include any of the following or other important factors. Criteria should be assigned weights or points, so that applicants know how much each factor counts. For example, the criteria for awarding maintenance contracts for office computer equipment may be: cost (40), experience (20), qualifications of staff (20), proposed work plan (15), and interview (5).

- Experience.
- Qualification of employees (higher education, technical skills, management structure, etc.).
- Reviews of customers/clients on the previous work of the participant.
- Evidence from site visit to applicant's work site.
- Proposed methods and organizational forms of work.
- Proposed price per client or service.
- Financial stability of competition participant during the previous year.
- Interview.
- Other.

Select and assign points to criteria for your competition.

2. Preparing a proposal/bid.

a. Contract Terms and Cost
- Types of services to be delivered and major areas of work (or indicate willingness to fulfill all tasks described in contract guidelines).
- Cost for services provided (e.g., price per client or per service provided). Bids must fully account for all costs.
- Information on clients or housing stock (or indicate willingness to fulfill all tasks described in contract guidelines).
- Period of service delivery.

b. Applicant Information
- Name of firm/agency/NGO.
- Experience.
- Qualifications of employees (years of experience, higher education, technical skills, management/supervisory structure).
- Proposed methods and organizational forms of work (how do you propose to get the job done—implementation of innovative technologies, new materials, efficient deployment of staff, etc.?)
- Evidence of past performance (positive ratings from previous customers/clients).
- Evidence of financial stability (absence of debts and salary arrears).

3. Evaluating the proposals. Using the criteria developed in Task 1, rate each of the applications submitted. Ratings can be done in a group with discussion, or each member can rate each application and total scores computed. Announce the winner.

4. Concluding the contract and monitoring.

- Types of services.
- Beneficiaries.
- Payment size and schedule.
- Rights and obligations of each side.
- Other considerations (if any).
- How government will monitor the work (including reporting and data collection requirements of the firm).
- Start date.
- Duration of the agreement.
- Conditions for canceling the agreement.
- How disputes will be settled.
- Procedure for making changes or amendments to the agreement.

PART 3

MONITORING AND EVALUATING PROGRAMS

Program Monitoring

If the broad goal of public policy is to have a positive impact on people's lives, then an important part of the policy process is to measure whether specific policies resulted in the intended public benefits. Policies can have unintended consequences, can be poorly implemented, and can otherwise fail to meet their objectives. Alternatively, policies can be highly successful. Agencies implementing policy decisions can improve upon the original policy notion. Generally, successes should be supported and used to inform other relevant policy decisions.

Most policy initiatives translate into specific programs, such as after-school programs for struggling students or tax incentives for small businesses. These programs may be administered by government or provided by a private entity, as described in Chapter 7. The crucial question is, are the policies or programs working?

Monitoring helps assess whether policies or programs are successful. Monitoring is the routine measurement and reporting of program operations and results. It means collecting and presenting data in a form that will help administrators and policymakers answer questions such as:

- How many clients are being served?
- What is the volume of each service that is being delivered?
- How many staff days were spent on each service?
- How much money or other resources were spent?

Most programs collect considerable data to comply with regulations or to assist in daily operations. Monitoring systematizes data collection and makes key findings available to program managers and others. These findings are used to improve program operations, supervise staff, inform policy, allocate resources, and inform stakeholders or the public. (Full program assessment generally requires an evaluation, which is the subject of Chapters 11–13.)

This chapter describes the benefits of monitoring and how to develop a monitoring system. It presents an example of financial monitoring of public housing in the United States to illustrate how monitoring can promote transparency and program improvements.

The Basics

• Benefits of Program Monitoring

A policymaker or program manager cannot know whether a policy or program is being effectively implemented unless they collect basic performance information. Laws and regulations require monitoring for many publicly funded programs, and for others it is simply good sense. Monitoring helps managers justify their budgets by demonstrating the results attained, such as the number of home visits conducted, kilometers of road maintained, or the number of arrests made.

Monitoring also helps administrators ensure that the program is serving its target audience and that the services provided are of a decent quality. Managing staff is one of the most important administrative tasks, and setting reasonable objectives, motivating staff, and holding them accountable for program outputs are tasks for which monitoring data is extremely valuable. There are several specific benefits of program monitoring.

Early Detection and Correction of Performance Problems. Monitoring data enables managers to identify and address problems before they become too serious. If a program serves only half its intended population at the end of a year, it risks losing some of its funding. However, if the program manager identifies low utilization early in the year, he or she can take active steps to improve participation— maybe the eligibility requirements are too strict, maybe clients do not know that the program is available, maybe the hours of operation need to be changed.

Staff Management. Monitoring provides useful information on staff performance and needs. Programs can establish basic guidelines so that staff know what is expected of them, such as the number of work requests completed or number of clients who express satisfaction with the services they received. Not all functions can be turned into a simple numerical objective, and obviously there are additional factors that need to be taken into account when assessing staff performance. Some tasks may be harder and more time consuming than others. However, basic performance data provide staff and their managers with useful information. It is important that data be used not just to identify low-performing staff, but also to recognize outstanding staff. In addition, monitoring data can identify staff needs, such as additional training or access to a computer or other resources.

Helps Identify More Efficient Uses of Resources. Monitoring identifies how well the program is working and at what cost. Program inputs (budget, staff, equipment, volunteers, and others) are compared to program results (the number of clients served, the number of clients placed in jobs, and so forth) to generate simple efficiency measures. Program managers may discover that one aspect of their operations is extremely costly and yields few positive results, whereas another function is oversubscribed and should be expanded.

Accountability to External Stakeholders. Monitoring informs stakeholders about how well the program is doing and how resources are being spent. Sharing these data with stakeholders can help build support for future program activities.

Develops Commitment to Improve Performance. Staff does not know that they should improve unless they have a clear sense of how well they are doing in the first place. Letting staff know that their actions contributed to an additional 100 clients receiving an essential service can help them strive for even better performance. Similarly, they need to know when their performance lags—that they served fewer clients than any other district office and that next month they need to do better.

Builds Confidence. Successfully meeting performance milestones helps to build staff morale, confidence, and pride.

• *Types of Indicators to Monitor*

Successful monitoring follows from a clear understanding of what the policy or program is trying to accomplish with what resources and through which activities. To monitor basic program functions and results it is necessary to develop measurable indicators. Each important program function must be translated into a concrete and measurable indicator. For example, a counseling program for the elderly may seek to reduce isolation and improve health and well-being. These general goals need to be translated into specific indicators, such as the number of social worker visits, increased elderly participation in community events, and number of referrals for medical care and other services.

Indicators are grouped into four basic types: inputs, outputs, outcomes, and efficiency:

- *Inputs.* Monitoring inputs means measuring the quantity of resources used. For an educational program, inputs include teachers, administrators, facilities, books, and other materials.
- *Outputs.* Monitoring outputs means measuring the quantity of service provided. The outputs of a municipal transportation department include the number of passengers served and the number of metro and bus trips provided.
- *Outcomes.* Monitoring outcomes means measuring the effect or result of the program on its clients or beneficiaries. For an employment training program, it might be how many clients get jobs.
- *Efficiency.* Monitoring efficiency means comparing outputs or outcomes produced to inputs used. How many clients were served per staff person? How many buildings were cleaned for how many months for a contract worth a specific sum?

Output vs. Outcome Indicators. The difference between outputs and outcomes can be somewhat confusing. An easy way to distinguish between outputs and outcomes is that outputs are what the program does and outcomes are what the participants actually get. For example, the output from a job training program is that fifty people received job training and the outcome is that twenty-five people obtained jobs. Table 9.1 offers additional examples of outputs and outcomes.

- **Types and Levels of Monitoring**

Types of Monitoring. Monitoring systems are designed to report on a variety of program functions. Many government agencies monitor budget spending, but

---

Table 9.1   Outputs and Outcomes

Outputs	Outcomes
Kilometers of road repaired	Percentage of roads (kilometers) in good condition
Number of clients served	Number and percentage of clients whose situation improved
Number of requests for service answered	Number of requests that led to a satisfactory response

Source: Harry P. Hatry, Louis H. Blair, Donald M. Fisk, John M. Greiner, John R. Hall Jr., and Philip S. Schaenman, *How Effective Are Your Community Services? Procedures for Measuring Their Quality,* 2nd ed. (Washington, D.C.: Urban Institute and International City/County Management Association [ICMA], 1992).

See Exercise 9.1: Assessing Monitoring Indicators on page 229.

This exercise involves identifying the type of indicator (input, output, outcome, and efficiency) for a number of program functions.

fewer actually monitor the outputs or the efficiency of that spending. Monitoring can focus on any or all of the following program aspects.

Program implementation. Monitoring focuses on basic inputs and outputs: number of clients, number of staff/other resources, services provided, policies/procedures followed, and so forth.

The quality of services delivered. Data is collected to provide feedback on the quality of services. Data may include evaluation forms completed by clients, complaints, site visits, and interviews.

Financial management. Basic financial monitoring involves tracking how resources were used and to what effect. Were funds used according to the program budget? What was the cost per service provided? What are the practices used by the agency to control project funds?

Client/citizen satisfaction. Monitoring systems to track client satisfaction include surveys, complaint logs, interviews, and client associations.

Levels of Monitoring. Monitoring programs can be designed to track the activities of an individual field office or to monitor the implementation of a specific program throughout the country. The type of service and number of sites or participants affects the design of the monitoring initiative. Monitoring the activities of a small team may include simple counts of services provided/tasks completed and a narrative on recent developments, whereas a regional cash allowance program will likely focus on quantitative factors such as number of families served, amount of benefits awarded, and similar factors.

Monitoring departmental functions or small programs. Such tracking may simply include weekly or monthly reports from each manager summarizing how many clients were served, the services provided, contributions of each staff member, and other basic functions.

Monitoring citywide or regional programs. Routine monitoring of this scale needs to be primarily quantitative and standardized reporting forms should be developed. Field offices may be required to submit reports (usually monthly) that are aggregated into citywide or regional program reports.

Some cities produce an annual report of key city indicators that illustrate basic economic and social trends, as well as the number or quality of public services provided. Examples of particular indicators might include the number of new small businesses, a reduction in automobile accidents, or the percentage of poor families receiving housing allowances.

Sector monitoring. Federal ministries are interested in the general trends for the entire sector in which they work. Quarterly or annual reports on key indicators can provide useful information on the overall health of the sector and the efficacy of major programs; and they can also serve as a useful planning tool. This report can be produced using routine monitoring data from regions/cities, periodic surveys, and other data sources. This document can be widely distributed to stakeholders (persons working in the field, other governmental departments, researchers, etc.).

• Monitoring Example: Financial Monitoring of the Public Housing Program

The following is an example of the financial monitoring system for public housing programs in the United States.[1] It is a good system because expectations are clear, the forms are easy to understand, and the results are used to drive program improvements. The monitoring data are collected in a timely manner and reports distributed to the relevant parties using the Internet.

Background. Social housing, or "public housing" as it is known in the United States, provides rental housing units for eligible low-income households (i.e., families, elderly persons, or persons with disabilities whose annual incomes are below 80 percent of the median income of the county or metropolitan area in which they live). Most, in fact, have incomes that are below 50 percent of area median income. Residents of public housing pay no more than 30 percent of their income for rent, which includes some but not all fees for communal services.

Public housing comes in all sizes and types, from scattered single-family houses to low-rise and high-rise multifamily apartments. The Department of Housing and Urban Development is the federal ministry that administers the program by providing funds to 3,300 state-chartered, local public housing agencies that build or acquire, own, and manage about 13,000 public housing developments (containing 1.3 million rental housing units and serving 3.3 million residents). To compensate these PHAs for receiving less in tenant rent than the cost of operating and maintaining their housing developments, HUD provides subsidies to PHAs.

HUD pays three principal subsidies to the local PHAs to support public housing. The Congress appropriates separate funds each year for each of the three subsidy streams:

1. A capital subsidy that pays 100 percent of the development and construction costs of public housing projects.
2. A subsidy covering operating expenses. The amount per unit month that a PHA receives is based on the cost of operating a well-managed PHA. So inefficient PHAs receive less than the excess of expenditures over tenant rents, a shortfall that the local government should in principle make up. In reality, reducing maintenance and repairs often funds the shortfall, which leads to larger long-term costs.
3. "Modernization subsidies," which are funded through a separate program. The amount of funds a PHA receives depends on the condition of its housing stock and the prospects that upgrading the housing is a good investment. An investment could be rated as poor either because of the low quality of PHA management or because of the combination of building type (high rise), occupancy (exclusively low-income and mostly single-parent families), and environment (severely adverse neighborhood conditions).

In exchange for these subsidies, a PHA agrees to abide by federally established rules that cover its operations and admissions policies. HUD monitors the PHA's compliance with these rules through its network of over fifty field offices and through its Real Estate Assessment Center (REAC) in its Washington, D.C., headquarters office.

The Real Estate Assessment Center is responsible for monitoring and evaluating all PHA housing for which the federal ministry provides some form of subsidy. In order to carry out this function, the REAC developed a four-pronged system that measures (1) physical condition, (2) financial condition, (3) management operations, and (4) resident service and satisfaction. Each component is measured using a specialized methodology. The four components are scored individually and combined to produce a Public Housing Assessment System (PHAS) score for a total score of up to 100 points. Table 9.2 summarizes the main components of the monitoring system.

PHAs Are Rated Based on Monitoring Results

- *High performers* achieve a score of at least 60 percent of the points available under each of the four PHAS indicators, and an overall PHAS score of 90 percent or greater of the total available points. A PHA is not designated a high performer if it scores below the threshold established for any indicator.

Table 9.2   Comprehensive Monitoring Program

Indicator	Component of Monitoring/Evaluation	Points
1	Physical condition	30
2	Financial condition	30
3	Management operations	30
4	Resident service and satisfaction	10
Total		100

High performers are freed from certain HUD regulations, given funding preferences, and publicly recognized for their achievements.

- *Standard performers* achieve a total PHAS score of not less than 60 percent of the total available points under PHAS, and do not achieve less than 60 percent of the total points available under the first three PHAS indicators (physical condition, financial condition, and management operations). A PHA that achieves a total PHAS score of 60 to 69.9 percent is required to submit an improvement plan to correct identified deficiencies. These PHAs risk being designated as "troubled" and must correct deficiencies and may be subject to additional oversight.
- *Overall troubled performers* achieve an overall PHAS score of less than 60 percent or less than 60 percent of the total points available under more than one of the first three PHAS indicators. Troubled performers are referred to one of HUD's two Troubled Agency Recovery Centers (TARCs). TARC works with troubled agencies to devise "performance targets, strategies to achieve performance targets, incentives for meeting such targets and the consequences of failing to meet the targets." If a PHA does not reach the goals set out in their agreement with TARC, it is referred to HUD's Enforcement Center, which either imposes sanctions designed to ensure compliance or places the PHA in receivership.
- *Troubled performers in one area* achieve less than 60 percent of the total points available under only one of the first three PHAS indicators. They are considered a substandard financial, physical, or management performer, and also referred to the TARC.

Financial Monitoring. Financial monitoring accounts for 30 of the 100 points in the monitoring system and is one of the primary performance indicators. HUD's financial assessment monitoring, referred to as the Financial Assessment

Subsystem (FASS), is a tool for evaluating the financial status of PHAs. The objectives of the system are to centralize and standardize the way HUD monitors and evaluates public housing, and to measure the financial condition of PHAs to determine the adequacy and effective use of resources.

FASS is an electronic system that enables auditors or independent public accountants to submit standardized financial forms to HUD over the Internet. Individual PHAs hire auditors/accountants to organize and submit their financial data. The system also provides the user with immediate feedback on the acceptability of financial information. Information submitted to HUD is scored by the system and then used to assign a status to the PHA. PHAs are also able to view the results of their financial assessment on the Internet. Table 9.3 summarizes the components of FASS and the number of points assigned to each indicator.

The PHA enters its financial data into the computer system. The system then performs basic internal checks on the submission to verify that the information appears correct. One example of an internal check is that assets and liabilities (plus equity) must match. If the information is rejected by the system, the PHA is provided with a detailed explanation of why the information was rejected. Monitors also review submissions for accuracy, and the analyst has the final say as to whether a submission is approved. A PHA may appeal submissions by calling its

Table 9.3   HUD's Financial Assessment Subsystem (FASS)

Component of FASS Evaluation	Points	Measure and Its Purpose
Current ratio	9.0	Liquidity: the PHA's ability to cover its current obligations
Months expendable fund balance	9.0	Viability: the PHA's ability to operate using its fund balance without relying on additional funding
Tenant receivables outstanding	4.5	Rent collections: the PHA's ability to collect its tenant receivables in a timely fashion
Occupancy loss	4.5	The PHA's ability to maximize rental revenues
Expense management/utility consumption	1.5	Operating cost per unit: the PHA's ability to maintain its expense ratio at a reasonable level relative to its peers (adjusted for size and region)
Net income or loss	1.5	Net income or loss impact against viability: how the year's operation has affected the PHA's viability

assigned analyst. Once the analyst approves the submission, the score generated by the system is sent to the PHA's HUD field office for review. The field office then has additional opportunity to appeal the score. Once the field office approves the score, it is communicated to the PHA.

Reports Generated. The PHAs, HUD field offices, and monitoring staff are able to view the following reports online:

- PHA's score on six main indicators (see Table 9.3).
- Summary balance sheet showing the major assets and liabilities of the PHA over the past year.
- Combined statement of revenues, expenses, and changes in equity over the past year.
- Comparative financial data schedule showing a two-year comparison of major balance sheet and revenue and expense items (see Table 9.4).
- Schedule of expenditures of federal awards showing the amounts and sources of federal dollars expended in the past year.

Table 9.4 presents a section of a comparison report. The report compares current and prior year performance of major balances and revenue and expense items. Variance and percentage change columns present the change in dollars and percentages.

Table 9.4   Sample Report: Comparative Financial Data (two-year revenue and expense report)

Account Description	Current Year ($)	Prior Year ($)	Variance ($)	Percentage Change
Net tenant rental revenue	2,465,018	2,453,450	11,568	1
Tenant revenue—other	88,777	24,039	64,738	270
Total tenant revenue	2,553,795	2,477,489	76,306	4
HUD PHA operating grants	6,133,256	7,435,834	(1,302,578)	(18)
Capital grants	843,564	0	843,564	—
Other government grants	616,541	564,444	52,097	10
Investment income—unrestricted	110,056	147,397	(37,341)	(26)
Other revenue	130,793	180,118	(49,325)	(28)
Gain/loss on sale of fixed assets	26,819	0	26,819	—
Total revenue	10,414,824	10,805,282	(390,458)	(4)

It is useful to look in greater detail at one indicator to see how the report is constructed. For example, one of the main indicators of financial management is the PHA's ability to maximize rental income. This indicator is worth 4.5 of the total 30 points. Maintaining high occupancy is the way to maximize rental income and occupancy loss is calculated based on the percentage of apartment units rented. See Table 9.5 for a sample occupancy report; the PHA depicted in the table had an occupancy rate of 95.8 percent—attaining 4.17 out of the possible 4.5 points.

Corrective Action. The HUD field office communicates final scores to the PHA. A PHA is required to submit a corrective action plan to its HUD field office if it receives a FASS score of less than 21 points (less than 60 percent of available points). Corrective action plans describe what the PHA will do over the course of a year to address the components of the FASS score that are bringing down the overall score. A PHA that receives a low score on the occupancy loss component is asked to provide a detailed explanation as to how they will adjust their current operations to turn units around within a thirty-day period. For example, one PHA wrote a corrective action plan that said:

> Wherein our existing inventory of Public Housing is being utilized as a primary resource, we reserved units, transferred tenants and repaired units out of sequence to meet the demand of the HOPE VI Program. As we expect to have New Brunswick Homes vacant during May 2001, our turnaround time at Robeson Village, Schwarz Homes and Hoffman Pavilion should not be an issue. We feel confident we can achieve an average unit turnaround time of less than 50 days with the quarter ending 9/30/01.

In this PHA's case, its occupancy rate was low due to the need to keep units unoccupied in preparation for renovations. That is, in order to make replacement units available for residents whose units were being renovated, the PHA purposely left

---

Table 9.5   Sample Occupancy Loss Details Report

PHA code: XXXXX
PHA name: XXX
Fiscal year: 6/30/04
Potential occupancy loss score: 4.5
Occupancy loss ratio: 4.17
Occupancy loss details: 95.8%

Numerator: number of unit months leased (units × months leased)	17,415
Denominator: gross number of units (units × 12 months)	18,172

units in other developments vacant. PHAs are expected to report their progress on reaching improvement goals on a quarterly basis to their HUD field offices.

If the HUD office believes that a PHA failed to address its problem adequately, the office may provide the PHA with recommendations. The following example illustrates how one HUD field office used quarterly reporting to encourage a PHA to meet its goals. In the example, the PHA attempted to improve utility consumption by performing an energy audit, but failed to meet its quarterly goal for expense management/utility consumption because it never implemented the audit recommendations. In response, the field office proposed the following measures:

- Immediately implement the audit recommendations.
- Hire an energy service company to identify additional cost-effective energy conservation measures.
- Discontinue energy allowances.
- Impose surcharges for excessive utility usage.

If PHAs are not able to bring their scores up during the year period, they are subject to additional oversight by the field office. Field office staff may visit the PHA periodically to administer technical assistance, or impose sanctions on funding.

Implementing a Monitoring System

The basic tasks of implementing a monitoring system include the following:

- Decide what to monitor (identify the questions to answer and select specific indicators).
- Develop written materials and forms.
- Distribute materials and forms.
- Conduct trainings for participating cities, departments, or staff.
- Complete monitoring forms (service delivery staff on a daily/weekly/ monthly basis).
- Collect monthly/quarterly data.
- Follow up with staff or departments that fail to submit data.
- Maintain the data (enter data into computer database every week/month).
- Check the quality of data.
- Analyze data (see Chapter 4).
- Produce periodic reports.
- Use monitoring data to inform program decisions.

This chapter describes each of these tasks. Important points to remember:

- What is being reported should be *well defined* and the measures should be *consistent* from one period to the next.
- Monitoring is *routine*. To be useful as a managerial tool, monitoring must be done *frequently* and at *regular intervals*. All reporting units must consistently provide their information. Monitoring loses its value if it is done haphazardly.
- Data and monitoring are not the same. Monitoring implies a careful selection and presentation of data that is used to identify problems or success. Monitoring tells not just what the program is doing, but also how well it is doing it.

Designating Responsible Staff. It is unlikely that monitoring data will be collected, maintained, and analyzed according to plan unless staff are assigned specific tasks and held accountable. In most transition countries, reporting information was not taken very seriously under the old regime, and this tradition is far from dead. Therefore, clearly assigning responsibility and monitoring the quality of the work, particularly for the first few submissions, is critical to establishing a system that generates reliable information.

Clearly explaining how and when forms are to be completed goes a long way toward the success of a monitoring program. Incentives or penalties also help ensure that monitoring tasks are completed. Finally, the biggest motivator is evidence that the monitoring data are being looked at and are contributing to program planning and policy development. Making the results public, charting improvements, recognizing exceptional staff or activities, and using monitoring results to modify program practices and policies reinforce the value of the monitoring initiative.

• Understanding the Program: Modeling

As an early step in developing a monitoring program it is essential to understand what the program does and how it is supposed to work. Many programs develop descriptions of their work based on what they aspire to do—rather than what is actually happening. Program modeling is a detailed description of how the program is currently functioning, including a description of all project resources, program activities, number of services provided, and benefits received by participants. The description of program activities should be as detailed as possible, such as describing how work orders are processed or how clients move through a program. See Figure 9.1.

The basic categories for the program model are inputs, activities, outputs, and outcomes.

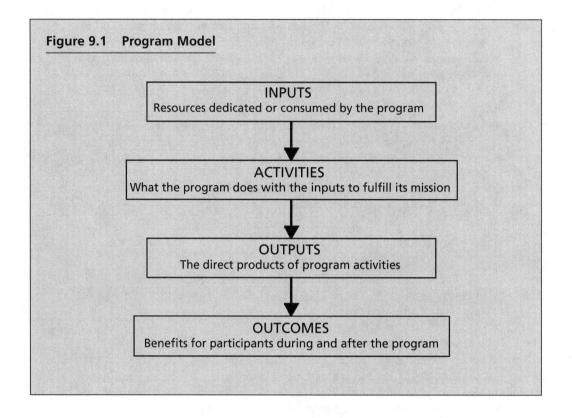

Figure 9.1   Program Model

INPUTS
Resources dedicated or consumed by the program

ACTIVITIES
What the program does with the inputs to fulfill its mission

OUTPUTS
The direct products of program activities

OUTCOMES
Benefits for participants during and after the program

- *Inputs* are resources dedicated to or consumed by the program. Examples are money, staff and staff time, volunteers, facilities, equipment, and supplies.
- *Activities* are what the program does with its inputs to fulfill its mission. Examples are feeding homeless families, street cleaning, maintaining parks, and sponsoring cultural events.
- *Outputs* are the direct products of program activities. Examples are the number of people fed, kilometers of streets cleaned, and the number of summer concerts.

See Exercise 9.2: Program Model on page 231.

The task in this exercise is to complete a program model for a program that you are familiar with.

- *Outcomes* are the benefits for participants during and after program activities. Examples range from initial outcomes such as increased skills and new knowledge, to long-term outcomes such as obtaining and retaining jobs, financial independence, and more healthy lifestyles.

Figure 9.2 presents a program model for the municipal jobs program described in Chapter 2, which helps participants find work.

• Determine What Is Most Important About the Program

After mapping how the program is supposed to function, the next step is to focus on

---

Figure 9.2   Program Model for the Municipal Jobs Program

Inputs
1. Municipal budget.
2. Employment and social services.
3. Social workers.
4. Employment centers.
   Resources dedicated to or consumed by the program.

Activities
1. Develop service plan and contract (responsibility of the social service agency).
2. Payment of monthly cash benefit (social service agency).
3. Provision of social services (social service agency).
4. Provision of employment services (employment center).
5. Active job search (client).
6. Employment (client).
7. Recertification of benefits (social service agency).
   What the program does with the inputs to fulfill its mission.

Outputs
1. Number of program participants.
2. Amount and number of benefits provided.
3. Number of employment and social services provided.
   Direct products of programs activities.

Outcomes
1. Number and percentage of employed participants.
2. Average salary of employed participants (and increase or decrease from previous employment).
3. Length of time employed.
   Benefits for participants during and after the program.

what questions need to be answered in order to understand what the program is doing and how well it is performing. These basic questions fall under the categories: *How many? Who? What? Where? When? How well?* and *At what cost?* The answers to these questions will provide indicators for inputs, activities, outputs, and outcomes. See Table 9.6 for an example of a program to provide social services.

These simple questions capture the basic functions of all programs. Asked with a certain amount of precision, the questions can be used to frame even the most sophisticated monitoring initiative. The question *Who?* captures all demographic characteristics. For a program like maintaining city buses, the *who* becomes a profile of the buses being serviced, with different models, ages, and mechanical histories as key attributes. *What?* can be used to track the different types of services provided. *When?* can be posed to trace whether services are provided in a logical sequence.

How well? assesses the quality or cost effectiveness of services. To make reasonable judgments about the quality of services, compare data to minimum standards, timeliness, and client satisfaction. For example, laws require a certain standard for drinking water, certification for doctors, and basic sanitary norms for orphanages. Some programs may need to set their own standards or compare performance over time or to similar programs to answer the question *How well?* The annex to this chapter includes more detailed descriptions of each of these questions and examples of forms and reports.

It is critical to limit monitoring requirements to indicators that really say something about the program. Asking too many questions or trying to collect too much data can be costly and can contribute to inconsistent data collection and too much data to analyze and study. Monitoring should provide the essential information that decisionmakers need to understand the program and guide improvements.

It is often helpful to engage stakeholders in a discussion on what to include in the monitoring program. This process will likely generate more indicators than are practical to use, but the process can help build commitment to monitoring and ensure that important indicators are not overlooked. A good way to eliminate excessive indicators is to ask what question does this answer and how will this information be used to improve program performance. It is a good practice to present the indicators and sample monitoring forms to program stakeholders and test the forms with several program clients. This process may reveal that some terms need to be clarified, that some questions need to be reframed, or that suggested responses need to be offered.

Keep in mind that all of these questions should be answered with respect to the same time period. This will allow you to create efficiency indicators (ratios of outputs to inputs) and compare one output with another output. (For example, during the winter there was particularly high demand for Service A, but not Service B.)

Table 9.6 Monitoring Categories

Question	Description	Purpose
How many?	How many clients does the department have? How many new clients did the department get in this reporting period? How many clients were discharged during this reporting period? How many of each type of service were offered? How many client contacts occurred?	Allows the director to know exactly how many persons have been served over a particular period and thus better identify service costs and demand.
Who?	Who is the population being served?	Ensures that the correct population is being served and helps identify which population(s) may be underserved.
What?	What are the services being provided?	Ensures that all services for which the client is eligible are being provided. In addition, ensures that clients are not receiving services for which they are not eligible.
Where?	Where does the agency provide its services—are the services provided at an office or off site? *Where?* also addresses the specific location if the program operates in several districts or cities.	Documents the location where services are provided so that the director can determine if more emphasis should be given to one location/region or another.
When?	What service period is covered by this monitoring report—is it a monthly report or an annual report, are these daily, weekly, or monthly services? When the number of services is identified, for what period were these services given?	Helps the director determine if there are periods when more services are required. This can help directors plan and budget services over the program year. Frequency of service delivery (onetime, ongoing, etc.) helps to gauge the resources required and likely outcome.
How well?	How well are services being provided? At what cost?	The whole point of monitoring program performance is to determine how well the program is operating and what areas need improvement. An important aspect of assessing *how well?* is comparing the costs to the program results.

Source: Adapted from Patrick A. Corvington, *Monitoring Social Assistance and Social Services* (Washington, D.C.: Urban Institute. November 2002).

Data Collection and Reporting

• Types of Data

There are many different sources of data that provide information about program operations and quality. The main types of monitoring data include administrative records, surveys, interviews, focus groups, and site visits.

Before organizing original data collection, it is important to identify existing data sources and assess their usefulness for monitoring purposes. Program offices maintain a host of information on their clients and services that will likely be the primary data sources. But administrative record keeping may need to be systematized and improved to serve as an effective basis for program monitoring. Other useful information may already be compiled as administrative records from other programs or statistics maintained by other agencies. (Administrative records are discussed in detail below.)

Collecting new data can be time consuming and costly, so it is important that the monitoring team limit new data collection to that which will answer important questions about the program. Some of these methods, such as surveys, interviews, or focus groups, may not be part of routine monitoring, but employed when monitoring reveals particular issues that need further investigation, as is discussed in Chapter 11.

The core monitoring data will likely be quantitative: number of persons served, number and percentage of clients receiving various services or having particular characteristics, the change in the number of graduating students, and so forth. Qualitative data are very useful in explaining the patterns found in the quantitative monitoring data, and it is a good idea for monitoring reports to have a short narrative section that presents additional pertinent information. This information may be the result of formal focus groups or observations from staff and informal conversations with clients. For example, "This month there was an increase in expenditures for snow removal due to higher than expected snowfall." Or, "Noticing a decline in participation in group activities, staff met with a group of teens who offered ideas for future group activities (different hours, acting club, writing a newspaper, etc.). Next month's report will reflect new group activities and hopefully an increase in participation."

See Chapter 4 for descriptions of different types of data and analytical techniques.

Establishing Reliable Administrative Records. Administrative records are most useful when they are routinely updated, well defined, and consistent. To use administrative records for monitoring may require some significant changes in what data are collected and how they are recorded.

What to include in administrative records should be driven by the basic questions or facts about the program. The main effort should be in creating an organized system of self-reporting and documentation by staff members that answer the questions: *How many? Who? What? Where? When?* and *How well?* Many programs and government agencies perform poorly at collecting and maintaining monitoring data, resulting in low-quality data. Ideally, programs and staff will come to see the value of monitoring, but most will require strict reporting requirements, deadlines, and clear instruction to comply.

Standardized case files or uniform records will help to ensure that monitoring data can be easily gleaned from the files (it may also help staff to deliver services). Standardized forms and reporting requirements need to be established and enforced. Develop simple, clear reporting forms so that program staff know what to report and how to report it. Establish firm deadlines, and if possible issue penalties and rewards to encourage compliance.

Staff and/or field offices should complete weekly or monthly reports that summarize the services provided. Weekly forms are recommended for reporting specific services provided, because if staff have not kept an ongoing log, they can recall their actions at the end of a week, whereas at the end of a month the data will be pure fiction. Staff can also summarize their weekly forms into a monthly report prepared for submission to their supervisor.

It is a good practice to regularly verify reports and records. Verification methods include reviewing case files or notes, field visits, on-site inspections, and trained observer ratings (staff or volunteers who regularly rate the conditions of a physical area or activity).

Collect data in a manner that is useful for maintaining and summarizing. Computer database programs are generally the most useful. It is essential that data are correctly entered and that all staff have a clear understanding of terms/conventions (useful tools are sample completed forms and a data dictionary that includes definitions of all terms, questions, or abbreviations).

It should be made explicit what forms staff members are required to complete and who is responsible for compiling summary reports. Staff may require training on how to complete forms, enter data into a database, or complete summary reports. This will take an initial time commitment, though once the program is in place it should require minimal effort from most staff.

• *Using a Logical Frame to Organize Monitoring Efforts*

A logical frame is a simple tool used to help design and implement a monitoring program. A logical frame organizes the pieces of the monitoring puzzle. Its three components are:

- Questions to answer or main objectives of the program.
- Indicators to measure.
- Source and methodology for collecting the necessary data.

A logical frame ensures that the data being collected answer the important questions about the program. The questions in the first column of a logical frame (see Table 9.7) should reflect program objectives. These can be written either as questions or as objectives. For example, "to provide elderly clients with home care services" or "what services did elderly clients receive?"

The middle column of a logical frame should outline the indicators that correspond to the objectives/questions and measure the program's inputs, outputs, or efficiency. Indicators must be well defined and specific. Some indicators are explicitly stated in program regulations, but often this is not the case and program managers will have to develop them.

The third column of a logical frame should outline data sources and collection methods. Most of the data sources for program monitoring come from administrative records. Therefore, the records must be maintained in a way that the indicators can be measured (e.g., separate activity logs for each worker). When other data sources or collection methods are necessary, it is important to make sure that they are administratively feasible and not cost prohibitive.

• *Assembling and Maintaining Data*

In order for monitoring data to be useful to program managers and other decisionmakers, it needs to be compiled into summary reports that present what the program did in the past month or quarter or how this period's performance changed from the previous.

The most efficient way to maintain data is to enter it into a spreadsheet or database program. Microsoft Excel or Access are common programs used for this purpose, though some agencies use more specialized programs.

If Using Excel. Excel is a useful program because it helps to organize the data and perform basic analytical functions. The program is easy to use and someone work-

See Exercise 9.3: Logical Frame on page 231.

The task in this exercise is to complete a logical frame for several public programs, such as housing subsidies, maternal and infant health care, primary education, and others.

Table 9.7 Logical Frame: Solid Waste Collection

Objective/Question	Indicator	Data Source/ Collection Method
Garbage is collected and ends up in legal landfills	Tons collected and disposed per month	Receipts for disposal at landfill
Garbage is collected regularly and residents are not inconvenienced	• Number and percentage of collection routes not completed on schedule (per month) • Number and percentage of households and businesses reporting missed collections (per month)	• Log of crew activities • On-site inspections • Log of complaints filed with the city and with the companies • Occasional survey
Pleasing aesthetics in city	• Number of curb-kilometers of streets cleaned (per week) • Complaints	• Log of crew activities • On-site inspections • Complaint log
Competition is used to ensure that garbage is collected efficiently (good service/price)	• Percentage of garbage collection that is competitively bid (measured in tons, routes, or households) • Decline in cost from the base value • Number and percentage of collection routes not completed on schedule (per month) for contracted and city agency routes • Number and percentage of households and businesses reporting missed collections (per month) for contracted and city agency routes	• Number of contracts signed • Number/percentage of households served (or tons collected) by competitive firms • Value of contracts • Change in budget outlays • Complaints, survey

ing in a secretarial capacity with basic computer skills could be made responsible for data entry and simple counts and averages. If your program has the staff and the need for more advanced analysis, the program can link spreadsheets, be programmed to generate specific types of reports, and perform advanced statistical analyses. It also has a graphics capability and can generate simple charts and graphs. Many of the tables in this chapter were composed from data in Excel spreadsheets.

If Computers Are Unavailable. Program-level data can be maintained without a computer by using simple summary forms. It is particularly important that these forms capture the important information, as once the monitoring initiative is under way, going back to retrieve additional information will be a time consuming task. Designated staff will have to collect all the weekly/monthly forms from other staff and complete a new form to record the totals for that time period.

Table 9.8 presents a sample monthly report for a tuberculosis program that compares March indicators with those of the previous month and includes a year-to-date (YTD) total. When computing by hand, the year-to-date total makes a year-end report very easy.

This report could be generated either using a computer or paper system. It clearly presents the number of patients served and the services provided (inputs and outputs). The YTD total is the sum of each month's services. Because most patients participate in the program for several months, the number of patients

---

Table 9.8   Tuberculosis Unit Monthly Report, March 2003

Services	March 2003	Previous Month	Year to Date
Total number of patients served	211	200	219
New patients this month	12	7	31
Cases closed this month	7	10	24
Total number of services provided	1,007	988	2,753
Average number of services provided per patient	5.7	4.9	4.6
Number of patients that received fewer than two services per month (include explanation in narrative section)	18	15	57
Number of patients receiving each of the following services:			Average
Diagnostic tests	114	121	117
Doctor consultations	78	66	72
Tuberculosis antibiotics	131	120	123
Medicine for other conditions	97	85	90
Other treatments	124	143	136
Referrals	120	101	109

receiving specific services needs to be averaged in the YTD. Adding the percentage of patients receiving each service would make it even easier to consider service levels, and including information on outcomes, such as number of patients to complete treatment, would make this table more interesting.

Time Series. Looking at changes in performance over time provides a useful context for monitoring data. Unless decreed by regulations, programs need to determine the most effective time period for comparison, such as changes from month to month or quarter to quarter, or changes from the same time period compared to the previous year. For programs with seasonal changes, comparing services delivered the present February compared to the past February may be a useful comparison. Table 9.8 is an example of a time-series report.

• *Developing Monitoring Reports*

Monitoring data must be summarized into concise and informative monthly or quarterly reports to be useful to the program manager and other responsible parties. The analysis and structure of these reports should allow busy administrators and policymakers to quickly understand the program's recent activities, changes in performance, effectiveness, and the like.

Reports should be generated on a regular basis. The frequency may be determined by regulation or by program administrators. Monthly or quarterly reports are most common, because they provide relatively fresh data and can be produced without overtaxing resources.

Deciding What Goes into the Reports. Monitoring reports do not need to be very long. If important factors about the program can be presented in a single page, there is no reason to make the report any longer. Other programs may be more complex and may require multiple pages of reports on client characteristics, services provided, resources spent, and results achieved.

To decide on the report contents, return to the basic questions *(How many? Who? What? Where? When? How well? At what cost?).* Develop a few sample reports and share them with key stakeholders. Ask yourself whether this information contributes to taking specific action steps to improve the program.

A program manager may decide to produce several different types of reports for different audiences. Department heads may receive monthly reports that provide breakouts by each staff member, for all services provided, and that include specific characteristics of clients. A central administrator or policymaker may receive only quarterly reports that include highlights of current and past program performance.

Let's take a look at the municipal jobs program example presented in Chapter

2. The following is a list of monitoring forms completed monthly for the program:

- Number of families participating and their characteristics (ages of children, number of pensioners and disabled members, education level of unemployed persons).
- List of participant names, wages (if any), and benefits received.
- Total benefits due to be paid by the program and actual benefits paid.
- Number of new agreements/terminations/sanctions.
- Employment services provided by type and statistics on acquisition of new jobs.
- Social services—number of each type provided to clients.

This list of forms captures the main functions of the jobs program. Each form is a simple table that includes the current month's data as well as data for previous months/quarters, and builds toward an annual total. Each table has a clear purpose and none of the information contained on one form is repeated on another. The tables that summarize employment and social services provided are likely constructed from staff-level weekly reports. The report on employment services and new job statistics is presented in Table 9.9. The table clearly summarizes services provided (outputs) and jobs attained (outcomes).

• Developing Action Plans

Collecting monitoring data and producing reports is only worthwhile if administrators and policymakers read the reports and use the information to understand and improve program performance. The information presented in a monitoring report should answer, either in the tables or the narrative, the following important questions:

- What is the general picture? How can recent activity be summarized?
- What are the most important findings? In what areas does the program appear to be particularly strong or weak?
- Are there any areas of concern? Areas where the program shows weakness or data are lacking?
- What issues require further investigation?
- Are there any follow-up actions that could be taken to improve performance? Are there any staffing or resource issues? Do program policies or procedures need to be reexamined? Are there improvements that should be publicly recognized?

Presenting Findings to Decisionmakers. Programs may be required to provide monitoring results on a quarterly or annual basis to city or regional administrators.

Table 9.9   Employment Center and Its Services

	January	February	March	Quarter 1
Number of families served by the employment center	45	39	42	53
Services received				
Professional consultation	29	20	23	72
Professional orientation	13	21	10	44
Professional training/refresher courses	12	16	9	37
Social adaptation	5	4	7	16
Information about job vacancies	32	26	24	82
Referral to job	14	9	8	31
Other	5	7	2	14
Number of families in which unemployed person got job during month indicated				
Number who got jobs during first three months of program participation	11	10	8	29
Number who got jobs months four to six of program participation	7	11	9	27
Number who got jobs due to employment center services	8	7	6	21
Number of families in which member got and lost job (lost job during month specified)	2	3	4	9
Number of families in which over one unemployed member got job	4	2	0	6

Regulations may be very specific about the reporting requirements and the city/region may develop specific forms. However, if there are no specific requirements, program leaders should develop a report format that they will use to keep decisionmakers informed.

Monitoring data are not always positive and sometimes program directors must present data that reflect poorly on their programs and themselves. Most programs have some problems or setbacks and the real test for an administrator is how well she deals with these problems. Monitoring reports must honestly disclose what is happening (or not happening) in the program. If there are problems, the accompanying narrative should describe the context or reasons for the problems and outline any strategies to remedy the situation.

Table 9.10 presents a sample annual report for the municipal jobs program. In addition to the monitoring findings, the report includes a summary of program accomplishments and explanations of outcomes and service provision. This report

Table 9.10   Municipal Jobs Program, Annual Report 2004

This was the first full year of operation for the Municipal Jobs Program (the program was start-ed in October 2003). The program served its projected 65 families (including 79 unemployed participants), and many more families expressed an interest in the program. Of the 79 unem-ployed persons served, 50 (63 percent) received jobs. Participants found jobs after an average of 3.5 months of program participation. The majority of clients received social and employ-ment assistance.

General Information and Employment Outcomes

Total number of families served	65
Total number of unemployed participants	79
Total number of participants to attain employment	50
Total number of participants to retain jobs for more than six months	15
Number of participants to get and lose a job	20
Average monthly wages for employed participants (rubles)	300
Number of employed participants who increased their earnings (number that got a job that paid higher than their last position)	5
Total cash benefits awarded (rubles)	120,000
Total cash benefits due (rubles)	156,000
Number of clients (unemployed participants) per social worker	26
Average length of time of program participation before clients attained employment (maximum program participation 9 months; average includes only those who attained employment)	3.5 months

Comments: The program exceeded its employment goal and 63 percent of clients attained employment (our performance target was that 50 percent of participants would receive jobs). Although many participants received jobs, only 15 managed to keep their jobs for more than 6 months (there were an additional 15 participants who were employed for less than 6 months at the end of the reporting period); 20 participants got and lost jobs during the year; only 5 received jobs that paid more than their previous positions. This suggests that the program is successful in moving clients quickly into jobs—but that they are low-paying jobs that partici-pants cannot or do not retain. It is unclear whether additional placement or follow-up services would help participants to retain jobs, whether these are short-term posts, or whether partici-pants have limited attachment to these low-paying jobs. The program has planned a focus group with participants to discuss these issues. Pending those results the program may alter its services or expectations.

   The program ran out of funds for the cash allowances and granted only partial payments in November and December. This aspect of the program needs to be fully funded for the coming year.

(*continues*)

Table 9.10   Continued

Services Provided	Number of Clients to Receive Services
Social services	
Child care or children's educational assistance	23
Discounts for public services	15
Social services at home	45
Social services (office)	35
Material assistance, gifts, food, etc.	12
Referrals for legal or psychiatric counseling	8
Housing subsidies	17
Employment services	
Skills assessment	53
Career counseling	27
Professional training/refresher courses	6
Information about job vacancies	38
Referral to job	9
Other	2

Comments: All clients were supposed to receive a skills assessment, yet assessments were completed for only 53. The assessments are completed by the employment center and either those workers failed to complete the assessments or clients failed to keep appointments. In addition, because several clients attained their own positions shortly after enrolling in the program, their contact with the employment center was limited. In the coming year, we will continue to work out the challenges of coordinating services with the employment center.

Staff social workers delivered a range of social services and referrals to program participants and their families. Social workers saw more clients in their homes than in the office, which is a poor use of staff time given that participants are deemed able to work. In the coming year, staff will spend less time conducting home visits and serving the entire family—and will instead focus on helping clients work with the employment center and providing services to help clients retain their jobs.

presents a mixed picture—wherein the program met its main goal of helping its clients attain employment, but had some problems with how it delivered services and with clients' retention of their jobs. (A full annual report would likely include more client characteristics and budget information.)

Presenting Findings to the Public. Presenting monitoring findings to the public and other stakeholders makes the program more accountable. When the results are positive, this can help build support for program activities or budget needs. Sharing negative results can be painful—but can also build momentum for needed change. Staff may resist changing practices or demands that they work harder, and performance results can help make the case for needed changes to internal and external stakeholders.

Chapter Summary

Monitoring is a useful tool to measure program performance, manage staff, allocate resources, and inform policy changes and program improvements. Monitoring requires articulating the primary objectives of the program, identifying indicators to measure those objectives, and collecting, analyzing, and reporting monitoring data. Asking the questions *How many? Who? What? Where? When? How well?* and *At what cost?* helps identify the main factors that need to be monitored. Data must be collected on a consistent and regular basis, and should be limited to indicators that really say something about the program and that have the potential to inform improvements. Monitoring often serves as the motivator and primary data source for evaluations, as described in later chapters.

The annex to this chapter provides additional detail on asking the basic questions about the program, and presents examples and forms in response to each question.

Recommended Reading

Center for Economic and Financial Research. *Monitoring the Administrative Barriers to Small Business Development in Russia: The Third Round.* Moscow: Center for Economic and Financial Research (CEFIR), November 2003. Available online at http://www.cefir.org.

This report summarizes the impact of Russia's recent reforms to reduce the administrative barriers to small business development. Between 2001 and 2003, Russia passed four new laws, affecting the licensing, inspections, registration, and taxation of small businesses. The Center for Economic and Financial Research is monitoring the implementation of these laws. The monitoring initiative began with a baseline study in 2001 documenting the high costs (both time and money) of these administrative practices to small business, including frequent inspections by the same public agencies requesting bribes. The second round of monitoring, in 2002, found significant improvements in inspections and licensing, and only modest improvements in 2003. Both rounds found that tax reforms simplified the tax burden for small businesses. Monitoring continued in 2004 and 2005. The report is a good example of monitoring major policy changes and illustrates how nongovernmental organizations can monitor government functions with objectivity and skill.

Annex: How to Ask the Basic
Questions About Program Performance

This annex describes in detail how to use the questions *How many? Who? What? Where? When? How well?* and *At what cost?* to frame a monitoring initiative.[2] These questions are a way of identifying the main characteristics of a program. This section provides a full description of how to use each question and specific examples of forms or reports based on the questions. An example of a social services program is used throughout.

• *How Many?*

The question *How many?* is posed for both the number of clients served as well as the number of services delivered. Clearly answering this question requires defining the client population and the services provided. However, for many programs this question is more complex than it appears. For example, programs working with families need to determine how to count clients: Is the family the client, the entire household, or the number of individuals from the family who are participating in the program? In developing a monitoring system, planners need to decide what is the most meaningful unit of measurement, make certain that everyone understands the definition of client (individuals or families) and other terms, and remain consistent over time.

Examples of some of the important *How many?* questions are presented in Table 9.11. Note that although many questions may need to be answered, many of these questions use the same basic data. If data are collected in an organized fashion, the effort will not overburden staff.

Table 9.12 illustrates how information on the number of clients served can be presented. It presents quarterly data on clients entering and leaving the program.

Based on Table 9.12, what might the program director ascertain?

1. The program director can determine that the program grew during the past year. In particular, the third quarter showed the most growth.
2. The fourth quarter has a high number of client exits, discharges in particular. This may be due to end-of-the-year operations, during which staff are catching up on program reviews they have not completed and so discover that some clients are no longer eligible to receive the benefits or services, or discover that budget funds have run out and the city can no longer provide the services until the new budget funds become available.
3. Finally, the program director knows how many *active cases* there were at the end of each quarter rather than just the number of enrolled cases.

Table 9.11 Defining "How Many?"

Question	Why do you need to know?	Where do you find this information?
How many clients received program services?	Tells you how the services provided match the client population. If you know that 100 services were provided you must also know how many clients benefited from these services—did one client receive all 100 services or did 10 clients each receive 10 services?	Case records and enrollment lists
How many active cases does the department have?	This sets context for service provision and allows the director to determine what proportion of active clients have been served in a reporting period.	Enrollment lists and case files
How many clients were enrolled or discharged during this reporting period?	Helps track the number of clients who enter and leave a program or receive a benefit over a specific period of time.	Intake forms, applications
How many services or benefits were provided at each site?	Enables program director to determine activity level at various program sites.	Case records, program office records, sign-in sheets.
How have services fluctuated over time?	Tracks increase in need in the client population and helps compare service periods, months, and years against one another. In this way a program director can determine if more or fewer services have been provided.	Case records

Table 9.12 Client Activity by Quarter

Quarter	Active Cases at Beginning of Period	New Clients	Discharged Clients	Clients Who Left Program	Total Client Exits	Net Gain/ Loss	Active Cases at End of Period
January–March	56	41	12	13	25	16	72
April–June	72	22	8	4	12	10	82
July–September	82	36	11	4	15	21	103
October–November	103	31	21	13	34	−3	100
Total	NA	130	52	34	86	44	NA

Based on the information provided, the program director can make some decisions about how the program is growing and thus plan for the next year. For example, the director can judge how the program grows in each quarter and can plan staffing patterns based on this information. In addition, the director can make the case for more money for staff or other resources based on demonstrating program growth. Finally, the director can more closely examine program exits and investigate the cause of program exits and develop an intervention to address this issue. Whatever the director decides, this information offers a clear picture of program activity over the year.

- *Who?*

Who Are We Serving? It is important to understand who is being served by the program. Some public programs are available to the entire population, while others may have regulations that determine the target population.

Depending on the targeting methodology, the program may end up serving some people not in its target population and/or denying services to people in the target population. Keeping track of statistics such as the age, sex, or residence of beneficiaries may provide useful information to better target services or introduce new services. The characteristics of the population may also affect program design or results. For example, a program serving mainly women may need to pay extra attention to child care and other family issues. A job program may find that the majority of its participants did not complete their secondary education, which would impact the types of jobs and salary levels that participants receive.

Being clear about who is eligible for services is important for monitoring, because a population can often be divided into subpopulations. The question any director should be asking is: "What information do I need about the client population?" The answer to this question will inform the decision about what information to collect.

For example, the director of a center for troubled children may want to know how the population is constructed by age and gender. This seems like important information and answers some basic questions, such as: "How many children are there in my shelter?" "How old are they?" "What is the breakdown of girls and boys?" The director may also want more information, such as how the population was referred to the shelter. The information can be presented as in Table 9.13.

Who Is Providing the Services? A second *Who?* question concerns who is providing the services. This *who* refers to the provider: regional or city administration, local district, NGO, private company, staff, volunteers, and so forth. For many government programs the answer to this question is simply program staff. However, for some programs, this question can be more complex, and who is pro-

Table 9.13 Client Population by Referral Source

Referral Source	Age Groups		
	7–12	13–18	Total
Girls			
Police	4	9	13
Social protection	6	5	11
Family/relative	1	3	4
Total girls	11	17	28
Boys			
Police	4	13	17
Social protection	9	3	12
Family/relative	1	3	4
Total boys	14	19	33
Total boys and girls	25	36	61

viding the services can be an output. For example, a government initiative to introduce competitive procurement into housing maintenance would consider the question of who is providing services not simply as one of program inputs but also as an important program output.

Looking at the services provided by individual staff members is an important personnel management tool. Take, for example, a social service agency that has many social workers serving clients. The supervisor needs to be able to compare social workers to one another. Thus it is a good idea to collect information not only by client and services as discussed earlier, but also by staff member.

Table 9.14 gives an example of how data can be collected at the worker level.

In this example, each social worker's clients utilized services at different rates. The supervisor can do several things with this information:

- The supervisor can investigate why there is a difference in how children use services.
- This information also reveals that the client load is not evenly distributed. The supervisor could investigate this to see if this is true over time or if it is a temporary situation.
- The supervisor can also see that Social Worker 2 seems to have particularly low client-participation numbers. It may be that this social worker has, by chance, received particularly difficult cases. If this were true, then the pro-

Table 9.14   Services for Children: Social Rehabilitation

Social Worker	Client Load	Number of Children Who Participated in:		
		Life Skills Training	Individual Counseling	Group Counseling
Social worker 1	25	21	22	22
Social worker 2	28	16	18	14
Social worker 3	35	22	31	26
Total	88	59	71	62

gram manger would want to ensure that difficult or challenging clients were equally spread across social workers.

Whatever the director chooses to do with this information, the fact that this information is available gives the director options. Worker-level information can be used to improve services. If a social worker is performing very well and has been able to engage children in programs by discovering an innovative practice, it would be beneficial to expand that new practice to other social workers. If a social worker has a particularly difficult set of cases, it might be good to shift the case-load a little to spread out the difficulty so that each client can receive full attention. It is important to note that Table 9.14 does not explain why there is a difference in performance, only that there is a difference. But based on this information, the program manager can begin to investigate these differences.

• What? Where? and When?

What Services Are We Providing? Measuring what services are being provided is surprisingly difficult. Table 9.15 describes the services of an agency serving troubled children. Notice how a clearer definition of services helps identify what services the children are receiving.

Where Are Services Being Provided? Often a program provides services in a variety of locations, such as neighborhood-based offices. Monitoring where services are provided is important, because it allows administrators to identify activity levels for each office—information that is critical to staff management and to ensuring that program resources are appropriately targeted. For example, a city

Table 9.15   Service Definition

Vague Definition of Services	Make It Clearer	Clear Definition of Services
Medical services 1. Medical investigations 2. Assistance in getting medical consultations from hospitals 3. Assistance in getting medical treatment in hospitals	What service is actually being provided? Is it the medical consultation, investigation and treatment, or is it the assistance in obtaining these services (referrals)?	Medical services 1. Medical exams by staff doctors 2. Referrals to hospitals for follow-up and treatment
Psychological training for decreasing conflict and aggressive behavior	Is this training or is it psychological counseling? If it is counseling, is it done in a group setting or on an individual basis?	Psychological services designed to reduce aggressive behavior including: 1. Individual psychological counseling 2. Group counseling
Pedagogical services 1. Basic life- training skills 2. Leisure activities 3. Assistance in getting school education.	Again, what is meant by assistance in getting a school education? Is it a referral to a school, tutoring, or providing schooling at the center?	Pedagogical services 1. Life-skills training including learning how to do laundry, use eating utensils, and mend clothing 2. Cultural outings to the theater and museums 3. Referral to appropriate school to complete educational training

may have several police precincts serving local communities. Gathering information at the site level, as presented in Table 9.16, allows supervisors to know which site has the highest activity and thus allocate staff and administrative resources properly.

What can be gathered from the information in this table?

- First, the supervisor can see how many complaints were processed by each location during the particular months. Totals provide the program manager information about the total number of complaints for the quarter as well as for the site.

Table 9.16   Police: Complaints of Minor Crimes Processed by Each District

	June	July	August	Total
District 1	360	420	470	1,250
District 2	780	710	840	2,330
District 3	1,290	1,340	1,380	4,010
District 4	190	170	210	570
Total	2,620	2,640	2,900	8,160

- Second, District 3 has the highest level of activity, while District 4 has the lowest level of activity. This may suggest that there is a higher level of crime in District 3 or that District 4 discourages citizen complaints. Further investigation may be required to determine whether there is a performance or resource issue in either district.
- Finally, the supervisor may want to investigate why activity is so low in District 4. It might be that District 4 does not have enough activity to warrant the resources expended to keep it open and thus needs to be closed, with citizens being diverted to another office.

When Are Services Being Provided?   Knowing when services are being provided helps administrators track fluctuations or increases in client needs. Some services may have seasonal patterns—such as schools, summer camps, or emergency heating programs. For other programs, changes may not be related to such external factors and may reflect increasing or decreasing client needs.

Logical sequence of service delivery.   Another aspect of measuring when services are being provided is to map whether services are being provided in a logical sequence. What happens when clients first come to an agency: Is an intake interview conducted? How long before clients receive needed services? How do clients access additional services? Do clients have to repeatedly present documentation for characteristics that do not change? If services or program requirements are not arrayed in a logical sequence, clients can be deterred from receiving the services they need. Work with staff to develop a logical sequence of how clients move through the program. Does everyone agree on how it is supposed to work? Are there any changes to the sequence that might improve access to services or program efficiency?

When to collect data. It is critical that all data are collected for a specific period of time. This allows administrators to put the various numbers together to understand key program operations, such as the client flows in and out of the program and how the number of clients change.

This information can be collected for any time period, though often, administrators must adhere to specific reporting requirements. Collecting this information on a monthly basis is the customary approach. It strikes a balance between the cost of collecting information too frequently and making it available on a regular basis to inform decisionmaking.

• How Well?

The question *How well?* takes monitoring to the next level. The previous questions were descriptors of program functions, whereas this question is a judgment about the quality of program performance. *How well?* is the part of monitoring that enables policymakers to determine whether the program is successful, whether it should be expanded, modified, or terminated. Supervisors can use this information to alter program policies, reassign staff, devote additional resources to key functions, and take other practical steps toward improving performance.

In order to monitor how well a program functions, we must be explicit about program expectations. Two critical measures of quality are the minimum quality standards met and the timeliness of service delivery.

Minimum Standards. Laws or regulations may set certain minimum standards; the program may develop other standards itself. For example, there are laws that require a certain standard for drinking water, doctors are required to be certified, and homes for abused children need to meet basic sanitary requirements.

Many programs have implicit minimum standards and staff often have a general sense of what is expected of them. A useful part of monitoring is making these expectations explicit. For example, a regional initiative to increase the number of low-income families participating in the housing allowance program could require municipalities to increase enrollment by a minimum of 5 percent each month until each city is serving at least 60 percent of eligible families.

Timeliness. Standards of timeliness govern the amount of time that the program has to deliver specific types of services. For example, emergency ambulance services may be required to respond to a crisis call within one hour or less. Note that, except where governed by law, each program will need to establish its own standards.

Client/Citizen Satisfaction. Client satisfaction is perhaps the most obvious and direct measure of how well a program delivers its services. Although clients may not always appreciate the budget constraints that limit benefits to well below the poverty level or restrict certain services to only the neediest, they can provide important feedback on the quality of services. Complaint logs, suggestion boxes, surveys, and periodic interviews are useful ways of collecting feedback from clients/citizens.

Costs/Efficiency. Measuring efficiency—the costs of the program results—is another way of answering the question *How well?* Monitoring the finances of a project includes tracking the inputs or resources used, as well as comparing the program costs to the benefits or outputs. One program may boast that it is less expensive than others, but if it has few positive results, it is clearly making inefficient use of budget resources.

Efficiency is a measure of the outputs produced in relation to the inputs used. Examples of efficiency measures are the cost per unit of services delivered or the number of clients served per staff member. Although it is difficult to establish what the ideal ratio should be, comparing these ratios across time and across different offices or cities can point to problems and inefficiencies.

To answer questions about how well and how efficiently a program is performing, administrators need to combine several sources of data. For example, knowing the number of buildings cleaned per week and the number of complaints about poor services helps the manager understand whether the program is meeting its minimum standards and timeliness of service delivery. See Table 9.17 for additional examples.

• *Quality Control*

Most of the monitoring practices described in this chapter involve self-reporting from programs or individual staff. Monitoring the quality of services and the veracity of monitoring reports entails some specific oversight from program managers or city/regional administrators. For educational programs, quality control may include reviewing student records, sitting in on a classroom, interviewing students/parents, and inspecting physical conditions and availability of resources and materials.

Reviewing Records. For a social assistance program, a manager might randomly select ten or more case files per month (or some number of cases from each social worker). These cases would be read to check that appropriate client information was collected and that services were provided according to standards of timeliness and other program expectations. City or regional administrators could conduct an annual review of field offices and review a sample number of cases.

Site Visits and Interviews. Site visits or interviews provide an opportunity for managers to observe service delivery and to question staff or clients about the quality of services and any unmet needs they may have. Developing a checklist of key

---

Table 9.17   Child Allowance Program Monthly Report, March 2004

Number of families served	2,000
Number of social workers	5
Amount of allowances granted (in rubles)	300,000
Number of new cases (applications completed, intake interviews conducted)	150
Number of recertifications	100
Number of cases closed	50
Total program budget (in rubles)	345,000
Efficiency measures	
The average number of clients per worker (total families ÷ number of social workers)	400
Average benefit per family (amount of allowances granted ÷ number of families served)	150
Percentage of program budget spent on allowances (amount of allowances granted ÷ total program budget). We can assume that the remainder of the program budget is spent on administrative expenses.	85%
Number of applications and recertifications processed per social worker (number of applications + number of recertifications ÷ number of social workers)	50

---

issues can help to structure a site visit or interview; this checklist might include the professionalism of staff, cleanliness of site, a list of activities observed, attitude of clients, and more. Site visits, including home visits, should be conducted on a random basis, because staff or program offices should not have the opportunity to make special preparations for the visit.

Financial Audits.   Programs have basic financial practices and controls in place to manage and report revenues and expenses. Most routine financial reporting is based on administrative reports generated by program staff and could be manipulated. An annual, independent financial audit is the best way to verify the use of program resources. However, such audits can be expensive and beyond the means of many programs.

Some audit techniques can be used to strengthen program monitoring. These include having the financial officer describe the systems in place for controlling the use of funds (i.e., Who has permission to approve the use of funds? Are bids required for large purchases? Are receipts maintained? etc.). Clients can be asked to verify receipt of payments, and equipment purchases can be visually inspected and compared to receipts.

Exercise 9.1: Assessing Monitoring Indicators

Each of the statements presented in the table below is a program indicator. Categorize each statement by the type of indicator, such as input, output, outcome, or efficiency. Some indicators may fall into several categories, depending on the context or objectives of the program.

Indicator	Type of Indicator (input, output, outcome, efficiency)
1. Kilometer of train track repaired daily	Output
2. Percentage of customers who have water meters	Input/Outcome
3. Number of teachers at the high school	Input
4. Rate of new AIDS cases reported per 1,000 population	
5. Number of high school students who go on to university	
6. Percentage of fees collected	
7. Number of health-related water quality characteristics exceeding standards one or more times during reporting period	
8. Number of small businesses participating in tax incentive program	
9. Percentage of customers with complaints who were satisfied with the handling of their complaints	
10. Number of students who graduate from grammar school	
11. Cost per square meter of housing maintained	
12. Percentage of costs covered by fees collected	
13. Number of regional staff working in the education department	
14. Percentage of households under the poverty line	

(continues)

Continued

Indicator	Type of Indicator (input, output, outcome, efficiency)
15. Total number of garbage pickups per week	
16. Cost per kilometer of road rated acceptable or better by trained observers	
17. Meters of water lines repaired each year	
18. Kilometers of train track rated "bad or worse" by trained observers	
19. Total cost of water service	
20. Number of patients seen by doctor	
21. Number of reported traffic accidents and the rate per 1,000 population	
22. Percentage of citizens who rated the timeliness of mail delivery as fairly slow or worse	
23. Number of households connected to the water service	
24. Percentage of citizens who have a family member needing assistance due to unemployment	
25. Cost per social assistance benefit recipient	
26. Total rubles spent on environmental protection	
27. Percentage of customers satisfied with water quality	
28. Average peak and off-peak travel times between key or representative origins and destinations	
29. Quantity of water produced per year	
30. Cubic meters of water lost for technical reasons	
31. Percentage of customers who have access to water four hours a day or less	
32. Cost of building a new hospital	

(*continues*)

Continued **Indicator**	**Type of Indicator** (input, output, outcome, efficiency)
33. Total number of valid complaints and requests for service per 1,000 customers, by type of complaint (including billing overcharge, water quality, broken or leaking pipe or meter)	
34. Cost per customer served	
35. Air-pollutant levels attributable to transportation sources; number of days that air pollution exceeded hazardous threshold; and number of persons possibly exposed to hazardous levels	

Source: Katharine Mark, *Module on Performance Measurement* (Budapest: Central European University, Intergovernmental Fiscal Relations and Local Financial Management course, July 2000).

Exercise 9.2: Program Model

Complete a program model for a program that you are familiar with. The program model should specify:

- *Inputs.* Resources dedicated to or consumed by the program.
- *Activities.* What the program does with the inputs to fulfill its mission.
- *Outputs.* The direct products of program activities.
- *Outcomes.* Benefits for participants during and after the program.

Exercise 9.3: Logical Frame

In the table on pages 232 through 234, complete the logical frame for each of the programs presented. The objectives are already listed in the first column. The last section of the table allows you to choose a program you are familiar with and to specify the objectives, indicators, and data to be collected for a monitoring initiative.

Logical Frame

Housing Allowance Program

Objective/Question	Indicator	Data Source/ Collection Method
A. Protect low-income households from full impact of rent increases 1. Participation of low-income households in the program 2. Targeting benefits to those who most need them		
B. Encourage more efficient use of the housing stock		
C. What is the efficiency of the program?		

(continues)

Continued

Maternal and Infant Health Care

A. Increase the number of pregnant women receiving prenatal care		
B. Improve birth outcomes		
C. Improve infant care		

Unemployment Assistance

A. Protect unemployed persons from loss of income		
B. Assist unemployed persons to reenter the job market		

(continues)

Continued

C. Efficiency of employment assistance program		
Primary Education		
A. Maintain/improve student performance		
B. Maintain/improve level of educational attainment		
C. Ensure adequate number and quality of teaching staff		
D. Maintain school buildings		
Other:		

CHAPTER 10

Performance Management

Performance management is a system of regularly measuring program results or outcomes and using this information to improve service delivery.[1] Performance management is a fairly new strategy to improve public services by using performance data to inform policy and build accountability and transparency. Performance measurement techniques aim to hold government agencies publicly responsible for the results of their activities through a set of performance indicators. A decade ago, the United States passed a federal law—the Government Performance Results Act (GPRA)—that requires federal agencies to provide annual performance data on program outcomes. Many other OECD countries are making extensive use of performance measurement for certain sectors. Performance-based contracts, where contractors are paid not for their activities but for the results attained, are becoming much more common throughout the world. Because performance management is a new tool with great potential to improve program performance, this book devotes a whole chapter to it.

The point of tracking government performance is to implement changes that improve services in ways that enhance the quality of life for citizens. Citizens are often regarded as partners in performance management. By offering feedback on the relative importance of services and service quality, citizens provide input that helps the government set priorities for service delivery and resource allocation. Focus groups, surveys, and ratings of public services are all ways that citizen feedback is collected.

Performance measurement is *not* a substitute for traditional program monitoring of the kind discussed in the previous chapter. A program manager still needs to know how resources are deployed and how many services are actually delivered to manage operations successfully. Performance or outcome measurements are other barometers of program success that should be used with traditional monitoring indicators, such as inputs, activities, and outputs.

This chapter is written primarily from the standpoint of implementing performance management for public services. NGOs can certainly use these same techniques. Private firms are more accustomed to such practices as it is clearly in their interest to focus on results or the bottom line. The chapter describes the benefits of performance management and then outlines how to implement a performance management system.

Definitions of Performance Measurement and Performance Management

Performance measurement provides useful information to decisionmakers and is a vital component of any effort at managing-for-results. Performance measurement refers to the regular, systematic collection of quantitative information about the results (outcomes) of public agency programs, organizations, or resources. The emphasis on outcomes means that performance measurement is concerned with specific objectives—for example, focusing on the percentage of a municipality's roads that are in good riding condition, rather than on the number of square meters of roads that are maintained.

Performance measurement of public services makes a sharp distinction between outputs and outcomes:

- Outputs are expected to lead to desired outcomes, but do not indicate the quality or results of the work performed. For example, the number of persons to complete a job training program does not indicate what useful skills they might have gained or how many will attain jobs.
- Outcomes indicate the results and accomplishments of the program or services. Outcomes reflect events, conditions, or changes in attitude or behavior that indicate progress toward the achievement of goals and objectives. Outcomes occur for the customers (students in educational programs, disadvantaged citizens in social programs), other organizations (businesses or NGOs), or the community in general (impact on environment).

Chapter 9 provides additional examples to help distinguish between outputs and outcomes.

It is useful to distinguish between intermediate and end outcomes:

- Intermediate outcomes are the early results that indicate government activities are moving in the right direction, even though such actions may not have produced the desired ultimate results. Intermediate outcomes also refer to characteristics of the quality of services, such as the number of students to graduate or those rating their educational experience good or excellent.

- End outcomes are the desired objectives or ultimate results, such as the number of graduates to secure jobs in their field.

Performance management uses performance information to make policy, allocate resources, and deliver services. The critical point of tracking government performance is to obtain reliable information that supports managers' abilities to implement changes that improve services in ways that are meaningful to improving the quality of life for citizens.

"Governing for results" has recently become a popular phrase. It is closely related to "results-based management" and refers to the need to strategically plan and manage public sector efforts. It encompasses the following:

- Focusing government decisions and activities on results—that is, the actual outcomes experienced by citizens (rather than the completion of work or the quantity of services that an agency provides).
- Emphasizing government efficiency or productivity:
  - Efficiency expresses the relationship between the use of resources (e.g., inputs such as costs or staff time) and the achievement of successful outcomes—for example, the cost per number of customers who rated drinking water as good or excellent quality (input/outcome).
  - Productivity is the inverse (outcome/input)—for example, the amount of success resulting from a given investment.

Box 10.1 presents examples of performance measurement from Montgomery County, Maryland.[2] The county has been using performance measurement and issuing performance reports for five years. It uses this information to allocate resources, manage programs, and report progress.

The first section of Box 10.1 shows major outcomes (results) for programs serving abused and vulnerable children and adults. It presents a fairly stable rate of child abuse and neglect cases (2.4 per 1,000), and a low percentage of families whose abuse and/or neglect cases are reopened within one year of receiving protective services (the percentage fluctuates, but declined in fiscal year 2002—the last year of actual data). The low rate of reopened cases suggests that protective services are an effective means to keep children safe in their homes. The report also presents remarkable findings on domestic violence: 85 percent of domestic violence victims establish safer living conditions after leaving shelters and 70 percent of abusers stop abusive behavior after treatment.

The second section of Box 10.1 provides more detailed measures on child welfare services. In addition to outcome measures, this report includes measures of service quality, efficiency, outputs, inputs, and explanations. In the most recent year, fiscal year 2004, reporting standards were changed to reflect the contributions

Box 10.1   Performance Management Examples, Montgomery County

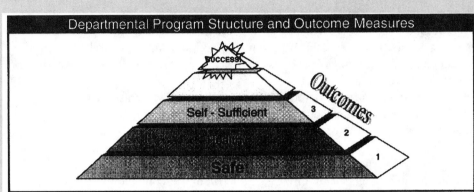

Departmental Program Structure and Outcome Measures

Outcome-based accountability in health and human services is built on a commitment to ensure that every dollar spent works toward improving the conditions of people living in Montgomery County. It means being able to look into the eyes of a child or a vulnerable adult knowing that the County has done the best possible job with the resources it has available. If the Department of Health and Human Services is to be accountable, we must be able to demonstrate that our programs make a difference in the lives of the people we serve—making them safer, healthier, and more self-sufficient.

DEPARTMENTAL OUTCOME #1

Children and Vulnerable Adults Are Safe

	FY00 ACTUAL	FY01 ACTUAL	FY02 ACTUAL	FY03 BUDGET	FY04 CE REC
Community Conditions					
Rate of indicated child abuse and neglect cases per 1,000 children	2.4	2.4	2.4	NA	NA
Rate of confirmed cases of neglect, self-neglect, or exploitation of seniors per 10,000 residents ages 65 or older	22.1	21.5	24.3	22.7	23.0
Program Outcomes					
Percentage of families whose abuse and/or neglect cases are reopened and confirmed within one year of receiving protective services	11	7	4	8	NA
Percentage of Montgomery County victims of domestic violence who establish safer living conditions after leaving shelters	84	79	85	85	85
Percentage of court-referred abusers who cease abuse following treatment	69	69	76	70	70
Percentage of elderly and disabled adults who remain safely in the community after receiving services	79	81	81	80	75

Department Programs Contributing to Outcome #1:

Child Welfare Services, Linkages to Learning, Outpatient Addiction Services, Addiction Services Coordination, Partner Abuse Services, Adult Assessment Services, In-Home Aide Services, Continuing Case Management, Persons with Disabilities Outreach Services, Senior Food Program, Ombudsman Services, Health Promotion and Prevention, Senior Mental Health Services, 24-Hour Crisis Center, Adult Outpatient Mental Health Services, Care Coordination Team, Child Care, Infants and Toddlers Program, Child and Adolescent Mental Health Services, School Health Services, Community Outreach, Prevention and Crisis Intervention, Public Assistance Benefits Certification, Rental Assistance, Shelter Services, Transitional Housing and Services, Victim Assistance and Sexual Assault Services, Community Health Nursing, Specialty Medical Evaluations, Income Supports, STD/HIV Prevention and Treatment, Adult Protective Services, Respite Care, Shelter Program, Income Maintenance Programs, Information and Assistance, Guardianship Program, Community/Nursing Home Medical Assistance and Outreach, Assisted Living Licensure Unit, Licensing and Regulatory Services, Partner Abuse Services.

Box 10.1   Continued

HEALTH AND HUMAN SERVICES
Children, Youth, and Family Services

PROGRAM: Child Welfare Services	PROGRAM ELEMENT: Adoptions				
PROGRAM MISSION: To achieve long-term stability for abused and/or neglected children who cannot be reunified with their parents					
COMMUNITY OUTCOMES SUPPORTED: • Children and vulnerable adults who are safe					

PROGRAM MEASURES	FY00 ACTUAL	FY01 ACTUAL	FY02 ACTUAL	FY03 BUDGET	FY04 CE REC
Outcomes/Results:					
Percentage of children in foster/kinship care who are adopted or placed for adoption within 24 months of entry[d]	NA	32.7	33.8	33.6	32
Service Quality:					
Average number of cases per adoption worker (State standard = 18)	NA	17	11	[e]18	16
Efficiency:					
Average cost per finalized adoption ($)[f]	NA	7,274	[c]18,641	23,029	37,087
Workload/Outputs:					
Number of guardianships granted to the Department from cases with a plan for Termination of Parental Rights (TPR)[a]	NA	42	25	50	50
Number of finalized adoptions[b]	69	62	39	34	34
Inputs:					
Expenditures ($000)[f]	NA	451	[b]727	783	1,261
Workyears[f]	6.0	7.0	[c]11.5	11.5	15.3

Notes:

[a]Termination of Parental Rights (TPR) must be considered if a child cannot be reunited with his or her family within fifteen months. When there is sufficient cause, the Court can terminate parental rights.

[b]The FY00 - FY02 results represent the number of finalized adoptions credited to the County by the State of Maryland. The FY03 target reflects a lower number of children available for adoption.

[c]Beginning in FY02, expenditures and workyears also include administration, supervision, community service aides, and clerical support.

[d]This measure was revised so that it was consistent with Statewide measures.

[e]The Adoption Unit is down one worker, so the average caseload is higher than usual.

[f]Effective FY04, Child Welfare Services realigned all of its program measures to ensure consistency with the outcome data already being collected by the State of Maryland's Department of Human Resources. The Foster and Adoptive Parents Services program measures, originally submitted as a separate display, have been incorporated into the revised measures shown above. As a result, it was determined that 26% of the latter unit's workyears and expenditures should be included in the Adoptions program element. This explains the increase in workyears, expenditures, and cost per finalized adoption. There have been no other budgetary or personnel changes.

EXPLANATION:

All children who enter foster care have a "permanency plan" that is intended to achieve long term stability for the child, either through reunification with the family or adoption. If a child cannot be reunited with his or her family within fifteen months, termination of parental rights to free the child for adoption must be considered. When there is sufficient cause, the Court terminates parental rights and grants legal guardianship of the child to the Department. The Department then prepares the child and the adoptive family for the adoption. The Court subsequently grants the adoptive family's petition to legally adopt the child. This ends the Department's clinical, but not necessarily financial, involvement with the family.

For those children who cannot be reunited with their families, success is measured by finalizing adoptions as quickly as possible - within 24 months of their first entry into the system. This ensures that children do not languish in temporary placements but move on to permanent homes with long-term caregivers as soon as possible. The data indicate that Child Welfare Services is meeting and exceeding its own and the State's targets for the number of children adopted in a timely manner.

PROGRAM PARTNERS IN SUPPORT OF OUTCOMES: County Attorney, District Court, Circuit Court, Police, Montgomery County Public Schools, Housing Opportunities Commission, Maryland Department of Human Resources, Department of Juvenile Justice, State's Attorney, Collaboration Council.

MAJOR RELATED PLANS AND GUIDELINES: Maryland Safe and Stable Families Act, Child Welfare League of America report, Montgomery County Council's Children First Agenda, COMAR 07.02.12.

Source: Office of Management and Budget, "Montgomery Measures Up!" Montgomery County, Md., 2003.

and expenses of all activities or departments engaged in child protective services. In general, however, it seems that outcomes, workloads, and service quality have remained stable in recent years.

Reasons to Undertake Performance Management

Performance management can be a powerful tool to better understand and manage public programs. Still, some managers resist performance management out of fear that such a system will expose the weaknesses of their operations. This is true and is a reason why performance management must have strong support from high-ranking officials if it is to be successfully implemented. It is also part of what makes performance management such a useful tool—by pointing to program weaknesses (or successes) attention can be rightly focused on how to improve performance. Reasons to undertake performance management include:

1. It helps managers use existing resources more efficiently by identifying programs that are not efficient or effective.
2. It helps prioritize services and investment policies based on citizen preferences and feedback.
3. Implementation costs are not high. Most government entities already gather information on service delivery, although they tend to focus on outputs (work completed by government staff or contractors) rather than outcomes (the results or accomplishments as experienced by citizens). Outcome indicators can frequently be added without wholesale changes in data acquisition or monitoring practices.
4. Performance indicators, like certain input and output indicators, can be used to track workload completion and results over time. For successful programs, this type of accountability (monitoring) and transparency (reporting) positions government managers to legitimately claim positive and improved results. For weak programs, this type of information permits managers to demonstrate that they (a) have proactively identified problems that interfere with positive performance and (b) are emphasizing corrective actions.
5. Performance information can be used to provide appropriate commendations or rewards to government staff when data show major improvements or maintenance of prior service levels in the face of adverse external factors.

Governments around the world are using different tools to govern-for-results. The following are examples of how performance management tools can be introduced on a manageable basis:

- Develop and track two or three performance indicators in each service sector. Disclose this information in the budget and make policy decisions based on the information.
- Develop service improvement action plans in one or two priority sectors.
- Do an in-depth analysis for one sector and implement performance management based on that information and lessons learned.

Good information on program performance and results lay the foundation for improvements in government services. In their book *Reinventing Government,* David Osborne and Ted Gaebler write, "What gets measured, gets done. If you don't measure results, you can't tell success from failure. If you can't recognize failure, you can't correct it. If you can't see success, you can't reward it. If you can't see success, you can't learn from it."[3]

Implementing Performance Measurement

Performance measurement and performance management represent a serious change in philosophy for most government agencies or NGOs. Most agencies are accustomed to measuring their success based on the amount of budget resources or staffing allocated, or activities completed (such as persons trained or roads maintained). Being accountable for real outcomes initially leaves many agency heads feeling that much of their work is no longer being counted or that they are being held responsible for things they cannot fully control, such as improvements in client lives or customer satisfaction. In developing a performance management system it is critical to set reasonable goals with corresponding milestones to chart the progress toward meeting those goals. Performance management does not expect that all clients participating in job training will attain good jobs or that all residents will be satisfied with city garbage collection services—but rather that reasonable results are achieved and that improvements are documented from one year to the next.

This section describes the eight key steps of implementing performance management, as enumerated in Table 10.1.

• *Step 1: Assign Responsibility for Oversight, Planning, and Implementation*

A high-level individual or group should oversee the performance management initiative. This person or group is responsible for planning the scope of the project and ensuring that it is implemented according to the plan. An initial performance management initiative may be limited to one agency or program area, and expanded to other agencies after it has successfully been established.

Table 10.1   Implementation Steps for Performance Management

Step 1: Assign responsibility for oversight, planning, and implementation.
Step 2: Identify the program's goals, objectives, and customers.
Step 3: Decide what outcomes to measure.
Step 4: Identify benchmarks and targets.
Step 5: Identify data sources and collect data.
Step 6: Analyze data.
Step 7: Prepare performance reports.
Step 8: Use performance information.

Performance management is often viewed as a participatory strategy and many stakeholders can contribute to implementing a performance management system. Because performance measurement is concerned with program outcomes—or how government services affect citizens—it lends itself to engaging many voices. That said, the process does not inherently need to involve all stakeholders and can be implemented by a small core group, with major findings and improvement plans shared with a broader audience.

In general, oversight is assigned to high-level officials or other leaders, and implementation is assigned to program-level staff. The oversight group sets general goals and time frames for the project, with an implementation group charged with establishing specific performance targets, measurement strategies, and action plans. The successive steps are generally considered the work of an implementation committee.

• Step 2: Identify Goals, Objectives, and Customers

For each sector, department, or program, specify a goal and several specific objectives. The goal states the overall purpose of the operation and the objectives summarize the specific results you want to accomplish.

Goals describe what the program seeks to achieve. Goals typically are general in nature and specify the long-term outcome desired for a program. For example, highway programs have a goal: "to provide safe, reliable transportation of people and products." A goal can be achieved through several objectives.

Objectives are generally results-oriented and measurable. A program may have several objectives to meet its goal. To continue with the highway program example, objectives could include: "to have fewer traffic crashes resulting in injury or deaths" and "to maintain road surfaces in excellent condition."

Goals and objectives also help identify customers. The primary customers of public functions are the principal beneficiaries—those individual citizens or groups whom the work is intended to benefit. Secondary customers are others whom the work benefits less directly. For example, students and their parents are the primary customers of school programs, but employers who plan to hire future graduates as skilled employees are secondary customers of these programs. In functions whose principal product is compliance, not service (e.g., militia/police, environmental protection agencies, tax collection), the primary customer is the community at large. (See Box 10.2 for examples of goals and objectives.)

• *Step 3: Decide What Outcomes to Measure*

Outcome indicators define the results you hope to achieve. Not all program outcomes are easily measured, and program outcomes must be translated into measurable performance indicators. Outcome indicators should be stable over time, and only the targets should change over time. For example, an outcome indicator for a job training program would be the number of participants to get and keep jobs for more than three months, whereas targets might be that 40 percent of participants will attain this outcome this year and 50 percent in the following year. Focusing on outcomes does not mean that government managers should neglect inputs and outputs. Instead, focusing on outcomes provides a framework for managers to analyze inputs and outputs in a more meaningful way.

When identifying and selecting performance indicators it is good practice to keep in mind their potential use. In most cases, major indicators should be reported to citizens via government budgets, newsletters, bulletin boards, brochures, or other media. However, detailed indicators also may be developed for internal reporting to program managers and their personnel. The process will be a failure if performance information is not helpful to program managers and their personnel in improving the program.

To identify what outcomes should be tracked for various activities, consider what results are expected from a program's completed work (outputs). Sources that can help identify which outcomes are important include legislation and regulations, policy statements, strategic plans, annual reports, customer complaints, and discussions with officials, staff, customers, and service providers.

Criteria for Selecting Performance Indicators. The overriding criterion for the selection of performance indicators is that they should provide information that will be the basis for program improvements. (See Box 10.2 for examples of performance indicators.) The following attributes can help guide the selection of indicators:

- *Relevance.* Choose indicators that are relevant to the goals and objectives of the program.
- *Importance.* Select indicators that provide useful information on the program and that are critical to the accomplishment of the department or program's goals.
- *Availability.* Choose indicators for which data are accurate and readily available.
- *Ease of implementation.* Use indicators for which measurement is easy to design, conduct, analyze, and report.
- *Validity.* Select indicators that are unambiguous and for which changes in the value are easily interpreted as desirable or undesirable and directly attributed to the program.
- *Uniqueness.* Use indicators that provide information not duplicated or overlapped by other indicators.
- *Timeliness.* Choose indicators for which you can collect and analyze data in time to make decisions.
- *Ease of understanding.* Select indicators that citizens and government officials can easily understand.
- *Costs of data collection.* Choose indicators for which the costs of data collection are reasonable.
- *Privacy and confidentiality.* Select indicators that can be measured without violating the privacy or confidentiality of respondents.

- ### Step 4: Develop Targets

It is useful to establish targets for each outcome indicator at the beginning of each year and then to compare actual values to the targets. Where performance management is in place, this is usually required for an agency's budget preparation process. Targets can also be set for shorter reporting periods, such as quarters. (See Box 10.2 for examples of targets.) Following are some pointers to keep in mind when selecting targets:

- A target does not have to be a single value—a range is perfectly reasonable.
- Consider previous performance when determining current targets.
- Consider benchmarking against the best (that is, setting targets at the achievement levels of the best similar programs).
- If benchmarking against the best is considered too great a challenge, use the average performance of all units.
- Consider the outcomes achieved in the past for different customer or workload categories.

Box 10.2 Sample Goal, Outcomes, Indicators, and Targets for Road Maintenance Program

---

Goal

Provide safe, functional roads to the citizens, by regular renovation and maintenance of existing roads and by upgrading of any unpaved roads in the municipality.

Outcomes

1. Maintain road surfaces in good, better, or excellent condition.
2. Reduce traffic injuries or deaths by improving the condition and clarity of road signs.

Indicators for Outcome 1

- *Input.* Cost of paving roads, personnel, equipment; amount of equipment used.
- *Output.* Kilometers of road paved; number of households having paved roads.
- *Outcome.* Road surface in good or excellent condition; percentage of citizens satisfied with road conditions.
- *Efficiency.* Cost per kilometer of road

paved; cost per kilometer of road in excellent condition.

Indicators for Outcome 2

- *Input.* Cost of new road signs; personnel costs.
- *Output.* Number of road signs improved; number of new road signs installed.
- *Outcome.* Traffic injuries or deaths; road signs in good or excellent condition.
- *Efficiency.* Cost per new or improved road signs.

Target

- *Outcome 1.* Ensure that 90 percent of the road surface is in good or excellent condition by the year 2003.
- *Outcome 2.* Reduce traffic injuries or deaths during the year 2004 by 10 percent through improved road condition and clarity of road signs.

- Consider performance levels achieved by other jurisdictions or by private firms with similar activities and workload or customer compositions.
- Make sure the targets chosen are feasible, given the program's budget and staffing plan for the year.
- Identify any new developments—internal and external—that may affect the program's ability to achieve desired outcomes.
- Target setting for periods shorter than a year should be done in the context of seasonal factors.

- *Step 5: Identify Data Sources and Collect the Data*

A major step is to identify data sources for each indicator and practical ways to collect the data. The primary sources of data for performance indicators are:

- Administrative records.
- Customer/citizen surveys.
- User surveys.
- Trained observer ratings (individuals are trained to visually monitor conditions using a standardized rating system).
- Technical equipment.

Costs can be an important factor affecting the choice of data collection method. There are progressively higher costs associated with agency records, user surveys, trained observer ratings, and customer surveys. Each method has its pros and cons. Agency records may be the cheapest form of data collection, but time taken by the agency in compiling the necessary data may cause significant delays. Agencies may need to establish revised information-gathering procedures, such as a new procedure to collect response-time information. Customer surveys are often expensive (depending on the scope); however, they are worth undertaking if sufficient resources are available. Surveys yield outcome indicators and data without burdening agencies and provide key outcome information directly from agency customers.

Chapter 9 discussed how to select outcome indicators and create reliable agency records, so agency records will not be reviewed here. However, it is important to recognize that if agency record keeping currently includes only input and output information, government managers will need to add outcome data requirements, since this is the essence of results-based management. Typically, the kind of information that might be added to agency record keeping is information that measures service quality (e.g., response time) and customer satisfaction.

The annex to this chapter describes different types of surveys and how to design a survey instrument, as well as how to implement a trained observer rating system.

Technical equipment can be used to measure outcomes for some programs. For instance, environmental programs measure the results of air or water quality using technical equipment. Similarly, health programs sometimes use equipment to measure changes in patients, such as vision or hearing equipment.

See Exercise 10.1: Indicators of Service Quality on page 259.

This exercise is similar to Exercise 9.3, which involved creating a logical frame, except that here, indicators should reflect program outcomes, such as response time, quality of service, and the like.

• *Step 6: Analyze Data*

Analyzing performance data is no different from analyzing other types of data. Most analytical techniques required are fairly simple, such as averages, changes over time, ranges, and so forth. Most important is highlighting changes in performance and providing the detail or breakouts for managers and staff to plan service improvements.

See Chapter 4 for information on basic analytical techniques, including measures of central tendency, distribution, and variation. Chapter 4 also discusses ways to organize the data to increase its usefulness for program managers and staff, as well as how to compare data findings to targets or benchmarks.

• *Step 7: Prepare Performance Reports*

Performance data should be summarized into reports for internal and external audiences. The general public and other external stakeholders will probably only be interested in key findings, whereas direct supervisors and program staff will benefit from detailed information about their activities and results. That said, the information shared with the public should be honest and not omit any important findings, including negative results.

Analysis of performance information starts by choosing breakouts and making comparisons. The analysis should result in data displays that show that the program has done better or worse than anticipated. Select only a short list of key indicators for external reporting, even though you may track a relatively large number of indicators for internal program use. The reporting format adopted by Montgomery County (see Box 10.1) is a good example.

Short narrative explanations accompanying the performance indicators are used to explain significant program outcomes, such as indicator values that were worse than expected. Important items to reference include internal and external factors that affected performance in unexpected ways, such as how road maintenance was affected by excessive freeze-thaw cycles or how a federal tax reform affected the regional budget. Narrative can also summarize and highlight important performance information so that readers focus on these findings, and provide additional detail on specific concerns, such as negative comments from customers.

See Chapter 4 for ideas on how to format performance reports, such as presenting changes over time, actual outcomes versus targets, geographical breakdowns, or client characteristics. Chapter 4 also includes descriptions of when to use graphs, charts, or maps.

• *Step 8: Disseminate Findings.*

As mentioned earlier, findings should be disseminated to the various stakeholders, with highlights (positive and negative) reported to officials, the press, and the general public, and detailed findings shared with managers and staff. Program managers may benefit from quarterly or monthly data, whereas annual reports usually suffice for the general public. For example, New York City produces an annual Mayor's Management Report. The full report is hundreds of pages long and includes program descriptions and performance indicators (inputs, outputs, and outcomes) for all city agencies. The report is available to the public, and Table 10.2 includes selections that were published in the local newspaper.

The table presents a mixed picture for 2003, with troubling increases in the number of people receiving food stamps, in infectious diseases other than AIDS, and in homelessness. However, the city can also be proud of decreases in major

Table 10.2   Municipal Report Card, New York City

	2001	2002	2003
Health, education, and human services			
New adult AIDS cases reported	5,378	6,355	6,017
Syphilis cases	188	357	456
West Nile virus cases reported	14	7	28
Teachers who are certified	84.0%	83.0%	89.6%
People receiving public assistance	497,100	430,400	421,500
People receiving food stamps	836,200	820,500	871,300
Children in foster care	30,858	28,215	25,701
Abuse/neglect reports for children in foster care	1,976	1,767	1,615
Adults in homeless shelters per day (average)	7,187	7,662	7,953
Infrastructure, administration, and community services			
Water main breaks	523	494	594
Citywide traffic fatalities	386	397	366
Pothole complaints	31,913	21,072	35,812
Streets rated acceptably clean	85.9%	84.2%	85.4%
Parks rated acceptable for overall condition	85%	88%	88%
Playground equipment rated acceptable	87%	85%	91%
Public safety and legal affairs			
Major felony crimes	172,646	156,559	147,669
Civilian fire fatalities	107	98	109
Arson fires	3,996	3,232	2,340
Average response time to structural fire (minutes: seconds)	4:16	4:14	4:17
Average response time to life-threatening medical emergency by ambulance	7:04	6:52	6:54

Source: Michael Cooper, "City Hall Gauges City Services, and Finds Them Not Bad," *New York Times,* September 18, 2003, citing data from the Office of the Mayor.

crimes, the number of persons receiving public assistance, and children in foster care. After a year of budget cuts and reductions in the public work force, one might expect that the quality of public services would decline. However, based on these indicators, ratings of public services improved and response times for fire and medical emergencies were reduced.

Making performance information public—literally publishing performance indicators in a newspaper or other public document—is a powerful measure:

- It shows concern for citizens' opinions and their satisfaction.
- It increases transparency.
- It motivates staff.
- It builds accountability.
- It takes a major step toward improving services.

Performance Management in Action—Uses and Tools

Performance management really only has value if performance data are used to inform program improvements. Performance data can be used as indicators in budgets, in report cards for communicating with the public, in evaluations, in comparing performance data across jurisdictions, in planning service improvements, in performance contracting, and in employee motivation and identifying training needs.

The early experience with performance measurement in Eastern Europe was characterized by an emphasis on data acquisition and the generation of indicators. Comparatively little attention was given to finishing the cycle of measurement, data analysis, plan development, and change implementation. At the heart of performance management is the use of indicators to create and implement an action plan for program improvement.

For example, Chapter 9 describes the US public housing monitoring system. It focuses on financial monitoring, though it also mentions a resident satisfaction component that is clearly outcome oriented. The description of financial monitoring outlines how monitoring results influence program improvements. The financial monitoring system requires that any program that does not meet minimum requirements must submit a corrective action plan. The corrective action plan describes the problem and proposes specific steps to improve performance. If the program does not demonstrate sufficient improvements within the designated time period, the oversight office may require specific steps, offer technical assistance, and ultimately reduce program funding or assume management control. Programs that demonstrate exemplary performance are granted greater autonomy, serve as role models for others, and are eligible for additional grants.

Table 10.3 provides additional examples of how performance indicators can contribute to program management.

Table 10.3   Uses for Performance Indicators

Uses and Tools	Description
Using performance indicators in decisionmaking, such as indicators in budgets	Using performance indicators in budgets—to improve decisionmaking and resource allocation—can be done initially for one or more sectors
Communicating with the public via independently published ratings of public services, such as report cards	Publishing performance information to make both citizens and local governments aware of the impact of municipal services on its customers
Evaluating programs	Performance indicators can provide essential information about program effectiveness for program evaluation
Comparing performance data across jurisdictions, such as comparisons across governments	Compare data by service sector across local or regional governments
Planning and prioritizing service improvements, such as service improvement action plans	Service improvement action plans (SIAPs) are a proactive sectoral approach that uses a working group to develop a plan or priority improvements, using indicators to identify and measure improvement targets; an SIAP is especially useful when just beginning to introduce performance management
Integrating performance information into regular ongoing reviews of public services	On a periodic or regular basis, performance data can be used to trigger in-depth examinations of why outcome problems exist and why the program is successful in some situations and not in others; this involves an integrated use of performance indicators for regular management of one or more service areas
Using performance measures in contracts—performance contracting	Inclusion of outcome-based performance targets in contracts with the private sector for government services
Motivating staff	Indicators can be used to orient employees to the agency's principal objectives (and encourage them to be more responsive to citizens' needs), and in some cases to evaluate employee performance
Identifying training needs	Use performance information to identify needs for technical assistance and training for program personnel

Chapter Summary

Performance measurement is a type of monitoring that focuses on program outcomes. *Performance management* uses performance data to inform program decisions and to guide program improvements. The focus on outcomes or results builds accountability and directs attention and resources to improving performance.

Implementing a performance management system includes project planning, identifying goals, objectives, and targets, collecting and analyzing data, preparing reports, and using performance data to improve the program. The annex to this chapter provides detailed information on surveys and trained observer ratings.

Annex: Gathering Data Using Surveys and Trained Observer Ratings

• *Surveys*

Customer Surveys. Citizen surveys are an important source of information for performance measurement. These surveys differ from opinion polls in several important ways:

1. They specifically measure government objectives and focus data collection on information about outcome indicators.
2. They ask respondents about their recent past or current situations, not about what they think might occur in the future.
3. The same instrument is used at regular intervals to measure changes in outcomes over time.

One type of survey is a *household or customer survey,* which collects information from a sample of all potential citizens in a jurisdiction. The sample includes citizens who have used the service(s) covered by the questions, as well as those who have not. This type of survey may cover only one program or service, or may be multiservice in scope. One advantage of multiservice surveys is that the costs of data collection and analysis are shared among a number of participating programs/services.

A *user survey* gathers information only from clients of the particular program or service. A possible advantage to this type of survey is that it may be easier to identify the potential sample, assuming the program keeps correct contact information for its clients. Also, because respondents are clients of the program, they are familiar with the program and can provide relevant and thoughtful information.

A *nonuser survey* is conducted less often than a household or user survey. Such a survey specifically samples citizens who are eligible for a program or service, but who do not participate in it. This type of survey may be helpful to managers who are concerned about (1) why a program or service is not attracting the population it is designed to serve and (2) what improvements are needed to make the service more useful and attractive to its intended customers.

Surveys Have a Number of Advantages. An important characteristic of surveys is that they can provide confidentiality so that people can respond honestly. In addition, surveys are extremely useful for obtaining information that might otherwise be hard to acquire:

- The extent to which people are aware of or actually use a particular service; such information can be helpful in improving public information campaigns.
- Data on people's experiences in using a service, and factual information on what results were achieved (or not achieved)—this is particularly useful if the survey occurs after service delivery has been completed, because it can give program managers and workers information about the longer-term consequences of their efforts.
- People's overall satisfaction, as well as satisfaction with specific features of the service help program staff identify specific service problems that can be corrected. Diagnostic questions, such as asking respondents to explain why they gave poor ratings, can improve the utility of the survey.
- Reasons why people have not used the service—this type of information is useful in helping program staff understand barriers that undermine proper use of government services.
- People's suggestions for how the agency might improve its current activities.
- People's characteristics (age, gender, income, education level, etc.) and locations—to help the program identify whether such differences influence customer perspective or the quality of services received.

Surveys Also Have Some Potential Disadvantages. Surveys require expertise or skill to properly design and can be costly. It is easy to write a bunch of questions that are interesting but lose track of the intended purpose of the data collection. Another disadvantage is that surveys may be subjective, as they rely heavily on participants' memories, perceptions, and abilities to accurately answer questions—all of which may be distorted.

• *Trained Observer Ratings*

The objective of trained observer ratings is to permit different persons (observers) to use an instrument with a clearly defined rating system, to obtain consistent, comparable results. Trained observer ratings can be developed to assess the quality of any activity or program that can be seen and judged by an expert or by other individuals trained to measure specific characteristics.

Applications include

- Conditions of public facilities, such as walkways, streets (potholes, grading, congestion), parks, and restrooms (supplies, odors).
- Attendance at programs or level of citizen use of public facilities, such as who uses park grounds (age, race), when, and for what purposes (recreation, exercise, dog-walking).
- Functional abilities of clients, such as mobility and capacity to groom or care for themselves if receiving rehabilitation.

Table 10.4 highlights some of the advantages and disadvantages of trained observer ratings.

Types of rating systems/scales include written descriptions, photographic displays, and other visual displays, such as drawings, videos, or a combination.

Table 10.4   Advantages and Disadvantages of Trained Observer Ratings

Advantages	Disadvantages
They provide reliable, reasonably accurate ratings of conditions that are otherwise difficult to measure	They are sometimes a "labor-intensive" method that requires time and training of observers
If ratings are done several times a year, allocation of program resources can be adjusted throughout the year	Ratings may need to be checked periodically to ensure that the observers are adhering to procedures
Ratings can be presented in an easy-to-understand format to public officials and citizens	Scales may require periodic review and recalibration
They are relatively inexpensive and an easy way to quantify outcomes.	Unsuitable for factors that are not readily observable
Can be performed by trained volunteers • Promotes citizen involvement • Reduces costs	Concern for observer safety

Source: Harry P. Hatry, *Performance Measurement: Getting Results* (Washington, D.C.: Urban Institute, 1999).

Written Rating Scales. The simplest and most familiar type of rating system uses specific written descriptions of each grade used in the rating scale. The scale verbally describes specifications for each category.

Table 10.5 shows a written set of grades for street signs. Visual rating of readability and appearance can be made from a car or by observers on foot.

The usefulness of this type of scale can be increased with the addition of comments about specific improvements that are needed. Assessing the need for repairs (determining needed action) is an additional, very important use for outcome information from observer ratings. The city of Toronto used the information obtained from the scale in Table 10.6 to monitor road conditions and determine what repairs were needed in each location.

Although the scale in Table 10.6 is more useful than the scale in Table 10.5, it is still not as useful as a photographic or visual scale.

Photographic Rating Scales. Photographic scales can be more precise than written scales in providing clear definitions of each ratings grade. Photos are used to represent each of the grades on the rating scale. Observers are given (and trained in the use of) the set of photos, with several representing each grade on the rating scale.

Box 10.3 on page 257 illustrates a photographic rating scale showing street drivability conditions. Visual ratings by trained observers are based on a scale described both photographically and in writing. This reduces the subjectivity of the ratings so that different observers using the rating guidelines give the same rating to similar street conditions. The box shows photographs representing four levels of rating, accompanied by verbal descriptions.

Other Visual Rating Scales. Visual rating scales can also use drawings or sketches that represent each grade on a rating scale. An example of this is sketches representing conditions of school buildings or classroom walls. This kind of rating scale was used by the New York City school system to track the physical condition of its schools and to help make decisions about building repairs.

See Exercise 10.2: Critiquing a Short Survey on page 263.

This exercise presents an example of a citizen survey to rate the quality of park facilities. The assignment is to identify the strengths and weaknesses of the survey instrument.

Table 10.5 Written Rating Scale: Street Sign Grades

1. Conveniently visible
   a. Sign head and support in good condition (tilted, twisted, or bent less than 5°); and
   b. Sign not defaced in any manner; and
   c. Sign continuously unobscured for the last 50 feet
2. Visible, but somewhat inconvenient to read or find, or unpleasant to see
   a. Sign head or support slightly tilted, twisted, or bent (between 5° and 30°), but visible even though inconvenient or unpleasant to see; or
   b. Sign partly obscured, or intermittently obscured within the last 50 feet; or
   c. Sign defaced but still readable
3. Missing, ambiguous, difficult to see or read
   a. No sign on any corner of the intersection; or
   b. Sign broken off pole; or
   c. Sign tilted, twisted, or bent more than 30°; or
   d. Sign ambiguous, misleading, or incorrect (sign twisted 45° to 90°, or with wrong street name—a sign twisted 90° may appear normal at first glance); or
   e. Sign totally obscured by a tree, bush, brush, pole, another sign, or other objects so that it cannot be read from the car continuously within the last 50 feet or approach; or
   f. Printing on sign not legible

Source: Harry P. Hatry, Louis H. Blair, Donald M. Fisk, John M. Greiner, John R. Hall Jr., and Philip S. Schaenman, *How Effective Are Your Community Services? Procedures for Measuring Their Quality* (Washington, D.C.: Urban Institute and International City/County Management Association [ICMA], 1992).

Box 10.4 on page 258 outlines how to establish a trained observer system.

Trained Observer Ratings in Fort Worth, Texas, and Washington, D.C. Groups of residents in Fort Worth and Washington, led by neighborhood-based NGOs, conducted trained observer ratings of their neighborhoods in the fall of 2001. Residents prioritized the conditions that were of the greatest concern to them, such as street cleanliness, street and sidewalk conditions (potholes, cracks), and vandalism. Rating scales were created to measure each of the indicators of interest to the neighborhood residents. Residents were trained how to use and interpret the scales, and were then sent out into the community to record information about the streets in their neighborhood.

Approximately fifty street blocks were rated in the Columbia Heights neighborhood of Washington. In the Near Northside neighborhood of Fort Worth,

Table 10.6   Written Rating Scale: Road Conditions

Rating	Condition	Description	Comments
9	Excellent	No fault whatsoever	Recently constructed work
8	Good	No damage, normal wear, and small cracks	
7	Fair	Average rating for Toronto pavements and sidewalks	Slight damage, crack fill, or minor leveling required
6	Repair	10 percent of complete replacement cost	Pavement requires preventive overlay
5	Repair	25 percent of complete replacement cost	Eligible for reconstruction program
4	Repair	50 percent of complete replacement cost	
3	Repair	75 percent of complete replacement cost	Total reconstruction probably indicated
2	Repair	More than 75 percent of complete replacement cost	Requires complete reconstruction
1	Impossible to repair		

Source: Harry P. Hatry, *Performance Measurement: Getting Results* (Washington, D.C.: Urban Institute, 1999).

approximately one hundred street blocks were rated. After data collection was complete, reports summarized each condition in the neighborhood.

Residents worked with the neighborhood-based NGOs to use the information to improve their community through partnership with local government. In this case, the involvement of an active NGO and volunteers to conduct the ratings were important factors in the successful completion of data collection.

Box 10.3 Photographic Rating Scale

- Condition 1: Smooth. No noticeable defects or one or two minor defects such as a small, open crack.
- Condition 2: Slightly bumpy. Several minor defects or small potholes, but none severe, or a sizable single bump or several minor bumps, or gravel or dirt road in good condition.
- Condition 3: Considerably bumpy. At least one section of the street is broken up or has easily visible bumps, but no single safety hazard is present.
- Condition 4: Potential safety hazard or cause of severe jolt. One or more large potholes or other major defects three and a half inches high or deep. Types of hazards should be noted.

Rideability Equals 1

Rideability Equals 2

Rideability Equals 3

Rideability Equals 4

Box 10.4 Basic Steps to Set Up a Trained Observer Rating System

1. Determine the scope of the trained observer initiative; determine what conditions to rate. Starting with measuring just a few conditions may make this data collection method more viable for some governments. Fewer conditions rated may lessen the training burden and allow the government to use resident volunteers to collect data. As capacity for collecting trained observer ratings develops, more conditions can be added at a later time.

You might also decide to collect trained observer ratings for a limited geographic area, such as specific neighborhoods or sample of sites in a larger target area. This "piloting" process affords opportunities to work intensely in one part of the community and then later transfer those lessons in the creation of a broader trained observer–rating program.

An additional factor mitigating cost is the frequency that observations are made. Agencies can choose to do more by observing quarterly instead of monthly, for example.

2. Develop and document explicit definitions for the grades for each condition measured. After determining the scope of the effort, decide specifically what to rate and create measurable scales for each condition. If you are using a photographic rating system, the following additional steps are needed:

- Take a large number of photographs in settings representative of the range of conditions to be rated—photos should reflect the actual types of conditions the program wants to assess.
- Select a panel of judges with varied backgrounds who are not associated with the measurement activities. Select labels— each representing a condition that the program expects to find, such as clean, moderately clean, moderately dirty, and dirty—and ask the judges to sort the photographs into groups that represent each condition.
- For each condition, select four to five photographs that the largest number of judges identified as representative. These sets of photographs then become the rating scale.

- Develop written guidelines to accompany the photographs.
- Develop the final scale. Package copies of the photographs selected for the final scale in a kit for each trained observer.

3. Develop and document procedures for selecting inspection locations and recording and processing data. It is important to have all aspects of the data collection process in place. Questions that need to be answered to accomplish this include:

- How will the observations be recorded? On a paper form? With a hand-held computer? With a camera?
- How will sites be assigned to observers? How long will their shifts be and how many sites will they rate per shift? How will they be transported to the sites they are rating? Will they be paid, and if so, how much?
- What do observers do with their data after rating? Record it in a central database? Have a government or NGO official process it?

4. Select and train observers. Observers can be community volunteers, part-time employees, recruits through an NGO (see the description of trained observer ratings in Fort Worth, Texas, and Washington, D.C., above), or staff members. The observers need to learn what each of the rating scales means and how the government expects them to be interpreted. Then observers should work together as a team to rate sites in the neighborhood. This group practice is important in developing the same understanding of the rating scales in each observer. To the extent that observers have the same interpretation of what a condition looks like on a given street, ratings for streets will be comparable. Revise the rating and procedures as needed.

5. Set up a procedure for systematically checking the ratings of the trained observers. In order to maintain confidence in the data, it is a good idea for someone, usually the project supervisor, to go back out and verify ratings for 10 to 15 percent of the area rated.

Exercise 10.1: Indicators of Service Quality

The quality of public services is important to citizens and is an important intermediate outcome of government efforts. This exercise builds on Exercise 9.3, which involved creating a logical frame for various government programs including housing allowances, job training, and maternal health.

In the table that begins on page 260, complete the logical frame and identify outcome indicators that indicate the result or quality of services. For example, one measure of service quality for police might be response time—how long do the citizens have to wait from their call for assistance or report of a problem and the arrival of the police?

Housing Allowance Program

Objective / Question	Indicator

A. Protect low-income households from full impact of rent increases
 	
    1. Participation of low-income households in the program
    2. Targeting benefits to those who most need them	

B. Encourage more efficient use of the housing stock	
C. What is the efficiency of the program?	

Maternal and Infant Health Care

A. Increase the number of pregnant women receiving prenatal care	

(continues)

Continued

B. Improve birth outcomes	
C. Improve infant care	

Unemployment Assistance

A. Protect unemployed persons from loss of income	
B. Assist unemployed persons to reenter the job market	
C. Efficiency of employment assistance program	

Primary Education

A. Maintain/improve student performance	

(*continues*)

Continued

B. Maintain/improve level of educational attainment	
C. Ensure adequate number and quality of teaching staff	
D. Maintain school buildings	
Other:	

Exercise 10.2: Critiquing a Short Survey

The following is an example of a citizen survey designed to rate the quality of park facilities and programs. It is to be administered to persons as they enter or exit several of the city's parks.

Identification

1. What are the strengths of this instrument?
2. What are the weaknesses of the instrument, and how would you improve it? Particular issues to focus on: Are the questions clear or could they be interpreted in several different ways? Are the categories comprehensive and mutually exclusive? Will the questions generate sufficient information for problems to be specifically identified so improvements can be made?

Citizen Survey: Park Facilities

1. How old are you?
   ___ Under 10
   ___ 10–15
   ___ 15–20
   ___ 21–25
   ___ Over 25

2. What is your marital status?
   ___ Single
   ___ Married
   ___ Widowed
   ___ Divorced

3. Do you go to the park to:
   ___ Use sports or recreational equipment?
   ___ Walk your dog?
   ___ Spend time with friends?

4. How would you rate the following?

	Excellent	Good	Fair	Poor
a. Hours of operation				
b. Cleanliness				
c. Condition of equipment				
d. Crowdedness				
e. Safety conditions				
f. Physical attractiveness				
g. Variety of programs				
h. Helpfulness and courtesy of staff				
i. Overall				

CHAPTER 11

Program Evaluation

Evaluations enable government and others to assess policies and programs. While monitoring provides routine feedback, evaluation offers a more in-depth study of particular issues or concerns. For example, an evaluation of administrative reforms in Arzamas, Russia, documented substantial savings and service improvements. An evaluation of how food assistance was being delivered in the United States revealed that the work requirements of another program were creating unwarranted barriers to households seeking food assistance. And an evaluation of the early implementation of housing allowances in Russia suggested important strategies to increase family participation.

Evaluations can have a significant impact on public policy—either steering resources away from failed strategies or making the case to expand successful interventions. They often lead to improvements in ongoing programs. Monitoring and evaluation are the final step in policy analysis, as described in Chapter 2. Policy analysts seeking to develop new policy can also learn from the evaluations of similar measures and use this information to better understand and estimate costs, impacts, and risks.

Program evaluation is the systematic collection of information about the activities, characteristics, and outcomes of programs to make judgments about the program, improve program effectiveness, and inform decisions about future programming. The key point is that evaluation requires making judgments about how well a program is working and achieving its intended results. The legitimacy of such judgments is based on the objectivity and rigorous analysis of the evaluation.

Because evaluations often document problems, many managers resist program evaluation. Evaluations often occur because a supervisor, funder, or regulator requires a formal evaluation. Yet for an evaluation to influence program improvements, managers and others in positions to make changes must be full partners in the evaluation process. This means that the evaluation should address issues that are of concern to them.

This chapter provides a brief introduction to three different types of evaluation: process evaluation, impact evaluation, and benefit-cost evaluation. Additional information on impact and benefit-cost evaluation is included in later chapters. This chapter outlines the benefits of evaluation, stresses the importance of designing client-focused evaluations, and describes process evaluation.

Introduction to Program Evaluation

• *Definition of Evaluation and Why to Do One*

It is useful to distinguish between evaluation and monitoring. Program monitoring is the regular reporting of program operations and results that stakeholders use to understand and judge program activities and results.

Unlike monitoring, evaluation is not routine and generally not very frequent. Evaluations are discreet analytical activities designed to answer questions about program performance (such concerns may have been identified through routine monitoring). The key component of evaluation is to recommend corrective action or to objectively document program successes. (See Box 11.1 for a brief history of the development of program evaluation.)

This book covers three major types of evaluations:

- *Implementation or process evaluation.* An implementation or process evaluation assesses whether the program is working as intended. Typical questions addressed by process evaluations include: Are the correct services being delivered? Are the intended persons getting the benefits or services?
- *Impact evaluation.* Impact evaluation measures the share of program outcomes that can be accurately attributed to the program. For example, unemployed persons participate in a training program and then are interviewed four years later to determine the long-run benefits associated with the program. Interviews reveal that 80 percent of those trained are employed. But over this period the economy has grown vigorously. So how can one be certain that the program caused the high employment rate? Answer: You cannot be certain without a control group (i.e., similar unemployed workers who did not receive the training).
- *Benefit-cost evaluation.* Benefit-cost evaluation (also called cost-benefit analysis) measures program efficiency, that is, the cost required to produce a unit of benefit—for example, the cost per job created that results in each increment of at least $100 income for program participants.

Analysts select an evaluation method based on the type of information sought. Table 11.1 further defines the different types of evaluation by describing the questions that each answers.

Box 11.1 History of Program Evaluation

The United States was an early pioneer in program evaluation. It conducted its first evaluations before World War I, for education and public health initiatives. By the 1930s, social scientists in various disciplines advocated the use of rigorous research methods to assess social programs. Evaluations became somewhat more frequent. A landmark evaluation of this time examined the impact of boiling water as a public health practice in villages in the Middle East.[a]

After World War II, the United States initiated many new programs and was keen to evaluate their impacts. Evaluations were conducted for housing, occupational training, delinquency prevention programs, psychotherapeutic treatments, educational activities, community organization initiatives, and international assistance programs.

The creation of integrated policy development and evaluation and research offices in the US government was very important in promoting program evaluation. Moreover, the integration of evaluation with policy development greatly facilitated getting the recommendations from evaluations implemented. From the mid-1960s, the US government routinely commissioned program evaluations. This spurred the development of the evaluation industry. Think tanks conducted evaluations mandated by the Congress and initiated by ministries.

From the early 1970s, social experiments and piloting new programs were popular with government agencies. These both required detailed and sophisticated evaluations. In the 1970s, evaluation became a distinct academic field and the first textbooks were introduced. Journals, such as *Evaluation Review,* were founded.

Since the 1980s, the United Kingdom, Australia, New Zealand, and most of the Scandinavian countries have been active in program evaluation. But most of Western Europe, Japan, and transition countries have done comparatively little.

Note: a. Peter H. Rossi, Howard E. Freeman, and Mark K. Lipsey, *Evaluation: A Systematic Approach,* 6th ed. (Thousand Oaks, Calif.: Sage Publications, 1999), p. 10.

Table 11.1 Questions for Different Types of Evaluations

Question	Type of Evaluation
Is a particular intervention reaching its target population?	Process
Is the intervention being implemented well? Are the intended services being provided?	Process
Is the intervention effective in attaining the desired goals or benefits?	Process or impact
How much does the program cost?	Process
Is the program cost reasonable in relation to its effectiveness and benefits?	Benefit-cost

Reasons for Evaluating Programs. Evaluation provides valuable insight into how a program is working and whether or not it is achieving its goals. Evaluation findings can be used to inform program improvements, document successes, and justify funding needs. For example, following the weak results of an impact study on its active labor market programs, the Kyrgyz government canceled the program and channeled the funds into other areas of social protection.[1]

Feedback and improvement. Evaluations should provide useful answers to questions that managers have about their programs. However, because evaluations often document problems with programs, most administrators resist having their programs evaluated. Although the evaluation may be instigated by a supervisor or mandated by regulation, the program manager is generally the one who is most likely to use the information. Evaluators need to be sensitive to the fact that administrators may oppose the evaluation and work with them to make it a thing of value.

Accountability. Evaluations provide detailed objective information on project performance that can be used to hold administrators responsible for program operations.

Funding. Evaluation results often have a strong impact on government and parliamentary decisions to increase, reduce, or even eliminate funding for a program.

Ownership. The process of program improvement can build staff commitment and a sense of ownership. Program improvements are greatly aided when staff identify with the program and take responsibility for its results.

Policy impact. Results of well-executed evaluations are very difficult for senior administrators to ignore, especially if they have agreed to the questions being addressed in advance. Evaluation findings shape discussions about program improvements and future policies, and evaluators can play a key role in these deliberations.

Who Should Conduct the Evaluation? Staff or independent consultants/research organizations can conduct evaluations. Independent experts are often hired both for their skills and their objectivity. An evaluation is only valuable if the client (and the public) considers the results objective. Although it is appropriate for supervisors and program directors to perform regular monitoring of program operations, it is usually best to hire an outside expert to conduct a major program evaluation. Major evaluation results should be made available to the public. This helps convince all parties that the evaluation was performed in the most unbiased manner. It may also create public pressure to implement the recommended changes.

Internal or self-evaluations can be valuable exercises if staff have the expertise to conduct a legitimate evaluation. Self-evaluations can be particularly useful when programs lack funding to hire an outside consultant or are addressing process issues—that is, evaluations that document ways to improve operations rather than evaluations that attempt to quantify program impacts or benefits. Although it is best to be as transparent as possible, a program director may wish to share the results of an internal evaluation with only a select audience. If the purpose of an evaluation is to identify internal problems, a manager may not want to publicize the findings, sharing instead an action plan to improve the program or the results of improvement efforts. The goal of transparency should not prevent managers from taking a critical look at their program operations.

• *Designing a Client-Focused Evaluation*

The purpose of an evaluation is to answer questions about a program or policy for persons who are in a position to use this information.[2] The wrong way to start an evaluation is for the evaluator to decide the objective of the evaluation and the analytic methods. The right way is to have a process for generating questions that stakeholders want answered about the program. Evaluation methods should be driven by the questions being asked, not the other way around.

The evaluator must build an audience among decisionmakers if the results are to be used. This step is often ignored. Too often, the evaluator assumes he or she knows the questions that are most important and molds the evaluation around them. The result is that the people actually responsible for the program have little interest in the findings.

For example, in the late 1970s evaluation experts within the US Department of Housing and Urban Development developed evaluation designs with insufficient input from the program offices. Later, after much effort and expense, the program offices too often had little interest in the completed evaluations.[3]

Who Are the Stakeholders for the Evaluation? The primary intended users are those who can make things happen or influence those in power. Primary intended users are often program administrators. Both senior and front line supervisors can be important. Line supervisors are particularly crucial where problems are documented in routine operations, such as work assignments or basic procedures. The people who can use the evaluation results to change the program or policy are the most important stakeholders.

Those funding the evaluation are often not the primary audience. For example, the World Bank may engage a firm to evaluate an education program in India. But it is only the Indian officials who have the power to change the program. So it is essential to engage them in defining the issues to be addressed.

For a national government program, stakeholders will likely include the ministry, apparatus of government (office of the prime minister), program administrators at the local level, advocacy NGOs working on this topic, clients, and service providers (if they are different from the administering agency).

The opinions of clients can be critical to defining an evaluation particularly where participation rates are low. In such an evaluation, the question is: What do they find objectionable about the program?

How to Engage Key Stakeholders.   The following are the types of questions an evaluator might ask stakeholders:

- What do you most want to know about the program? Name three pieces of information that would be at the top of your list.
- What do you consider the strengths and weaknesses of your program? (Then follow-up with questions about how the person knows this; if not founded on real analysis, then these are candidate questions for the evaluation.)
- What information is your boss likely to ask you for about the program?

The following is another technique to engage groups of diverse stakeholders and generate evaluation topics. Ask each person to list ten things they want to know about the program. Then divide the people into groups of three or four and ask them to make one list of ten things from their individual lists. After ten to fifteen minutes, assemble the group and create a consolidated list of ten things. The evaluation will likely not address all the issues raised by stakeholders, but this engagement process should at least identify the most important topics.

Ultimately an evaluation has one primary client and the principal research questions are negotiated with that person/organization. But evaluators may well have to broker the interests of the other groups—who will be in a position to utilize the evaluation results.

See Exercise 11.1: Stakeholder Evaluation Role-Play on page 287.

In this role-playing exercise, the primary parties affected by a recent change to municipal transportation privileges for the elderly are gathered to discuss their concerns and identify research questions for a process evaluation.

Chapter 3 provides additional information on identifying stakeholders and their interests.

Criteria for User-Focused Evaluation Questions.   During the evaluation design, the evaluator needs to consider whether the necessary data are available and if there is a real audience for the results. Note that not all questions can be answered. Issues of time and resources may also limit data collection. That said, it is important not to investigate a question that has already been answered. For example, the question of whether the bus system is financially viable as currently operated may not be a good evaluation question if it is readily apparent that the system is not viable. A good research question must have several potential answers.

To assess whether there is a real audience for the evaluation, the primary intended users must express a willingness to utilize the information to inform policy or improve program performance. Without a committed primary intended user, it is doubtful that the evaluation should proceed.

Six Evaluation Mistakes

1. Evaluators make themselves the primary decisionmakers, and therefore the primary users. This is a big mistake, because evaluators do not have the power to make program or policy changes.
2. Identifying vague, passive audiences instead of specific individuals to be your partners. An example of a passive audience is when an evaluator emails a questionnaire to thirty administrators of a program to solicit their input on key program issues. It is likely that the administrator will get few responses, because no one feels responsible. A better strategy is to engage a few administrators intensively.
3. Focusing on decisions rather than decisionmakers. The evaluator may focus on correcting a defect in the program (how to improve outreach to the target population) without considering who has the power to change the outreach procedures now in use.
4. Assuming the evaluation's funder is automatically the primary stakeholder. A contractor may assume that the funder (public or private) is the primary stakeholder. Again, it is program administrators who actually make changes.
5. Waiting until the findings are in to identify users. If one waits this long, the program administrators or other key users are likely to take offense at not being consulted first and may adopt an adversarial attitude toward the whole project.
6. Taking a stance of standing above the fray of people and politics. The evaluator must mediate among various interests to get an agreed upon list of evaluation questions.[4]

Box 11.2 shows how to use a logical frame to organize an evaluation.

Process Evaluation

Process or implementation evaluation is the systematic documentation of key aspects of program performance that indicate whether the program is functioning as intended *or* according to some appropriate standard. Process evaluation generally examines program implementation in the domain of (1) service utilization or (2) program organization and operations.[5]

Process evaluation permits program managers to understand how the program actually operates. An incisive understanding of how a program functions is essential to changing policy or improving program performance.

• *Judging Programs Based on Standards or Similar Programs*

Evaluation does more than describe a program; it makes judgments about how well the program functions. The strength of an evaluation is in its objectivity, thus judgments must be based on standards or similar programs. Sources of defensible standards include program regulations, similar programs, and widely accepted administrative practices.

Regulations often set standards for minimum performance expectations and/or timeliness of service delivery. Examples of using regulations for defensible standards are sanitary norms, clean water regulations, or acceptable error rates for social protection eligibility certification.

Similar programs can be used to compare participation rates, outputs, or outcomes. For example, in the United States, participation rates for many programs targeted to the poor are 50–60 percent of those believed eligible to receive benefits. This benchmark is an important factor in assessing the utilization of similar programs.

To determine standards for administration practices look at the practices of well-regarded programs. Practices to examine include program documentation (e.g., guidelines for intake workers), personnel management and supervision, training, record keeping, quality control, and reporting. When there are few such programs in a country to use as models, turn to guidebooks for good program management in other countries.

Understand How the Program Should Work. A key evaluation task is to understand how the program is supposed to work and how it actually operates. This task may include assessing needs, how services are delivered or utilized, and the administrative and monitoring practices in place. There are several strategies for accomplishing this task:

Box 11.2   Organizing the Evaluation: The Logical Frame

Use a logical frame, introduced in Chapter 9, to organize an evaluation. This simple framework helps keep track of the evaluation questions, indicators, and data sources.

A useful exercise is to compare the questions generated by the stakeholders with the objectives defined by program regulations and make certain that the evaluation is not missing a key point. It is the evaluator's job to compile a complete list of research questions.

Once the main objectives or questions are specified, the subsequent criteria should become increasingly specific: what indicators to use, and what data source to use for each indicator.

The logical frame helps make certain that the evaluation questions can be addressed. It helps track data sources, costs, and feasibility, and is a fundamental planning tool.

In this example, most of the questions can only be answered by contacting the elderly recipients and asking them about the new subsidy and their travel arrangements. A survey is probably the best way to collect this information—though focus groups could provide useful feedback and are a good strategy if survey costs are prohibitive. If using a survey, evaluators need to determine the size of the sample, draft the survey instrument, and decide whether to administer it in person, by mail, or phone. Administrative records could be used to verify timing of payments and combined with demographic (census) data to assess participation level.

Logical Frame: New Transportation Benefit for the Elderly

Objectives	Indicators	Data Sources
To provide transportation for the elderly		
1. Improve their travel experience	Number/percentage of elderly reporting improved travel experiences/options	Survey
a. Change in types of transportation services used	Number/percentage of elderly using shared taxis or other transportation options	Survey
b. Minimize problems with new services	Number/percentage of elderly reporting problems with new arrangement; potential problems: receiving payments on time adequacy of payment availability of new transportation options such as shared taxis	Survey and administrative records
2. Income assistance to low-income elderly	Number/percentage of eligible low-income elderly receiving benefits Benefit used by elderly person (not by other members of household) Amount of benefit available per month for other needs (amount in excess of regular travel)	Administrative records and local demographic data; survey

- The program modeling process described in Chapter 9 is one way of understanding how the program works.
- Another way of looking at a program or policy is to use a top-down approach, which examines the program by each level of activity. For example, a national program is governed by law; the law identifies a department that is responsible for program oversight; and implementation is then delegated among several regional or local offices. Clearly delineating the roles and activities of the players at each level is a good way to understand how the program works.
- Other effective strategies are to follow a client through the program, or to trace the specific components of a program activity, such as understanding how a work order for a road repair is completed.
- To understand program operations it is useful to study regulations, guidelines, and program manuals, and consult program staff. Program administrators can describe how the program is intended to operate, but frontline workers are more likely to describe how the program works in practice. The difference between intention and actual practice may be an important aspect of the evaluation.

See Exercise 11.2: Designing a Process Evaluation on page 288.

This exercise involves outlining an evaluation plan for one of several public programs.

There are two types of process evaluation—those that answer questions about service utilization, and those that answer questions about program organization and operations. Evaluations of service utilization address whom the program serves, and evaluations of organization and operations address how the program works.

• *Evaluations of Service Utilization*

Service utilization evaluations are concerned with the number of persons receiving services, whether those receiving the services are the intended population, and whether the target population is aware of the program. The first question, concerning how many persons are receiving services, addresses the *coverage* of the program. The second, concerning targeting, addresses whether the program has a *bias.*

To study *coverage*—the share of eligible persons or households actually receiving services—one must have information on the number of persons or households eligible for the service. Sometimes information on the size of the eligible population can be determined from published data (secondary source), but quite frequently a special survey is necessary (primary source).

For infrastructure programs, "eligibility" may be defined as the kilometers of highway needing a certain level of repair, or the number of kilometers of expressways needed to bring transportation services up to a defined standard.

Bias includes errors of exclusion (leaving out those whom the program wants to serve) and errors of inclusion (serving those whom the program is not intended to serve). These two types of errors have very different effects and are often weighted accordingly. The welfare loss of excluding eligible applicants has a serious negative impact on those persons and represents a failure of the program to fulfill its basic goal. However, from a government budget perspective, this failure may not be so obvious, because low participation rates mean lower expenditures. On the other hand, there is no welfare loss associated with errors of inclusion, except insofar as resources spent on those not in need represents an opportunity cost to society. Budgeters are against inclusion errors because they drive up costs. Many would say, however, that a 5 percent error of exclusion has worse overall consequences than the same inclusion error.

Bias can be measured by a careful review of case records for errors and for unintended beneficiaries (those who technically qualify for participation but are clearly not the intended population). For example, bias errors in eligibility of benefit determination include wrong household type (e.g., no children present), income too great, income level in application not supported by documents provided by the client, and clerical errors in adding income from various sources.

With respect to unintended beneficiaries, a review of participant records could reveal that a significant share of income-eligible participants have large assets (e.g., own a second dwelling or a late-model car). These may be unintended beneficiaries in that their overall economic position is better than that of the households the program seeks to help. The discovery of unintended beneficiaries may prompt a change in rules if it is determined that such persons should not participate.

- *Example Service Utilization Evaluation:*
Coverage and Targeting in Russia's Housing Allowance Program

In Russia, the state owned 80 percent of the urban housing stock until it transferred ownership to local governments in 1991.[6] The skyrocketing costs of housing maintenance and operations (caused by general hyperinflation) coupled with severe rent controls soon overwhelmed local budgets. By 1993 the typical local government was spending half of its total budget to operate the housing stock, including associated subsidies for utilities.

In December 1992 the state Duma (parliament) passed a framework housing reform law. It called for raising rents and utility fees on municipal housing to full cost recovery levels over a multiyear period. The timing of the increases was left to local governments, because they owned the stock. The law specified that the process was to begin in January 1994. Municipalities could only raise rents after establishing the housing allowance program to protect poor renters. The housing allowance program provides rental subsidies to low-income families and is a locally and federally funded program that is locally administered.

An evaluation was conducted in 1994 and 1995 to assess the early implementation of the housing allowance program and to ensure that it provided adequate protection to poor renters.

Evaluation Issues. The evaluation addressed the following questions:

- What share of eligible households was participating (program coverage)?
- Were benefits concentrated on poorer households (targeting)?
- Were participants satisfied by their treatment in administering offices (client satisfaction)?

The question of client satisfaction was especially important in 1994, because housing allowances were the first means-tested program introduced in Russia.

Program Structure. The housing allowance paid a gap benefit that represented the difference between what the family could afford and the actual rent. (See Chapter 5 for additional information on gap benefits and other subsidy structures.)

The basic formula for the benefit was:

$$S = MSR - (t \times Y)$$

Where

S = the amount of the subsidy

MSR = the maximum social rent, which is the cost estimated for a unit of a suitable size for the family applying for the subsidy. It is based on unit size (square meters) and standard use rates for utilities. A participant household can occupy a bigger unit or use more utility services but the subsidy is fixed for the standard unit and consumption.

Y = household income

t = the share of its own income the household must spend on housing before receiving the subsidy

Cities had the right to establish the share that families contributed toward their housing expense *(t)*. Household contributions were capped at 22 percent of household income by federal law, though most cities chose much lower shares.

Eligibility. Eligibility was means-tested and families with insufficient incomes were eligible to participate in the program:

a.　　$Y < Y^* = MSR \div t$

Where

Y^* = the income cutoff (i.e., the lowest income a family can have and not receive a subsidy)

b. Households living in state housing, including those who had privatized their units, and households living in cooperative housing were eligible under the national law; local authorities set the eligibility policy for households in other types of housing.

The number of households eligible and program costs fluctuate according to the values cities set for maximum social rents and share of household income contribution. For example, a higher standard rent generally increases the number of households eligible for housing subsidies—as the difference between rent obligation and what families can afford increases. A higher household contribution level limits eligibility, whereas a lower threshold qualifies more families. Because local governments pay most of the costs, they had an incentive to cut participation in years when transfers from higher governments were unexpectedly small, which has happened fairly often since the program's implementation.

Data Collection. The housing ministry and the evaluation team wanted to get an early reading on how the program was working, so two cities that implemented rent increases and housing allowances in the spring of 1994 were selected for the evaluation. Vladimir and Gorodetz are small, European Russian cities.

The team conducted a survey of the population in each city to estimate the share of households who were eligible to participate. Three hundred households were surveyed in Vladimir and five hundred in Gorodetz. An additional sample of program participants was surveyed to ensure that the sample for analyzing participant satisfaction with the program would be large enough. (This extra sample was necessary because if program participation rates were low, then there would only be a few participants included in the general survey of the population.)

The initial evaluation was conducted in the spring of 1994 and repeated in 1995 to assess whether there had been any improvement.

Housing Allowance Evaluation Results

Participation rates. Participation rates in 1994 were extremely low in both cities. By 1995, both cities had improved their outreach efforts and increased participation rates. See Table 11.2 for additional details.

1. The share of households eligible for payment changed considerably in Gorodetz between the two years. This is because the city raised the household contribution rate *(t)* between the two years to control the cost of the allowance program. (In 1994 the household contribution rate was determined on a sliding scale, with the poorest households paying only 2.5 percent of their incomes on rents.)
2. Participation in 1994 among eligible households was very low. This was a surprising finding. In part this is explained by the fact that rents remained low in absolute terms, so that the benefits of participating in the program were low. Nevertheless, the finding created great concern in the housing ministry, because it feared that poor households not participating would refuse to pay their rents or, worse, protest rent increases. Based on these findings the housing minister sent a letter to every state governor urging him to press cities to conduct information campaigns about the availability of the subsidy before the next rent increase.

Table 11.2   Participation Rates

	Vladimir		Gorodetz	
	1994	1995	1994	1995
Percentage of household income contributed toward housing expenses *(t)*	10	15	2.5–10.0	0.15
Percentage of households eligible	46	45	55	19
Participation rate for eligibles (%)	2.1	20.4	3.6	37.8

3. Participation rates rose considerably by 1995, especially in Gorodetz, where the information campaign was more effective. A second round of rent increases, which increased the value of the subsidies (*MSR* increased), also encouraged participation.

Targeting. Program targeting was very successful, as benefits were strongly concentrated on poor families. Table 11.3 shows that more than half of all recipients were in the lowest income quintile.

Client satisfaction. Clients gave positive ratings to the timeliness of service delivery (see Tables 11.4 and 11.5). These ratings were particularly surprising, because in Russia terrible service levels traditionally characterized interactions with the bureaucracy.

Table 11.3   Distribution of Participants by Income Quintile

Income Quintile	Vladimir	Gorodetz
1 (lowest)	63	58
2	23	37
3	11	4
4	2	—
5 (highest)	1	1

Table 11.4   Client Satisfaction: Timeliness

Evaluation of Speed with Which Client's Case Was Handled	Vladimir	Gorodetz
Very slowly	13	1
Slowly	14	4
Average	38	12
Quickly	28	44
Very quickly	4	38
No answer	2	—

Table 11.5   Client Satisfaction: Staff Performance

Evaluation of Treatment by Housing Allowance Employee with Whom Client Had Most Contact	Vladimir	Gorodetz
Fully satisfied	62	62
Satisfied	23	27
More or less satisfied	7	11
Not satisfied	4	1
Not satisfied at all	2	—
No answer	2	—

The exceptional ratings for Gorodetz are partly explained by the fact that the interviews with applicants to determine eligibility were very brief. This likely signaled a problem in the eligibility certification process rather than efficiency. So the figures are not all good news.

Client satisfaction with program staff was again remarkably positive. Client satisfaction was used as an indicator of attitudes toward income testing, and such findings clearly suggested that the participants were not rejecting means testing.

Conclusions.   The program got off to a good start overall. The initial evaluation results (from 1994 surveys only) demonstrated low participation rates. In response to this finding the housing ministry sent letters to the state governors urging the housing allowance offices to better advertise the program so more families would participate when tariffs and rents would increase in 1995. Participation rates increased in 1995, but continue to remain lower than anticipated. In 2001 about 30 percent of eligible households participated across the country.

The housing allowance program has served as a model for other means-tested programs in the country.

• *Evaluations of Program Operations*

Organization and operations evaluations address whether the program is being appropriately and effectively implemented.

Examples of questions addressed by organization/operations evaluations include:

- Are necessary program functions being performed adequately? For example, for program outreach, are the expected numbers of people applying for services?
- Is program staffing sufficient in numbers and competencies for program functions to be fulfilled? How long do clients have to wait for services? What are the error rates in processing them? How long are potholes on the streets before they are repaired?
- Is the quality of garbage pickup (or any other public service) consistent with the city's standards?
- Does the program coordinate effectively with the other agencies with which it must interact?
- Are program resources used effectively and efficiently?

An assessment of social service operations, for example, would include the flow of clients through the system, accessibility of services, and the quality of case management, record keeping, management planning, staff training, program documentation (e.g., procedures manuals), and monitoring. This basic assessment applies to all programs, with the exception of client flow and case management.

As described earlier in this chapter, to conduct an operations/organizational evaluation it is a good practice to "map" the operations of the program. That is, how are tasks assigned? How are clients or work orders processed? As before, study the documentation and ask staff how the program is supposed to work.

Implementation Failures. The following describes different types of implementation failures, that is, ways in which a program does not meet its objectives.[7]

Nonprograms and incomplete interventions. An example of a nonprogram is a funding initiative in which money is sent to schools for special services for children from low-income families but no special services are found. An example of an incomplete intervention is a housing initiative in which funds are given to an NGO for a community improvement project but little is accomplished (funds "disappear" into general administration functions).

Wrong interventions. For example, schools agree to participate in an experimental program using new teaching techniques but in fact the teachers sabotage the project by not changing their teaching approach. Or housing funds are given to an NGO to fund provision of stand pipes in a poor housing area but funds are used instead for dwelling upgrading loans.

Unstandardized interventions. Too much discretion is given to those determining service provision, so that the kinds of interventions—and results—vary excessively across sites and clients.

How to Measure? Evaluators assess program operations or service organization through site visits, examinations of records, and interviews with program staff, clients, NGOs or private firms working in the field, and cooperating agencies.

Site visits to program offices enable evaluators to witness program operations and speak to staff. Evaluators generally interview a range of persons, not just program staff and not just the supervisor. NGOs are sometimes used as surrogates for clients, but this must be done carefully, as they may have their own agendas. Staff at cooperating agencies may have interesting views on interagency cooperation, the quality of relations, and feedback from shared clients.

To conduct a successful office visit, evaluators generally must have a clear idea of how the program should work in concept prior to the visit. Part of being prepared is to draft a basic interview protocol. This provides structure to the discussion and, if there is more than one interviewer, ensures some consistency. However, it is important that the protocol not be followed so rigidly that interviewees cannot fully express themselves. Staff should be interviewed without supervisors present, so that they can be as open as possible.

• *Example Program Operations Evaluation: Changes in Participation in Food Stamps After Implementation of Welfare Reform in the United States*

This evaluation sought to assess changes in participation in food stamps after the implementation of welfare reform.[8] The food stamp program in the United States is a large federally funded program that provides food vouchers to low-income people. The vouchers (which used to look like play money and are now distributed using something like a debit card) can be used in any participating market to purchase food. Regional and municipal offices implement the program according to federal regulations. The same offices that administer food stamps also typically administer income support programs.

Implementation of reforms of the income support program appeared to restrict eligible households from participating in the food program—an unintentional and undesirable impact.

The original income support program was called Aid to Families with Dependent Children and served low-income families. A female-headed family could receive benefits indefinitely under the program (that is, until the youngest child reached eighteen years of age). Approximately 25 percent of those receiving benefits at any time were long-term recipients (ten or more years). The program was widely criticized for promoting dependency. For decades the program had very weak job-search requirements, but these were gradually strengthened over time.

In 1996, broad legislation, referred to as welfare reform, was enacted that fundamentally changed the structure of basic assistance for low-income families. The new program, Temporary Assistance for Needy Families (TANF), emphasized putting recipients to work, while providing support for a limited period of time.

The food stamp and TANF programs work closely together and are frequently administered from the same office. After implementation of welfare reform, a decline in the participation of food stamps was observed. Program administrators, advocates for the poor, and the media raised concerns about the access to benefits.

The objective of the evaluation was to determine if changes in program administration caused the decline.

Fieldwork. The evaluation entailed detailed analyses of the local administration of the two programs. Evaluators studied twenty-four offices—three offices in each of eight states. Because local variation in administration is permitted, the evaluation design sought to analyze operations in multiple states and multiple sites within each state. The team examined client services, with a focus on program accessibility, quality of service, and availability of employment services.

Evaluators conducted interviews with state and local staff. State agencies regulated the administration of the program and generally delegated benefits administration to local offices. Interviews with local agency staff included the director, casework supervisors, and caseworkers. In addition, focus groups were conducted with service providers (firms conducting job training programs for clients and telephone call centers that contact clients for the agency) and client advocates (NGOs).

Results. The analysis showed that in some offices new administrative practices created for the TANF program discouraged applicants for the food stamp program. In these offices the new procedures required multiple interviews with employment-related staff before the food stamp application could be completed. Sometimes applicants were required to visit the employment office before applying for food stamps. Employment offices are generally located separately from the agency administering the TANF and food stamp programs. So being sent to the employment office is typically a significant effort for applicants, many of whom do not own a car.

Also, punitive food stamp sanctions were sometimes enacted for participants in some states that violated rules under the new welfare program. Agencies punished clients for not fulfilling their work requirements by reducing or eliminating food stamp benefits for three or six months. This practice was in violation of federal food stamp regulations.

The federal Department of Health and Human Services and the state agencies that administer the program used the results of the evaluation to improve client access to food stamps.

• Factors Influencing Program Success

This chapter has focused on accurately documenting program functions and making judgments about how well a program or policy is implemented. Some generalizations can be made about the important features of successful programs. The following are lessons about good program design drawn from analyses of over a hundred program evaluations:[9]

- *Characteristics of the policy being implemented.* The greater the clarity and specificity of goals and procedures, the greater the likelihood that the program will achieve its objectives. Still, some flexibility is necessary to deal with unforeseen obstacles and to adapt to changing environments.
- *Availability of resources.* Did program implementers have sufficient resources with which to work? While the literature often refers to financial resources, other inputs are important as well (e.g., adequate office space, copying services, and qualified staff).
- *Number of implementing actors.* It is often held that the more people and agencies involved in implementing a program, the greater the chance that implementation will be retarded or less successful if full implementation proceeds.
- *Attitude of implementing personnel.* Another factor is the support for the innovation among the staff (i.e., are the changes viewed as reasonable?). Acceptance of new procedures depends implicitly on the establishment of new norms in the relevant policy community. Some studies emphasize peer-pressure and professionalism as powerful agents in revising norms.
- *Alignment of clients.* Client support is particularly important in programs where success is seen as depending on the involvement of all stakeholders. Support can result from consultation with clients in the design stage or the willingness of agency staff to negotiate changes in procedures or even standards during implementation, if needed.
- *Opportunity for learning among implementers.* Exchanges among implementers give administrators tips on how to improve services and promote professionalism.
- *Past experience.* Programs are easier to implement when staff can draw on past experience with similar issues. For example, when designing and implementing the Arzamas school lunch program, the social protection agency did a strong job of means testing, because it had recently incorporated this into other programs, but it was weak in areas where it had little

experience, like determining oversight for the quality of meals delivered to students.

- *Local environment.* Attributes that clearly matter are the state of the local economy, the incidence of poverty, and the profile of the poor (e.g., young/old, disabled). Success of a program to help unemployed workers find a job will be heavily affected by local labor market conditions.

- ## *"Bottom-Up Perspective"*

The bottom-up perspective acknowledges that frontline offices and workers often have considerable power over implementation.[10] It is not a prerequisite for success, but a factor that policymakers and program administrators are wise to consider. Much of this chapter and public administration in general is presented from the perspective of a higher-level government or official assigning program implementation to a subordinate office. The subordinate office is viewed as generally lacking decisionmaking authority and passively fulfilling directives. Frontline offices do, however, often exercise considerable power and discretion. This can occur whether or not policymakers and higher authorities formally delegate such authority.

A substantial quantity of research shows that the bottom-up perspective is most important when frontline workers have discretion in program administration, when there is ambiguity in the formal policy, and when policy implementation involves change in organizational practice (lots of room for discretion).

Research shows that practices differ mostly according to the context in which the workers operate: how much training they have, the quality of management, the adequacy of program resources, the incentives staff are given for good performance, and the quality of equipment they have.

To a significant degree the bottom-up perspective has been incorporated into implementation evaluation. It is generally recognized that the way a program is administered at the local level can have a dramatic impact on whether the program is successful in a particular location. Recall the importance of the interviews with frontline staff and managers about exactly how they do their work; this is the heart of mapping or understanding a program.

See Exercise 11.3: Understanding Process Evaluation on page 290.

The task in this exercise is to answer a series of questions that assess basic understanding of process evaluation.

Chapter Summary

Three types of evaluation strategies are process evaluation, impact evaluation, and benefit-cost evaluation. Each method addresses different types of questions about program performance. Process evaluation assesses how well a program is operating. Impact evaluation is used to measure program results (see Chapter 12). Benefit-cost evaluation assigns monetary values to the program's benefits and costs and assesses program efficiency based on whether benefits outweigh costs (see Chapter 13).

Two basic types of process evaluation are service utilization evaluation and organization and operations evaluation. A service utilization evaluation focuses on whether the program is reaching its intended audience. An organization and operations evaluation explores how a program functions and what might be done to improve program operations or procedures. Useful practices in conducting process evaluations include meeting with stakeholders to generate research questions, mapping the program (describing how it functions), and using a logical frame to summarize the evaluation questions and identify key indicators and data sources.

Focusing on clients is an important part of evaluation. Because the purpose of any type of evaluation is to inform policymaking or improve program performance, it must be responsive to the needs of key stakeholders—those who are able to set policy or drive improvements.

Recommended Reading

L. Jerome Gallagher, Raymond J. Struyk, and Ludmila Nikonova. "Savings from Integrating Administrative Systems for Social Assistance Programmes in Russia." *Public Administration and Development* no. 23 (2003): 177–195.

This article describes an evaluation of administrative reforms in Arzamas, Russia. The city created a unified application process for all social benefits. Previously, low-income families needed to apply separately for housing allowances, child allowances, school lunch subsidies, and other programs. Each program had its own application and required families to present documentation and meet with eligibility staff. The new "one-window" approach resulted in significant time and efficiency savings for clients and staff, with the average client saving between 1.3 and 2.4 hours, and with each staff member processing 127 benefits per month compared to 85 under the old system. The article describes the evaluation methods (interviews, case reviews, focus groups, and analyses of budget expenditures). The evaluation clearly supports the project, and the city could use the evaluation findings of significant savings to justify this and other reforms.

Exercise 11.1: Stakeholder Evaluation Role-Play

This exercise is designed as a role-play involving an evaluator and several stakeholders. The evaluator is a private consultant hired by the mayor's office, and his or her task is to assemble the primary stakeholders and generate a list of evaluation questions based on their concerns. The stakeholders include the head of the social assistance department, a representative of a local NGO, and the director of the finance department. After the stakeholders have had a chance to raise their questions, the evaluator should summarize the main points. It is likely that the same point will be raised by more than one of the stakeholders, so three to five main issues or questions should be identified. After the exercise, observers can be asked if the stakeholders generated good research questions, and asked how they would measure each question and what data could be used.

Background. The new mayor of Szaboz (fictional city) is interested in improving the efficiency of public services. Six months ago, he implemented a new policy regarding transportation benefits for the elderly.

Previously the elderly were allowed to ride local buses for free and the city paid the transportation company $14.40 per person per year (or 5¢ per trip for twenty-four trips per month). The actual number of rides used was unknown, though the city generally assumed that the subsidy was in excess of actual usage. Only 40 percent of the population use buses, and buses run on approximately 65 percent of the routes. Other routes are served by privately operated shared taxis that cost 10¢ per ride.

The new policy cashed out the transportation benefit and granted elderly persons $12 per year that they could use for transportation or other expenses. The payments were made two times per year directly into the bank accounts of the elderly. The program gave the elderly the option of spending the money as they chose and, if using it for transportation, allowed them to choose between buses and shared taxis. The subsidy was reduced from $14.40 to $12, thereby saving the city money.

The new program has been operating for six months and the mayor has requested an implementation evaluation.

Stakeholder Roles

Head of social assistance department. The department provides social services to the elderly. Staff have frequent contact with the elderly and fully understand the program. The social assistance department is responsible for compiling a list of all elderly and their bank account information. Elderly persons with questions about the program or problems receiving money report to the social assistance department.

Representative from NGO. The organization and its volunteers provide free social services to low-income elderly. The city often seeks the opinion of the organization on issues affecting the elderly. Several volunteers report that frail elderly have problems using the shared taxis, because they are hard to enter and drivers are sometimes rude and unhelpful.

Director of finance department. The finance department is responsible for making the payments to the elderly. The reduction in the benefit has saved the city money, despite a slight increase in program participation. The director is interested in whether the elderly are actually receiving the benefits (or whether the benefits are being used by other family members or for other household purposes).

Exercise 11.2: Designing a Process Evaluation

Select a program from the following list to use for designing a process evaluation.

Employment
- Job placement program

Education
- Teacher training program
- Computer literacy program
- Program to repair school buildings, increase energy efficiency, and improve building utilization (e.g., closing or combining schools with few pupils)

Health
- Programs to treat persons with tuberculosis
- Programs to reduce the spread of AIDS

Economy
- Evaluation of recent reforms to reduce regulatory burdens on small businesses (registration, licensing, certification, and inspections)

Courts
- Evaluation of recent judicial reforms

Housing
- Evaluation of regional/local mortgage programs to determine how a new federal program might help to further develop mortgage market

Environment

- Program to reduce industrial pollution

Next, outline a process evaluation strategy using the list below. You will need to make up some details about how the program might operate. The task is to outline an evaluation design—not to actually make judgments about the program.

1. Program description:

2. Evaluation objectives:

3. Research questions (a logical frame can help identify these questions; see Exercise 9.3 for a sample logical frame):

4. Program modeling (describe how the program works):
   Inputs:

   Activities:

   Outputs:

   Outcomes:

5. Analysis plan:
   Key data elements:

   Analytical methods:

   Report outline (e.g., summary, project description, analysis, conclusions/ recommendations, appendix):

6. Data collection (summarize data requirements needed to answer the research questions):

7. Data analysis methods:

8. Strategy for getting the evaluation used:

Exercise 11.3: Understanding Process Evaluation

This exercise assesses basic understanding of process evaluation. You work for the Ministry of Social Welfare in Bulgaria and are assigned the task of assessing the degree of income targeting of the national child allowance program in the city of Sofia. Main characteristics of the program:

- It is means-tested: only families with children under age sixteen and with incomes below the poverty line can participate.
- The benefit structure is flat (i.e., benefits are on a per-child basis and it is the same benefit amount regardless of the family's income).
- There is only one office, located in the center of the city, where families can apply to receive benefits.
- In Bulgaria a typical poverty reduction program with open enrollment has a coverage rate of about 60 percent.

Answer the following questions by circling the letter next to the correct answer:

1. To study the degree of targeting the evaluator should examine
   A. the income distribution of beneficiaries.
   B. the income distribution of beneficiaries compared with a reference group (e.g., of all households in the population).

If you answered "B," go to Question 1.2

1.1. (If you answered "A" to Question 1.) What type of analysis would you do with the information on the income of beneficiaries?
   A. Compare the income distribution of participating families with and without the money from the child allowance program.
   B. No additional analysis is necessary, the distribution of income including the child allowance is sufficient.

Go to Question 2.

1.2 (If you answered "B" to Question 1.) The evaluation should compare the income distribution of beneficiaries with the income distribution of
A. all households.
B. only households with children.

2. In assessing errors of inclusion and exclusion, policy analysts usually assign greater weight to
A. errors of inclusion, because these error increase program costs.
B. errors of exclusion, because these errors result in large social welfare costs.
C. neither inclusion or exclusion; actually, they treat both the same.

3. Your boss wants you to analyze a sample of beneficiary records taken from the files in the administrative office. What *valid* purpose for *this* evaluation is served by studying these records?
A. Gives a sample for conducting a survey of beneficiaries about their satisfaction with the program.
B. Can use the names to determine if the beneficiaries are getting benefits from other programs.
C. Can determine if those receiving benefits are actually income-eligible to participate.
D. Can assess the workload of the office.

4. Examine the information in the following table.

Income Quintile	Percentage of Households in Income Group Eligible to Participate	Percentage of Eligible Households in the Income Group Participating
Lowest	15	30
Second	25	60
Third	5	60
Fourth	4	22
Highest	0	0

(The low eligibility figure for households in the lowest income quintile is explained by the large number of elderly households in this group.)

Characterize the degree of targeting:
   A. Strong (progressively targets the neediest).
   B. Moderate (is generally proportionate to the population or roughly equal for all groups).
   C. Weak (the neediest receive less than their proportional share).
Characterize the degree of program coverage:
   A. Strong (most of those eligible participate in the program).
   B. Moderate (a reasonable number participate—basically on par with similar programs).
   C. Weak (only a fraction of those eligible participate).

5. What might be the reasons for low participation of the lowest-income households? (circle the two most important)
   A. They have no knowledge of the program.
   B. The benefit is too small to bother with.
   C. Program requirements—particularly the documents one has to bring—are too hard to meet.
   D. Cannot afford to travel to the administrative office.
   E. They are opposed to accepting "charity" of this type.

6. What would be the best way (in terms of reliability and cost-effectiveness) to confirm your answers to Question 5?
   A. Ask the head of the office administering the program.
   B. Hold two to three focus groups with eligible households who are not participating.
   C. Do a scientific survey of eligible households, both participants and non-participants, to gather the information.

CHAPTER 12

Impact Evaluation

Impact evaluation assesses how well the project has achieved its intended goals and identifies factors affecting their achievement.[1] Impact evaluation compares program outcomes with measures of what would have happened without the program. For example, a job training program may report that 60 percent of its participants attained jobs. An impact evaluation compares this result to that of a control group to determine how much of this outcome can be attributed to the program's efforts or how many participants would have found jobs on their own. The evaluation may determine that 40 percent would have secured employment without the program, and thus that the program's impact is the 20 percent of participants who would not have found jobs without the training.

The key characteristic of impact evaluation is that it attempts to subtract extraneous factors—whether broad social or economic changes or differences among the motivations of individuals—from the reported results of the program. The evaluation measures the impact of an intervention and enables policymakers to confidently say that the program caused a specific result. This type of evaluation can be very important to major policy decisions. Even in the absence of an impact evaluation, policymakers who are cognizant of how program results can be inflated or depressed by general social and economic changes or the particular characteristics of participants can make better judgments.

This chapter describes impact evaluation and the main methodological approaches. Examples of each approach are offered and strengths and weaknesses outlined.

What Is Impact Evaluation?

An impact evaluation is a technically rigorous way of assessing the results of policies or programs. Formal impact evaluation is generally beyond the capacity or need of most small programs. However, for major programs or policies, impact analysis is one of the most effective ways to determine the impact or effect of the intervention. This book has already suggested a variety of ways to monitor and evaluate program outcomes or results, including routine program monitoring and performance measurement. The use of control groups distinguishes impact evaluation from these other methods.

Table 12.1 is a useful review of the various program functions that lead to an intended impact. The example is for a health program to reduce mortality rates of young children through the use of oral rehydration therapy (ORT). Diarrhea and the resulting loss of fluids is a leading cause of infant mortality in many developing countries. Oral rehydration therapy involves training mothers treat their sick children with a simple solution of water and sugar that aids in rehydration.

The table distinguishes between simple program outputs (media campaigns and trainings), intermediate outcomes (increased access to services), outcomes (improved use of ORT), and the ultimate impact (a reduction in child mortality rates). An actual impact evaluation of this project would compare the child mortality rates of families or communities who participated in the program with those who did not.

Table 12.1   Model of Implementation and Results for Health Intervention Program

	Implementation		Results		
Inputs	Activities	Outputs	Intermediate Outcomes	Outcome	Impact
Trainers ORT supplies Funds	Launch media campaign to educate mothers Train health professionals in ORT	Fifteen media campaigns completed 100 health professionals trained in ORT	Increased maternal knowledge of ORT services Increased access to ORT services	Improved use of ORT for managing childhood diarrhea	Reduce mortality rates for children under five years old

Source: Adapted from Jody Zall Kusek, Ray C. Rist, and Elizabeth M. White, "How Will We Know the Millennium Development Goal Results When We See Them? Building a Results-Based Monitoring and Evaluation System to Give Us the Answers," draft, October 10, 2002.

The impact is defined as the net effect of the intervention and is assessed based on the gross outcome minus the effects of other processes. Other processes include extraneous confounding factors such as changes in the economic or social context or motivations of the population. The gross outcome is the social or physical condition that the program seeks to address.

Presented as a simple formula, an impact evaluation looks like this:

impact = net outcome of intervention = gross outcome − effects of other processes

The difference between outcome and impact is that an outcome is the status or result, which may or may not be due to the program's intervention. An impact is clearly linked to the program. The usual practice is to identify the impact by contrasting the outcomes for an experimental group that receives a treatment and a control group that does not.

For example, medicines are usually tested using an impact evaluation methodology. A new drug may appear to reduce heart attacks in half of all patients; however, an impact study with a control group of similar patients who are given only placebo drugs may also witness a reduction in heart attacks. The control group is essential for quantifying how much of the impact is actually caused by the intervention.

The following is a slightly more complicated example that gets at the difficulty in assessing impacts: The objective of the housing allowance program is to protect low-income households from having to pay the full cost of housing. As a result, participants have more money to spend on nonhousing consumption. Can the impact of the program be measured by knowing the size of the housing allowance a family receives?

Unfortunately it is not that simple, because of the possibility of a substitution effect. Consider the following case: An elderly widow receives income from her son to help her with expenses. When she begins receiving the housing allowance subsidy, she tells her son. He in turn reduces his monthly support by about half of the value of the housing subsidy. So the impact on this woman's nonhousing consumption is only half of the value of the subsidy payment.

Confounding Factors

A confounding factor is any situation that may influence program results, such as a broad social or economic change, a concurrent intervention, motivation of participants, or a program parameter that distorts the measurement of impacts. Different types of confounding factors are described below.

- *Selection bias.* Selection bias occurs when errors are made in selecting the study participants, either in the assignment of targets (participants) in a random process or when "similar" controls are selected that were not matched with the treatment group on a critical factor. For example, the evaluation of a program to improve the reading scores of primary school children selects schools as the unit of study and matches the schools on the socioeconomic characteristics of their neighborhoods. But it could be that for some reason students in some schools systematically read better than those in others. (The reason for higher student achievement may depend on the general reading curriculum, more talented teachers, or other factors.) If this is not taken into account, the evaluation results will be biased.

- *Secular drift.* Secular drift pertains to changes that occur for the general population. For example, a general increase in homeownership rate makes it hard to isolate the effect of a mortgage lending initiative. In the United States in the late 1980s, the Federal National Mortgage Association (FNMA; also known as Fannie Mae)—the secondary mortgage market firm—announced a major change in its underwriting standards to make it possible for families with lower incomes to purchase a home. A general increase in homeownership occurred over the next twenty years. However, many argue that this has less to do with FNMA's policies, and is more accurately attributed to household preferences, significant real income growth, and low mortgage interest rates.

- *Interfering events.* A hurricane batters an area that is the target of a slum upgrading project. The intervention—the project—is very badly disrupted and the comparison with the control neighborhood (that was not hit by the storm) is no longer valid.

- *Hawthorne effect.* The Hawthorne effect occurs when those in the treatment group respond to the treatment just because they receive it. This is especially problematic where satisfaction is being measured, as results may only reflect that someone is paying attention to the clients rather than the impact of the specific intervention.

Principal Design Strategies

The two main design strategies are randomized controls and quasi-experimental designs. With random controls, subjects are randomly assigned to either an experimental or a control group. This is generally viewed as the best way to measure impacts. But because this method is costly, complex, and time consuming, many analysts turn to other methods—quasi-experimental designs. With quasi-experimental designs, participants are matched according to specific characteristics, where differences in the characteristics of members of the treatment and control groups are statistically controlled, or where participants themselves act as controls in a before-and-after model.

- ### *Summary of Design Strategies*

Randomized Controls. Targets (participants) are randomly assigned to an experimental group or a control group from whom the intervention is withheld. One example is from the Housing Allowance Demand Experiment, conducted in the United States in the 1970s. At that time, all US assistance to improve the housing of poor people was in the form of constructing housing for these families. There was great uncertainty about how effective a demand-side approach would be in improving participants' housing. So the experiment was structured to determine what share of a housing allowance subsidy would be spent on housing and how much would be spent on other things.[2] The program required participants to live in a unit meeting certain minimum physical standards, and households were expected to use the subsidy to improve their existing housing conditions or move to a unit meeting the standards if their current unit failed them. The study took place in two cities that were selected for their market conditions: Pittsburgh, with a surplus of available housing, and Phoenix, with a tight housing market.

To test the hypothesis, subjects were randomly assigned to various subexperiments. One compared the changes in housing circumstances of those receiving a housing allowance with those getting an equivalent cash payment without any special housing requirements. Families who thought they were eligible to participate in a "new housing program" advertised in the local media, applied to participate. As they applied they were randomly assigned to the treatment and control groups. By comparing the housing outcomes of the two groups, the evaluators documented the effectiveness of housing requirements on actual housing conditions. In fact, the effectiveness was very modest.

Quasi-Experimental Designs. There are a variety of designs of this type. The three most commonly used are described here.

1. Match-constructed controls. Targets to whom the intervention is given are matched on selected characteristics with individuals or entities (e.g., schools) that do not receive the intervention to construct an "equivalent" group to serve as a control. For example, in a school reading program, the evaluator's primary interest is in the difference in mean reading scores. Schools defined as similar—in terms of the test scores of pupils, income of families in the neighborhood, percentage of students from single parent households—are assigned to treatment and control groups. Students in the treatment group get intensive assistance with reading.

2. Statistically equated controls. Statistical methods are used to compare the differences between participant and nonparticipant targets on selected characteristics. For example, in a project to test the impact of lower (subsidized) interest rates on the price paid for housing, samples of units purchased are created of those receiving the subsidized loans and those with similar incomes paying market interest rates. The analysis is of the price per square meter paid for housing after controlling for other property characteristics. (Regression techniques are used to control for other factors such as size, number of bathrooms, building materials, neighborhood attributes, and other potentially meaningful characteristics, and a variable is included to indicate if a family got a subsidized loan.)

3. Reflexive controls.   Targets who receive the intervention are compared with themselves before and after the intervention. For example, measuring the impact of a training program by measuring participants' work and pay experience before and after the training experience. Reflexive controls are especially vulnerable to the problem of secular drift. It is easy to imagine how general wage or employment trends might make it difficult to determine the impact of an employment program using reflexive controls.

Random Assignment: Key Points

The key element is that persons or entities (schools) are randomly assigned to treatment or control groups. If done successfully, *in aggregate* the two groups should have identical composition, identical predisposition toward the project/treatment, and identical experiences in terms of confounding factors. An *identical predisposition* is defined as equally disposed toward the project or treatment and equally likely without the treatment to achieve the same outcome—for example, similar test scores for an educational program. An *identical experience* refers to the experience of the two groups, in that each is exposed to the same time-related processes, such as aging, secular drifts (incomes increase equivalently), and more.

Other ways to obtain "near random assignments" include:

- *Serialized lists.* For example, student ID numbers. This process is acceptable if the numbers are not assigned in some systematic way (e.g., different tables at registration had different numbers to assign and students drifted by sex to one table or another).
- *Overcapacity controls.* Households or persons who apply for the program, but do not receive services (that is, those who meet eligibility criteria but who do not receive services due to a lack of resources or similar issue), are used as controls. This method is effective because such controls have revealed that they have the predisposition to participate in the program.

• The Challenges of Random Assignment

Large samples are needed if differences between controls and the treatment group are expected to be small. For example, consider the actual case of an evaluation of an experimental counseling program for new homebuyers that attempted to assess the impact on mortgage delinquency and default rates. Three thousand households were randomly assigned to control and treatment groups, and their experiences tracked for five years. At the end of the experiment there was a difference in default rates, suggesting that counseling might be effective, but the difference was too small to be statistically significant with the sample size used.

Randomized field experiments are challenging to implement (rules, logistics of assignment, costly if large, and usually time consuming). Care must be taken to enforce the random assignment rules (people ask for special treatment in assignments or administrators are not rigorous in applying the rules). Workers at local service offices often object to not being able to provide services to clearly needy potential clients who are assigned to the control group. In addition, adjustments may need to be made in the analysis for differential attrition between the experimental and control groups. Such adjustments involve sophisticated statistical methods.

Random experiments are also time consuming because they take time to set up, the assignment process is typically lengthy, and then the analysis takes more time. Compared with statistical matching, random assignment is a lengthy and involved process. Often those in senior positions who support undertaking these analyses have moved on before the evaluation is complete—leaving the evaluator with the challenge of finding a new champion for the work.

Standard statistical tests are employed to ensure that the two groups are similar. If all differences between the treatment and control groups have been controlled through the assignment process, then simple parametric tests work, such as *t*-tests and analysis of variance. Controlling for other factors is not needed in principle. But if the strong conditions for comparability are not met, then multiple regression similar to that used for statistically equated controls is needed.

- *Random Assignment Example: Job Corps*

Evaluation Question.   Does the program have a positive effect on the employment and earnings of participants?[3]

Program Description.   The Jobs Corps is a long-established training program for young men and women. It is distinctive because participants are taken to rural locations—often former military bases that have been retrofitted—where they receive intensive job training and counseling on appropriate life behavior and skills. Participants spend approximately six months at the training facility, so the program is expensive.

Evaluation Design.   The evaluation was based on a national random sample of all eligible applicants in 1994 and 1995, with experimental and control groups formed. The design is a good example of the use of applicant overflows as the source of the control group. Participants and controls were interviewed multiple times over a four-year follow-up period.

Evaluators also conducted site visits and interviews at the training centers. The site visits were included to understand if the program was being administered the same everywhere (i.e., if it was operating as a single unified program or multiple programs). If there were important variations in program composition among sites, then the evaluation would have to try to control for these in the analysis.

Results. Program services were delivered comprehensively and consistently in centers across the country. The program increased education and job training of participants by 1,000 hours (equivalent to one school year). These initial findings could be part of a process evaluation on how the program operated and provide a good example of the complementarity between implementation and impact evaluation. That services were delivered consistently confirms that there really was only one program to be evaluated, not multiple programs.

In the fourth year after enrolling in the program, participants earned about $1,150 per year (12 percent) more than the controls. The program significantly reduced involvement in crime (by about 16 percent) and receipt of public assistance. The program had no measurable effect on illegal drug use or fertility.

The program is cost-effective, although at an expense of about $14,000 per participant. The positive cost-effectiveness is based on all benefits, including higher earnings and savings to society from lower crime rates (prosecution, court, and prison costs).

Quasi-Experimental Designs

• *Control Group by Matching: Key Points*

Match-constructed controls, by which a control group is selected based on similar characteristics, were widely used in the 1960s and 1970s for evaluations of programs where participants were individuals or families. For example, a project based in London gives youths who have committed auto theft an opportunity to work on cars and learn about how they function and are maintained. The effectiveness of the program in reducing new crimes was evaluated by comparing arrest data for thirty-five probationers in the project with those of a matched group of forty probationers who did not participate. The youths in the comparison group were selected based on similar offense careers to the youths in the treatment group. This yielded groups who were similar in age and criminal records. (Random assignment was *not* used.)

The program did have a significant impact on crime rates. The analysis involved a simple comparison of differences in the average share of each group who committed crime again during the observation period.

Match controls are still used for comparisons of small numbers of aggregate units, such as schools, neighborhoods, or cities. For example, in 1994, "Kids Voting USA" administered a civics curriculum that was used by 2.3 million kindergarten to twelfth-grade students in twenty-one states. The objective was for students to discuss political issues with their parents. The evaluation question was whether this had an impact on parents' voting participation. To assess the effects, voter turnout in areas where the program was implemented was compared with that in nearby areas that did not use the program. Various data sets were used to match the areas in terms of racial, socioeconomic, and partisan characteristics. In the end reasonable matches were produced for areas in only fifteen of the twenty-one states. Creating good matches can be quite difficult, even at a fairly macro level. In this case, the matching problems undermined the evaluation.

The basis of matching should go beyond simple attributes and evaluators often try also to match on "behavior." Even with careful matching, an evaluation can have significant selection bias. For example, it could be that in an evaluation of the impact on health of providing water stand pipes in urban slums, the control areas have active neighborhood organizations that work with families on basic sanitary conditions. This could have an impact on the degree of improvement observed and bias the findings toward showing no impact of the program.

Another example is of an evaluation of a program to improve math scores in elementary schools. Schools could be carefully matched on math scores and the socioeconomic status of the neighborhoods, but significant differences could remain. Some schools could have active parent associations that work with struggling students. If the work of the associations is not taken into account, the evaluation results could be biased.

• Example of Matched Control Evaluation: Success for All

Success for All (SFA) is a program designed to help young students (ages six to eight) in low-performing schools improve their reading skills.[4] Success for All offers a comprehensive array of interventions, including tutoring and working with parents.

Evaluation Design. Evaluators examined one SFA school and one control school in Charleston, South Carolina. Schools were matched on neighborhood characteristics and standardized reading scores of the children. The cohorts of children—experiments and controls—were followed for three years.

Results. Regression analysis (described below) was used, and the unit of observation was the student. The regression controlled for prior test scores (i.e., the student's capability at the time the program began). This was important because it is possible that students who received the treatment had systematically done better in the past than had controls. The impact of the program could have been overestimated without controlling for this factor. Significant impacts were found for the first year (kindergarten) but not thereafter. Evaluators noted interpersonal difficulties between the SFA in-school facilitator and some teaching staff.

In other words, this program may have failed because it was not implemented as designed, due to personality conflicts and the opposition of some teachers (i.e., confounding factors). Also note that the selection of schools is an example of controlling by matching, whereas the analysis with multiple regression is an example of statistically controlling for other differences.

• *Equating Groups with Statistical Procedures: Key Points*

Matching using statistical techniques is now the primary approach for quasi-experimental designs. It employs *regression analysis.* Regression is a statistical tool used to establish the causal relationship between a dependent variable (the one being acted upon) and one or more independent or causal variables.

For example, say an analyst wants to establish the relationship between observed hourly wage rates and the number of years of workers' education in a particular city. For this analysis, the dependent variable is the wage rate and the independent variable is education. The analyst assembles data for a random sample of 200 workers on the number of years of education and their wage rates. Figure 12.1 shows the plot of these observations (dots), with wage rates on the vertical axis and years of schooling on the horizontal axis. The line *AB* is the fitted regression. The regression procedure is such that the placement of the line is the one that minimizes the sum of the squares of the distance between the dots and the line. (Hence, regression is often called "least squares regression.") Note that the line cuts the vertical axis at *a*. In other words, this is the wage that someone with no education receives in the city.

The complete estimated model is:

$$W = a + (b \times Ed)$$

Where

> W = wage
> a = constant (i.e., it is the value of W when all of the independent variables are equal to 0)
> b = slope of the regression line
> Ed = years of school completed

The slope of the regression line indicates the average value of one more year of education. In other words, it is the value *at the margin* of one more year of educa-

Figure 12.1   Wage Rates and Years of School

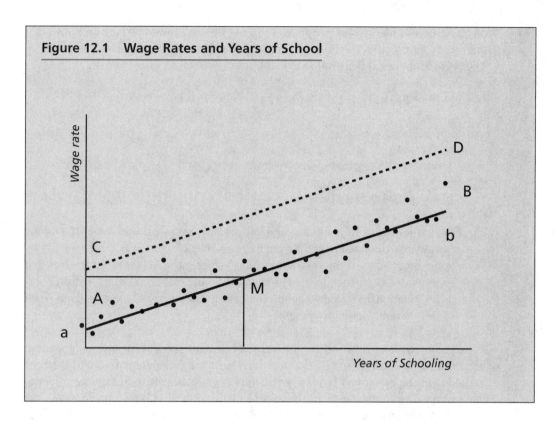

tion. An actual model of this sort could look like the following for a city in Germany:

$$W = \$2.55 + (\$1.11 \times Ed)$$

So the wage for someone with 8 years of education is $11.43; for someone with 14 years, $18.09. One property of the regression is that the regression line passes through the mean values of the dependent and independent variables, shown in Figure 12.1 as point M. There are statistical tests that determine if the relationship between the variables is statistically significant—that is, if it cannot be attributed to chance, at various levels of rigor (e.g., there is a 5 percent chance that the relationship is not valid, or a 1 percent chance). The widely used R^2 statistic, which has values between 0 and 1.0, indicates that the share of the variance in the dependent variable (W in our case) is explained by the variance in the independent variable *(Ed)*.

We can now take a somewhat more complicated example to illustrate the use of regression in identifying program impacts. This example is based on a program that provides computer training to unemployed persons to improve their wages. The regression model is as follows:

$$W = a + (b_1 \times Ed) + (b_2 \times Exp) + (b_3 \times A) + (b_4 \times Tr) + e$$

Where

> a = constant
> b = slope of the regression line
> Ed = years of school completed
> Exp = years of work experience
> A = age
> Tr = participation in a job training program; it takes on the value of 1 if the person participated in the program, otherwise its value is 0
> e = the error term of the regression (this is present to account for the fact that the model is stochastic, meaning that because we are dealing with a complex relationship among people in determining wages, there will be some idiosyncratic elements present)

In a multiple regression (i.e., a regression with more than one independent variable), the interpretation of the coefficients of the independent variables (the b variables in the equation) is very particular: the coefficient indicates the effect at the margin of a unit change in the independent variable *after controlling for the other variables included in the model*. In other words, the regression allows the analyst to identify the program impact.

So if the analyst estimated the model shown above for a validly drawn sample of program participants and controls three years after the training was completed, then the coefficient of *Tr* would indicate the increase in the wage rate due to participating in the program. Say the coefficient has the value of 83¢ (i.e., participants earn 83¢ more an hour on average because they participated). In Figure 12.1 this effect is shown by the shift upward in the line *AB* to its new position at *CD*.[5]

Critically, the validity of the estimate of the program impact requires that the model is correctly specified (i.e., that all the relevant variables are included in the model). If the analyst omits an important variable, then the program variable could be capturing some of the effects of the omitted variable. The bias in the estimated program impact could be positive or negative.

Types of Independent Variables in a Regression Model. Control variables are those that account for presumed initial differences that are important for outcomes and for adjustments for selection bias.

The treatment variable may be either "yes/no" or indicate variations in the intensity of the treatment. In our case, the variable "training" could be specified as:

1. A dummy variable: 1 = received training, 0 = no training. The coefficient then indicates the increase in the hourly wage rate associated with the program.
2. A continuous variable that indicates the depth of the program (e.g., number of hours or weeks of classes). The coefficient then indicates both a significant effect and whether more training promotes greater wage increases.

• *Example of Statistical Controls: Big Brothers–Big Sisters Program*

Big Brothers–Big Sisters is an intensive mentoring program designed to help troubled or disadvantaged youth stay in school and out of trouble.[6] The program assigns an adult mentor to each young person participating in the program. The mentor and youth spend time together regularly (two to four times per month for three to four hours). Both mentors and youths are screened for suitability for the program. The interaction is not school oriented and is intended to demonstrate the support and role model of a caring adult. The pair might participate in various activities, such as attending sports events, going to the movies, and eating together.

Evaluation Design. The evaluation examined programs from eight cities. Applicants to the program were randomly assigned to experiment and control groups. There were 1,138 young people enrolled in the study and their behavior was monitored over an eighteen-month period. The evaluation sought to determine whether the program contributed to improved educational outcomes and reduced illegal drug use and violent behavior among participants.

Regression analysis was used to control for variations in the situation at enrollment, agency differences, and length of participation in the program. Control variables—factors that could affect outcomes besides program participation—included age, gender, race, repeated a grade in school, victim of abuse, and family characteristics (income, receiving welfare, etc.). The coefficient for the dummy (0/1) treatment variable indicates if program was effective.

Results. Participants in the Big Brothers–Big Sisters program were 45 percent less likely to start using drugs, and 32 percent less likely to have hit someone. Participants also had stronger relationships with their parents than the control group. On the other hand, there were no significant differences between program participants and controls in the frequency with which they participated in organized social activities and culturally enriching activities.

• Reflexive Evaluation: Key Points

Reflexive evaluations use participants as their own controls by assessing them before and after the intervention. *Secular trends* can be a very serious confounding problem with this model. The longer the study period, the greater the chance that this problem could invalidate the results. Examples of secular trends:

1. Does providing health insurance improve the health of the elderly? The aging process could overwhelm any positive effect.
2. Programs to reduce fertility of women of childbearing ages. Propensity to have children declines with age independent of any interventions. In addition, there have been wide swings in fertility rates in industrialized countries over the past seventy years; the baby boomer–baby bust cycle following World War II is perhaps the best known. If one were trying to use a reflexive evaluation design to determine the impact of a contraceptive device any time during this period, the large secular trends would make this very difficult.

• Example of Reflexive Design: Contracting for Housing Maintenance Services in Moscow

This evaluation sought to assess the impact of competitive contracting on the quality of housing maintenance services in Moscow.[7]

Hypothesis: Private firms will perform better than municipal firms.

The basic question under analysis was whether private firms selected through a competitive process would do a better job maintaining municipal housing than the city companies that had enjoyed a monopoly on providing these services for many years.

Context. In 1993, 90 percent of Moscow's housing was managed by the city (a smaller share was city-owned due to housing privatization that began in 1991). City housing maintenance companies maintained the buildings with a complete absence of competition. Public spaces were very dirty, repairs requested by tenants received a slow response, the quality of work was poor, and payments were often required for service.

The pilot project included two competitions for the maintenance of approximately 7,000 units. Only private firms were eligible to compete. The first competition, held in March 1993, included 2,000 units in multifamily buildings that included all types of housing (e.g., five-story walkups built following Khrushchev-era designs, high-rise panel buildings, prewar multifamily buildings, high-quality brick buildings). The units were divided into three groups of about 700 units each for the competition. Three different firms won. The second competition, held in September 1993, included 5,000 elite units divided into four packets of units (about 1,250 each). The elite buildings had three distinguishing characteristics: they were occupied by families of high-ranking officials (the old nomenklatura); they were of high-quality brick construction; and they had been very well maintained. Two firms were each awarded two packets.

Reflexive Design Using Tenant Surveys. Housing conditions were evaluated using tenant surveys, with 300 households surveyed from the March competition and 379 households surveyed from the September competition. For both the March and the September buildings, the first survey was conducted two weeks before the private firm assumed responsibility for maintaining the buildings. For the March buildings, two later surveys were conducted—one in May and one in November. For the September buildings, only one later survey was done, in January 1994.

Importantly, interviewers returned to the same households in each survey round and almost always the same person in the household was interviewed. Thus, differences in perceptions and opinions among respondents were minimized.

Respondents were asked to categorize a specific condition for a specified period of time. So one question was, "How often in the last month were the lights in your hallway not working?" They were not directly asked about satisfaction, which can be subjective. (A chi-squared test was used throughout to test for significant differences in the response distributions between responses after the private firms began working and those at the baseline.)[8]

Results

March Buildings

Repairs. Tenant surveys indicated clear improvements in building repairs from March to May (baseline survey to first change survey). From May to November (first change survey to second) there was a slight decline in performance, but tenants still rated repairs higher than in the baseline survey.

Maintenance. Tenants noted broad improvements from March to May—significantly better in nine of eleven categories. The results from May to November were mixed, with reductions in service quality noted in six of the eleven categories. Some of the poor scores were in areas where the firm itself was not fully responsible, such as security systems.

During the May–November period the city was very slow in paying the company, and this may have led to a reduction of effort (at the time, annual inflation in Russia was about 800 percent, so delays were very costly).

September (Elite) Buildings

Repairs. Tenants reported that the private firms were better at completing repairs on the first visit; however, fewer respondents were fully satisfied with the repairs.

Maintenance. Tenants rated performance at least as good as city firms. Improvement was noted in eight of eleven categories; however, deterioration of services occurred in two important areas—the condition of entryways and working lights.

Note that the analysts monitored city policies and funding levels for housing maintenance over the period of the experiment. No changes occurred. So the analysts were confident that the results were not associated with general improvements in housing maintenance in the city (i.e., secular drift).

Evaluation Conclusions. Private firms did a somewhat better job maintaining buildings than city firms. Under the terms of the competition, the private firms had to bid a price less than the cost of services from the city firms. So by definition, private firms cost less. Initially private firms were about 10 percent cheaper.

The evaluation results were used to convince Moscow and other cities to select maintenance firms through competitions, and to encourage the federal housing ministry to adopt competitive procurement as a national policy. The actual decision to implement the policy rested with local governments. Some cities, like Moscow and Nizhni Novgorod, adopted competitive procurement for maintenance services, but the majority did not.

Which Impact Evaluation Design Is Best—Randomized or Quasi-Experimental?

A fundamental question is whether one obtains the same results from impact evaluations done with experimental and quasi-experimental designs. A modest number of studies compare the results from randomized experiments with those with matched and statistical techniques. Often the results differ. The presumption is that the results obtained from those with an experimental design are more accurate. The following section describes the conflicting results on one policy question obtained over a number of years from a large number of studies.

• Comparison of Methodologies: Impact of Class Size on School Achievement

Reducing class size is a strategy to improve student learning (as measured by scores on standardized tests). The notion is that with fewer students in each classroom, teachers are better able to target their instruction to student needs. Dozens of studies using constructed controls (comparison schools) have yielded mixed results. The lack of consistent results from many evaluations has raised questions about the wisdom of devoting additional funds to smaller class sizes (an expensive intervention because it requires hiring additional teachers) rather than, for example, changing the curriculum to emphasize acquisition of basic skills in the early school years.

This section reports the findings of econometric studies of class size and a randomized study.

A Review of Econometric Studies on Class Size.[9] By way of context, pupil teacher ratios fell from 27:1 to 17:1 between 1950 and 1995, with no improvement in student performance. However, pupil-teacher ratios do not necessarily indicate smaller classes, because even though there are more teachers, various nonteaching assignments may result in fewer classroom teachers or less time in the classroom for each teacher. In addition, student populations have changed and students with special needs (including learning disabilities and other challenges) have higher teacher-student ratios—which can skew the teacher-student ratio while saying little about the academic achievement of the mainstream student population.

By 1997, 277 econometric studies had analyzed the relation between class size and student achievement. The studies used both school-level and individual student-level data. Statistical measures controlled for the influence of family income and other inputs to education. The results of these studies are highly inconsistent. Only 28 percent produced statistically significant results for class size. Of these, slightly more than half the studies found a positive effect on learning and 46 percent found a negative effect.

The most significant results came from studies that analyzed test scores for individual students. In addition, some studies restricted their samples to a single state to control for differences in state policies, though of these 83 percent reported insignificant findings.

Random Assessment: Tennessee STAR Project.[10] The Student/Teacher Achievement Ratio (STAR) project was an assessment of the impact of smaller class sizes mandated and funded by a state law in Tennessee in the southern United States. The evaluation was an experimental design with random assignment of students and teachers to various learning situations. Schools had to volunteer to participate and had to be large enough to have all three types of "study situations" present (i.e., small schools were excluded).

STAR design. The study was longitudinal (followed the same students over a period of time). Both students and teachers were randomly assigned to three types of classes:

- Small classes: 13–17 students.
- Regular-sized classes: 22–25 students.
- Regular classes with a full-time teacher aide.

After the initial assignment, students were to stay in the same type of class for four years.

Over the four years, 11,600 students from 80 schools participated. Some "noise" occurred from a limited amount of shifting between class sizes, mostly because of student discipline problems or in response to parents' demands for children to be placed in smaller classes. These changes affected about 10 percent of the sample.

Measuring performance. Changes in student achievement were measured using the annual reading and math exams offered each spring (these standardized tests included the Stanford Achievement test [kindergarten through grade three] and the Tennessee Basic Skills First test [grades one through three]).

Analysis. Performance was analyzed as the differences each year among groups and the change in achievement over time for each group. Regression analysis was used to control certain student and teacher characteristics. For students, these factors included race, ethnicity, and receipt of free lunch (a measure of poverty). Teacher characteristics included race, advanced degree, and years of experience.

Results. Table 12.2 summarizes the basic results of the STAR program. The first three rows are designed to show that students in different class configurations were similar at the start (the minor differences indicated in the table are not statistically significant). Student characteristics include the proportion of students receiving free lunch (a measure of poverty, since this is a means-tested program), race (because white and Asian students typically receive better scores than do black children), and age (a potential indicator of the child's maturity and skill level). The percentile score indicates student achievement as measured by the kindergarten test (that is, after one year in the program). The difference in student achievement is statistically significant, with students in smaller classrooms scoring approximately four percentage points higher. In later years, differences in scores increased by about one percentage point per year.

Regression analysis controlled for differences among classes in several potentially important variables and did not affect the estimate of the impact of class size. Variables included in the model: sex of student, free lunch, white teacher, teacher experience, and teacher with master's degree. Most of these variables are significant, but the random assignment succeeded in controlling for their impact on mean differences in achievement with class size.

Table 12.2   STAR Program: Basic Results

Variable	Class Size		
	Small Class	Regular Class	Regular with Aide
Free lunch (%)	0.47	0.48	0.50
White/Asian (%)	0.68	0.67	0.66
Age at start (years)	5.44	5.43	5.42
Percentile score in kindergarten	54.7	49.9	50.0

• *The Debate Continues*

In spite of the positive findings of the STAR evaluation, the debate over whether class size is an effective intervention continues. Critics raise several questions about the methodology of the evaluation:[11]

- The treatment groups had high attrition rates and were replaced by new students. (By the fourth year, only 48 percent of those who started in kindergarten were left in the small-class group. While replacements were in principle randomly assigned, the effects of such large-scale additions are not known. There was also significant [10 percent] shifting among the treatment groups.)
- Groups were randomly assigned; however, there was no baseline assessment of students when they entered the program.
- Schools were not randomly selected. Schools had to volunteer (self-select), and only large schools were eligible to participate.
- The process of teacher assignment was not clear.

Hence the effect of class size on academic performance remains a topic of further analysis, although the STAR Project provides the best information to date.

• *Which Is the Best Methodological Approach?*

Table 12.3 summarizes some of the main strengths and weakness of each methodological approach. Selecting a design strategy depends heavily on the characteristics of the program or policy being studied and the resources and time available.

One point that is clear from numerous recent "replication studies" is that only the experimental approach can eliminate selection bias in the control group, and

Table 12.3   Summary of Strengths and Weaknesses of Design Strategies

Design Strategy	Strengths	Weaknesses
Randomized controls	Thought to be most objective for large clinical trials	Time consuming Costly Does not control for differences prior to group assignment
Quasi-experimental controls		
Matched controls	Good for small number of subjects (such as matching schools or cities)	Difficult to obtain accurate matches
Statistically equated controls	Inexpensive Short time frame Easy for others to replicate or identify potential problems of the analysis/conclusion Can help to eliminate selection bias	Results can be highly dependent on how the model is set up and what methods were used
Reflexive controls	Because participants act as their own controls, avoids some of the selection problems of random or matched controls	Especially vulnerable to secular drift

that the larger the differences between controls and those in the treatment group, the harder it is for statistical procedures to work well.[12] In training programs, for example, there is strong self-selection among those who want to participate versus those who do not. To have a valid impact evaluation is likely to require that the controls be formed from persons who applied for the training program and were then assigned to the control group rather than a sample of unemployed persons in general.[13] This could be done either through random assignment or by forming the control group from those who apply after all slots in the program have been awarded.

Yet the experimental approach is also limited in several ways:

- It fails to compare the intervention's services to no services at all (its comparison is to what else people might receive).
- Experiments often create more capacity in other programs, and controls get more services than they would have without the experiment.
- Random assignment does not control for differences before the assignment,

such as intake procedures or, as in the example above, prior student achievement levels.

- In the case of entitlement programs, it may not be possible to form a valid control group.

In short, there is no simple rule on what is the best method for impact evaluations. A reasonable rule of thumb is that random assignment is preferred. If that is not possible, then work hard to make members of the experimental and control groups as similar as possible in terms of their characteristics before participation in the program and their general experiences after participation.

Chapter Summary

Impact evaluation assesses what results can be attributed to a specific intervention. Its key attribute is the creation of treatment and control groups. Control groups are used to determine how much of the result is actually due to the program.

Among several different design strategies are randomly assigned controls and quasi-experimental methodologies. With randomized controls, participants are assigned to either an experimental or control group on a random basis and the intervention is withheld from the control group. The quasi-experimental methods include match-constructed controls, statistically equated controls, and reflexive controls. Match-constructed controls intentionally pair experimental and control groups based on similar characteristics (such as income, race, education level,

See Exercise 12.1: Designing an Impact Evaluation on page 314.

The task in this exercise is to make several basic methodological decisions on the design of an impact evaluation for a neighborhood improvement program.

See Exercise 12.2: Designing an Impact Evaluation for a Job Search and Income Support Program on page 315.

The task in this exercise is to answer several multiple-choice questions on the proper methodology for this evaluation.

etc.). Statistically equated controls go further by using regression analysis to control for any differences between subjects. And reflexive controls use the participants before and after the intervention, with the individual essentially acting as its own control.

Impact evaluations are clearly beyond the need or capacity of most small programs, which can generally obtain the feedback they need from monitoring, performance measurement, and process evaluation. However, for major programs and policies, impact evaluations are absolutely essential for assessing the effects of those interventions. Without impact evaluation, it is impossible to know how many unemployed persons would have found jobs without assistance or how many persons would have recovered without costly treatments. Such information helps policymakers to target resources to interventions that have the greatest impact on the public good.

Exercise 12.1: Designing an Impact Evaluation

Instructions and Background. Design an impact evaluation for a neighborhood improvement program in a city in the Philippines. The program provides loans to low- and moderate-income owners of single-family units to fund improvements to the dwelling. Housing is very simple and the poorest families live in units with dirt floors, and walls and roofs made of temporary materials. Better-off families have homes constructed with permanent materials. The interest rate on the loans is about one-half of the rates charged for similar loans by commercial banks.

The evaluation seeks to answer the following questions:

1. Does the loan program result in better housing for participants over a one- to two-year period?
2. Is better housing quality for participants versus nonparticipants sustained over four to five years? This question is asked to determine whether the loan program only makes a difference in the timing of the improvements but not in their ultimate realization.

Evaluation Design. Answer the following four questions:

1. What should be used as outcome indicators? Options include: physical conditions of the housing or changes in property values. Explain your reason for selecting the indicator.
2. What is the appropriate unit of analysis—the neighborhood or the individual dwelling unit? Why?
3. What characteristics should be taken into account in selecting controls?
4. What would the estimated regression model look like? Define the independent and dependent variables.

**Exercise 12.2: Designing an Impact Evaluation
for a Job Search and Income Support Program**

Read the description of this job search and income support program, and then answer the questions that follow.

Program/Evaluation Description
Program objective. To help participants obtain permanent jobs.

Eligibility. Eligibility is limited based on family composition and household income. An eligible family is defined as a household that (a) includes at least one child under sixteen as well as at least one able-bodied, temporarily unemployed adult; and (b) has a total per capita household income of less than 60 percent of the per capita subsistence minimum.

Program cash benefits. Participants receive a cash benefit for their time in the program, usually nine months, including after they have found a job. After they have a job, the benefit is reduced by 75 percent of each euro earned, after the first 200 euros, which are not counted as program income. This structure is seen as a strong incentive for quickly finding a job. According to program regulations, the amount of a family's benefit is dependent upon two main variables, family size and income.

Employment services and other requirements. While the monetary benefit is given only once per quarter, there are ongoing requirements for both the client and the caseworker. Once determined eligible for the program, recipients complete an individual social assistance plan under the guidance of caseworkers. As part of this plan, all able-bodied adults in recipient households are required to participate in employment activities sponsored by the local employment office in order to improve their chance of finding and maintaining employment; these include formal training programs. Not all participants receive training or other services from the employment center.

Questions

1. Some impact evaluations need a control group; others use a reflexive method in which participants act as their own controls. What would you recommend for this evaluation? (circle one answer)
   A. Use of the reflexive design—that is, no control group—so one would compare the status of program participants before and after their participation in the program.
   B. Use a random sample of unemployed workers.

C. Use a sample of unemployed persons who applied for the program but could not participate because the program did not have enough resources to include them.

If you answered "A," go to Question 2.

If you answered, "B," go to Question 1.1.

If you answered, "C," go to Question 1.2.

1.1. (If you answered "B" to Question 1.) What was your reason? (circle one)

A. The sample would represent all unemployed persons, not just a subset.

B. They could be easily found through the employment office.

Go to question 2.

1.2. (If you answered "C" to Question 1.) What was the basis for the choice? (circle one)

A. These persons are easily identified as unemployed, so it would be easier than constructing a random sample.

B. These persons have demonstrated a similar motivation to participate as have those in the program.

2. What indicators of program impact would you select? (circle not more than two)

A. Changes in work effort of other members of the household.

B. Finding a job.

C. Finding and keeping a job for at least a particular number of months.

D. Changes in the household's standard of living.

E. Hourly earnings of the participant.

3. In determining outcomes, which of the following factors would be the most important to control for? (circle not more than four)

A. Age.

B. Place of birth.

C. Education level.

D. Worker expressed desire to move to another city.

E. Years and type of work experience.

F. Number of children.

G. Dresses well and makes a good impression.

H. Received training in the program.

4. In a regression model to estimate the impact of the program, what variable do you think would best capture the impact of the program (i.e., independent variable)? (circle one)

A. How many months it took the person to find the job.

B. A 0/1 variable indicating the persons had received training.

C. A simple 0/1 variable for participation in the program.

D. The number of months the person received training.

CHAPTER 13

Benefit-Cost Evaluation

Benefit-cost evaluation and cost-effectiveness analysis are methods to evaluate the efficiency of various policy options. Benefit-cost evaluation determines what action or what level of action will achieve the greatest net economic benefit. It assigns a monetary value to each program expense and benefit, and a program is deemed positive when benefits outweigh costs. Benefit-cost evaluation can assist in public decisionmaking in situations such as determining whether and what type of capital investments to make—for example, whether to develop a high-speed rail system or invest in a new sports stadium. Benefit-cost evaluation is also called cost-benefit analysis, but we use the former term to stress the public benefit.

Cost-effectiveness analysis assesses which option best achieves a specific objective at the least or most effective cost. For example, determining the most effective strategy to reduce a particular type of pollution by a set amount, or selecting among various strategies to reduce the spread of HIV by a certain rate. Evaluators use cost-effectiveness when they cannot confidently assign a monetary value to a program benefit, such as the value of saving or extending a life.

This chapter outlines how to conduct a benefit-cost evaluation, including how to specify costs and benefits and how to account for costs and benefits that occur at different times. We also describe cost-effectiveness analysis, including how to measure marginal values (that is, the difference among the impacts of the various alternatives) and the importance of using good data and presenting all options fairly.

It is important to examine the costs and outcomes of government actions. However, cost is rarely the only criterion in government decisionmaking. These evaluation methods are most useful when used with other analytical and political decisionmaking processes. The chapter describes the limitations of each method.

Definitions

Benefit-cost evaluation is a set of practical, systematic procedures that program evaluators use to assign monetary values to all costs and benefits of a program. Benefit-cost evaluation defines an efficient program as one where aggregate benefits exceed aggregate costs: benefits ÷ costs > 1.0. The simplicity of the benefit-cost ratio is very attractive to decisionmakers because it provides a simple standard and the ability to compare projects explicitly. Often benefit-cost evaluation assesses or compares major capital projects, for which costs are significant and most benefits are tangible. The procedure, however, is challenging, because the analyst must assign monetary values to all costs and benefits. Deciding on what factors to include and what values to assign costs and benefits makes this a more subjective method than it appears.

Benefit-cost evaluation was popular in the 1970s and 1980s, but is less so now. This reflects both the difficult measurement issues involved and a loss of confidence in studies that distort results (as described later).

Evaluators use cost-effectiveness analysis when monetary values do not capture program benefits but the program's objectives are clear and singular or sufficiently related so that the relationship between objectives is evident. Examples of programs for which it is difficult to assign monetary values are initiatives that aim to improve health or prolong life. In both cases it is very difficult to place a reliable monetary value on an improvement—for example, extending by a year the life of an elderly person with a certain type of cancer. However, it is possible to determine with some precision the cost of the additional life-year achieved with different technologies. Cost-effectiveness analysis can compare several alternative programs or approaches and identify the most effective or least costly.

Benefit-Cost Evaluation

• *The Basics*

Table 13.1 presents a basic benefit-cost evaluation for a project to replace and maintain a city's fleet of buses. The costs are the capital expenditures (to purchase the buses), maintenance, and operations. These costs fall fairly evenly over the three- and six-year term, with capital costs declining somewhat while operating expenses slowly rise. Total project costs for the first phase are $3.58 million. There is a single benefits figure that includes the value to commuters of improved bus service. Benefits begin to accrue from year one. Values are adjusted to compare costs and benefits occurring over time. Note that with many capital projects, especially those that involve construction, costs accrue early in the project life and benefits occur only later. This standard pattern has a powerful influence on project assessments that value benefits and costs from today's perspective, as described below.

Box 13.1   Net Present Value

The formula for calculating net present value (NPV)—total discounted benefits of a project minus total discounted costs—is:

$$NPV = (B - C)^{y1} + [(B - C)^{y2} \div (1 + r)] + [(B - C)^{y3} \div (1 + r)^2] + [(B - C)^{y4} \div (1 + r)^3] \ldots$$

Where

B = benefits
C = costs
y = year
r = discount rate or real rate of return

Apply this formula to benefits and costs for each of the project years to determine the net present value. The effect of the discount rate grows with each additional year. In the first year, the discount rate (r) is not applied. Calculate the second year as: benefits minus costs, divided by 1 plus the discount rate. Year three is: benefits minus costs, divided by the square of 1 plus the discount rate (the latter quantity is squared to reflect two years of interest payments). Clearly, values further in the future receive sharply reduced values when converted to NPVs. See Table 13.1 for an example using actual figures. (Most spreadsheet programs and scientific calculators have a net present value function.)

This project, like most, has benefits realized and costs incurred over several years. The analyst needs some way to take into account the difference in the time distribution of benefits and costs. Therefore, to determine whether this is an effective project to pursue, one discounts costs and benefits to obtain present values.

The concept of discounting attempts to standardize the value of the use of money now or in the future. Benefits in the future are worth less than the same benefits today. So someone who wants to purchase a new car would rather do so today than wait two years; he or she prefers to enjoy the services now. Postponing the car purchase may become attractive if interest rates are sufficiently high to induce saving the money. The rational person adjusts his or her consumption until today's saving is just balanced by the interest rate reward of doing that much saving.[1]

Box 13.1 provides a fuller explanation of the net present value, including the formula for its calculation.

A discount rate reflects the cost of waiting for benefits from publicly funded projects. Selecting an appropriate discount rate can be difficult, and changes in the discount rate can determine whether a program meets the benefit-cost threshold. Table 13.1 shows the benefits and costs for a bus replacement program over two successive three-year periods. So, for example, in the second year the company incurs costs of $1.2 million for bus purchase and maintenance but has benefits of only $0.9 million. In terms of present values, the net benefit is –$0.28 million at a 5 percent discount rate and –$0.27 million at a 10 percent discount rate. In this

Table 13.1   Benefit-Cost Evaluation: Bus Fleet Replacement (in $ thousands)

Year	Costs			Benefits	Net Benefits	Present Value Benefits-Costs at 5%	Present Value Benefits-Costs at 10%
	Capital	Maintenance and Operations	Total				
Phase 1: 70 buses							
1	1,000	100	1,100	800	–300	–300	–300
2	1,000	200	1,200	900	–300	–286	–273
3	800	280	1,280	1,100	–180	–163	–149
Total/NPV	2,800	580	3,580	2,800	–780	–749	–721
Phase 2: 40 buses (data for Phase 2 investments only)							
4	800	80	880	800	–80	–80	–80
5	800	160	960	900	–60	–57	–55
6	400	200	600	1,000	400	363	331
Total/NPV	2,000	440	2,440	2,700	260	226	196

case, the NPV for the project is not terribly sensitive to the discount rate. Indeed, at either a 5 or 10 percent discount rate the project has a negative benefit-cost ratio for the first five years and a large positive value only in the sixth.[2]

Because of the uncertainty about the appropriate discount rate, governments often specify the rate for assessing projects. A reasonable value is the government's cost of long-term money (that is, the cost or interest rate on bonds of ten or more years).[3] In the example provided in Table 13.1, the NPV is fairly insensitive to the discount rate. However, the discount rate will generally make a significant difference on project feasibility ($B \div C > 1.0$) when there is a large difference in the time profile for benefits and costs.

Total Net Benefits vs. Marginal Net Benefits. Policymakers frequently confront the question of whether to continue a program. In making this decision, policymakers should only consider the marginal net benefits—that is, the value of continuing the program for the coming year or years. At this point, looking at the total net benefit is irrelevant.

Continuing with the previous example, policymakers must decide whether to launch the second phase of the bus replacement program. They will make their decision in the third year, so the fourth year is the first future year. The second half of Table 13.1 presents the costs and benefits for the fourth through sixth project years.

Too often policymakers argue that "we have invested so much in the project already that we cannot quit now." This is not an economist's logic and has led to fantastic money pits where public funds continue to flow into projects that have no marginal value. *Sunk costs* refer to all previously incurred expenditures and have no bearing on the future desirability of the project. The question is: At the margin, is it wise to continue the program?

In the example in Table 13.1, clearly the decision should be to proceed with years four to six. The aggregate benefits exceed aggregate costs over the period and the positive benefit-cost ratio is insensitive to the discount rate used.

• Framework for Analysis

Benefit-cost evaluation requires identifying all benefits, costs, and transfers and then assigning a monetary value to them. Transfers involve payments from one person or business to another without any net increase in income. (See the description of transfers later in this section.) Correctly accounting for these factors and assigning an appropriate monetary value can be challenging and, if done poorly, highly subjective.

Table 13.2 presents a benefit-cost framework for a slum clearance and housing relocation project. This project aims to demolish substandard and dangerous housing, relocate residents to decent housing, and prepare the cleared lots for resale. The project will run for ten years and the enabling legislation includes annual budget estimates and specific annual targets for the square meters of housing demolished. The table includes several categories of costs and benefits that are discussed below.

Tangible vs. Intangible.   Tangible benefits and costs convert easily to monetary values. Intangible benefits and costs are those for which you cannot or choose not to assign an explicit price (nonmeasurable). Examples of tangible benefits from Table 13.2 include the improved housing and neighborhood conditions for families relocated to decent housing. Tangible costs are equally obvious, the cost of new housing and the cost of destroying the old units. The intangible benefits include qualities that are difficult to measure, such as the improved quality of life for former slum dwellers or the improved appearance of the city. Intangible costs might include the dislocation of extended families and social networks. Correctly identifying all of these factors is a very demanding task. (Published works provide guidance on measuring most benefits and costs.)

Direct vs. Indirect.   Direct benefits and costs relate to the primary objectives of

Table 13.2 Benefit-Cost Framework for Slum Clearance/Housing Relocation Project

Type of benefit/cost	Indicator/Nature of Benefits/Costs	Value/Cost Calculation	Assumptions
Benefits			
Direct			
Tangible	Families in new housing	Value of new units occupied by relocated families at the time of initial occupancy minus the value of prior units	
	Substandard/dangerous housing demolished	Value of cleared land (resale price and reduction in emergency service expenditures)	
Intangible	Improved quality of life/family life	NA	
Indirect			
Tangible	Improved city appearance/conditions	Property values and tax increases of blocks without blighted housing (excluding housing sites)	Do property values/ taxes reflect improvements?
	New jobs created	Wages earned	
	Reduced crime rates	Cost avoided: police investigations, court costs, prison costs; value of stolen goods	
Intangible	Improved demographic conditions	NA	
	Reduced mental and physical paid and suffering on the part of crime victims	NA	
Costs			
Direct			
Tangible	Housing construction	Cost for housing construction	
	Housing demolition	Total demolition cost	
	Land acquisition	Cost of land acquisition	
	Improved infrastructure to the area	Cost of any related infrastructure improvements	
	City's management of project	Cost of city administration of the project	

(continues)

Table 13.2   Continued

Type of benefit/cost	Indicator/Nature of Benefits/Costs	Value/Cost Calculation	Assumptions
Intangible	Displacing communities/ families (through scattered relocation)	NA	
Indirect			
Tangible	Administrative overhead of government	Cost of city administrative overhead	
Intangible			
Transfers			
	Taxes to support budget project	Budget allocation	

Source: Table framework from James Edwin Kee, "Benefit-Cost Analysis in Program Evaluation," in Joseph S. Wholey, Harry P. Hatry, and Kathryn E. Newcomer, eds., *Handbook of Practical Program Evaluation* (San Francisco: Josey-Bass, 1994), p. 465.

the project. Indirect or secondary benefits and costs are by-products, multipliers, spillovers, or investment effects of the project. Direct benefits and costs are all the basic items you would normally include (such as benefits and costs of new housing construction).

Table 13.2 lists indirect benefits as new jobs created, improved city appearance, and reduced crime rates. Indirect costs include the city's general administrative costs. Administrative costs should reflect not just the cost of the frontline office in managing the project (a direct cost item) but also the time of higher-level administrators.

For another example of indirect or secondary benefits and costs, consider a government road construction project. The primary benefits are the reduction in transportation costs (time and fuel savings) for individuals and firms. Secondary benefits are the increase in profits of nearby hotels, restaurants, and other businesses. The new road could lead to economic development impacts. The cost side includes not only the cost of building the road but also the secondary costs associated with the loss of profit of businesses that were along the old road, assuming there was one.

Assigning items in the direct versus indirect and tangible versus intangible categories requires a certain amount of judgment. However, correct categorization is not the most important part of the exercise. Most important is to ensure that all benefits and costs are included in the analysis. Listing any assumptions made about the categorization or assignment of values helps readers to evaluate the objectivity of those decisions.

Types of Costs. A nother perspective on costs is how they occur over the life of a project. Note that costs in most of the categories reviewed above (such as direct and indirect costs) can be disaggregated in terms of how they arise over a project's life. This kind of breakdown is important in capturing all relevant costs. These kinds of costs include:

- *Onetime, fixed, or up-front costs.* Research and development, planning.
- *Investment costs.* Land, buildings and facilities, equipment and vehicles.
- *Recurring costs.* Operations and maintenance.

Table 13.1 lists program costs using several of these categories (i.e., capital or investment costs and operations and maintenance costs). The costs outlined for the slum clearance project in Table 13.2 could be disaggregated in this way.

Two other costs, similar but slightly different from those just listed, are noteworthy:

- *Compliance costs.* Time for citizens to fill out forms, cost to firms to comply with regulations.
- *Mitigation costs.* Measures to prevent a cost to others (e.g., pollution control equipment).

An example of a mitigation cost is the expense required to relocate households in a contaminated area to prevent them from developing cancer.

Measuring Costs in Government Programs: Selected Issues. Measuring costs for government programs is somewhat more complicated than that for private firms. Market prices for government activities are often unclear and government must balance transfer issues so costs do not unreasonably burden specific groups.

Indirect costs should include part of the direct and administrative costs of an organization that are difficult to allocate to individual activities. This is usually a factor for organizations running multiple programs or activities. Examples include rent, vehicles, the accounting department, and other overhead expenses.

Certain costs of government projects are borne mostly by the private sector, such as costs of water or air pollution control (compliance costs). These expenses should be included in total costs.

Benefit-cost evaluations should reflect *interest costs*. If the government is running a deficit, the analyst should assume that this is a marginal project (i.e., that the government will have to borrow the funds to execute it).

Common costs are difficult to allocate. Consider, for example, a dam constructed for multiple purposes: water supply, irrigation, electricity, and recreation. If the analyst wants to compute a benefit-cost ratio for each purpose, how should the costs be allocated across purposes? There are rules devised for this, but they are in fact quite arbitrary except for elements that are clearly distinct (e.g., turbines for electricity production).

Shadow prices reflect the true economic costs to society of the resources invested and the true economic benefits of the outputs produced. If one were analyzing the benefits of a housing program, one clear benefit would be the value of the months of housing services provided to families awarded the new units. If the units rent at controlled rents, then the controlled rent would not reflect the actual value of the services. In this case, the analyst would use the shadow price of these services (i.e., the rents paid in the market for similar units).

Transfers. Transfers are different from real benefits and costs. Transfers involve payments from one person or business to another without any net increase in income—they are not payments for goods or services. For example, a welfare payment is a transfer from one person (a taxpayer) to another (the welfare recipient). From society's perspective, there is no net change in income. There is a change in income distribution, but benefit-cost evaluation does not account for this.

The role of transfers depends on the perspective considered—individual versus society. From the perspective of the individuals involved, taxes and payments definitely have an impact on welfare. From society's perspective, there is no net change from transfers.

Take an example of a government investment, such as the construction of a dam that alters agricultural productivity. Farmers in some areas will have higher productivity and hence higher incomes; but if the demand for agricultural products is relatively price-inelastic, then the income of other farmers will fall as surplus produce comes to the market. From society's perspective, this is a transfer—income-losing farmers transfer income to income-gaining farmers. In this case, at least some of the increased farmer income from dam construction is a transfer, not a benefit. This illustrates that net benefits can be very demanding to measure for many investments.

Benefit-cost evaluation must have a defined perspective—person, city/region, or nation. It is simply not possible to assign benefits and costs from the perspective of multiple stakeholders. Most benefit-cost evaluations have a particular perspective or client in mind. For example, a city considering a new water treatment facility might conduct a benefit-cost evaluation. From the city's perspective, costs imposed by its action on another jurisdiction would not be included.

> *See Exercise 13.1: Allocating Costs for a*
> *Youth Orchestra Program on page 343.*
>
> The task in this exercise is to allocate costs and identify transfers for an educational program.

> *See Exercise 13.2: Understanding*
> *Benefit and Cost Categories on page 345.*
>
> The task in this exercise is to identify the correct benefits and costs for a Romanian dam construction project. Costs and benefits have been assigned under the categories of direct, indirect, tangible, and intangible. Misassigned costs and benefits, and examples of transfers, need to be identified.

• *Measuring Benefits*

Measuring benefits can be more challenging than measuring costs, because monetary values are not always obvious. These decisions can be guided by several basic economic theories and standard indicators used to measure benefits. Of course, the same broad economic framework underpins measurement of both costs and benefits, but the economic assumptions are more prominent with benefits.

Economic Assumptions. We mention only a few of the more important economic concepts here. Even these brief notes, however, should make clear that benefit-cost evaluation requires very strong conditions for the results to be strictly valid.

A state of *consumers in equilibrium* requires that the price paid equals the marginal utility for the good or service. That is, the price a citizen pays for bus transportation is equal to their need or value of the ride. In a benefit-cost evaluation, the benefit of bus transportation is often estimated as the price per ride.

A second important concept is the *Pareto criterion,* wherein gains to the beneficiaries are more than great enough in principle to compensate for the losses or costs to others. If the gains are not sufficient to compensate for the losses to others, the change is not Pareto-optimal. For example, if the cost of purchasing food for low-income people costs taxpayers a particular amount, yet the recipient households value the food at less than this amount (reselling the food at a discount and using the cash for other needs), the transfer is not Pareto-optimal.

Willingness to pay is the amount of money an individual would pay to make a particular change in his or her circumstances. This can be a positive amount—the person purchases more of a service he or she wants—or a negative amount. It is negative when the person accepts a payment to give up some favorable position. As one can readily imagine, this concept is closely related to the meeting of the Pareto criterion.[4]

Measurement in practice. There are two closely related approaches to actually measuring benefits, both resting on the same conceptual underpinning. One is to use a program's *estimated impact* as determined by an impact evaluation. An example could be the additional lifetime earnings and other gains resulting from a training program. If the impact evaluation takes a broad view of the kinds of impacts a program could have, then this approach has genuine merit. In the example just given, the analysts would have to consider benefits beyond just higher wages to get a full picture of benefits. The Job Corps program example later in the chapter includes multiple benefits.

Willingness to pay, discussed just above, is the other major approach to measuring benefits. It rests on the idea that market valuation is the most direct and objective measure of a benefit. For example, the benefit of flood protection to agricultural land subject to flooding is the increment in land values associated with this protection. If an impact evaluation has used market valuations of benefits, it will arrive at the same values as a willingness to pay analysis. In the flood protection example, the impact evaluation seeks to value the impact of providing flood protection to the affected land. One way to do this is to rely on market information—observed increases in the price per acre that buyers are willing to pay for the now-protected land. In other words, willingness to pay for the improved land.

Measuring willingness to pay can be accomplished in two ways:

1. It can be based on observed behavior, such as measuring the value of avoiding risk through the wage differential between hazardous and nonhazardous work or the willingness to pay for protection, such as automobile air bags. In these cases the analyst can observe actual differences—differences in hourly wage rates and the cost of crash protection (the cost of the air bag times the probability of an injury-causing accident gives the value the person places on avoiding an injury).

2. It can involve surveys that ask people how much they would be willing to pay for a service or to avoid a problem. Such surveys are obviously much less reliable than observed behavior. The main problem is that the respondent often has an incentive to manipulate the answer. If the person really wants the service (e.g., more reliable water service), they may quote a higher price than they are willing to pay if they think that this will influence the decision to provide services. On the other hand, the person may anticipate

service improvements and name a low price with the goal of ensuring a low cost. Such surveys are typically employed only when there are no actual market transactions to observe, as when the government is considering providing a new service, such as water stand pipes in an urban slum in a tropical, developing country.

Special Topics in Benefit Measurement

Valuing a life.   Valuing the benefit of lives saved presents special issues. Lives saved are clearly tangible benefits—and important results of public interventions—yet assigning a monetary value to a life presents several challenges. Evaluators generally generate estimates of the value of a life based on lost earnings or willingness to pay to avoid risk.

A review of numerous studies shows that, on average, people in high-income nations in the early 1990s were willing to pay $3–7 for each reduction of one in a million in the risk of death. Taking the midvalue of $5 and applying this to the million total chances of death just noted, the aggregate willingness to pay or value of a life is $5 million.[5] The value of human life (based on workers' willingness to accept risk) varies considerably among nations, with the Japanese valuing a life at about $10 million, the United States at $7 million, Britain at roughly $4 million, and South Korea at approximately $1 million.[6]

Or to use an example from an earlier period when people paid extra to have a seat belt in their car, drivers made the decision based on the cost of the belt and installation compared to the benefit, avoidance of the probability of having an accident, and the average cost of an accident in terms of bodily injury.

Willingness to pay for risk reduction appears approximately proportional to income. Whether it depends on age or life expectancy is an open question.

An alternative method for valuing a life is to use discounted future earnings to value the risk of death. This is an older technique since discredited, because it does not apply the willingness-to-pay principle. It also attempts to value the full transition between life and death rather than the small changes in risk that people actually face as a result of public policies. Nevertheless, some analysts used this method to value the lives lost in the 2001 World Trade Center terrorist attacks for purposes of determining payments to surviving family members.

Cost avoidance.   Benefits can be measured by costs avoided. For example, the value of a burglary prevented is difficult to assess. One might be able to determine it through examining the willingness to pay for various kinds of additional home protection. An alternative approach is to use dollars saved from the avoidance of burglaries (police searching and holding an offender, and value of goods stolen). Or, for an environmental improvement, the value is often determined as the cost of achieving the same result. So the value of cleaner water is the investment that industry would have to make to cut toxic discharges into a river.

Time saved. The measure of time saved assesses benefits in traffic improvement studies and in evaluating program administration. For example, an administrative reform in Arzamas, Russia, consolidated all public benefits so that poor families needed only to fill out one form at a convenient location. This change resulted in significant time savings for both staff and clients.

Wage rates or proxies are often used to value time savings. Wage rates are not terribly accurate, because the wage rate is based on the assumption that persons work to the point that leisure is more valuable than work. However, the problem is that most people cannot actually vary their hours to suit their preferences. So the wage rate may overstate or understate the value they place on one more hour of work.

Estimating time savings is even more challenging for those who do not receive wages. For example, what is the value of the housewife's time? Options are to assign values based on the hourly wage of others with similar education or based on what the housewife might pay for someone else to clean her home. Clearly, assumptions inform time valuations. Importantly, many past benefit-cost studies have established routines for measurement that provide guidelines for such problems.

Willingness to Pay for Good Schools.[7] Here is an additional example of the willingness-to-pay concept. Local governments operate primary schools in the United States and serve children living in the community surrounding each school. Significant quality differences exist among school districts, as indicated by test scores, the share of students going to college, and the quality of the colleges students attend. Local property taxes are a primary funding source for public schools. Because there are many separate towns in most US metropolitan areas, families can select the package of taxes and services that maximizes their utility and move there. Two-thirds of US families own their homes. Some parents are willing to pay extra for a home in order for their children to attend better schools. If it is systematic, this should be reflected in house prices.

Evaluation design. This study uses a basic regression model. It then specifies two different samples to address the question of how access to quality schools affects housing prices.

In the first, researchers used a broad sample of all housing units, where the dependent variable is the price of housing and the independent variables are the dwelling attributes, neighborhood attributes, and test scores. The central problem with this sample is that better schools are broadly associated with better neighborhoods (higher-income families demand both). So the issue is how to separate the impact of neighborhood conditions and test scores on house values.

In the second, the study employed a new approach in which the sample includes only dwellings near the boundaries of school districts. Because houses are so close to each other, neighborhood effects associated with the immediate area are controlled for by virtue of being essentially identical.[8] The only real difference is which school district children attend. Independent variables include dwelling attributes, variables for broad neighborhood characteristics (e.g., travel time to the city center), and test scores. The study used variables on broad neighborhood conditions because the sampled neighborhoods are from throughout the metropolitan area. So although the immediate neighborhood conditions are controlled using the house matching approach, differences among pairs of houses still remain and have to be controlled with these variables.

The control variables included:

- *Broad neighborhood attributes.* Distance to city; percentage black, percentage Hispanic, percentage elderly, median household income; education distribution of households (these factors are measured using census tract data).
- *School district attributes.* Per-pupil spending; pupil-teacher ratio; property taxes.
- *Dwelling characteristics.* Number of bedrooms and bathrooms; age of building; lot size; internal square footage.

Sample Characteristics

- Single-family houses only in city-area suburbs.
- School districts: 39.
- Attendance school boundaries: 181.
- Number of observations: full sample, 22,679 observations; matched sample, 4,494 observations within 0.15 miles (about 250 meters) of a boundary.

In the United States, most public school students attend the school that serves the neighborhood in which their home is located. Therefore, there is a one-for-one relation between the location of the home and the public school attended by children residing in it. Families electing to send their children to private schools may obviously select any private school that meets their needs. In addition, some public school districts allow students to choose their schools; the study excludes districts of this type from the sample of properties and school districts.

To measure differences in school quality the analyst used the average of the test scores for fourth-graders for 1988, 1990, and 1992 for each school. The study used average scores to control for possible special situations in a given year (e.g., a very good or very bad teacher).

Results. The results, reported in Table 13.3, are the increase in house values for students with fourth-grade reading test scores one standard deviation or higher than the average. The model regression with all units in the district includes the neighborhood and school district attributes, as described earlier. The mean value of units is about $188,000 (in 1993 dollars).

Researchers draw two conclusions from the numbers in Table 13.3:

1. Some parents are willing to pay higher prices to get their children into better schools. But their willingness is limited—the difference in purchase price is equivalent to about the one-year-per-pupil expenditures of the average school district. If the average family stays in its home for eight years, then it is paying only about $500 per year for better schools on a present value basis.

2. Differences in the two models illustrate the sensitivity of the willingness-to-pay estimates to model and sample specifications. The model with all housing units imperfectly controls for variation in neighborhood quality, which correlates with school quality. The result is that the school quality variable (test scores) picks up some of the variation in house prices that is correctly associated with neighborhood quality and thereby substantially overestimates the value of better schools.

Table 13.3 Housing Price and Quality of Education

	Model with Boundary Units Only	Model with All Units in Districts
Percentage increase in house prices	2.1	4.9
Increase in house prices ($)	3,948	9,212

See Exercise 13.3: Willingness to Pay for Clean Air on page 347.

This exercise specifies the variables used for a study of the willingness to pay for clean air. The task is to identify information sources for the variables on neighborhood characteristics, housing characteristics, and pollution levels.

- *Alternative Time Frames for Benefit-Cost Evaluation*

Benefit-cost evaluations assess either proposed policies or existing programs. *Retrospective analysis* is used for ex post evaluation (evaluations conducted after implementation of the project). Retrospective analysis looks at historical data and converts them to NPV for the program. *Snapshot analysis* assesses benefits and costs for the current year. And *prospective analysis* estimates future benefits and costs for the program based on projections (using NPV to standardize costs and benefits).

Prospective analysis offers an ex ante assessment of the value of enacting the program. For example, in the United States in the 1980s the Reagan administration required most programs to demonstrate a positive benefit-cost ratio before considering them for federal funds.

- *Calculations: From Whose Perspective?*

A societal level is the broadest perspective from which to consider costs and benefits. At this level transfers are more common, because both the persons contributing the money and those receiving it are in the same jurisdiction—the nation.

From the perspective of the national government, the emphasis is on its net benefits from undertaking an activity. The point here is that the net-of-transfer benefits must be sufficient to justify the project.

From the perspective of a particular jurisdiction, such as a city or region, federal spending is treated as a benefit. So in allocating costs and benefits, a grant from the national government to upgrade the water system is a negative cost and the benefits from spending the money on water improvement are computed as usual. Of course, from the national government's perspective, the grant is a cost. (One enters a "negative cost" rather than just ignoring the gift, because a complete accounting of all resources is essential in benefit-cost evaluation.)

The perspective of program clients might include welfare recipients of long-term poverty assistance in a chronically depressed region. The cash payments to them are benefits paid for by negative costs.

The following example provides an assessment of benefits and costs from multiple perspectives.

Example of Benefit-Cost Evaluation from Several Different Perspectives: The Job Corps Program.   The Job Corps is a training program for low-income young people to increase their skills and improve attitudes about work. The program is a six-month residential program that teaches skills while imposing strict discipline on participants.

Table 13.4 presents the benefits and costs of the Job Corps program from the perspective of society, clients (corps members), and others. In this case, clients and nonclients together constitute society. So societal-level benefits and costs are the

Table 13.4 Estimated Net Present Values per Job Corps Member (1977 dollars)

	Perspective		
	Social	Non–Corps Member	Corps Member
Benefits			
1. Output produced by corps members			
In-program output	757	673	83
Increased postprogram employment output	3,276	0	3,276
Increased postprogram tax payments	0	596	−596
2. Reduced dependence on transfer programs			
Reduced public transfers	0	791	−791
Reduced administrative cost	172	172	0
Increased utility from reduced welfare dependence	+	+	+
3. Reduced criminal activity			
Reduced criminal justice system costs	1,253	1,253	0
Reduced personal injury and property damage	1,366	1,366	0
Reduced stolen property	300	462	−162
Reduced psychological costs	+	+	+
4. Reduced drug/alcohol abuse			
Reduced drug/alcohol treatment costs	31	31	0
Increased utility from reduced drug/alcohol dependence	+	+	+
5. Reduced utilization of alternative services			
Reduced costs of training and education programs other than Job Corps	244	244	0
Reduced training allowances	0	33	−33
6. Other benefits			
Increased utility from redistribution	+	+	+
Increased utility from improved well-being of corps members	+	+	+
Total benefits	7,399	5,621	1,777
Costs			
1. Program operating expenditures			
Center operating expenditures, excluding transfers to corps members	2,796	2,796	0
Transfers to corps members	0	1,208	−1,208
Central administrative costs	1,347	1,347	0
2. Opportunity cost of corps-member labor during program			
Foregone output	881	0	881
Foregone tax payments	0	153	−153
3. Unbudgeted expenditures other than corps-member labor			
Resource costs	46	46	0
Transfers to corps members	0	185	−185
Total costs	5,070	5,735	−665
Net present value (benefits minus costs)	2,327	−115	2,442
Benefit-cost ratio	1.46	.98	1.99

Source: Mathematica Policy Research, "Evaluation of the Economic Impact of the Job Corps Program: Third Follow-Up Report" (Washington, D.C.: Office of Policy and Evaluation and Research, Employment and Training Administration, Department of Labor, 1982).

sum of those for these two groups. All figures are net present value and were generated four years after completion of the program. Intangible (nonmeasurable) benefits and costs are indicated in the table by plus or minus signs.

Benefits

1. Output produced by corps members:
   - *In-program output.* Nonclients get most of the benefits, because they are staffing the program; the corps members receive less than their market wage for the work they do, because they do not produce much.
   - *Postprogram employment output.* Clear net gain is to participants.
   - *Increased tax payments by participants.* This is an example of a transfer—participants pay taxes, which reduces their benefits; but this is a positive benefit to other taxpayers, who pay less tax (under the assumption that the size of government does not change). Tax is a negative benefit to participants.
2. Reduced dependence on transfer programs:
   - *Reduced public transfer.* This refers to various poverty assistance programs or other public services. Reduced public transfer results in no net savings; rather it is a transfer from participants to non–corps members (taxpayers).
   - *Reduced administrative costs.* Real savings to society and nonclient taxpayers.
   - *Increased utility from reduced welfare dependence.* Clearly intangible and not measurable.

Costs

1. Program operating expenditures:
   - Includes operating expenses, transfers to corps members, and administrative costs.
2. Opportunity cost of corps-member labor:
   - *Foregone output.* Refers to the lost wages of those corps members who would have been employed during the time of program participation.
   - *Foregone tax payments.* Refers to the income tax payments of lost wages. This is a transfer, because if participants do not pay the taxes, then the rest of society must.

Benefit-cost ratio. The program is highly successful from the perspective of both society and participants. This is interesting given that the cost is quite high per participant per year—about $5,400 in nondiscounted dollars.[9]

> *See Exercise 13.4: Ex Ante Evaluation of Downtown Auto Restraint Policies on page 349.*
>
> The task in this exercise is to identify the costs and benefits associated with a policy proposal to limit traffic congestion at the center of a city.

• *Limitations of Benefit-Cost Evaluation*

Although benefit-cost evaluation can be a powerful analytical instrument, it has several limitations that diminish its utility as a public decisionmaking tool. It is a method that can be easily misused:

- Its appeal is that it generates a seemingly objective "bottom line." There are, however, many subjective decisions in measuring costs and benefits, and multiple assumptions are frequently required.
- Intangibles, such as improvements to the quality or length of life, are not included in the benefit-cost ratio. The failure of this method to reflect what are often essential public criteria is a significant limitation.
- The method ignores distributional issues. Who benefits and who pays are critical policy issues, and this is one of the most serious arguments against the method.
- Poor measurement of benefits is sometimes another limitation. Outcomes that are treated incorrectly as impacts sharply overstate project benefits.
- Lack of consistency in the application.
- Reviews of benefit-cost evaluations within the same agency have sometimes found very wide differences in assumptions and measurement practices.

But perhaps most worrisome is that the results are subject to manipulation. This is a real problem for projects when benefit-cost evaluation determines whether to undertake the investment. One analysis of prospective benefit-cost studies prepared for eight subway projects built recently in eight different US cities found very systematic overstatements in the volume of passengers who would be carried by the new systems and large understatements of the costs of building and maintaining the systems.[10] In the median case, capital and operating costs were underestimated by 33 percent and ridership was overestimated by 300 percent. So the average cost per rail passenger turned out to exceed the forecast in every case by at least 188 percent and by more that 700 percent in three cases.

The US government agency that funds the subway projects requires benefit-cost evaluation as part of the application for funding. The benefit-cost ratios are an essential determinant of allocating funds to competing projects. So the agency in effect encourages inflation of the benefit-cost values. Moreover, the Congress tends to allocate funds to specific ongoing construction projects to cover cost overruns. So there is little incentive to correctly identify costs at the project's onset.

Finally, the procedure has become politicized in the United States. For example, the Reagan administration in the 1980s used benefit-cost evaluation as a tool to block new programs. In particular, the Office of the President required the use of unjustifiably high discount rates in the analyses presented to it for consideration. This had the effect of systematically reducing benefits relative to costs because benefits tend to accrue a few years after most costs.[11] The politicization of the tool motivated very sharp attacks on benefit-cost evaluation.

Cost-Effectiveness Analysis

Evaluators use cost-effectiveness analysis when they cannot place a monetary value on program benefits but the objectives of the program are clear and singular or sufficiently related so that the relationship between objectives is evident. An example of a single benefit to which it is difficult to assign a monetary value is saving a life. Cost-effectiveness analysis could determine the cost per life saved of installing safety belts in automobiles.

Cost-effectiveness analysis is a technique for choosing among competing strategies to achieve the same objective when resources are limited. The US military first developed cost-effectiveness analysis and the practice expanded to other sectors, notably health care, in the 1960s.

"Cost-effective" simply means that the new strategy is the cheapest way to achieve a stated objective. Note that being cost-effective does not mean that the strategy saves money—and of course, just because a strategy saves money does not mean that it is cost-effective (that is, it may be inexpensive but may not have the desired effect).

The overall approach is to value the project using some variable other than money, such as the number of lives saved, number of live births, or reduction in cholesterol count. Cost-effectiveness analysis is used when there is a single objective (e.g., to improve reading performance or to protect poor persons from rising tariffs) and the decision is among several alternative policies or programs. In its most common form, cost-effectiveness analysis compares a new strategy to the current practice.

Examples of cost-effectiveness analysis:

- To reduce lifetime drug consumption by individuals:
  Cost per kilogram of cocaine ingestion averted over a lifetime.
- To increase the number of secondary school graduates:
  Cost per student who graduates.
- To improve reading skills of illiterate adults:
  Cost per student to raise their score on the Test of Basic Adult Education by a particular number of points.

• *The Basics*

$$\text{cost-effectiveness ratio} = \frac{\text{cost of new strategy} - \text{cost of current practice}}{\text{effect of new strategy} - \text{effect of current practice}}$$

Cost-effectiveness analysis is concerned with marginal or incremental costs and benefits. The cost-effectiveness ratio is the cost of the new strategy minus the cost of the current strategy, divided by the marginal effectiveness (effect of new strategy minus the effect of current practice).

Table 13.5 looks at the cost-effectiveness of residential and outpatient drug treatment programs. The outpatient program may include group and individual counseling and periodic drug testing. The residential program would provide room and board, in addition to intensive counseling services for six months or longer.

For simplicity, assume that doing nothing has no cost and no effectiveness. So the marginal cost of the simple, outpatient strategy is the difference between the cost of that strategy and the cost of doing nothing. The marginal cost of the resi-

Table 13.5   Cost-Effectiveness Analysis for Drug Treatment Programs

Strategy	Cost	Marginal Cost	Effectiveness	Marginal Effectiveness	CE Ratio
Nothing	0	—	—	—	—
Outpatient	$3,000	$3,000	30% drug-free	30% drug-free	$10,000[a]
Residential	$20,000	$17,000	60% drug-free	30% drug-free[b]	$56,666

Notes: a. Calculate the CE ratio by dividing the marginal cost by the marginal effectiveness.
   b. Although the residential option is effective with 60% of its clients, when compared to the outpatient option, it is, at the margin, only 30% better. This inflates the CE ratio to $56,666 ($17,000 ÷ 0.30).

dential strategy is the difference between the cost of the residential program and the cost of the outpatient program (not the cost of doing nothing). Effectiveness uses the same calculation methodology. The final outcome measure for the analysis is the cost-effectiveness ratio: the ratio of marginal cost to marginal effectiveness.

• *Are the Relevant Strategies Being Compared, and How Good Are the Data?*

As in benefit-cost evaluation, the results of cost-effectiveness analysis are highly dependent on the strategies compared and the assumptions about costs and effectiveness/benefits.

Looking again at the drug treatment example, the cost-effectiveness ratio is dramatically different when the analysis excludes the outpatient strategy. In Table 13.6 the cost-effectiveness ratio (comparing doing nothing to the residential intervention) drops from $56,666 per recovered addict to $33,333. By not considering the outpatient option, Table 13.6 biases the decisionmaking process by lowering the cost-effectiveness ratio of the residential option. Cost-effectiveness analysis is very sensitive to the choice of strategies compared. Users of cost-effectiveness analysis need to examine whether the strategies presented are really those that are most relevant to public decisionmaking.

How good are the cost and effectiveness data? Are the data based on real practice or estimated? Evaluators make assumptions when the effectiveness or cost of a new strategy is unknown, and should detail how they arrived at each assumption.

• *An Additional Example of Cost-Effectiveness Analysis*

Table 13.7 is a summary of a cost-effectiveness analysis conducted by the World Bank for a Latvian welfare reform project.[12] The project considers how to improve social service administrative capacity in order to implement new welfare reforms.

Table 13.6   Cost-Effectiveness Analysis of Residential Drug Treatment Compared to Doing Nothing

Strategy	Cost	Marginal Cost	Effectiveness	Marginal Effectiveness	CE Ratio
Nothing	0	—	—	—	—
Residential	$20,000	$20,000	60% drug-free	60% drug-free	$33,333

Table 13.7   Costs and Effectiveness Summary: Latvia Welfare Reform Project

Scenario	Investment Cost ($ millions)	Administrative Cost Saving	Other Impacts	Meets Criteria	Comments
1. Nonproject scenario	1.0	None	Cannot administer modern welfare system; difficult to control fraud and abuse; clients' time wasted	No	The administration will be overwhelmed within a year by massive information system failure
Option 1: Keep current organizational structure; modest information technology upgrade; no new accounting system	10.0	None	Cannot implement new pension system; difficult to control fraud and abuse; clients' time wasted	No	A system similar to other FSU countries; no transparency; information to clients is limited and thus behavioral incentives do not work
Option 2: Limited investments in a client-oriented organization; new information technology system but without full national network	20.8	Payoff in 6.5 years	Modern welfare system implemented, leading to lower expenditures and higher growth; fraud and abuse control tightened in 70% of country	Partly	Weak client service and information in nonnetworked offices; weaker financial management; fewer efficiency gains and weaker sustainability

(continues)

Table 13.7   Continued

Scenario	Investment Cost ($ millions)	Administrative Cost Saving	Other Impacts	Meets Criteria	Comments
Option 3: Full investments in a client-oriented organization; new information technology system with full national network and new financial management system	24.7	Payoff in 6.7 years	Modern welfare system implemented, leading to lower expenditures and higher growth; fraud/abuse control in 100% of country	Fully	A modern system meeting all requirements of the reform; nationwide network allows better financial management for all welfare system programs

The basic criteria for the alternatives considered are that a solution must increase the administrative capacity to implement welfare reforms, improve information systems, and be client oriented. Although this summary table does not present the marginal cost-effectiveness measures described previously, it is a good example of the various kinds of cost-effectiveness analysis.

Based on its analysis, the World Bank selected Option 3. Option 1 does not yield any cost savings. It actually wastes money. Option 2 is viable and cost-effective. However, it would leave roughly one-third of the country out of the network. Processing time in these offices would be slow, wasting clients' time. Nationwide cross-checking of individuals to detect fraud would be much slower and less rigorous. Local social assistance offices would not be able to tap into the network to check income information during means testing. Option 2 requires more staff and consequently the cost of Option 2 is not much different from that of Option 3, though only Option 3 fully meets the project criteria.

• Problems with Cost-Effectiveness Analysis

Cost-effectiveness analysis cannot effectively treat programs with multiple benefits. For example, building a dam protects a downstream city against floods, saves lives (from averted floods), and provides water for irrigation of farmland. So there are three benefits: urban property protected, lives saved, and additional food production.

To obtain a unified estimate of the benefits the evaluator assigns weights to the various benefits and adds them together, which is a highly subjective exercise. What weight is appropriate for saving a life versus five additional tons of corn production? In addition, there is no simple bottom line, as in the benefit-cost ratio.

Chapter Summary

Benefit-cost evaluation can determine what action achieves the greatest net economic benefit. Although the rationale for comparing costs and benefits of public actions is straightforward, valuing costs and benefits in dollar terms and translating future costs and benefits into present-year dollars is not. Distributional effects of policies, ignored by this method, are also a major consideration for most public actions.

Cost-effectiveness analysis can determine the least costly or most effective activity toward a single, specific goal. It offers an assessment when monetary values of benefits are indeterminable.

In applying either method, the burden is on the analyst to think broadly about the nature of the costs, benefits, and transfers involved and to be explicit about how each is measured. Published sources give guidelines and examples for addressing most measurement issues.

The objective of using these tools in policymaking is to provide an assessment of positive and negative economic and other impacts, and to facilitate a ranking of the alternatives. Analysts work hard to calculate benefits and costs to rank various proposed projects. It is challenging to conduct rigorous and fair cost benefit and cost-effectiveness analyses, and analysts and policymakers should be aware of the limitations of each method. Not all impacts can be assigned a monetary value and assumptions about costs and benefits can distort results. Moreover, cost is rarely the sole evaluation criterion in policymaking, and these methods fail to address other factors such as political considerations, stakeholder interests, and distributional effects. See Box 13.2 for a summary of the technical aspects of benefit-cost evaluation and cost-effectiveness analysis.

Box 13.2   Technical Summary

Benefit-Cost Evaluation
A technique used to assess the efficiency of expenditure decisions.

Basic Steps

- Identify all project benefits, costs, transfers (include direct/indirect and tangible/intangible).
- Determine which costs and benefits are onetime and which are recurring and assign to specific project years.
- Assign monetary values to benefits, costs, transfers.
- Apply discount rate to calculate net present value.
- Project is positive if benefits outweigh costs ($B \div C > 1.0$).

Definitions of Key Terms/Formulas

- *Discount rate.* Used in the treatment of time in valuing costs and benefits. A discount rate adjusts costs and benefits to their present values. Because of the uncertainty in determining an appropriate discount rate, governments often specify the rate to use in assessing projects. A common measure is government's cost of long-term money—the interest rate on bonds of ten or more years.
- *Net present value.* The total discounted benefits minus the total discounted costs. Used to calculate benefit-cost ratio:

$$NPV = (B - C)^{y1} + [(B - C)^{y2} \div (1 + r)] + [(B - C)^{y3} \div (1 + r)^2] + [(B - C)^{y4} \div (1 + r)^3] \dots$$

- *Total net benefits versus marginal net benefits.* In deciding whether to continue a program, policymakers should only consider the marginal net benefits for the coming year or years. Previous expenditures or sunk costs have no bearing on the decision to proceed.
- *Transfers.* Payments from one person or business to another without any net increase in income. For example, welfare payments are transfers from taxpayers to poor people.
- *Consumers in equilibrium.* The price paid for a good or service equals the marginal utility of the good or service. For example, the price a citizen pays for bus transportation is equal to their need or value of the ride. In benefit-cost evaluation, estimate the benefit of bus transportation as the price per ride.
- *Pareto criterion.* The gains to beneficiaries should more than compensate for the losses or costs to others.
- *Willingness to pay.* The amount of money an individual would pay to make a particular change in his circumstances, such as the willingness to pay for better schools or to avoid risk of auto accidents. This is an important concept in measuring benefits.

Cost-Effectiveness Analysis
A technique used to determine which intervention best meets a specific objective at the least cost or achieves the greatest gain at a given cost (e.g., increase in life-years per $1 million spent). Evaluators use this method when a monetary value cannot be assigned to benefits, such as the value of extending life.

Basic Steps

- Determine the singular project objective, such as to improve reading performance or

(continues)

Box 13.2   Continued

to protect poor persons from rent increases.
- Assign value to the project using some variable other than money, such as the number of lives saved or reduction in cholesterol count.
- List the cost of each intervention considered and the value gained (e.g., number of lives saved).
- Compare the marginal costs and effects of the interventions (see formula below).

The "best" program is the one with the best cost-effectiveness ratio—lowest marginal costs or highest marginal effectiveness.

Definitions of Key Terms/Formulas

$$\text{cost-effectiveness ratio} = \frac{\text{cost of new strategy} - \text{cost of current practice}}{\text{effect of new strategy} - \text{effect of current practice}}$$

All relevant strategies must be included in the cost-effectiveness analysis in order to achieve a fair result.

Exercise 13.1: Allocating Costs for a Youth Orchestra Program

Instructions. This task requires you to allocate the costs of an educational program among various stakeholders.[13] The exercise addresses types of costs, who bears the costs, treatment of user fees, and treatment of subsidies. The task is to allocate the costs among the four contributors: the school, city, orchestra, and parents/students. The table on page 344 shows total costs in the second column. Note that some of costs are transfers (i.e., payments by one group offset expenses made by another). Where this is the case, you should enter a positive and a negative entry in the same row.

Background. The school district in Prague has decided to form a special youth orchestra for gifted young musicians. The school district could not afford to develop the project by itself. So the head of the school solicited assistance from the city government and the Prague Symphony Orchestra. The city agreed to make a contribution of $10,000. The orchestra will contribute the time of one conductor and contribute instruments for half the students. Parents will pay a fee for their children to participate in the project. Two parent volunteers will assist with the program.

Costs Include

- *Personnel.* Instructors, conductor, opportunity cost of volunteers.
- *Facilities.* Extra costs of keeping facility open, cleaning, and the like.
- *Required client inputs.* Transporting kids, extra time of parents to attend meetings with instructors and volunteers.

Annual Costs for the Youth Orchestra

Cost Item	Total Cost ($)	Cost to School	Cost to City	Cost to Orchestra	Cost to Students and Parents
Personnel					
2 high school music teachers	9,000				
1 orchestra conductor	14,800				
2 parent aides (volunteers)	3,600				
Facilities					
High school music room	2,000				
Materials and equipment					
Music/photocopies	800				
Instruments	15,000				
Other					
Maintenance and janitorial services	1,500				
Insurance	1,100				
Energy	900				
Required client inputs					
Transportation (time, vehicle cost)	625				
Total input costs	49,325				
User fees	($1,000)				
Other cash subsidies	($10,000)				
Net costs	38,325				

- *User fees.* Costs to the parents and a reduction in the cost to the program sponsor (school). Total cost does not change.
- *Cash subsidies.* From the city to the school.

Exercise 13.2: Understanding Benefit and Cost Categories

The task is to identify correctly the benefits and costs for a Romanian dam construction project. Costs and benefits are assigned under the categories of direct, indirect, tangible and intangible. Identify the costs and benefits that are erroneously assigned, and identify examples of transfers.

Background. The Romanian government is considering whether to construct a dam to protect a middle-sized city further down the river from frequent flooding. The national government will finance the dam from general tax revenues. When the dam is completed, it will cause a reservoir to fill that will cover about eighty-five square kilometers. A number of farms and one village will be flooded.

1. The government has requested a benefit-cost evaluation of the project. The table on page 346 contains several indicators for the costs and benefits associated with the dam and reservoir. For each type of cost and benefit, circle the items that do not belong in this category.
2. From a national perspective, some benefits and costs are actually transfers from one group of citizens to another and have no net effect on the expenses of the government. Circle all of the following statements that you believe are examples of a transfer from a national or social perspective.
   A. The loss in agriculture income from the area flooded by the reservoir offsets the increased income of farmers in other locations.
   B. The increased value of land in the newly protected areas of the city offsets the decrease in land values in other parts of the city, as business activity relocates.
   C. Increased tax payments resulting from the economic activity in the protected area offset other taxes that would have been paid if the dam had not been built, assuming that government revenues are held constant.

Costs

Direct-tangible	A. Design costs for the dam B. Construction materials, labor, etc. C. Time of legislature spent considering the allocation of funds D. Government agency direct supervision E. Maintenance and operation of the dam
Direct-intangible	A. Cost of purchasing land and improvements on farms and village that will be flooded B. Loss of sense of home by those who are forced to move from the flooded area
Indirect-tangible	A. Additional travel time and cost for river traffic B. Vacationers have a sense of loss from not having the former beauty of the river to enjoy C. Loss of agricultural output from land flooded by the new reservoir D. General costs of the agency supervising dam construction

Benefits

Direct-tangible	A. Gain in land values of locations benefiting from the protection B. Savings to shippers who can build warehouses closer to the river C. Gain in retail sales in already protected sites from the economic development of the city D. Business and households in area subject to flooding no longer pay for flood insurance E. Government savings on subsidized flood insurance program
Indirect-tangible	A. General economic development of the city B. Increased sense of security of residents

Exercise 13.3: Willingness to Pay for Clean Air

This exercise involves listing important variables and identifying information sources for a study on willingness to pay for clean air. The city that has commissioned the study has two sides, one with factories and dirty air and another with cleaner air and favorable breezes. The study will examine how much families are willing to pay for clean air based on an analysis of the variation in housing values. The analysis will involve data on dwelling conditions, neighborhood characteristics, and measures of pollution. The task is to specify, in the table on page 348, what factors need to be controlled and how to measure these factors.

Variable	Information Source
Dependent variable: Value of housing (market rent or sale price)	
Factors to Control for	
1. Dwelling characteristics	
Specify:	
2. Neighborhood characteristics	
Specify:	
3. Measures of pollution	
Specify:	

Exercise 13.4: Ex Ante Evaluation
of Downtown Auto Restraint Policies

Identify the benefits and costs of the mayor's proposal to reduce car traffic. Complete the table on page 350 by categorizing benefits and costs according to direct/indirect, tangible/intangible, and suggest how to measure these items.[14]

Background. The mayor has decided that there is excessive car traffic in the city's center. This produces an unfavorable environment for retail activity and even office workers are complaining to their bosses about potential health problems. To combat the poor-quality air, the mayor decides, with the support of the city council (legislature), to impose restraints on the number of cars that can enter the city center. His program consists of the following:

1. Those motorists who want to enter the city center on weekdays during the early and afternoon rush hours (that have been extended to cover all but the middle three hours of the day) will have to have a device on their car that will charge them a high fee for access. The fee is being set initially at a level that should reduce traffic by 75 percent.
2. Buses have unrestricted access to the city center.
3. Construct additional parking facilities at various locations. There will be an attempt not to concentrate them just outside the restricted area, but several will be there.
4. Bus service will be increased in two ways: (a) more lines and more frequent service will be added where services are already provided; (b) shuttle service from the new parking structures to the city center will run every ten minutes.

Other factors to note:

- Buses operate at a loss under the current fare structure, but the higher ridership rates (more riders per bus) are likely to eliminate the losses on the home-to-center runs. Parking fees and fees for riding the shuttle buses will cover costs.
- The analyst should take a city-level perspective.
- This is a prospective analysis (i.e., you are trying to determine if the proposed policy makes sense—as a result, many of the indicators will be estimates).

Identification of Benefits and Costs of Imposing Downtown Auto Restraints

	Item/Indicator	How to Measure?
Costs		
Direct- and indirect-tangible		
Direct-intangible		
Benefits		
Direct- and indirect-tangible		
Direct-intangible		
Transfers		

PART 4

PREPARING POLICY RECOMMENDATIONS

CHAPTER 14

Writing and Presenting Policy Recommendations

Good ideas have power. In some situations, innovative ideas rule the day. For example, Chapter 1 describes Russia's decision to solve a housing crisis by introducing vouchers rather than rely on slow and costly new construction. At that time, vouchers were a new idea and the capacity of the fledgling private real estate market still untested. Such public-private solutions are now commonplace.

Often there is a range of generally accepted options offered in response to particular problems and the policymaking process involves sorting through or developing support for those positions. For example, many nations are currently struggling with the need to reform their pension systems. As populations in developed nations age and birth rates continue to decline, pension systems are quickly becoming unaffordable and the needs of the elderly are pitted against the needs of the young and the ability of the current and future work force to support such benefits. Reform strategies include politically unpopular ideas such as raising the retirement age, reducing benefits, and various schemes to encourage private investment. It is unlikely that any truly innovative ideas will solve this pending crisis, and most countries will select from the standard mix of options in the configuration that best meets local needs and politics. In such cases, the policy process is one of finding balance among the alternatives and slowly building support for the necessary reforms.

The analyst's task is to stimulate and facilitate good decisionmaking—regardless of whether a highly innovative solution is on the table or whether the candidate solutions are well known. Written policy recommendations must forcefully present the facts, analyze the alternatives, and carefully balance administrative, budget, effectiveness, and political acceptability factors.

Preparing policy recommendations draws on all the topics covered in this book. Developing effective and creative solutions requires rigorous analytical thinking. Analysts are required to sort through a confusing array of data, mediate among competing interests, generate creative solutions, evaluate the options, and select not just the "best" solution but also the most feasible. This reality check of what is economically or politically feasible makes policy analysis an art of compromise and opportunity. Policy recommendations present decisionmakers with the ideas and information they need to advance an issue or solve a problem. In this chapter, we return to the policy analysis method described in Chapter 2 as a primary problem-solving tool.

This chapter also focuses on writing and presentation, because good ideas are not enough. It is important to convey ideas clearly and powerfully. We provide examples of good policy statements and tips on structure, tone, and other writing issues. Although the chapter stresses writing skills, the same organizing principles apply to oral presentations.

The exercises for this chapter require you to write policy recommendations for a variety of public problems. These case studies draw on the concepts of targeting, incentives, subsidies, evaluation, assessing costs, equity, and more. The case studies are included in the book's appendix.

What Makes a Strong Policy Recommendation?

A strong policy recommendation demonstrates a solid understanding of the problem, thorough analysis, and posits creative, doable solutions. Equally important, a strong policy statement is well written and organized.

• Content

An effective policy recommendation must demonstrate understanding of the problem, available options, and constraints. Real problems tend to be complex. A good analysis must methodically sort through an array of data and interests, present a cogent understanding of the problem, and identify a reasonable solution or solutions. The recommendation memo presents the key findings of the analysis—showing how the strengths and weaknesses of the options stack up against explicit criteria, such as how well each option serves clients, ease of implementation, cost, or political acceptability.

• Organization/Presentation

Any number of formats may be used for the presentation. However, it is critical that the statement be clearly written and well organized. The points below further detail writing and organization issues.

The Problem Is Clearly Stated. The problem needs to be well defined, with relevant data used to help explain its nature.

The Options Are Clearly Defined. Where alternatives for addressing a problem are available, the report must include various alternatives—it should not be just a case for a favored solution.

The Recommendation Is Clear. The reader should not be left guessing. State your recommendations clearly at the beginning and/or end of the report. Never assume that the recommendation is obvious.

The Recommendation Is Justified. Use evidence and analysis to support the recommendation.

The Report Is Concise and Well Written. The report must include the important facts and a strong analysis. Excess information will distract from your recommendation. A good policy recommendation is measured by its quality not by the number of pages. Good writing is that which conveys ideas clearly. Complicated ideas may require lengthy sentences and precise terminology, but avoid needless clauses and language that is overly verbose or legalistic. Always proofread your work. A sloppy typo or spelling error can undermine the entire presentation.

What Makes a Poor Policy Recommendation?

Poor policy recommendations are those that exhibit sloppy thinking, weak research, and poor presentation. Examples of specific pitfalls follow.

An Opinion—Not Based on Facts. This is the worst and most common mistake. The recommendation should be based on your analysis and presentation of the facts of this specific case. Many of us have opinions about particular problems and even about the efficacy of different types of government actions—but what worked in one situation may not be the best solution in another. Previous knowledge or experience can provide a useful "reality check," but it must not be allowed to obscure the facts or limit new solutions.

New Information Introduced That Is Not Mentioned or Supported in the Discussion of the Problem/Options. The recommendation is like a conclusion—it must not introduce new factors. Recommendations should not come out of the blue or unveil startling new data or options that were not included in the analysis.

Too Political.   A recommendation that is not politically acceptable is unlikely to be implemented. In addition, a recommendation that requires too much political deal-making is likely to be compromised or unrealized. The analyst should not try to prejudge political acceptability too finely him- or herself. Analysts often lack full information in this sphere and can easily accidentally eliminate a viable option.

Costs or Administrative Constraints Ignored.   Policy recommendations must be doable. If the recommendation requires money, time, staffing, and other resources that are simply not available, it is not a viable option.

Incomplete Analysis.   The recommendation may seem reasonable, but the analysis of criteria and/or options is so limited or poor that it is difficult to trust the recommendation.

Plagiarized Report.   Always use your own words and properly attribute the ideas and works of others.

Examples of Policy Recommendations

This section presents two examples of policy recommendations. The examples have different structures and illustrate the range of presentation options available. Both are generally strong policy recommendations that demonstrate a clear understanding of the issue, good problem solving, and are presented in clear and concise language. As you read each example, ask yourself what might make it a stronger policy statement. How might you improve either the substance or organization of the statement?

The first example is the executive summary of a process evaluation conducted for a new job search and income support program. It makes several broad recommendations and offers a series of specific recommendations for improving the program. Some of the analysis and data to back up the recommendations are not included in this summary, but are included in the full evaluation report.

The second example is a policy brief from the Brookings Institution, a well-known US public policy organization. The policy brief promotes the idea that greater work participation and higher marriage rates would reduce poverty and dependence on public assistance programs. The brief compares data on five options: increasing the education of the poor, increasing marriage rates, greater work participation, fewer children, and doubling the public assistance allowance.

Both examples address similar topics of work and income support. However, the first example looks at how a specific, small municipal program might be improved, whereas the second addresses broader policy issues and the reform of the major national income support program. Only the second example follows the policy analysis method and compares several different policy options.

• Policy Recommendation Example 1:
The Perm Motovilikhinsky District Targeting Pilot

Jerome Gallagher. *Implementation Assessment: Motovilikhinsky Targeting Pilot, Perm.* Perm, Russia: Urban Institute/Institute for Urban Economics, 2001.

In November 2000, the city of Perm, Russia, initiated an innovative pilot project designed to provide low-income families with both income support and employment services. Operating in three neighborhoods of the Motovilikhinsky district of Perm, this pilot program employs an integrated approach to benefit delivery—in addition to a targeted cash benefit for the alleviation of poverty, families are also connected with services provided by municipal agencies and NGOs that assist families in social and economic matters, primarily focused on employment. For the first time in Perm, the provision of cash benefits requires unemployed beneficiaries to make efforts toward obtaining a job.

The Urban Institute (Washington, D.C.) and Institute for Urban Economics (Moscow) conducted an evaluation of the Perm targeting pilot project after the first five months of operation. It focuses on the implementation procedures and initial outcomes based on program monitoring data, interviews with client and administrators, and a review of program documents.

Assessment.   Overall, the evaluation findings suggest that the program is operating in line with program goals. Most important, the implementing agencies worked together to successfully launch the program—interviewing clients, paying benefits, and delivering services. During the first four and a half months of the program, sixty-five households received approval and quarterly benefits averaging about 690 rubles. Despite whatever problems occurred in implementation of the program, this alone is a significant achievement. Other early pilot implementation successes include:

- Interviews with clients and staff revealed a high degree of understanding of the program goals and a high degree of acceptance of these goals as appropriate.
- Program administrators at all levels made many positive contributions in preparing for the program launch, including developing the program policy, disseminating information about the program, hiring and training staff, developing procedures, and coordinating the various agencies involved in the program.

- Clients interviewed were enthusiastic about the location of the benefit office in their neighborhood and the convenient and helpful service of the benefit workers.
- Reviews of the client case records reveal that despite some variation among staff in creating client case records, the number of application mistakes was not large.
- The program appears to have had considerable success in moving clients into jobs. Although not all those referred to the employment center actually sought its services, about 60 percent (twenty-three of thirty-eight) of those who did receive employment services were successfully placed in jobs after job search assistance or a combination of training and job search assistance.

Despite these positive aspects of the program, the evaluation revealed a number of areas of concern regarding program policies and implementation. Many of these problems are typical of municipal social programs in Perm as well as many other cities. Early pilot implementation weaknesses include:

- Program policies offer insufficient detail regarding many key policy areas. In addition, the benefit calculation policy initially undermined program goals, although later regulations resulted in improvements in this area.
- Recertification of benefits and payment of second-quarter benefits did not occur on schedule.
- Program documents and manuals detailing staff program procedures and coordinating cooperation among various agencies were conspicuously lacking.
- Benefit offices were not adequately equipped to serve the new clients.
- There is excessive reliance on upper-level staff for eligibility determination and enforcement of program requirements, and a lack of reliance on standardized procedures.
- Although program monitoring data was strong in some areas, much of the program monitoring data provided to the Urban Institute/Institute for Urban Economics team were neither internally consistent nor consistent between agencies.
- Due to low client to caseworker ratios, the sustainability of the program is a cause for concern.

Recommendations. Based on these findings, the Urban Institute/Institute for Urban Economics team made a number of general recommendations intended to improve program policies and operations:

1. Revise the pilot program regulations in order to provide sufficient detail and greater clarity to policies regarding sanction, appeals procedures, client monitoring, applicant budgeting, the role of the district commission, and caseworker procedures.
2. Create a policy and procedures manuals for benefit caseworkers with detailed instructions for benefit caseworkers, and update it regularly in order to ensure accurate implementation of policy and equitable treatment of clients.
3. Redefine the role of the Motovilikhinsky district's Benefit Commission to one of helping in interdepartmental/organizational cooperation and resolving disputes. Remove from it the responsibilities of determining eligibility, calculating benefits, and imposing sanctions, since these should be determined by strictly following program regulations.
4. Develop formal written agreements between agencies participating in the program specifying the duties and responsibilities of each agency.
5. Provide the office equipment necessary for the benefit of caseworkers in the pilot program office to improve their efficiency, particularly a photocopier, but also a computer and other necessary equipment.
6. Promote the effects of the benefit calculation formula's earnings disregard to clients so that they are better informed about how obtaining employment will affect their benefit.
7. Revise the sanctions policy to include gradations of penalties so that less severe offenses are not heavily penalized and more severe or repeated offenses are more severely penalized. The sanction policy should also clearly define "good cause" for noncompliance and the process for appeals.
8. Provide the benefit on a monthly basis instead of a quarterly basis and ensure on-time delivery of benefits.
9. Improve program monitoring efforts and the coordination of monitoring efforts between participating agencies.

In addition to these general recommendations, the Urban Institute/Institute for Urban Economics team shared the concerns of many program administrators regarding the pilot program's sustainability. Many of the program administrators interviewed noted the considerable administrative resources currently consumed by the pilot program and the low client to staff ratio (less than twenty-five households per caseworker). As officials in Perm consider extending the program into the future or expanding the program geographically, we suggest a number of recommendations related to reducing administrative burden and improving project sustainability:

1. Reduce administrative procedures for clients, particularly requirements that

they bring to recertification meetings documents that do not change, such as birth certificates.

2. Eliminate home visits for all clients; only require home visits for special cases—for instance, when fraud is suspected.

3. Reduce the number of administrative levels involved in reviewing applications prior to their approval; a review by one competent supervisor should be enough.

4. Change the certification period from three to six months, in line with other social assistance programs, such as child allowances. Use monitoring data from the employment center to determine if recipients obtained employment during the certification period.

5. Reduce staff involvement in obtaining nonemployment-related services for clients.

6. Consider how to integrate the program into the overall network of social policy programs in the city, so that it can take advantage of shared resources.

Overall, we recommend that the program continue, with the possible expansion to other districts, but only after careful consideration of changes and considerable restructuring of the program to address the issues described above. We also advise further evaluation of program outcomes following improvements in monitoring data.

- *Policy Recommendation Example 2:*
Work and Marriage—The Way to End Poverty and Welfare

Ron Haskins and Isabel V. Sawhill. "Work and Marriage: The Way to End Poverty and Welfare." Welfare Reform and Beyond Policy Brief no. 28. Washington, D.C.: Brookings Institution, September 2003.

Many advocates for the poor believe that the solution to poverty involves giving people more money. After all, if poverty is defined as having an income below some socially acceptable level, then the easiest and most direct way of raising poor people above that level is to boost their incomes. Such assistance is usually called welfare, although it may include, in addition to cash assistance, noncash benefits such as food stamps and housing subsidies.

Providing such assistance has been the dominant strategy for combating poverty in the United States for many years. Yet it has been remarkably unsuccessful. There is no state where a welfare check will raise a four-person family above the government's official poverty line ($18,104 in 2001). And given the fact that the official poverty line is a rather stingy standard that has not kept pace with rising standards of living over the past half century, these data become even more disheartening.

In this brief, we contrast making cash and related forms of public assistance more generous with strategies that encourage work and marriage. The data suggest that the latter are more effective ways of reducing poverty and demonstrate the wisdom of the increasing attention that has been given to encouraging work and marriage in recent policy discussions.

The Poor Work and Marry Less Than the Nonpoor.   Most of the poor in the United States are poor because they either do not work or work too few hours to move themselves and their children out of poverty. More specifically, the heads of poor families with children worked only one half as many hours, on average, as the heads of nonpoor families with children in 2001, according to the Census Bureau (see Table 14.1). There are many reasons the poor work fewer hours than the nonpoor, including difficulty in finding jobs, the demands of caring for young children, poor health, transportation problems, substance abuse, and other personal problems. Although a shortage of job opportunities is often cited as an important reason for the poor's lack of involvement in the work force, the gap in the work hours between poor and nonpoor families with children is observed in good years as well as bad. The state of the economy and the availability of jobs surely play some role, but are not the primary reasons for these differences in work effort. In short, the poor have less income in large measure because they work far fewer hours than their more affluent counterparts.

Another striking difference between the poor and nonpoor is the much smaller proportion of the poor who are married. In 2001, 81 percent of nonpoor families

Table 14.1   Key Differences Between Poor and Nonpoor Families

Characteristic	Poor	Nonpoor
Family income ($)	9,465	75,288
Hours worked in 2001	1,017	2,151
Married (%)	39.5	81.0
Education	High school dropout	Some college
Number of children	2.13	1.78

Source: Ron Haskins and Isabel V. Sawhill, "Work and Marriage: The Way to End Poverty and Welfare," Welfare Reform and Beyond Policy Brief no. 28 (Washington, D.C.: Brookings Institution, September 2003). Reprinted with the permission of the Brookings Institution.

with children were headed by married couples. This compares to only 40 percent among poor families with children (see Table 14.1). In part this reflects higher marriage rates among the better educated or more skilled, and in part it reflects the fact that such families increasingly have two earners, lifting them out of poverty whatever the size of their individual paychecks.

Still a third difference between the poor and the nonpoor is in levels of education. The average head of a poor family with children is a high school dropout, while the average head of a nonpoor family has completed some college (see Table 14.1). While lack of education is commonly cited as a prime source of poverty, it is less important in depressing family incomes, as we will see, than are work and marriage.

Finally, poor families have more children than the nonpoor, requiring that their limited incomes support more people. Among families with children, the typical poor family has slightly more than two children whereas the typical nonpoor family has less than two (see Table 14.1). While this difference is small, it not only requires that available income be stretched a little further, but more importantly could inhibit work and marriage among single parents.

Reducing Poverty by Changing Behavior.   The poverty rate for families with children was 13 percent in 2001. Using census data and some simple modeling, we can simulate what would happen to the poverty rate under different assumptions about work, marriage, education, and family size among the poor. One can think of these as a series of tests to see which changes in behavior have the biggest effects in reducing the incidence of poverty.

The first simulation assumes that all nonelderly and nondisabled family heads work at least full-time. They receive the same hourly wage they currently earn—or could earn based on their education and other characteristics. This test shows that full-time work would reduce the poverty rate more than 5 percentage points, from 13 to 7.5 percent (see Figure 14.1). Thus, full-time work eliminates almost half of the poverty experienced by families with children. (If work-related expenses were subtracted from income, the effects would be somewhat less dramatic. For more details, see Isabel Sawhill and Adam Thomas, *A Hand Up for the Bottom Third: Toward a New Agenda for Low-Income Working Families* [Washington, D.C.: Brookings Institution, 2001].)

A second simulation assumes that the same proportion of children lived in female-headed families in 2001 as in 1970—before divorce and out-of-wedlock childbearing dramatically increased the proportion of children living with a single parent. The idea behind this test is to ask what would happen if as many people married and stayed married now as before. The test simulates marriages between single mothers and unmarried men who are similar in age, education, and race. These virtual marriages take place between real people who report their status to the Census

Figure 14.1   Factors Influencing Poverty Rates

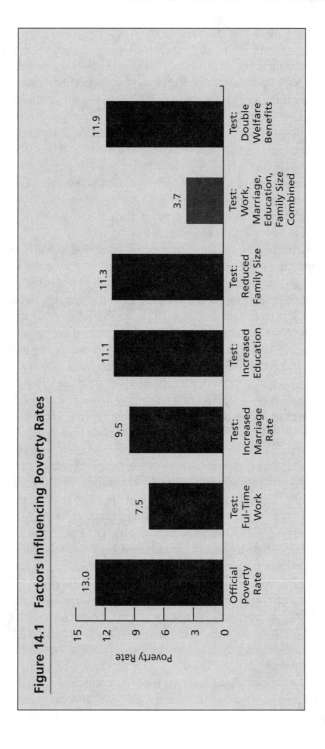

Bureau. Thus, if there is a shortage of men, or if they have limited or no earnings, these conditions are reflected in the results. Once married, we combine the incomes of the two households. (The details of this simulation are described in Adam Thomas and Isabel Sawhill, "For Richer or for Poorer: Marriage as an Antipoverty Strategy," *Journal of Policy Analysis and Management* [September 2002].)

The marriage simulation reduces the poverty rate among families with children by 3.5 percentage points, from 13 to 9.5 percent (see Figure 14.1). With a few exceptions, we find no shortage of unmarried men for these women to marry. The major exception is within the African American population, where there is a shortage of potential mates in some age and education categories. This shortage may be the result of the large number of young minority men who are incarcerated or dead or it may reflect the difficulty the Census Bureau has in finding and interviewing minority men in lower-income communities.

The third simulation assumes that every family head has at least a high school education and earns at least as much as high school graduates normally receive. Although not as big a poverty reducer as full-time work or marriage, this test lowers the poverty rate among families with children by nearly two percentage points, from 13 to 11.1 percent (see Figure 14.1).

The fourth test estimates how much less poverty there would be if families had no more than two children. With the same income but fewer mouths to feed, they are better off. This simulation reduces the poverty rate among families with children by only 1.7 percentage points, from 13 to 11.3 percent, not as much as the other three simulations (see Figure 14.1).

Finally, we conduct a combined simulation implementing each of the four individual tests sequentially. The full-time work test is conducted first, then the high school education test, followed by the marriage test, and finally the test that assumes families have no more than two children. After each test, each family's poverty status is reevaluated and only those families who are still poor are eligible to participate in the next test. The combined effect of these four tests is a 9.3 percentage-point drop in the poverty rate among families with children, from 13 percent to 3.7 percent. Thus the poverty rate among families with children could be lowered by 71 percent if the poor completed high school, worked full-time, married, and had no more than two children.

What About Welfare? For many years, liberals have advocated increasing welfare benefits as the best way to reduce poverty, especially among single parents. Many liberals remain concerned that the welfare law of 1996, by requiring work and encouraging marriage while time-limiting benefits, would have adverse consequences for the poor.

But just how helpful are welfare benefits compared to work and marriage in lifting people out of poverty? To answer this question, we conducted a simulation to determine the effect on poverty of doubling the amount of welfare benefits received by potentially eligible families. Because welfare benefits are underreported to the Census Bureau, we first corrected for this underreporting, and then simply doubled the (corrected) amounts received by each family. The result is revealing. Even a doubling of current benefit levels does less to reduce poverty than any of the simulations of behavioral changes reported above. We have to triple welfare benefits before they reduce poverty as much as any of the behavioral changes. Work, marriage, education, and family size are all more powerful determinants of the incidence of poverty than the amount of cash assistance received from the government. This conclusion is reinforced to the extent one believes that increasing cash benefits would undermine incentives to work, marry, complete one's education, and limit the size of one's family. None of these indirect effects of increased welfare is incorporated in these estimates.

Perhaps making all benefits—not just welfare—conditional on work could further reduce poverty. Research has shown that such conditionality increases employment. For example, since the mid-1980s, employment rates among single mothers have risen dramatically in part because of the increasingly generous wage supplements provided by the Earned Income Tax Credit (EITC), the increasing availability of child care subsidies, and the very substantial increases in health care coverage for families leaving welfare.

The Special Case of Single-Parent Families. Poverty is concentrated among single-parent families. For families with children, 32 percent are poor if the family is headed by a single parent, but only 7 percent are poor if the family is headed by two married parents. Full-time work would more than halve the very high poverty rate among single-parent families. However, advocating work, and especially full-time work, among single parents is controversial. Indeed, current proposals from the George W. Bush administration and House Republicans to require forty hours of work or other work-related activities each week from welfare mothers have been sharply criticized, not least by Republicans in the Senate.

This criticism may be justified if the focus is today's single mothers and their children. Juggling work and family responsibilities is hard for any family and especially for those with limited income and education. And it is doubly difficult if child care is not available or affordable. At the same time, there is good evidence that the children in these families are likely to do better if placed in high-quality child care or early education than if left at home until the time they enter school. Thus the opportunity exists to reduce both current poverty rates and improve children's development by a two-generation policy of requiring work and placing children in high-quality care.

A Vision for the Future. Looking beyond the circumstances of today's single mothers and focusing instead on a vision for the future leads us to suggest a comprehensive, behavior-based strategy for reducing poverty. The strategy is based on a set of normative expectations for the youngest generation. They would be expected to stay in school at least through high school, delay childbearing until marriage, work full-time to support any children they chose to bear outside marriage, and limit the size of their families to what they could afford to support. Existing policies would be aligned with this set of expectations. Income assistance would be conditional on work with some exceptions for hardship cases, including serious disability. Benefit programs (including tax credits and exemptions) would be capped at two children per family. This policy would not deny people the right to have more children, but it would require that they do so at their own expense. Marriage and work disincentives in existing benefit programs would be reduced wherever possible, not just by extending benefits up the income scale but also by making marriage and work a condition for receiving more types of assistance.

At the same time, some other benefits would be made more generous. Sawhill would guarantee good-quality child care to all low-income parents and add up to six months of paid leave for parents with infants or young children. Such leave would be conditional on having a substantial work history, would be available to all families, and would be subsidized on a sliding scale basis. Haskins does not support increases in family leave, but supports increased spending on child care, especially for poor children.

Paid leave would be combined with a more generous set of supports for low-income working families (including not only child care but also health insurance and the EITC). Unemployment insurance and community service jobs would be available for those unable to find work in the private sector, but only for a limited time, and only at minimum wage. Welfare as we know it would wither away. It would not be needed. After some future date it would simply not be available. The savings from eliminating welfare would be reinvested in some or all of the above programs. An initial demonstration of this system in one state, under waivers from the federal government, could be used to test this new approach and would help to establish its feasibility, net costs, and antipoverty effectiveness. In fact, the system that has been operating in Wisconsin for many years is already close to the model program we have in mind. However, many of its effects would not be clear until it had been in operation long enough, and on a large enough scale, to affect the attitudes and behaviors of the youngest generation.

Would It Work? Public opinion polls suggest that such a system would be far more popular than existing programs. Ending welfare resonated with the voters when Bill Clinton first proposed it in his 1992 presidential campaign and when sweeping reforms based on work and personal responsibility were enacted on a bipartisan basis in 1996. Polls have consistently shown that the public is much more willing to support those who work than those who don't.

The data reviewed above suggest that work is a powerful antidote to poverty. Moreover, the expectation of work has implications for education, marriage, and family size. Young people who know that they are going to have to work would be more likely to finish school. Those who aspire to be stay-at-home mothers for an extended period would be more likely to delay having children until they are married, since the government would no longer subsidize them to be full-time mothers. And those required to work would have less time to care for additional children and might plan their families accordingly. Indeed, serious work requirements may be more of an incentive to finish school, delay childbearing until marriage, and limit the size of one's family than all the combined government programs directly aimed at these objectives.

In addition to the data and arguments about the strong antipoverty effectiveness of work reviewed above, a number of demonstration programs point in a similar direction. For example, the Canadian Self-Sufficiency Project (SSP) requires that in order to qualify for generous wage supplements, former welfare recipients must work at least thirty hours a week. Studies suggest that it has been one of the most cost-effective antipoverty policies ever implemented, because every dollar of government assistance produces several additional dollars of earnings within the target population as a result of the strong work requirements embedded in the program. Thus the program has dramatically increased employment and incomes among recipients, reduced welfare dependency and poverty, and done all of this while imposing modest additional costs on government.

Contrast this to the current system in the United States, where disincentives to work are large. As incomes rise, various forms of assistance are scaled back and payroll and other taxes begin to take a larger bite out of people's earnings. For example, a couple each earning 1.5 times the minimum wage gets to keep less than 20 cents of each additional dollar they earn, according to a study from the National Center for Policy Analysis. If this couple moves from working part-time to full-time, they do not gain at all. Every dollar of additional earnings is offset by higher taxes and lower benefits. One way to reduce these disincentives is to make existing assistance conditional on work, including full-time work, and to eliminate anything other than temporary assistance for those who do not work at all.

Conclusion. Advocates for the poor have too long argued that welfare was the solution to poverty. Yet most evidence points in a different direction. The reform of welfare in 1996 has had far more positive effects on employment, earnings, and poverty rates than almost anyone anticipated. The data summarized in this brief suggest that this is because work is a powerful antidote to poverty and that, in its absence, no politically feasible amount of welfare can fill the gap as effectively.

The short-term implication of this finding is that fiscally strapped states need help if they are to continue to fund programs that move welfare recipients into the work force and keep them there in a softer economy. The longer-term implication is that steps should be taken to move the entire system of benefits targeted to lower-income Americans more toward encouraging work and marriage and less toward providing unconditional assistance to those who do not work and who bear children outside of marriage. Because work-related benefits are more politically popular than those not tied to work, the system would not only be more effective per dollar spent, but it might also well enjoy the political support that would make it more generous than the one it replaced.

How to Write Effective Policy Recommendations: Summary

• 1. Define and Solve the Problem

The first challenge to writing effective policy recommendations is having a clear understanding of the problem and generating a solution supported by careful analysis. You must solve the problem. For this we return to the policy analysis method covered in Chapter 2 (the next section provides a brief review). Using a scenario table or other method to organize data, options, and criteria can also be a very useful way to sort through a complex problem. (The scenario table was introduced in Chapter 2 to summarize how each of the options compared based on the evaluation criteria. A blank scenario table is included at the end of this chapter, on page 378.)

The process of writing can actually help to clarify the problem, identify additional data needs or options, and improve the logic of the analysis. Some practitioners advocate working on a rough draft as part of the problem-solving process.[1]

• 2. Outline and Write the Report

The report should be well-structured and clearly written. Begin with a simple outline. Plug in the important points. Then go back and connect the points with good, clean prose. Because policymakers are generally busy people with no shortage of memos, people, and tasks vying for their attention, your recommendations must be structured to meet their needs. This means that the structure should be obvious—a reader can scan the headings, understand the format of the report, and even seek out just the parts that are of interest to him or her. The purpose of the report is to recommend a course of action. Therefore the report should not waste time or space describing all that you know, but should focus on what the decisionmaker needs to know.[2] The tone must be professional, because in just the first few paragraphs the reader will decide whether the writer and the ideas have any merit. So avoid opinionated, flowery, or needlessly legalistic writing—the goal is to communicate information and ideas with clarity.

Review: Basic Policy Analysis

Chapter 2 introduced a basic method of policy analysis. Throughout the book we have returned to these basic themes of defining a problem (collecting data), establishing evaluation criteria, considering alternatives (using appropriate analytical techniques), making informed decisions, and monitoring the outcomes.

In writing policy recommendations, consider the six major steps in policy analysis:

1. Verify, define, and detail the problem.
2. Establish evaluation criteria.
3. Identify alternative policies.
4. Evaluate and compare alternative policies.
5. Select the best policy among the alternatives considered.
6. Outline a strategy to monitor and evaluate the proposed policy.

• Step 1: Verify, Define, and Detail the Problem

The first step is to understand the problem within the given context. How your client, boss, or other decisionmaker defines the problem may establish key parameters. Other stakeholders are also critical in the success of a policy or program, so it is a good idea to conduct a stakeholder analysis or at least consider stakeholder interests (see Chapter 3).

Gather the information needed to conduct an analysis of the problem. Examples of types of information/data needed: Who does the problem affect? Is the problem growing? How is the problem addressed currently? Is it working? And more. As you work through the six policy analysis steps, you may discover that additional information would be helpful or that the problem needs redefinition.

Consider, for example, the problem of excessive trash around garbage containers outside multifamily apartment buildings. The problem was initially defined as being one of collections crews not taking sufficient care in their work. But the investigation reveals that the problem is actually tenants throwing their trash on the ground around the bins, in part because in the rainy weather pools of water collect near the bins—pools that tenants will not wade through. Obviously, possible solutions would differ dramatically between these two problem definitions.

• Step 2: Establish Evaluation Criteria

Evaluation criteria set parameters for potential solutions and underscore the goals and objectives. Select which evaluation criteria are most appropriate for the particular problem and most relevant to major decisionmakers. Evaluation criteria may include:

1. The *cost* of the program to taxpayers (e.g., the cost of implementing the program in terms of staff, equipment, benefits paid out, etc.).
2. The *net benefit* from the perspective of the beneficiary. What are the costs to participants? Costs may be direct costs such as paying to obtain documents, but they can also be indirect costs, such as time lost and the loss of other assistance.
3. Program *efficiency*. Is this the least costly way to produce the desired good or service (e.g., help a certain number of beneficiaries)?
4. Most social programs *redistribute* money from taxpayers to the unemployed or the working poor with the goal of creating more *equity*. Keep in mind the equity or distribution of benefits among program participants and between program participants and other poor families (especially the working poor). It is often important to define the distributional impact among various groups (such as women, men, school-age children, pensioners, disabled, and others).
5. *Administrative, legal, and political criteria.* These concerns may be of particular importance to the political or agency leadership. How easily can the solution be implemented? Will it require a new law or only a directive by the mayor? Will it be popular among the general citizens?
6. How much *uncertainty* is there in implementing the policy (especially if it is a new program)?

- ### Step 3: Identify Alternative Policies

This book explores several key concepts in public policymaking. Before focusing on specific policy options, it is useful to consider the following concepts:

- *Targeting.* Who does the problem affect? Can targeting help to allocate scarce resources? Main targeting approaches include categorical, means testing, self-targeting, and community-based targeting. (See Chapter 5.)
- *Subsidies.* What is the best way to offer assistance? In-kind, cash, vouchers; flat benefit, tiered benefit, gap formula, earnings disregard? (See Chapter 5.)
- *Stakeholders/incentives.* What are the interests of each group of stakeholders? How can interventions be structured to meet the needs of most stakeholders or to limit any opposition? (See Chapter 3.)
- *Role of government.* Is it a problem that can be solved by local government?

What are the responsibilities and resources of other levels of government? (See Chapter 6.)

- *Public vs. private.* The role of government in a market economy is to set market conditions—not to compete in the market. If the problem or program does not affect the public good, perhaps it should be left to the private sector. (See Chapter 6.)
- *Competition.* Competition can be an effective tool to improve the delivery of services and/or to reduce costs. Options include: contracting, leasing, concessions, and privatization. (See Chapter 7.)
- *Efficiency.* Will the proposed solution have a meaningful impact on the problem? Is it an efficient use of resources?
- *Measuring and evaluating success.* Do we have clear goals in mind? How will the policy/program be implemented? How will we define and measure success? (See Chapters 9–13.)

Options: Types of Policy Actions. It is worth reviewing the types of policy actions from Chapter 2. Most policy recommendations fall into one of these main types of policy actions. In making recommendations you may be asked to select the best type of action or asked to select the best alternative from a specific type of intervention, such as recommending the best way to structure a tax subsidy.

The types of policy actions are:

- *Provision* (e.g., police protection).
- *Purchase* (e.g., communal services, from a private contractor).
- *Prohibition* (e.g., driving under the influence of alcohol).
- *Requirement* (e.g., licenses for street vendors).
- *Tax/fee* (e.g., charging for use of market space).
- *Subsidization* (e.g., health care).
- *Information* (e.g., about services for small business owners).
- *Imploration* (e.g., asking citizens not to litter).

- *Steps 4 and 5: Evaluate and Select Policy*

Evaluate and Compare Alternative Policies. Measure each of the strongly competitive policy options against the evaluation criteria established for this particular policy problem. Doing nothing or no action should always be considered an option. It is likely that there will be trade-offs among the different options and it may even be that there is no real winning solution. It is important to note any important constraints and to weight the criteria accordingly. If budget constraints are very severe, then the program cost will be a critical factor. Consider the involvement of different actors (participants, various parts of the government, NGOs, private firms, interest groups) in the evaluation criteria as either a constraint or an opportunity.

The use of a scenario table or other organizing tool can be a useful way to keep track of the various elements and findings of your analysis. A comparison of benefits and costs or analyses of quantitative or qualitative data may be important to the analysis depending on the issue or the demands of the audience.

Select the Best Policy from Among the Alternatives Considered.   This is a good time for a reality check. Although a certain option may sound good on paper, can it be accomplished based on the constraints facing your jurisdiction? Keep in mind the difference between a technically superior alternative and a politically viable one. The goal is to provide policymakers with the ideas, information, questions, or tools to advance an issue or decision.

- *Step 6: Outline a Strategy to Monitor and Evaluate the Proposed Policy*

Policy recommendations should consider what would define success and how it would be measured. It is not necessary to describe a specific monitoring or evaluation plan—but it is important to indicate measurable outcomes or clear expected results. Where the recommended solution is controversial, indicating a date for a thorough performance assessment can mollify opponents.

How to Structure a Policy Recommendation

There are several different ways to structure a policy recommendation. The format selected may depend on the audience or the issue at hand. The examples of policy recommendations earlier in this chapter illustrate two very different approaches. The following is a suggested outline of how to structure a policy recommendation. This is a standard structure and readers can easily follow the logic of the argument.

Enough information must be presented about the proposed policy (or policies) to encourage enactment. This means accounting for any budget issues, suggesting legislative language (if required), describing staffing needs, and highlighting challenges or obstacles.

- *I. Summary of Problem and Recommendation*

This section should be brief and should give the reader a clear understanding of the problem, important findings/criteria, and alternatives or recommendation. Often the recommendation is briefly mentioned at the beginning and elaborated more fully in a conclusion section. Because some readers will only read the summary of a policy memo, it is important to include the main points.

- *II. Background*

A fuller description of the problem including essential facts and why the problem is important.

- *III. Analysis or Summary of Key Findings*

Present the criteria, options considered, results of data analysis, interviews, and other research conducted. It is generally best to present only the essential findings of your analysis. Additional data and documentation can be included in an appendix.

- *IV. Proposed Policy*
  - A. General description of proposed policy/policies.
  - B. Administration—what it will take to implement the policy and who will be responsible:
    - i. Requirements (including staffing, time, and an assessment of feasibility).
    - ii. Cost. Consider costs to all major stakeholders not just those accruing to the government or your client.
    - iii. Location of activity within the government or responsible agency. Who is responsible?
  - C. Budgetary implications:
    - i. Short-term costs or benefits.
    - ii. Extended-horizon costs or benefits. For example, an economic development project could have short-term costs and long-term benefits to the local budget.
  - D. Challenges (if not covered elsewhere). Are there any additional factors (political, organizational, environmental, etc.) that could influence the problem or the implementation of the proposed solution?

Forms of Policy Recommendations

The recommendations or solutions can take many forms, such as a single recommended course of action or a comprehensive agenda. The nature of the problem, feasibility of available options, or demands of the client should dictate the form of the recommendations.

- *Single Recommendation*

One proposed solution to a problem. A single solution is often used when one option is clearly superior, the problem is simple or narrowly defined, or when constraints limit the number of potential policies.

- *Comprehensive Approach: Several Complementary Recommendations*

When addressing a complex problem (one that involves several sectors or a reform of an entire sector), you may need to offer several policy recommendations. Be realistic. In offering several recommendations, you will need to take into account the costs and administrative burdens for the entire package of recommendations, or offer a way to prioritize. A comprehensive agenda to fight domestic violence might include a range of interventions, such as, improved law enforcement, emergency shelters and counseling services for victims, and public education efforts. Specifying the sequencing of actions is often essential for complex programs.

- *Graduated Approach*

The same or similar recommendations are offered at different levels of intensity, with simple or deluxe variations. For example, a program to improve the skills of new teachers could be as simple as an after-school seminar or as involved as an advanced degree and apprenticeship program. This approach is good for when it is unclear how much money or effort a decisionmaker wants to invest in the project.

- *Pilot Interventions*

Pilot interventions test the impact of new projects or significant changes in policies when the outcome is uncertain. Pilot interventions or demonstration projects involve a limited number of participants or operate for only a limited amount of time and have a full evaluation as an integral element.

- *Conditional Recommendations*

Conditional recommendations—of the form "if *x,* then *y*"—should be used only when dealing with significant uncertainties (e.g. "if *x* is elected, then *y* will be possible"; "if funding is provided, then build mass transit system"; etc.).

- *Recommendations for Existing Problems/Programs*

When addressing existing programs you will likely have several specific recommendations addressing particular concerns about the program. These recommendations will tend to be quite detailed, such as how to train or supervise staff, how to track costs, or how to more efficiently deliver services.

Oral Presentations

Many of the basic tenets of good writing are the same ingredients of a strong oral presentation. An oral presentation must be well structured, concise, and informative. Because the listeners do not have the ability to scan the document, beginning with a few words to describe the structure of your comments can be helpful. For example, "I will speak for approximately five minutes and during that time present our recommendations and analysis of the city's affordable housing crisis."

Reading from a prepared statement is boring for listeners. Better to work from a prepared outline of key points, and to make eye contact and otherwise interact with the audience. Be aware of any verbal crutches that you might use, such as frequently inserting "um," "ah," or "like" into your speech while you collect your thoughts. These little habits undermine your message and professionalism.

Consider distributing written materials or using visual aids. These materials could include a formal policy statement, key tables, or other data. Such materials can help bolster your presentation, and charts or tables are an efficient way to present budget or other numerical data.

Rehearse your presentation in front of colleagues or even simply aloud to yourself. This process will help you to become more familiar with the flow, will give you a sense of timing, and will highlight where you might need to fill in your notes or eliminate some detail.

Dissemination

Conveying recommendations to decisionmakers can be a challenge. The merits of your ideas or report notwithstanding, it can be difficult to gain the attention of major decisionmakers. Getting your recommendations into the policy arena may require something like an outreach campaign.

If the recommendations are at the behest of a specific client, delivering the policy memorandum to that client may be the beginning and the end of your responsibility. However, it is much more common that recommendations developed by organizations, government departments, or even elected officials need to be circulated among a variety of stakeholders and momentum for the ideas developed. This may require sending the report to many stakeholders, issuing several different versions of the report (going into greater or lesser detail), arranging meetings with key players, attending public hearings or other forums where the issue will be discussed, and contacting the media.

Timing can be an essential factor. Ideas that may have been unacceptable just a

> *See Exercise 14.1: Writing Policy Recommendations below.*
>
> The task in this exercise is to solve policy problems and write recommendations.

few years ago may find new support due to recent events, evolving political or economic conditions, or other factors. Although such factors can rarely be controlled, it is imperative that policy recommendations be offered in a timely manner and that recommendations reflect the current context.

Chapter Summary

Preparing policy recommendations is the culmination of this book. Except for actually seeing your recommendations put into action, it is the high point of the policy analyst's work. Working through complex policy problems requires rigorous and creative analytical thinking, and draws on many of the skills and ideas presented here.

Policy recommendations must be well written, concise, and client-oriented. Tips for writing strong policy memoranda include demonstrating an understanding of the problem and context, rigorous analysis, careful consideration of alternatives, and clear, effective writing.

Although any number of formats can be used to structure a policy statement, we recommend the following basic outline: summary (including summary of recommendation), background, analysis, and proposed policy.

The policy problems in the book's appendix provide an opportunity to write recommendations on topics including reforming social assistance, improving municipal heating and water systems, reducing urban traffic congestion, addressing the drug problem, prison overcrowding, fighting AIDS, and more.

Exercise 14.1: Writing Policy Recommendations

Now it is your turn to solve a policy problem and write a recommendation. From the book's appendix, choose a case study, then conduct your analysis and prepare your recommendation. Use the outline below and scenario table on page 378 to help organize your efforts. The cases each include specific instructions.

    I. Summary of problem and recommendation.
   II. Background.

III. Analysis (or summary of the key findings of your analysis).
IV. Proposed policy.
    A. General description of proposed policy/policies.
    B. Administration. What it will take to implement the policy and who will be responsible.
    C. Budgetary implications.
    D. Challenges (if not covered elsewhere).

Scenario Table

Evaluation Criteria	Policy Option 1 Status quo (current lunch program)	Policy Option 2	Policy Option 3
Cost			
Net benefit			
Efficiency			
Equity			
Administrative ease			
Legal issues			
Political acceptability			
Extent of uncertainty			

Appendix
Policy Case Studies

This appendix includes case studies to use for writing policy recommendations and for general policy analysis practice. The cases are based on contemporary issues in Russia, other transition countries, and the United States. Cases vary in difficulty and address many of the topics covered in the book (targeting, equity/efficiency, monitoring, evaluation, and others).

Case 1: Reforming Local Social Assistance

• *Background*

The city of Tomsk, Russia, has a new vice mayor for social problems.[1] The vice mayor has little experience in this field and so begins her new assignment by reviewing the programs for which she is responsible. The city has two district offices that handle all social protection programs administered by the city. The city has responsibility for administering housing allowances, veteran benefits, and benefits to single-parent families and families with disabled children. The city also has several locally funded social assistance programs that provide an array of in-kind benefits. The oblast office administers the Child Allowance Program and some smaller benefits such as those for victims of the Chernobyl disaster.

In visiting the district offices, the vice mayor observes that certain services are being provided on-site to clients. These include haircuts, shoe repair, and limited furniture and appliance repair. In addition, clients receive vouchers to purchase certain other goods and services such as a bath at the municipal bathhouse and food at municipal stores. A separate voucher is issued for each purchase. She is struck at how much administrative effort goes into issuing each voucher for such a small value; administration is complex because only members of households with incomes under one-half of the subsistence level are eligible for these benefits. The need for each benefit is addressed separately. Her rough estimate is that about fifteen to twenty minutes of staff time are required to issue a voucher or authorize a repair.

She is also impressed at the seeming inefficiency of the city being directly involved in providing these services. While she is present the barber stands about idle and the shoe repair counter exhibits little activity. Those providing the services generally are working with outdated equipment and therefore frequently provide lower-quality services than do others.

- *Analysis*

Following this visit, the vice mayor formed a committee consisting of the directors of the agencies under her control and charged them to prepare options for simplifying the administration of these benefits and making their delivery more efficient. She makes clear her view that determining the need and eligibility for each of these small benefits separately must be replaced with a more efficient (i.e., less staff intensive) alternative.

The committee has developed two options, both of which give clients much more choice over what goods and services they can purchase with the city's assistance, and sharply cut administration. In both cases the city staff now providing haircuts and similar services are laid off.

Option 1: Vouchers. The city will determine the average value of benefits now provided to clients under all of the small programs of the type listed above; it will also determine the number of beneficiaries. Using these data, the average value of the benefits distributed can be determined. This is the value of the new voucher. All persons eligible for these services in the future will receive a voucher with which they can purchase the services they want from all of the services now provided in-kind or with the current vouchers. More specifically, clients will receive six vouchers (one for each of six months) at the time they are determined eligible for the assistance. (Income recertification would occur each six months under both options.)

Each voucher is a booklet; the front page shows the total value of the voucher and lists the items that the voucher can be used to purchase. Each time the person makes a purchase using the voucher, it is recorded on a page in the booklet, the entry stamped by the provider, and the amount of the purchase deducted from the unused voucher balance. The provider receives a copy of the page.

The voucher system limits the range of goods and services that can be purchased with the city's help. Its use will also be restricted to those stores that are willing to accept payments in this form; but this is an expansion beyond the few municipal stores where they can now be used.

Administration remains an issue. Although the front end of the process is simplified through issuing a voucher that can be used for a range of purchases, some complexity is added from the process of verifying the payment claims made by providers (those selling the goods and services).

Option 2: Cash. This proposal is the same as the previous one except that instead of eligible households being given a voucher they receive a monthly cash payment paid directly into the person's bank account. The person then uses the cash to purchase the services now provided in-kind or through vouchers.

The advantages to the cash payment are two. First, beneficiaries can shop anywhere, not just at the stores that will accept vouchers. Second, program administration is further simplified. However, there is a risk in using cash—the beneficiaries may not spend it on the necessities for which it is intended. The common view is that it will be spent on alcohol and cigarettes.

To address this particular problem, the committee considered but did not formally recommend that the new law include a provision on this point. The provision would state that city agencies would not provide emergency services to households who had received this cash benefit *unless* the emergency arose from an event clearly beyond their control (e.g., a fire in the apartment or death in the family).

- *Your Task*

You are an adviser to the vice mayor and she asks you to prepare a recommendation for her on which option to follow. It is critical that you defend your recommendation forcefully, because she plans to employ your arguments when meeting with the mayor.

Case 2: Fostering Small Business Development

- *Background*

As the countries of Central and Eastern Europe and the former Soviet Union (CEE-FSU) make the transition to market economies, they have witnessed a large increase in the number of small and medium enterprises (SMEs).[2] These entities have experienced substantial employment growth while the older, former state enterprises have generally experienced a long and precipitous decline in both numbers and aggregate employment.

Despite the growth in SMEs, they continue to face substantial obstacles. They are subject to oversight from local governments in the areas of licensing, inspections, and tax collections. They are also subject to national taxes, and the combined tax rates from all levels of government are very high. Representatives from several inspectorates visit a single enterprise and the visits and attendant interruptions to daily operations are not coordinated. Visits are frequently accompanied by demands for extralegal fees and other considerations. The cumulative effect of these administrative impositions is to retard the pace of business development in CEE-FSU countries.

To avoid administrative hassles and high tax rates, many SMEs do not officially register as business entities. This results in unfair administrative and tax burdens for those enterprises that are registered.

• *Analysis*

The mayor and the local chamber of commerce want to foster the growth of SMEs in order to increase employment and enhance tax revenues for the city. You are given the task of devising a plan that will help SMEs to play a larger role in improving local economic performance.

The national government also has an interest in local economic development and wants to encourage successful local initiatives. However, the national government has major budget constraints such that its support is conditional on a requirement that the net local contribution to national revenues not be diminished by SME development.

The chamber of commerce is concerned that the program be designed to aid a wide range of firms. In a letter to the mayor, the chamber argued that in devising a development plan, the following considerations are important:

- It is important to recognize the diversity of SMEs. They vary along the following dimensions: number of employees, the mix of physical and human capital, degree of reliance on local infrastructure, seasonality of operations, and complexity of business processes. This diversity implies that individual companies have different needs for support and services.
- It is also important to explicitly recognize areas where company interests and the interests of public administration diverge. Business success is higher if costs (including local taxes) and regulatory requirements are kept low, but municipal administration and the public interest require adequate local tax revenues as well as safe products and workplaces. Every business must have a tax identification number and must satisfy local (municipal) registration and licensing requirements. For existing entities, there is an ongoing requirement for reregistration as well as periodic inspections and financial audits.

• *Options for a Development Strategy*

In devising a local development strategy the following four considerations are important:

1. Be aware of best practices. Successful models may be available based on other areas of the country. If local conditions are comparable, importation of these models may be appropriate.
2. Successful development will need to rely on a mix of market signals (prices and costs) and administrative regulations to achieve its objectives. Develop an understanding of the situations where each mechanism is appropriate.
3. Identify key constraints on economic development. To gather information, it may be appropriate to commission a survey of local business to better gauge the most important impediments that they face. It also can be instructive to solicit the opinions of businesses on how to address these impediments.
4. Tailor the development approach to the situation of individual industries. It is likely that different approaches will be appropriate depending on the circumstances of different industries and companies.

The tools available to assist SMEs consist of two types: reduction and simplification of local regulations, and active assistance to startup firms with key development tasks.

Administrative Regulations. Administrative regulations and (local and national) tax administration affecting enterprises are typically not coordinated. Several innovative approaches can be considered to reduce burdens on enterprises and improve tax compliance:

1. Implement one-stop registration of new business entities.
2. Coordinate tax audits.
3. Coordinate inspections.
4. Work with local tax inspection offices to develop innovative ways to avoid tax-filing requirements when taxes are not due. For example, allow enterprises to phone a preset number to indicate that they were inactive during the most recent tax period.
5. Create a hotline to identify inspectors and/or auditors who attempt to extort bribes from enterprises. This needs to be done in such a way that whistle-blowers remain anonymous.
6. Create publicity in the local media that identifies companies that avoid tax obligations. One or several of these approaches may be appropriate in individual situations.[3]

Support Services. SMEs, particularly in their early months, are subject to a high rate of failure. While business failure is a necessary situation, actions to reduce the failure rate may exert a positive effect on economic development. Support services of various kinds may be useful in reducing business failure rates. Areas where proactive support from a local economic development agency may be helpful may include the following:

- Help potential new businesses to draw up business plans.
- Provide support in one or more of the following specialized areas of business operations: accounting, marketing, and financial management.
- Conduct a survey of existing SMEs to identify the area (or areas) of greatest need.

- *Your Task*

Your assignment has two parts. First, use the information provided above and other relevant considerations to develop a program to encourage SME development in your city. In some areas where only limited information exists, you may have to first obtain more information on which to base a detailed plan in a second phase. At this point in the process, limitation on what the city can afford to spend is not an issue. But timeliness is: the mayor wants a full program to be working in six months. He believes the city Duma will act expeditiously on the legislation required. Your initial statement for the mayor's review should not exceed two pages.

The second task concerns program effectiveness. As the development plan unfolds, questions will arise as to its effectiveness. What is the marginal effect on business development and the local economy, both in the aggregate and in individual sectors? In no more than one page, describe a strategy to assess the effectiveness of the local economic development program (i.e., How will the project monitor its activities/outcomes/effectiveness? What would be the major research questions of an evaluation?).

Case 3: HIV/AIDS in Russia

- *Background*

HIV, the virus that causes AIDS, is spreading faster in the former Soviet bloc than anywhere else in the world.[4] In Russia, the numbers of those infected have nearly doubled each year since 1998. In 1995 there were only 200 reported cases of HIV in Russia; in 2001 more than 75,000 new cases were recorded, with a total of over 190,000 infected. According to the federal AIDS center the actual number of people contracting the disease last year was considerably higher, as diagnosis and the onset of symptoms often lag infection by as many as five years.

Intravenous (IV) drug use is the source of 93 percent of reported HIV cases in Russia, and the vast majority of those infected with HIV are young people. Drug use is three times more prevalent than it was five years ago. Although IV drug use is considerably higher among young men, the ratio of men to women newly infected with HIV has narrowed to 2:1, indicating that young women are increasingly at risk. Because many drug users are sexually active and/or fund their habit through prostitution, the disease is increasingly being spread through sex.

In Russia, the epidemic began among drug users in Kaliningrad, spreading quickly to Nizhney Novgorod and Tver, then striking the nation's big cities. The greatest number of cases is in the Moscow region (15,746), Sverdlovsk region (12,187), and St. Petersburg (11,973). However, the prevalence of the disease is highest in the Irkutsk region (with 398 cases per 100,000), Khanty-Mansiisk (376), Kaliningrad (367), and Samara (339).

Although the disease is spreading at record rates in Russia, it is still considered to be in its early stages, and it is believed that massive prevention activities could curtail the disease. The cost of prevention programs and resistance to publicly discussing drug use and sexual behavior has limited the response to this deadly disease. However, there is a growing concern about the economic, social, and population impacts of AIDS—as costs of treating those infected loom and as the disease targets young and working-age people.[5]

Your city has been identified as having a high rate of HIV infection, and the mayor has asked you to submit a memo recommending what the city's AIDS policies should be.

• Analysis

The city currently has no official AIDS policy, and basic treatment and prevention services are provided through a loose array of public agencies and NGOs. The regional AIDS center in a nearby city provides testing and counseling. There are 2,600 reported cases of HIV in your city. The vast majority has been recently infected and only a few people have developed full-blown AIDS and exhibit related illnesses. The AIDS drugs that might prevent people with HIV from becoming ill have generally been unavailable. Persons that are ill receive basic health services through local hospitals and polyclinics. There are two drug treatment programs and several NGOs provide AIDS awareness/prevention information and free condoms to young people and other vulnerable populations.

AIDS Education and Prevention. Public awareness about the dangers of AIDS and how it is transmitted is very low. Several NGOs provide AIDS awareness information to young people, sex workers, drug addicts, and prison inmates. The programs explain how the disease is transmitted and how abstaining from dangerous behaviors, using condoms (some distribute free condoms), and using clean needles can prevent it (some programs instruct addicts on how to bleach their needles). The programs also encourage people who might be at risk to get tested for the virus.

Currently the municipal government does not support or participate in any public education efforts.

Options. Increase the city's participation in public education activities either through direct action or through grants/contracts to NGOs. Important policy decisions in this area include whether the city should sponsor public service announcements or advertisements, whether to allow AIDS education in the public secondary schools, whether to fund the distribution of free condoms, and whether to actively encourage residents to be tested for the disease.

Public service announcements and advertisements could be inexpensive (only the cost of producing the materials), as the city is granted free time on the local cable station and can place advertisements on public buses and municipal-owned billboards. The city (or NGOs) could also prepare materials on AIDS to distribute at schools, train stations, bars, police stations, hospitals, and other high-traffic areas.

The city could provide or contract for outreach services to educate vulnerable populations (young people, drug addicts, prostitutes, etc.) about the risks of HIV infection. If the city were to provide this service directly, it would require hiring and training new staff for the department of social protection. Alternatively, the city could provide grants or contracts to encourage NGOs to increase their services. Several NGOs already have expertise in this area and could expand their services.

Drug Treatment. The city's two drug treatment programs are operating at full capacity and both report that they are forced to turn away addicts seeking help each day. Both are short-term, detoxification programs, where addicts go through drug withdrawal and are discharged without any other type of treatment. The rates of recidivism are quite high and the majority of their clients return to drug use.

Options

1. Expand drug treatment programs. Both programs have indicated that they would be interested in serving additional clients if they received sufficient funding.
2. Improve drug treatment programs. Programs that combine detoxification with treatment are more effective in ending drug use. An effective and cost-efficient approach is a twelve-step method by which addicts participate in support groups, and learn to speak about and take responsibility for their addictions. A contract could be negotiated with either provider to implement such a program.

Harm-Reduction Strategies. Needle exchange programs are a controversial but successful approach to preventing the spread of AIDS among IV drug users. Needle exchange projects have been tested in thirty-six regions of Russia and have won some support. The programs offer clean needles to IV drug users in an effort to reduce the spread of the disease through sharing dirty needles. Most programs require that addicts turn in a dirty needle for every clean one they receive. Some people are opposed to the programs because they view them as enabling an illegal activity. An international aid organization is willing to offer free training and needles to any city or NGO (with the city's consent) willing to pilot a needle exchange project. The NGO Clean Life has stated that it is willing to run the needle exchange program without cost to the city.

Option. The city or an NGO could implement a needle exchange program.

Criminal Justice Intervention. Drug use and prostitution are crimes, and many addicts and sex workers eventually come into contact with the police. A sizable percentage of the city's prison population is drug-addicted, and the spread of HIV, through drug use and homosexual sex, is a growing problem in the city's prisons. Although an NGO provides AIDS education seminars in one of the prisons, the prison population is generally considered underserved (both in terms of AIDS awareness and health care services). Police officers and prison guards have little knowledge about the disease and are concerned about their own health. Moreover, officers and guards represent a missed opportunity in that they lack the knowledge and training to recommend safe behaviors, testing, and treatment to the addicts and sex workers that they encounter.

Options. Expand education and/or health care services to the prison population. Provide training on AIDS to police officers and prison guards. Offering AIDS education for either inmates or guards is obviously cheaper than improving services— though clearly does not replace the need for health services.

Treatment. The cost of treating patients with HIV/AIDS in municipal hospitals and polyclinics has just begun to grow as the number infected increases and as patients' health deteriorates. City hospitals and clinics treat AIDS-related illnesses, including pneumonia, tuberculosis, certain cancers, sexually transmitted diseases, and others. The city does not provide AIDS drugs, although a few HIV-positive residents have obtained such treatments through the regional AIDS center.

Option. Improve treatment and services for people with HIV/AIDS. There are several ways that the city might improve services; each has different costs associated. The city could improve medical services for people with HIV/AIDS through its provision of basic health care, better coordination with the oblast's AIDS center, or by making AIDS drugs available. The city could also better coordinate services for people with AIDS, as some victims require not only medical care but also drug treatment and social services.

• *Your Task*

The mayor has asked you to present recommendations for how the city might respond to its growing AIDS crisis. The mayor would like to take some proactive steps, but is also concerned about upsetting the public and about current budget constraints. Your statement should recommend specific prevention and/or treatment options, and suggest how the city might collaborate with NGOs.

Case 4: Traffic Congestion in Ivanograd

• *Background*

The city of Ivanograd, Russia, population 400,000, suffers from severe traffic congestion in its core downtown area—a region consisting of about fifty square blocks.[6] This zone is the economic heart of Ivanograd, where the city and regional administrations are located, along with numerous banks, insurance companies, and other white-collar employers. Additionally, this zone houses the main shopping opportunities in the region.

Traffic congestion has been building for the past five to six years as more families have been able to afford to purchase a car and nothing has been done to increase the capacity of downtown streets. Actually, capacity has fallen thanks to the combination of motorists parking their cars on the street in what should be traffic lanes and the lax enforcement of parking violations by the militia.

The congestion affects not only automobile occupants but also the passengers of the city's bus and trolley systems. These systems have deteriorated over the past several years because of the huge losses the companies experience due to the high number of riders who have privileges and the unwillingness of the previous mayor to press the city Duma for fare increases. There has been no fare increase since summer 1997; so in constant rubles, fares today (2002) are only a fraction of what they were in 1997.

The new mayor was elected six weeks ago mainly on the promise to do something to reduce the congestion problem and to improve public transportation. In his campaign he was able to be vague about what he intended to do. But now he is rushing to develop a set of recommendations to place before the people and city Duma while he still has the momentum of his victory. The mayor, understanding the city's financial problems, has ruled out any significant increases in spending on transportation services.

• *Analysis*

The team the mayor commissioned to investigate the situation has developed the following information and ideas but no coherent set of recommendations.

Public Transportation. The low quality of bus and trolley service—infrequent service, overcrowding, and unreliable schedules—has pushed a significant number of former patrons into automobiles, particularly for their journeys to work.

Several cities have introduced private firms to use vans to provide a higher quality of service. They charge more than public companies, but citizens seem to be willing to pay for the better service. Initial investigation indicates that several local firms would be willing to bid for route contracts, but they would want an exclusive right to provide services on the routes where they won the tender. The basis for the competition would be the price the firm would charge and the quality of service it would provide—type of vehicles and frequency of service.

Given the mayor's prohibition on increased city expenditures, the only way to improve the quality of public transportation is to raise more revenue from trips provided. The team, working with the Transportation Committee, has on an experimental basis introduced two conductors on some buses and trolleys to rigorously collect fares that now should be paid. They found that revenues collected increased by 55 percent on the same routes under this system. After paying the cost of the extra conductor, there was still a 30 percent increase.

The team estimates that with the two-conductor system in place, service frequencies could be increased by about 20 percent by increasing expenditures on maintenance that would put more buses and trolleys on the streets. If fares were increased by 25 percent (and sustained at that level in real terms), new equipment could be acquired and service frequencies increased by 40 percent compared to today's level.

These actions would result in definite improvements, but much decrease in travel times would be hard to achieve without cutting congestion in the center of the city.

Addressing Congestion. One option is to ban all but official vehicles and public buses, vans (if this option is adopted), and trolleys from the city center. There is concern that this would not be politically feasible: the important people who funded the mayor's campaign would demand that they be exempted from such restrictions. But the exceptions would be highly visible and could create a major problem for the mayor with the voters.

A second option is to restrict access to the city center during workdays by requiring all private vehicles (except taxis) with access to have a sticker on their windshield indicating that they had paid the annual fee for the sticker. The stickers would be numbered and registered to a particular individual and car; so it would fairly easy to identify cheaters.

The team thinks that the price for the sticker should be set so that only about 5 percent of car-owning households could afford it (about 1,000 households). But they expect only about half to actually purchase the sticker. They estimate that businesses would purchase stickers for about 300 vehicles at almost any price. They think the annual price should be 9,000–10,000 rubles.

There are four potential problems with the sticker idea that must be addressed in any plan:

1. *Enforcement.* Fines for entering the central zone without a sticker and a larger fine for a false sticker are essential. Somehow incentives will have to be created for the militia to enforce the new restrictions.
2. *Parking at the periphery of the central zone.* Many drivers may try to park their cars in the neighborhoods surrounding the city center. This would have an adverse impact on the quality of life for those living there and on the efficiency of business operations.
3. *Resistance by merchants.* The shopkeepers and bankers in the central zone will likely object, because they will be worried about a decline in customers.
4. *Commuter discontent.* Those who cannot afford the stickers may be angry that they cannot drive to the center. While the hope is that the faster service for all the passengers using public transportation will compensate for this, it remains a concern.

A third option is to address congestion through restricting the number of parking places in the city center, charging high fees for them wherever possible, and rigorously fining those parking illegally. This approach has the advantage that it is far less dramatic than the direct restrictions on access. But the problem of developing incentives for the militia to enforce the new parking ordinance remains. Thus a critical part of this option is establishment of a new training program for the militia on parking enforcement and traffic management more generally. Nevertheless, worries about the effectiveness of the program remain. (This would involve minor budget expenditures to bring in outside experts.)

A fourth option to is to supplement the stronger enforcement with the provision of more parking in off-street parking structures. Preliminary analysis shows that there are lots available, owned by the city, for the construction of the structures. At reasonable rates (45 rubles per day) structures accommodating 400 cars could be built. A key assumption in the financial analysis is that on work days at least 300 of the parking places are occupied. There are two related concerns with this initiative:

- Unless the militia enforce the parking restrictions, utilization may be below the 300 level.

- Since the city does not have the funds for the construction, private developers have been contacted. They are deeply worried about the ineffectiveness of the militia and are asking for a city guarantee under which they would receive payment from the city of the difference between their actual revenues and revenues from a 300-space utilization rate on all workdays.

A fifth option is to engage traffic management experts to improve the efficiency of the utilization of the existing road network. The consultant may recommend implementation of one-way streets, better synchronization of stoplights, and similar measures. A review of the literature suggests that such improvements typically add 15–20 percent to the effective street capacity. Engaging the consultant is expected to cost around 2 million rubles; implementing these improvements would cost approximately 10–15 million rubles.

- *Your Task*

Use the information provided above and other ideas you may have to develop a concise policy program for the mayor to address the congestion problem. Your initial statement for the mayor's review should not exceed two pages.

The policy recommendations at a minimum should contain at least one initiative to address congestion and one to improve public transportation and make a case as to how they complement each other.

Other criteria for judging the recommended program:

- It meets all of the mayor's constraints.
- It is likely to have a significant impact on congestion. For example, the improved enforcement of current parking regulations is likely not to have a significant impact.
- It addresses issues of administrative feasibility and indicates how to address/overcome various problems associated with the recommended actions.

Case 5: Selection of the Child Allowance Calculation Method

- *Background*

Families with children have the greatest probability of living in poverty, according to an analysis of poverty risks among different segments of the population conducted by the International Labour Organization's Moscow bureau.[7] According to Russia's state Statistics Committee (Goskomstat), families with one or two children account for 19 percent of very poor families (households with a disposable income below the subsistence minimum), while families with three children account for 41 percent of such families. Single-parent families account for 23.4

percent of very poor families. The average level of extreme poverty for all households lies between 12 and 14 percent.

• *Analysis*

From the viewpoint of government spending, the most significant social program is the monthly allowance to families with children. Child allowance payments from the federal Compensation Fund amount to about 24 billion rubles annually. This testifies to the government's efforts to reduce the burden on poor families with children through government transfers. In addition, previous reforms of the child allowance program reflect the government's efforts to target scarce budget resources to the most vulnerable groups of the population. For example, child allowances were previously paid to all children under sixteen (or eighteen if they continued to study at secondary educational institutions). In 2002 these benefits were targeted to families whose income is below the official subsistence minimum in the region where they live. At present, 22 million children are entitled to allowances, or about two-thirds of all children in Russia, according to Russia's Ministry of Labor. Monthly allowances to citizens with children are currently 70 rubles per child in Russia.[8] According to 2001 statistics, such allowances amounted to only 6 percent of the child's subsistence minimum. So it is obvious that such allowances do little to reduce the level of poverty in families with children.

The problem can also be analyzed from the viewpoint of households' average budget deficit, that is, the difference between the subsistence minimum and the average per capita household income. In 2002 the average household budget deficit amounted to 1,200 rubles per month, or 360 rubles per family member. However, in families with children the average monthly budget deficit is larger. It amounts to 1,500 rubles in families with one or two children, 2,500 rubles in families with three children, and 2,600 rubles in single-parent families with three children. Consequently, the monthly child allowance covers only 5 percent of the average family budget deficit.

Assume that proposals to increase the child allowance are being considered. Preparation of such proposals requires an analysis of the budget expense of larger allowances, the allowance's impact on the level of poverty in families with children, and the probability of increased demand for higher allowances.

A specific option to consider is a revision of the child allowance calculation formula—replacing the fixed benefit with an allowance whose amount would be determined by the difference between the total family income and the poverty line (gap benefit). Proponents of this option suggest that 50 percent of the subsistence minimum should be adopted as the "administrative poverty line" and used to determine eligibility and calculate child allowances. One reason for using 50 percent of subsistence is that the government does not have the resources to raise all families to the subsistence level. Given these limitations, this option concentrates resources to the "poorest among the poor"—families whose income is lower than a half of the subsistence minimum.

The main options are to keep the benefit program as is or to adopt a gap formula offering benefits up to 50 percent of the subsistence level.

- *Options*

    Option 1. Eligible families receive a fixed allowance in accordance with legislation. Income distinctions are not drawn among eligible families. An example of fixed allowances is the current monthly allowance, with a base amount of 70 rubles.
    Option 2. The allowance guarantees total family income of 50 percent of the subsistence minimum. The allowance fills the gap between family income and 50 percent of the poverty line. The amount of the allowance depends on the family income. Each additional ruble in the family income means a reduction of the allowance by one ruble.

- *Your Task*

As a government ministry adviser, you are required to write recommendations for changing or preserving the formula for monthly allowances for citizens with children.

Criteria. Your recommendations must follow the basic principles of government social policy, which include the following:

- The more children a poor family has, the larger the government aid to that family should be.
- The poorer a family is, the larger the government aid to that family should be.
- A family with working members should have a larger total income than a family living only on government aid.
- The system of allowance payments must not create negative incentives for the aid recipient (such as an incentive to conceal their income).

When preparing recommendations, you must complete a comparative analysis of the two options based on the criteria listed above, as well as analyze the options from the viewpoint of financial limitations and the importance of the allowance to the income of families with children. Your assessment of financial limitations should include a rough estimate of the cost of Option 2. For the cost estimate assume that roughly half of the 22 million children living in poverty will be eligible. Information included in the case about the subsistence level and household budget deficits can be used to estimate the benefits. Include notes indicating what data are required for a more precise cost estimate. If Option 2 appears to be too expensive, ask yourself whether there are other ways that child allowances might be restructured to better meet the needs of families living in extreme poverty.

Case 6: Overcrowding in US Courts and Detention/Correctional Facilities Due to Illegal Drug Cases

• Background

In the late 1980s the US government passed several anti–drug abuse acts that forced changes in local law enforcement policies and practices.[9] Cook County, Illinois, with its major city of Chicago, offers a good example of these changes and the related policy issues.

Cook County has 120 police departments, including the Chicago Police Department, which is the third largest in the United States. In Cook County, most arrests for marijuana are considered misdemeanors (i.e., less serious offenses), while arrests for other narcotics are considered felonies (i.e., more serious offenses).[10] Arrests in the county for illegal drugs, except marijuana, increased from 10,000 in 1986 to more than 30,000 in 1988. Marijuana arrests actually declined during that period, from 17,000 to 10,000, but later increased. By 1995 the annual number of drug arrests in the county was more than 50,000.

Each year, the Cook County Courts, which constitute the largest court system in the United States, handle more than 40,000 felony and 300,000 misdemeanor cases. As a result of increased felony drug arrests, the number of court cases nearly doubled in the 1980s and 1990s. Drug offenses now account for more than half of all Cook County Courts felony case filings. Overall, including arrests for marijuana use, Cook County Courts handled more than 50,000 drug cases per year in the mid-1990s. In addition, more that 58 percent of felony probation sentences and 50 percent of prison sentences involve drug violations.

The increase in drug cases has overwhelmed the criminal justice system. Court dockets are booked to maximum capacity, and unable to keep pace with the new cases that need to be tried. Also, because court schedules are so heavily booked, it takes longer for a case to come to trial. As a result, some people are spending more time in jail awaiting trial—this has compounded the problem by causing overcrowding of the detention facilities.[11] In addition, both jail and prison facilities are now overcrowded, as more individuals are found guilty and sentenced to serve time in a correctional institution. In order to continue to incarcerate drug offenders, the state will need to build additional regional prison cells, or the county will need to expand its jail space.

Furthermore, prosecutors, judges, and other criminal justice staff (e.g., probation officers) are becoming frustrated, because many of the same offenders keep being recycled through the system—arrested, sentenced, placed on probation or incarcerated, then rearrested, resentenced, and placed on probation again or reincarcerated. High probation violation rates are one sign that court mandates are not deterring drug use. Some estimates suggest that more than 50 percent of drug offenders reoffend within two to three years. Criminal justice system practitioners want a more effective way to handle drug offenders to reduce substance abuse relapse and criminal recidivism.[12]

Aside from the impact on the criminal justice system, citizens are increasingly unhappy with the impact of drug use—particularly injection drug use—on their neighborhoods. They worry that drug users may contribute to increases in other crimes, such as theft to support their drug addictions. Also, citizens are concerned about drug equipment (e.g., dirty needles, syringes, etc.) that users discard in the streets or in alleys. Not only do they dislike seeing the trash in public places, but they also express concern about public safety, particularly for small children, who may pick up the litter and be hurt by a needle or even the drug substance.

The governor of Illinois has asked the mayor of Chicago to establish model approaches that can be introduced in Chicago and later replicated in other cities in the state. The mayor has convened a Task Force on Improving Responses to Drug Crime to identify the policies that should be implemented. The task force includes representatives of several police departments, two judges, the district attorney, a public defender, the administrator of the jail, the chief probation officer, and the director of the city's Public Health Department.

• Analysis and Options

The Task Force on Improving Responses to Drug Crime held a two-day meeting during which participants shared a wealth of information about the impact of drug crime, and possible solutions that should be considered. However, the task force did not draft a concise set of recommendations. Key information discussed during the meeting is summarized below.

Option I: Addressing the Overcrowding in Courts and Detention Facilities

a. More efficient processing. Given the increasing demand for court services, the county invested in a reasonably sophisticated automated scheduling system several years ago. Most local law enforcement and criminal justice staff believe the system is very good; it automatically schedules courtroom time, and notifies judges, prosecuting and defense attorneys, defendants, and victims of the date, time, and courtroom for each specific case. As it stands now, all judges and courtrooms are fully booked during daytime business hours, so there is no way to process more cases during the day.

b. Increasing the courts' capacity. The current courthouse is only five years old, and ran wildly over budget when it was built, much to the disgust of citizens. Everyone at the meeting agrees that local political leaders will not be willing to make a capital investment in more courtroom facilities. One option that has been suggested, but to the task force's knowledge has never been tried by any other jurisdiction, is to schedule drug cases for a "night court." This would involve holding sessions in the evening only for drug offenders after the rest of the court's business has been concluded. All of the court's rooms would be available for use at that time. This not only would reduce the court's backlog, but also could help alleviate the overcrowding of the detention center. However, it will be necessary to find staff to hear the evening cases. Some incentive will have to be offered to motivate judges, attorneys, and other staff to work evening hours.

Option II: Reducing the Number of Cases Flowing into the System by Not Bringing Misdemeanor Offenders to Trial. Several other cities that have experienced dramatic increases in drug offenses have implemented policies to reduce the demand for criminal justice resources.

a. Ticketing. One option is to have police issue tickets to misdemeanor offenders, rather than arrest them. The offenders then are expected to pay a fine, much like a traffic ticket. The tickets would be tracked just as traffic tickets are tracked, and offenders would be liable to pay a more expensive fine if they fail to pay the initial ticket within the prescribed period of time. The police seem to approve of this idea, suggesting that it would provide the city with extra revenue, which could be used to support other crime-fighting efforts or to improve neighborhoods in other ways.

The district attorney and the judges want to send offenders the message that misdemeanor drug use is more serious than a parking infraction. To make this point, and also to serve as a deterrent to future drug use, they insist that the amount of the original ticket should be set higher than that for traffic tickets (e.g., $200 for marijuana use, as compared to $75 for a parking ticket or $100 for driving through a red light or making an illegal turn). Failure to pay within thirty days would result in a 10 percent penalty for each additional thirty days of delinquent payment (e.g., an offender who pays sixty days late will owe $240). This could generate upward of $5 million per year in new ticket revenue.

The public defender (who provides free legal services to people who cannot afford to pay for legal services) likes the idea of ticketing misdemeanants rather than arresting them, but points out that many of these people will not have the money to pay the amount of the original ticket. She is concerned that poor offenders will fail to pay the initial fine, and then receive reminders asking for increasing payments associated with each delay. She points out that if such offenders were unable to afford the initial fine, they are even less likely to be able to pay the higher penalties. And she suggests that eventually the agency monitoring collection of fines will ask the courts to serve a warrant so police can arrest these individuals for nonpayment. Ultimately, this might undercut the gains that could be made in reducing courtroom caseloads.

b. Diversion programs.   Another option is to offer misdemeanants, and possibly first-time felony offenders, an alternative to going to trial. Several jurisdictions have introduced diversion programs. To be eligible for inclusion in a diversion program, the offender must admit his/her guilt and sign an agreement with the district attorney. This is a kind of quid pro quo: the county, district attorney, public defender, police, and probation departments are saved the costs associated with a courtroom trial; in return, the offender is placed under probation supervision in the community for a shorter period of time than would have been likely if the person had been found guilty in a court proceeding. Currently, the average period of probation for drug offenders who are actually sentenced to such supervision is two years, at an annual cost of approximately $2,751 per probationer.

Either option is likely to reduce the number of cases that clog courtroom dockets; however, there are various trade-off decisions or costs associated with the two options. There is concern that Option II(a)—ticketing—may not be politically acceptable. The current federal administration has a central campaign platform built around the "war on drugs." The mayor and the governor are both members of the party in office, and are unlikely to approve a program that has the appearance of being "soft" on drug users, despite public opinion polls that suggest citizens see marijuana use differently from use of other illegal drugs. In addition, estimates of offender ability to pay drug fines vary considerably: approximately 28 percent of misdemeanor drug offenders are employed; and recent studies on felony offenders have estimated that anywhere from 19 to 54 percent are employed. The reports do not estimate the average income for those who are employed.

Option II(b)—diversion programs—also has some drawbacks. As it stands now, about 40 percent of all misdemeanor offenders (including drug offenders and those arrested on other low-level criminal charges) leave courtroom trials without receiving a punishment such as probation supervision or referral to needed services. The data are muddled, so it is not easy to determine whether this includes most misdemeanor drug offenders or whether they are more likely to receive a sentence. However, if offenders believe they stand a good chance of receiving no punishment in a court trial, they will be unlikely to voluntarily plead guilty and enter a diversion program. Furthermore, if they do agree to enroll in the diversion program, it may greatly increase the numbers and costs of offenders under probation supervision. One possibility is to provide incentives. For example, an agreement that probation will be limited to a one-year period and that, if offenders agree to voluntarily seek drug treatment and provide documentation showing they successfully completed such treatment, the DA will not formally charge them and their arrest record will be erased.

Option III: Preventing Relapse and Recidivism.   Regardless of what decisions are made to reduce the flow of drug abusers entering the court system, some decisions must be made to reduce the public harms associated with drug criminals.

a. Sentence more serious offenders to longer prison terms.   One possibility is to sentence the more serious offenders to longer prison terms. However, the prisons are already filled to capacity. Therefore, increasing the prison time of offenders would entail having to build new jails or prisons, or expand existing incarceration facilities. Use of this approach would involve increasing costs of two types: an average annual per-person incarceration cost of $25,607; and the cost of new construction, at approximately $28,600 per bed or $43 million for an annex of 1,500 additional beds.

What's more, eventually the imprisoned offenders will reach the end of their sentence and have to return to their home communities, raising the possibility of relapse and recidivism. New approaches to drug treatment appear promising. For most substance abusers, the treatment can be as effective when offered on an outpatient basis as when provided in a residential facility.

b. Implement a drug court.   Another option that can be considered is a new approach called a drug court, a specialized court to which the offender returns on a weekly basis. The court program, which combines therapeutic practices with legal sanctions, includes intensive supervision and monitoring, court-ordered outpatient drug treatment, and supportive social assistance services such as employment preparedness training. The judge orders the individual into treatment and checks his or her weekly progress, and a probation officer does frequent drug tests to ensure the individual is not using drugs.[13] If the test shows the person has relapsed, the judge immediately enforces a punishment, and punishments become more and more severe with each relapse. Ultimately, if the individual cannot progress with treatment, the fallback position is to send him or her to prison.

Drug courts that have been implemented elsewhere show a one-year treatment retention rate of 60 percent, compared to 10–30 percent of substance abusers who agree to voluntary treatment. Also, there is some evidence of lower posttreatment rearrest rates. The cost per participant of a community-based drug court, including treatment and drug testing, is $3,248 ($10.48 per day for an average of about 301 days).

While the costs of this approach are lower than those of incarceration, this shifts the perspective from a criminal justice problem to a health problem. The public health arena is not currently prepared to offer outpatient drug treatment to meet this new demand. In fact, it already must contend with waiting lists of people who have voluntarily sought treatment.

• *Your Task*

The potential interventions identified by the Task Force on Improving Responses to Drug Crime fall into three major categories:

1. To more efficiently process cases once they enter the system.
2. To reduce the number of cases flowing into the system.
3. To treat drug addiction to avoid future relapse and recidivism.

Use the information provided above, and other ideas you develop, to concisely draft a policy program that can be implemented in Chicago. Bear in mind the costs of the various interventions, the administrative burden, and the potential political issues.

Case 7: Municipal Heat Supply

• *Background*

At the beginning of the transition period in Romania, the district heating company's assets and liabilities were transferred to municipal ownership in Pluku along with the responsibility to provide the heat supply to the residents, commercial and industrial institutions, as well as municipal budgetary organizations.[14]

In general, the district heating systems were transferred at the time when most of the equipment was close to or beyond its useful life and in poor condition due to long neglected maintenance. For the past ten years, the overall political and economic situation, uncertainty of ownership, sharply rising fuel and equipment prices, and economic difficulties of the population have caused a severe shortage of public (budget) funds. Due to a low collection rate and inability to increase heat tariffs, the district heating company is unable to create positive cash flow. So it had no choice but to cut maintenance expenses and defer or eliminate investments. This caused a sharp deterioration of equipment and a fall in the quality of service even as costs increased. In this situation, dissatisfaction with district heating services has increased the problem with payment collection from residents and from commercial institutions. Customers were not properly supplied with heat, the cost was ever-increasing, and many users started to disconnect from the system, turning to "micro heating solutions." This in turn escalated the cost of heat, as the revenues decreased and the fixed costs remained at the same level or increased due to increased operating costs.

• *Analysis*

The main problem the municipality faces is the inability to obtain financing for the system upgrade and operation. Cost of heat sold to residents is regulated at the municipal level, and the municipal council is not willing to allow higher heat tariffs in an attempt to protect citizens from high prices. The low level of income of the general population contributes to a high percentage of nonpayment. This adds to the financial problem of the heating company, causing secondary debts (gas, water, electricity), and frequent shutoffs of supplies. Currently, the company operates with negative cash flow.

In order to rectify this situation, the system must be upgraded to working condition, with careful attention paid to energy efficiency. The cost of fuel is very high, which drives the high cost of heat. The supply-side energy efficiency (boiler houses and distribution system) should be evaluated and based on the findings, an investment program should be implemented.

The municipal administration, including the mayor, vice mayor, and technical staff, spends a substantial amount of time and effort addressing heat problems throughout the city, including using emergency measures to supply heat to hospitals, schools, and other critical users. Severe dissatisfaction with heat supply among the residents causes a low rating of the elected officials, and also unwise use of resources for emergency measures.

The mayor sees a chance to improve the situation as a result of three factors:

1. The national policy to increase cost recovery from the population and other users will generate a positive cash flow for the district heating company.
2. The city Duma (legislature), under great pressure from residents and businesses, has just passed legislation creating an interagency commission to regulate tariffs that will have full power to set tariffs in the future, subject only to an ex post review of the supporting calculations.
3. A new national program will guarantee loans taken by municipalities from commercial banks to finance improvements. The district heating company must submit a sound business plan for loan repayment as part of its loan package. Local banks are interested in participating.

The mayor's office has created a Municipal Energy Commission and charged it with resolving the heat supply issue with three main goals:

• To provide reliable heat supply to all connected users.
• To produce and deliver heat at lowest possible cost (heat tariff).
• To minimize the investment requirement.

The requirements set by the mayor's office contradict each other (that is, to provide reliable service with minimum costs and investments) and a reasonable compromise must be reached. As the basis for such a decision, detailed, comprehensive information must be prepared. The commission investigated the system of heat delivery in the city and determined the following:

- The present district heating system was built in the 1970s and no major investment or retrofit has been made since. Boiler-house equipment uses original low-tech controls, pumps, and regulating valves, and other equipment is controlled manually. Boilers are inspected according to the safety regulation and are maintained to comply with these requirements. The plant was originally built as a combined heat and power plant, but the turbines and generators were decommissioned and removed, leaving empty space.
- The distribution system was also built in the 1970s. The magistrala is in relatively good condition, but the other primary pipes are poorly insulated and have substantial heat loss and very large water leaks. Repairs are being done only to resolve critical defects.
- Substation equipment is in poor condition. The majority of heat exchangers are leaking or have already been bypassed, a circulator station typically has only one pump (i.e., the reserve pump is not functional), and all controls are manual.
- The fuel, electricity, and water consumption data for the past several years are available, as well as other cost data from the operation. Heat sale data are also available; however, this information was generated based on a calculation/accounting formula, and estimates of losses and other factors are not reliable.
- There is a natural gas distribution network in the city, with sufficient capacity. The gas supply company is willing to provide gas for individual boilers if desired. However, the gas company is not willing to invest in a building-to-building gas distribution system for small-building boilers. Such investment would have to be made by the users.
- The central district heating system has already lost 80 percent of its industrial customers, and 15 percent of residents are also disconnected. The total load has decreased by 40 percent since 1990, with a leveling off occurring in 1998–2000.

Based on the audit and its findings, the team has developed three main alternatives of heat supply reconstruction with subsequent issues in each alternative. The following alternatives were presented to the municipal council for its decision:

- *Options*

Option 1: Reconstruct the Central District Heating System. In this alternative, the existing district heating system would be preserved, the central heating plant upgraded, distribution pipes replaced to eliminate major leaks and heat losses, and replacement would continue over the next several years as part of an increased maintenance program. All substation equipment would be replaced by a new modern heat exchange system. The upgrade of the central heating plant could be achieved using one of the following three alternatives:

> *1.1: Coal-fired boilers with heat production only* (no electricity production). The advantages of this alternative are the low cost of fuel, relatively low cost of heat, and use of existing fuel-handling equipment and systems, including fuel yard, conveyers, and pulverizing mills. Disadvantages are the higher cost of equipment ($100 per kWt), high emission levels, and ash disposal problems.
>
> *1.2: Gas-fired boilers with heat production only.* This alternative offers clean operation with low emissions, relatively low investment cost ($50 per kWt), and simple installation. Disadvantages include the relatively high cost of fuel, resulting in high heat tariff.
>
> *1.3: Installation of a combined heat and power system.* This alternative assumes removal of some of the oldest equipment from the plant and installation of a combined heat and power system consisting of a gas turbine, heat recovery steam boiler, and steam turbine. The combined heat and power system would produce the required heat and electricity. This alternative offers the best economic results, lowest heat tariff, high efficiency, and low emissions, and improves the reliability of electricity supply in the town. Disadvantages include the high investment cost ($600 per kWt), difficult negotiations with the electric distribution company, and need for skilled turbine operators.

Another issue related to the district heating alternatives is the ownership of the plant and the system. The options for ownership and operation are:

- Owned and operated by the city as a municipal department. This arrangement is considered impractical and difficult to implement. The city lacks personnel resources, facilities, and overall experience in operating the district heating system.
- Owned by the city and operated by a concessionaire under a long-term contract (twenty years). This option is considered reasonably easy to implement, attractive to operate, and high-performing, assuming a well-written

contract. This option is also found in many other Eastern European cities, and favored by the commission.

- Sale of the system to a private investor prior to investment (as is). A potentially viable option, but the assumption of interest by an outside private investor is weak. The disadvantages are a very low book value, low expected revenue from sale, and little to no municipal control over the performance.
- Sale of the upgraded system to a private investor (after the investment). This option is viewed as unlikely to be implemented, due to the limited capacity of municipal staff and the inability to obtain an investment loan.

Option 2: Construct Local Boiler Houses. This alternative assumes decommissioning the current heating plant, eliminating primary network pipes (pipes connecting the plant with substations), and constructing small boiler houses in existing substations. Investment would include installation of boilers in existing substation buildings, necessary replacement of secondary pipes (pipes between the substations and buildings), installation of new pumps, controls, and metering equipment, and necessary gas supply pipes, water piping, and electrical installation.

Advantages of this alternative include elimination of primary pipe heat losses and water leaks. Eliminating these losses would increase the efficiency of the system, lower investment cost, provide better and more responsive heat supply, eliminate the need for the substation heat exchange system, and facilitate relatively easy maintenance. The main disadvantage is the slightly higher operating costs (more personnel in each boiler house).

The operation and ownership issues were identical with the central system alternative (owned and operated by the city, owned by the city and operated by concessionaire, and sale to private investor—either as is or after investment).

Option 3: Install Building-Level Boilers. This alternative assumes decommissioning the entire district heating system and installing a small boiler in each building throughout the town. This represents a major change in heat supply service and many issues must be considered, including the following:

> *3.1: Ownership, financing, and operation responsibility would be transferred to users* (residents, town, commercial users). The city would install boilers on users' property, but would not maintain, operate, or bill for ongoing heating services.
>
> *3.2: A substantial investment would be required.* Extensive installation of natural gas pipes would be needed, including high-pressure lines, reduction stations, and low-pressure pipes. The gas company is not likely to pay

for this investment, as total sales would not increase due to a loss of load in the central plant.

> *3.3: The investment cost of this alternative is substantially higher than that of any other alternative.* It is approximately 20–25 percent higher than central district heating investment due to a need for gas piping, construction of stacks, and higher cost of small boilers (dollars per kWt). The advantages of this alternative are elimination of heat losses in distribution piping, much better controls in the building, better incentives for energy saving, and heat cost reduction.

> *3.4: The difficult issue for this alternative is obtaining financing.* It is not possible to secure a loan for each individual owner, and it is very difficult to "organize" financing through the town assistance programs. Users, especially residents, lack the resources for self-financing.

• *Your Task*

The decision of the mayor will be based on all available technical and economic information and the balance of the advantages and disadvantages. Use the information provided above to prepare and defend a recommendation for resolving the critical problem with heat supply in the town. Your recommendation should include both an investment plan and an ownership form for the utility.

In preparing your recommendation, keep in mind that the interest rate on any loan taken by the municipality will be high, and so keeping investment cost low is an important criterion. However, all parties involved understand the trade-off between low investment costs and higher operating costs.

Case 8: Whether to Use Federal Funds for Modernizing Housing and Utility Services

• *Background*

Russian housing and utility services need investment to reverse the rapid depreciation of fixed assets and ensure normal functioning of the utility infrastructure.[15] Housing experts estimate the current housing investment needs at 550 billion rubles. Such needs result from inadequate financing of housing and utilities in the 1990s, which deferred necessary repairs and investments and reduced the quality of services. One consequence of this situation is an increased number of accidents and a corresponding need for emergency repairs.

These "debts" must be paid soon to prevent further deterioration. There is considerable pressure on governments to invest in housing and utility services. However, at some point in the future, private investors are expected to be the main source of funds for the utility service complex, with repayments to investors made from utility tariffs. Utility privatization remains controversial and it is not clear when or how such a transition would occur.

Amid this uncertainty, it is clear that the housing and utility service complex needs a significant amount of funds and economic restructuring to increase efficiency.

• Analysis

During budget negotiations in the state Duma, one of the political factions proposed to establish a federal fund for financing housing and utility modernization. The idea is that the most effective modernization projects should be cofinanced on a competitive basis. The proposal states the following potential impacts:

- The regions and municipalities will be stimulated to invest in modernization of the housing and utility sector, because such investment will make it possible to attract federal government funds to their regions.
- Competitive procurement will help regions learn how to assess the efficiency of projects and prepare business plans correctly.
- Private investors will see investment in the housing and utility sector as profitable and begin to invest their funds, eventually reducing the need for government investment.

• Your Task

You, as a government expert, are required to prepare a response to the state Duma's proposal. When doing this, you should remember that the budget prepared by the government provides only for federal spending to help Russia's regions eliminate emergencies that threaten human lives and health. The proposed spending item is much smaller than the actual amount needed to establish a federal fund for modernizing the housing and utility service complex. However, even this proposal provokes objections, because the housing and utility sector falls within the jurisdiction of local authorities and is not financed from the federal budget. Opposing Duma deputies may cite the division of expenditure responsibilities as a reason to reject the proposed fund.

Your task is to write an expert opinion containing recommendations on the following:

1. Should federal government funds be used for the modernization of the housing and utility service complex?
2. If so, what are the priorities for investment (e.g., the largest, the most obsolete, or the most profitable facilities of the housing and utility service complex, or those located in the poorest regions)?

Consider the following factors when evaluating the policy options:

1. Impact on the financial situation in the housing and utility service complex.
2. Incentives to reform the housing and utility service complex (e.g., resource saving, reduction of power consumption, etc.).
3. Potential administrative costs at the federal level.
4. The expenditure responsibilities of the federal authorities, and their responsibilities in the eyes of the regional and local authorities and the population.

Case 9: Supporting Homeownership

• Background

The city of Dutik in central Russia has a population of about 500,000 and has suffered from a housing shortage for many years.[16] Municipal data show that 22 percent of dwellings are occupied by three-generation families and that, on average, newly married couples live with the parents of one of the partners for eight years before acquiring an apartment of their own.

In the last mayoral election the winning candidate promised to expand the supply of housing in Dutik. The new mayor is aware that the city has limited funds to devote to the housing sector. So he is opposed to the construction of more municipal housing, where the city pays the full cost of a new unit. Since privatization of municipal housing is still in force, most new units are quickly privatized after occupancy (and lost to the city for further use). Rather, he wants a solution under which the city only pays for part of the cost and the beneficiary household pays the rest.

• Analysis and Options

Staff of the Committee for Housing and Communal Services have developed three options. In each of these options, eligible households would be those with moderate incomes, which the staff defines as a *maximum* monthly income of 24,000 rubles,[17] and currently occupying a unit smaller than the standards defined in the city's housing allowance program. Families on the waiting list would be given priority.

The city's assistance would be limited to subsidizing the cost of a standard apartment. The family could purchase a larger unit, but only the standard number of square meters could be subsidized.

Option 1: Interest Rate Subsidy on Mortgage Loan Through a Commercial Bank. Under this scheme the city would provide a subsidy to cover 2 percentage points of the interest on a dollar-denominated, ten-year mortgage loan to the family. The maximum interest rate the bank could charge the borrower is 13 percent. So the maximum total interest rate would be 15 percent. The city would pay the bank each year for the interest subsidy. Credit risk would be the sole responsibility of the bank originating the loan.

An advantage to using commercial banks for the lending option is that it would encourage banks to be more active in making mortgage loans generally. Banks also have greater lending expertise than municipal agencies.

Option 2: Interest Rate Subsidy on Mortgage Loan Through a Municipal Agency. Some have expressed the view that commercial banks will not give sufficient weight to social considerations in making decisions on granting loans to potential borrowers. For this reason they propose that the city establish its own agency to administer the program. A major disadvantage of this approach is that the city would have to use its own funds for the full loan amount and therefore would be able to provide assistance to fewer households.

Option 3: Downpayment Subsidies. In this case the city would provide a subsidy of 20 percent of the cost of the standard unit directly to the seller when the unit is completed. The advantages are several: the value of the subsidy is very clear to everyone; there is no uncertainty about the city making payments year after year to the commercial bank; and the city still leverages the funds it has available.

- *Issues*

Banks have expressed general interest in the mortgage program. But they are very concerned about the risk of the city not making subsidy payments over the full ten-year life of the mortgage loan.

The option of municipal agency–as-lender raises several issues: whether the city would be able to attract competent staff; how long it would take to make a new agency operational; and the problem of possible lax loan underwriting and of the agency making loans to "favored clients" in exchange for bribes.

A principal issue is whether the subsidy should only apply to newly constructed units or whether it could be used for the purchase of existing apartments as well. Some argue that it is not necessary to directly subsidize construction to encourage more housing to be built. They say that some of those who would sell their apartments to those using the city subsidy would use the proceeds of the sale to purchase a new, probably larger, apartment or a cottage. Real estate agents consulted report that the price per square meter of existing units is about 10–15 percent less than that for new units. So a program that let the households receiving the subsidy buy either a new or existing unit could save money. Of course, this would require that the city set separate cost limits for new and existing units.

• *Your Task*

The vice mayor charged with preparing a proposal for the mayor has asked you to write up a policy recommendation. You are to make recommendations in two areas:

1. The type of subsidy program to adopt.
2. The type of housing eligible for the subsidy—only new construction or new and existing apartments.

Your justification for the recommendations should address the relevant issues noted above, and your presentation should not be longer than three pages.

Case 10: Developing a Child Care Assistance Program

• *Background*

City officials in Trivtov, Russia, have become increasingly concerned about the social and economic costs of unattended children.[18] The problem is that parents, while they are at work, are leaving their children alone or in the care of siblings who are too young to care for others. More and more children are showing up in emergency rooms of the local hospital, and in public health clinics, with serious injuries and untreated illnesses. Four-year-old children are found roaming the streets while their older siblings are in school.

In more serious cases, children are taken out of the home by the state for placement in an orphanage due to severe neglect. Children are also being abandoned to orphanages by their parents in what are called "voluntary placements." In some cases parents are truly unable to care for their children—due to problems with alcohol, mental illness, or abusive behavior. However, officials believe that many children could remain with their families if parents were provided child care assistance and other support (either social services for themselves or additional support and guidance in caring for children, especially those with disabilities).

• *Analysis*

The child care problem has arisen, in part, because more households are headed by single mothers and because more mothers (in both one- and two-parent families) are working and unable to make appropriate child care arrangements. In earlier decades, there were plenty of grandmothers, aunts, and other adult relatives available to care for the young children of working parents for free or modest wages. But now those formerly caregiving adults are, themselves, in the marketplace working for higher wages than they earned as child caregivers.

City officials have decided that they must reduce the number of emergency hospitalizations and children entering orphanages. To achieve this goal, the city is interested in increasing the child care options available for low-income families. Obviously, child care will not solve the problems of the more deeply troubled families—but the city is interested in increasing the supports available for families as a way of preventing common problems from leading to neglect and abuse.

Needs Assessment and Funding Availability.   There are approximately 6,000 low-income families with young children in Trivtov, although not all of these families have working mothers or are in need of child care services. The city estimates that approximately 2,500 families with 3,100 children are in need of child care. The mayor is willing to increase spending on child care services with the expectation that a substantial portion of these expenditures will be offset by a reduction in the costs of hospitalization and institutional care.

• *Options*

Option 1: Child Care Centers.   The city could open child care centers that it would run or operate under contracts with private or nonprofit agencies. The city has several underutilized kindergartens that could be converted to child care centers at a very low cost. Several agencies have expressed interest and have experience providing child care (including to disabled children), early childhood education, and health services. The city estimates that it could serve approximately 500 young children in six former kindergartens. The limitations of this option are its high cost compared to home care (due to facilities expenses and salaries for more specialized staff), limited locations, and capacity for only 500 children.

Option 2: City Contracts with Individual Child Care Providers.   The city would advertise in the local papers, on radio, and on television that it is launching a new child care program for low-income families, and is looking for quality caregivers. The advertising campaign would include information about the payment rate per day per child that the city proposes, depending on ages of children and whether the caregiver will take children with disabilities. The advertising campaign would run for six months, during which time caregivers could submit applications indicating their intent to become child caregivers, their experience, whether they will provide services in their homes or their clients' homes, how many children they can take and the age range of children they are willing to care for (e.g., infants, toddlers, only before- and after-school care for school-age children), whether they will accept children with disabilities, the space and total area of the home that the children will have access to, what child development activities the caregiver plans to offer during the day, plans for installing safety equipment, and so forth.

Low-income families applying for the child care program would come to the social services office to fill out an application, and show pay stubs to prove they are employed and to verify their income. Within thirty days they would receive a notice of eligibility and information on providers.

The department of social protection would review all the proposals and select child care providers proposing high-quality care. Through the city's procurement process, contracts would be negotiated with providers to offer child care services for eligible low-income families. The city would not necessarily purchase all child care slots from any given provider, and it is assumed that some portion of the slots would be bought by higher-income families in the open market, as those parents could pay the full amount of the care themselves. Eligible low-income parents would obtain care from the contracted provider by presenting their notice of eligibility to the provider.

The city would contract with providers for one year and make payments at the beginning of each month. This means that providers have no up-front costs for which they must await reimbursement. Contracts would be renewed each year, depending on whether parents report on a semiannual survey that the provider is meeting quality measures developed by the social services agency staff, and whether the provider indicates a willingness to renew at the agreed upon price per child. The social services agency would execute contracts, monitor payments to the contracted providers every month, and conduct the semiannual survey.

Contracting for child care slots would be fairly easy and inexpensive for the city to administer. Contracting also facilitates budgeting, as the city knows in the beginning of the year how much money it needs for the program, because it knows how many slots it plans to issue contracts for.

On the other hand, there is some waste inherent in this approach. Some slots may go unfilled, because officials may overestimate demand by low-income families, but the contracted providers must be paid for those slots nevertheless. In addition, contractors would have to be paid according to their contracts, regardless of whether some children end up receiving less than full-time care, or are absent due to sickness or holidays.

Contracting with child care providers limits families' choice of child care providers to only the pool of contracted slots. While there may be a perfectly good child care provider around the corner from a family's house, the only contract provider may be five miles away and not in the direction of the mother's workplace. Moreover, directing low-income families to certain contracted providers could lead to social and economic segregation of the children, though integration of low-income children with more advantaged children would be socially and developmentally preferable.

Option 3: Child Care Vouchers for Licensed Providers. The city could develop provider agreements with caregivers whose applications appear to meet minimum quality standards and issue vouchers to eligible parents. Provider agreements would be open-ended arrangements between the city and the provider. They would stipulate that if a family with a notice of eligibility presents their voucher to the child care provider, the provider would serve that family/child for a predetermined fee (written into the provider agreement and/or on the voucher). The provider would not be required to accept any particular child. The fee structure would depend on ages and disabilities of the children for which the caregiver indicated a willingness to provide service. Caregivers serving children with greater needs would receive higher payments.

The city would establish as many of these agreements as possible in each neighborhood, to give families the maximum number of choices of child care provider. Families would theoretically have maximum choice, and could exercise their own values as to what constitutes quality, and have the flexibility to select a provider in the geographic location of their preference. Eligible families could recommend that their current provider apply to participate in the program.

The city would have to establish an office in the social services agency to receive vouchers from the providers and authorize payments to providers every month. It is assumed that the office would not review applications and monitor quality to the same extent required in Option 2, whereby the city would contract directly with providers. It is assumed that with so many choices, parents will "vote with their feet"—that is, if parents find the quality lacking in the first month of using one provider, they can simply switch to a better provider in the same neighborhood. However, there is the possibility that parents may make poor choices or find that they have few choices of providers willing to accept their child—this issue may be of particular concern with special needs children.

Although the city could budget the cost of this program based on the number of families that it grants vouchers to, it is uncertain how many slots would actually be made available to meet low-income families' needs. It remains unclear whether a sufficient number of providers would be interested in providing child care at the rates offered by this program. It may also be that providers might not want to get involved in serving low-income families, or might not want to deal with the bureaucracy and wait a month for reimbursement of their up-front service costs.

An issue with either home care option (Options 2 and 3) is whether other family members would be eligible to participate in the program and receive subsidies for caring for children that they may have willingly served without the subsidy. If family members are allowed to participate, this would certainly increase the cost and the number of potential participants. However, excluding family providers may limit options that could best serve children and may also raise equity issues.

- *Your Task*

You are an adviser to the mayor and he asks you to prepare a recommendation for him on which option to follow. It is critical that you defend your recommendation on grounds that take into account the following:

- The need for administrative efficiency.
- Minimizing cost.
- Maximizing child care quality and child well-being.
- Maximizing the supply of child care slots for low-income children.

Do not forget to consider the cost savings that the program may create from fewer emergency hospitalizations of children, and from caring for children in orphanages.

Case 11: Federal Funding for Housing and Communal Service Subsidies

- *Background*

In Russia, housing and utility services that were previously funded through subsidies to enterprises are being transformed into subsidies targeted to low-income households.[19] Regional and local budgets bear the brunt of housing and communal service expenses, including subsidies to residents. Federal law requires that regional/local governments provide housing subsidies for needy households as a precondition for increasing tariffs from their current cost-recovery levels, which remain below full cost-recovery levels. Local governments are given considerable latitude in how they implement the subsidy program. For example, localities are allowed to determine what portion of household incomes must be contributed toward housing expenses. The maximum allowable rate is 22 percent of household income, though cities can, and most do, opt for lower rates.

According to current estimates, the burden of payment for utility services—that is, the relationship between the average cost of utility services and per capita income—varies considerably among different Russian regions.

Regions facing the most difficult economic and financial situations are not able to adequately fund the housing subsidy program. In such regions, the housing and utility sector is subsidized mostly at the expense of utility enterprises' income (the city does not fully pay its bills for services provided to its housing units) and through cross-subsidizing of utility service rates.

- *Analysis*

Under such conditions, part of the spending on the housing subsidy program will now be financed from the federal budget in the form of joint financing of consolidated budgets of subjects of the Russian Federation, under Resolution of the Government of the Russian Federation no. 354, of May 27, 2002. This recent resolution outlines criteria for federal funding, but specific program guidelines for allocating resources to the various regions still need to be finalized.

Federal housing expenditures must meet the following criteria:

- They must smooth differences in payments for utility services in different regions and thus facilitate the transition to subsidy-free operation of the housing and utility service complex.
- They must promote adoption of uniform principles (federal standards) in the transition to a new economic model of utility operations in Russia's regions.

Federal allocations will be based on the following guidelines:

1. A fixed sum of federal funds will be allocated to support the housing subsidy program.
2. The amount of funding received by various regions will depend on the health of their budgets and the social and economic situation in each region.
3. Information about regional spending on housing subsidies will be factored into federal allocations. Regional housing subsidy expenditures that do not fully conform to federal standards but are close to meeting them will be multiplied by reduction coefficients that characterize the degree of actual spending from federal standards (hereafter referred to as the "adjusted spending on housing subsidies payments").
4. Federal government funds are transferred to Russia's regions. The amounts transferred are calculated as follows: the amount of federal government funds allotted for a particular region is multiplied by the adjusted spending on housing subsidies in that region during the accounting period.

The following federal standards apply to the calculation of housing and communal service subsidies:

- The federal minimum housing space standard.
- The federal standard for the population's share of payments for utility services.
- The federal standard for payments for utility services per square meter of housing space.
- The federal standard for the maximum share of citizen payments for utility services according to the minimum housing space standard.

Under current conditions, the majority of regions will be unable to meet federal standards in the coming year. Federal authorities are particularly concerned that federal funds be used to motivate regions to work toward compliance. Among the concerns are that regions may manipulate the household contribution rate to increase their need for federal assistance (e.g., lowering the household contribution from 20 percent to 5 percent will increase the eligibility for the program and drive up subsidy expenses). Such regions would shift the housing burden to the federal budget without fundamentally addressing the needs of its housing sector—yet technically, the region could be credited with attracting federal funds to a troubled sector, providing subsidies to its population, and increasing the share of targeted assistance in the total amount of funds spent on the housing and utility sector.

• *Your Task*

You are an analyst charged with finalizing how federal housing subsidy funds will be allocated to the regions. You must answer the following questions:

1. What indicator(s) should be used to determine the base level of federal contributions toward financing regional housing subsidies? (See Guideline 2 described above.)
2. To what extent should regions be "punished" for the failure to observe federal standards? How?

Case 12: Municipal Water and Wastewater

• *Background*

In Russia, severe fiscal constraints have dramatically reduced the large subsidies that vodokanals (water utilities) and local governments used to receive from the national budget for the operating and investment costs of water utilities.[20] Vodokanals suffer from large financial shortfalls that preclude proper maintenance and operation of existing systems and do not allow for much needed asset rehabilitation, replacement, and expansion. If the present trend of increasing costs and diminished revenues continues, the provision of safe water and wastewater services in many Russian cities will be in jeopardy.

The gradual introduction of full cost recovery for operations and investments is essential for vodokanals to generate the resources required to meet current needs. At the same time, vodokanals must become more efficient, as scarce income is wasted in poor administration, inefficient operation (losses, excessive water consumption, hydraulically inefficient networks and plants with high energy consumption), and poor investment choices.

The federal government has announced a special program that will provide additional funding and technical assistance to selected municipalities that are committed to reforming their water and wastewater systems. Your city's water/wastewater system is fairly typical and suffers from the problems described in the analysis section below. Your mayor, with the governor's strong support, is interested in reforming the city's water system and competing for the federal funds.

• *Analysis*

A water sector study prepared by the Russian government and the World Bank in 1996 found a serious deterioration in the capacity of most of the country's vodokanals to provide reliable and safe water and wastewater services. The financial base of vodokanals has eroded alarmingly, with most suffering from large financial deficits. Maintenance has been inadequate and investments in system rehabilitation and new construction have ground to a halt. The population is dissatisfied with the quality of services and worried about the safety of the supply, as inadequate water treatment is responsible for an increasing number of water-related diseases. If the country's water and wastewater infrastructure is allowed to continue to deteriorate, public health concerns will rise and the quality of life of a large segment of the population will further decline.

The water utility study points out that the past system of central command and the government's subsidy policies are responsible for disincentives and distortions that prohibit efficient sector management and development. These include:

- *The poor state of repair of facilities.* The water and wastewater networks and treatment plants are in a state of severe disrepair due to inadequate funding, poor planning and design, low quality of materials and equipment used, and inadequate maintenance and repair.
- *Inefficient operations.* Potable water and wastewater treatment plants have been poorly designed, maintained, and operated, which results in poor output and inefficiency. For example, water networks suffer from excessive leakage—loss rates of 50 percent are not uncommon. This, combined with improper design, burdens sewer pipes with excessive leakage and infiltration demands.
- *Lack of incentives for consumer water conservation.* Negligible water charges provide very weak signals to water users about the value of the resource. There is no incentive for users to reduce demand or improve their internal plumbing or industrial systems.
- *Lack of financial viability.* Low tariffs combined with poor collections fail to make up for the traditional budget subsidies of the past. Vodokanals face a tax structure that penalizes efficient use of financial resources. This financial situation leads vodokanals to delay needed maintenance and investment, and accrue substantial wage arrears and other debts.
- *Institutional and regulatory weakness.* Water utilities are poorly regulated,

overstaffed, technically oriented entities with insufficient concern for efficiency and little autonomy or control of the crucial aspects of their business.

- *Poor management.* Management lacks adequate financial and technical information to manage and develop their systems efficiently.

• *Options*

The Russian Federation has endorsed the following principles as part of its overall program to reform the communal services sector. The federal government is soliciting proposals that address these reform strategies. Cities with the best proposals will be eligible for additional funding, loans, and technical assistance. Cities may submit proposals for any one or all of the reform options. A certain number of contracts will be granted to cities that pursue all reforms—those cities will be considered model cities and will be eligible for larger grants and/or assistance.

Reform Options (choose any or all)

1. Transform the present vodokanals into independent utilities regulated by local government.
2. Gradually turn vodokanals into financially self-sufficient institutions through tariff reform and better collection.
3. Reform past investment policies by introducing least-cost strategies and giving preference to plant and network rehabilitation and efficiency enhancements.
4. Include consumers in vodokanal decisionmaking.

Uses of Funds

- To support essential investments needed to improve system operations, reduce operations costs, and improve service quality (such as replacement of critical pumping equipment, rehabilitation of water or wastewater treatment plant components, rehabilitation of specific sections of water mains that frequently break, etc.).
- To implement specific institutional and commercial reforms aimed at improving the physical operation and financial performance of vodokanals.

Main Criteria

- Scope of project and benefits clearly defined.
- High priority from a technical and service quality perspective.
- Capacity to effect small but noticeable improvements in services.
- Improvements in system operations that reduce costs and/or improve service quality.

Local Context. The governor is strongly urging the mayor to apply as a model city. It is likely that an effort to privatize the water utility would be met with considerable opposition both from within government and from consumers. Consumers' main concerns are the threat of tariff increases and any further reduction in services, and some are ideologically opposed to privatizing public utilities.

The problems outlined above about vodokanals in general can be assumed to accurately describe your city's water system.

• *Your Task*

The mayor has asked you to draft an overview statement on which of the reforms the city should apply for. For each of the reforms you recommend, include some information on what problems will be addressed, what the city proposes to do (include administrative and other implications), and how it would fulfill the evaluation criteria. If there are any options that you do not recommend, outline for the mayor your reasons for rejection.

Notes

Preface

1. P. deLeon and T. A. Steelman, "Making Public Policy Programs Effective and Relevant: The Role of the Policy Sciences," *Journal of Policy Analysis and Management* 20, no. 1 (2001): 164. This is consistent with similar views expressed in Laurence E. Lynn, "The Changing Public Policy Curriculum," *Journal of Policy Analysis and Management* 20, no. 1 (2001): 161–162; and Francine S. Romero, "The Policy Analysis Course: Toward a Discipline Consensus," *Journal of Policy Analysis and Management* 20, no. 4 (2001): 771–779.

2. To learn more about the work of the Institute for Urban Economics (Moscow) and the Urban Institute (Washington, D.C.), visit http://www.urbaneconomics.ru and http://www.urban.org/tpn.

Chapter 1

1. European Bank for Reconstruction and Development (EBRD), *Transition Impact Retrospective* (London: EBRD, 2001).

2. World Bank, *Transition: The First Ten Years—Analysis and Lessons for Eastern Europe and the Former Soviet Union* (Washington, D.C.: World Bank, 2002), p. 17.

3. Description of the East German situation from World Bank, *Transition*, p. 37.

4. Clare Romanik and Raymond Struyk, "Assisting De-Mobilized Russian Officers Obtain Housing: The Housing Certificate Option," *Review of Urban and Regional Development Studies* 7 (1995): 97–118.

5. The book is based on curriculum developed for the Policy Fellows course, a public policy training program offered to government officials and NGO representatives in Russia and Bosnia. The course was developed in 2001 by the Urban Institute (Washington, D.C.) and the Institute for Urban Economics (Moscow) and underwritten by the US Agency for International Development.

6. See, for example, Carl V. Patton and David S. Sawicki, *Basic Methods of Policy Analysis and Planning,* 2nd ed. (Englewood Cliffs, N.J.: Prentice Hall, 1993); Eugene Bardach, *A Practical Guide for Policy Analysis: The Eightfold Path to More Effective Problem Solving* (New York: Seven Bridges Press, 2000); Edith Stokey and Richard

Zeckhauser, *A Primer for Policy Analysis* (New York: Norton, 1978); David L. Weimer and Aidan R. Vining, *Policy Analysis: Concepts and Practice,* 3rd ed. (Upper Saddle River, N.J.: Prentice Hall, 1999); and Jessica R. Adolino and Charles H. Blake, *Comparing Public Policies: Issues and Choices in Six Industrialized Countries* (Washington, D.C.: Congressional Quarterly Press, 2002).

Chapter 2

1. The recommendations appear in Jennifer Turnham and Jill Khadduri, "Issues and Options for HUD's Tenant-Based Housing Assistance Programs," report prepared for the Millennial Housing Commission (Cambridge, Mass.: Abt Associates, September 2001). The full report includes analysis and recommendations on nine aspects of the program.

2. Based on interactions with association members and a survey of twenty individuals who work in apartment leasing.

3. In recent years, lead poisoning has emerged as the most common environmental disease among young children, eclipsing all other environmental health hazards found in the residential environment. HUD estimates that approximately 60 million occupied homes, or 80 percent of homes built before 1980, have some lead-based paint. Higher childhood blood lead levels are associated with lower household income, residence in large urban areas and older homes, and non-Hispanic African American residents. The effects of childhood lead poisoning are well documented and include reductions in IQ and attention span, reading and learning disabilities, hyperactivity, and behavioral problems.

Chapter 3

1. This chapter is based on Jennifer Rietbergen-McCracken and Deepa Narayan, *Participation and Social Assessment: Tools and Techniques* (Washington, D.C.: International Bank for Reconstruction and Development/World Bank, 1998).

2. Tata Energy Research Institute, "Report on Regional Environmental Assessment and Social Assessment," Bangalore, India, March 2001, pp. i–xxviii, sec. 6.2.

3. Gaelle Fedida, "Field Exchange March 2003: Disparate Responses to Need in Southern Africa," Emergency Nutrition Network, March 31, 2003, pp. 1–5.

4. The situation described is based on Fedida's report "Field Exchange March 2003" and has not been independently verified.

Chapter 4

1. Ritu Nayyar-Stone, Katharine Mark, Jacob Cowan, and Harry Hatry, "Developing a Performance Management System for Local Governments: An Operational Guideline," report prepared for UN Habitat and the World Bank (Washington, D.C.: Urban Institute, July 2002).

2. Ibid.

Chapter 5

1. Louise Fox, "Safety Nets in Transition Economies: A Primer" (Washington, D.C.: World Bank, March 2003), available online at http://www.worldbank.org.

2. Ibid., p. 5.

3. This presentation draws on L. Jerome Gallagher, "Key Issues of Targeting in the CIS: Briefing Note," paper presented at the international conference "Reform of Social Assistance in the Commonwealth of Independent States," Moscow, November 15–16, 2002.

4. L. Jerome Gallagher, "Means-Tested Targeting in Social Assistance Programs: An Overview of Benefit Calculation Issues" (Moscow: Urban Institute Field Office, n.d.).

5. David Coady, Margaret Grosh, and John Hoddinott, "The Targeting of Transfers in Developing Countries: Review of Experience and Lessons" (Washington, D.C.: World Bank, April 16, 2002).

6. Tomas A. Mroz, Laura Henderson, and Barry M. Popkin, "Monitoring Economic Conditions in the Russian Federation: The Russia Longitudinal Monitoring Survey, 1992–2000," report submitted to the US Agency for International Development (Chapel Hill: Carolina Population Center, University of North Carolina at Chapel Hill, March 2001), p. 17.

7. Fox, "Safety Nets," p. 11.

8. Coady, Grosh, and Hoddinott, "Targeting of Transfers," pp. 51–55.

9. Aline Coudel, Sheila Marnie, and John Micklewright, "Targeting Social Assistance in a Transition Country: The Mahallas in Uzbekistan" (United Nations Children's Fund, 1998).

10. Fox, "Safety Nets."

11. Coady, Grosh, and Hoddinott, "Targeting of Transfers."

Chapter 6

1. This section includes passages from Francis J. Conway, Brian Desilets, Peter Epstein, and Juliana H. Pigey, *Sourcebook on Intergovernmental Fiscal Relations in Eastern Europe* (Washington, D.C.: Urban Institute, August 2001).

2. John Norregaard, *Tax Assignment: Fiscal Federalism in Theory and Practice,* edited by Teresa Ter-Minassian (Washington, D.C.: International Monetary Fund, 1997), p. 5.

3. This section draws substantially from Conway et al., *Sourcebook.*

Chapter 7

1. These and other devices for governments to execute their responsibilities are discussed in Lester M. Salamon, ed., *The Tools of Government: A Guide to the New Governance* (Oxford: Oxford University Press, 2002).

2. Gabriel Roth, *The Private Provision of Public Services in Developing Countries* (Washington, D.C.: Oxford University Press/World Bank, 1987), p. 224.

3. John D. Donahue, *The Privatization Decision* (New York: Basic Books, 1989).

4. Trevor L. Brown and Matthew Potoski, "Managing Contract Performance: A Transaction Costs Approach," *Journal of Policy Analysis and Management* 22, no. 2 (2003): 275–297.

5. World Bank, *Toolkits for Private Sector Participation in Water and Sanitation* (Washington, D.C.: World Bank, 1997), p. 6.

6. Ibid.

7. Ibid., p. 8.

8. World Bank, *Transition: The First Ten Years—Analysis and Lessons for Eastern Europe and the Former Soviet Union* (Washington, D.C.: World Bank, 2002), pp. 76–78.

Chapter 8

1. John D. Donahue, *The Privatization Decision* (New York: Basic Books, 1989).
2. Ibid., citing Barbara J. Stevens, "Scale, Market Structure, and the Cost of Refuse Collection," *Review of Economics and Statistics* 60 (March 1977).
3. Ibid., citing E. S. Savas, "Policy Analysis for Local Government: Public vs. Private Refuse Collection," *Policy Analysis* 3 (Winter 1977).
4. Ibid., citing James C. McDavid, "The Canadian Experience with Privatizing Residential Solid Waste Collection Services," *Public Administration Review* 45 (1985).
5. Ibid., citing John Cubbin, Simon Dornberger, and Shirley Meadowcroft, "Competitive Tendering and Refuse Collection: Identifying the Sources of Efficiency Gains," *Fiscal Studies* (August 1987).
6. For example, in Russia the announcement must be published at least forty-five days before the deadline for submitting proposals (Federal Law no. 97 [May 6, 1999], para. 1, art. 16).
7. Based primarily on the experiences of the Urban Institute and the Institute for Urban Economics in contracting out for housing maintenance and social services in Russia. Experience shows, however, that in industrialized countries local officials often need to be proactive to maintain conditions for effective competitions. See, for example, Trevor L. Brown and Matthew Potoski, "Managing the Public Service Market," *Public Administration Review* 64, no. 6 (2004): 656–668.

Chapter 9

1. Elizabeth Cove and Marty Abravanel, "Monitoring Financial Condition and Resident Satisfaction in Public Housing Developments in the United States" (Washington, D.C.: Urban Institute, October 2002).
2. This material is excerpted with some editing, with the author's permission, from Patrick A. Corvington, *Monitoring Social Assistance and Social Services* (Washington, D.C.: Urban Institute, November 2002).

Chapter 10

1. Ritu Nayyar-Stone, Katharine Mark, Jacob Cowan, and Harry Hatry, "Developing a Performance Management System for Local Governments: An Operational Guideline," report prepared for UN Habitat and the World Bank (Washington, D.C.: Urban Institute, July 2002).
2. Office of Management and Budget, "Montgomery Measures Up!" (Montgomery County, Md., 2003), pp. 72, 110.
3. David Osborne and Ted Gaebler, *Reinventing Government: How the Entrepreneurial Spirit Is Transforming the Public Sector* (New York: Penguin Books, 1993).

Chapter 11

1. World Bank, "Kyrgyz Republic: Enhancing Pro-Poor Growth," report no. 24638-KG (Washington, D.C.: World Bank, 2003), p. 148.

2. The broad ideas outlined here come from Michael Quinn Patton, *Utilization-Focused Evaluation,* 3rd ed. (Thousand Oaks, Calif.: Sage, 1997), pt. 1, pp. 1–115.

3. Information from Raymond Struyk, who served as the deputy assistant secretary for research and evaluation at the US Department of Housing and Urban Development at that time.

4. These are six of seven items discussed in Patton, *Utilization-Focused Evaluation,* pt. 1, pp. 51–58 and menu 3.2.

5. Based on the definition in Peter H. Rossi, Howard E. Freeman, and Mark K. Lipsey, *Evaluation: A Systematic Approach,* 6th ed. (Thousand Oaks, Calif.: Sage Publications, 1999), p. 192.

6. Raymond J. Struyk, Lisa Lee, and Alexander Puzanov, "Monitoring Russia's Experience with Housing Allowances," *Urban Studies* 34, no. 11 (November 1997): 1789–1818.

7. The three types of failure and some of the examples are from Rossi, Freeman, and Lipsey, *Evaluation,* pp. 215–217.

8. Vivian Gabor and C. Bsotko, "Changes in Client Service in the Food Stamp Program After Welfare Reform," report to the US Drug Administration, Food and Nutrition Service (Washington, D.C.: Health Systems Research, 2001).

9. This list comes primarily from Laurence J. O'Toole, "Policy Recommendations for Multi-Actor Implementation: An Assessment of the Field," *Journal of Public Policy* 6, no. 2 (1986): 181–210.

10. Evelyn Z. Brodkin, "Street-Level Research: Policy at the Front Lines," in M. C. Lennon and T. Corbett, eds., *Policy into Action: Implementation Research and Welfare Reform* (Washington, D.C.: Urban Institute, 2003), pp. 145–164.

Chapter 12

1. Joseph Valadez and Michael Bamberger, *Monitoring and Evaluating Social Programs in Developing Countries: A Handbook for Policymakers, Managers, and Researchers* (Washington, D.C.: World Bank, 1994).

2. Raymond J. Struyk and Marc Bendick Jr., *Housing Vouchers for the Poor: Lessons from a National Experiment* (Washington, D.C.: Urban Institute, 1981).

3. P. Z. Schochet, J. Burghardt, and S. Glazerman, *National Job Corps Study: The Impacts of Job Corps on Participants' Employment and Related Outcomes* (Princeton, N.J.: Mathematical Policy Research, 2001).

4. Elizabeth M. Jones, Gary D. Gottfredson, and Denice C. Gottfredson, "Success for Some: An Evaluation of a Success for All Program," *Evaluation Review* 21, no. 6 (1997): 643–670.

5. In reality the impact of training on wages is not likely to be uniform for workers with different education and work experience levels. The analyst could use a more complex specification to capture such interactions.

6. This evaluation is described in Jean Baldwin Grossman and Joseph P. Tierney, "Does Mentoring Work? An Impact Study of the Big Brothers–Big Sisters Program," *Evaluation Review* 22, no. 3 (1988): 403–426.

7. Raymond J. Struyk, Karen Angelici, and Marie Tikhomirova, "Private Maintenance for Moscow's Municipal Housing Stock: Does It Work?" *Journal of Housing Economics* 4 (March 1995): 50–70.

8. A chi-squared test is a statistical procedure used for data that are arranged in cate-

gories. It assesses whether the number of responses in different categories fit a null hypothesis (the expected number of observations in each category). In this example, one would expect a change in the quality of building services from the baseline survey to the survey conducted after private firms assumed building management. Chi-squared is used to assess the reliability of differences in two distributions of categorical data.

9. The studies are summarized in Eric A. Hanushek, "Assessing the Effect of Schools Resources on Student Performance: An Update," *Education and Policy Analysis* 19, no. 2 (1997): 141–164.

10. STAR results reported in Alan B. Kruger, "Experimental Estimates of Education Production Functions," *Quarterly Journal of Economics* (May 1999): 497–531.

11. Hanushek, "Assessing the Effect."

12. There has been considerable work done on ways to reduce the selection bias in analyses using quasi-experimental methods. One widely used technique for addressing this problem is described in James Heckman, "Sample Selection Bias as a Specification Error," *Econometrica* 47, no. 1 (1979): 153–161; and James Heckman, "Addendum to Sample Selection Bias as a Specification Error," in Ernst Stromsdorfer and George Farkas, eds., *Evaluation Studies Review Annual*, vol. 5 (San Francisco: Sage, 1980), pp. 970–995.

13. On the new evidence, see Stephen H. Bell, "Review of Alternative Methodologies for Employment and Training Program Evaluation," draft (Washington, D.C.: Urban Institute, 2003).

Chapter 13

1. In the precise jargon of economists, the consumer adjusts the consumption-savings mix until the marginal rate of time preference in consumption just equals the rate of return on savings.

2. In principle, the discount rate should reflect that investment as well as consumption are involved in these projects. Private firms undertake investment to the point at which the marginal productivity of capital just equals the interest cost of funds. So the discount rate for a project could be defined as the weighted sum of the return to savings and the return to investment, where the weights are the proportions of the estimated financial flows from consumption and investment. That is, a firm will invest in a project only when the return to that investment (profit) is equal or greater than its interest or opportunity cost. As an example, consider a project where over the life of the project, capital costs are 70 percent of the total costs and operating costs are 30 percent. If the cost of funds to corporations for long-term finance is 9 percent and the return on savings to consumers is 4 percent, then the discount rate should be 7.5 percent $[(0.7 \times 9) + (0.3 \times 4)]$.

3. There are important economic concepts involved in selecting a discount rate. For a discussion, see Mark A. Moore, Anthony E. Boardman, Aidan R. Vining, David L. Weimer, and David H. Greenberg, "'Just Give Me a Number!' Practical Values for a Social Discount Rate," *Journal of Policy Analysis and Management* 23, no. 4 (2004): 789–812.

4. Willingness to pay is measured with reference to consumer surplus, a more complex concept that we leave to presentations that are more comprehensive. For a full explanation, see Kenneth Small, "Project Evaluation," in Jose Gomez-Ibanez, William B. Tye, and Clifford Winston, eds., *Essays in Transportation Economics and Policy* (Washington, D.C.: Brookings Institution, 1999), pp. 137–177.

5. Small, "Project Evaluation."

6. *The Economist,* "The Price of Prudence," January 24, 2004.

7. Sandra E. Black, "Do Better Schools Matter? Parental Valuation of Elementary Education," *Quarterly Journal of Economics* (May 1999): 577–599.

8. Tests done of the similarity of dwelling and neighborhood attributes of homes at various distances from the attendance district boundaries confirm that units and neighborhoods closer to the boundaries are more similar that those farther away.

9. This figure differs from that cited in Chapter 12 because they refer to different years—1977 and 1994.

10. Don H. Pickrell, "A Desire Named Streetcar: Fantasy and Fact in Rail Transit Planning," *Journal of the American Planning Association* 58, no. 2 (Spring 1992): 158–176. There is also a perception that the US Army Corps of Engineers, which has broad responsibilities for waterway infrastructure projects on rivers and lakes that cross state boundaries, biases its analyses to make projects look economically justified.

11. Described in Peter H. Rossi, Howard E. Freeman, and Mark W. Lipsey, *Evaluation: A Systematic Approach,* 6th ed. (Thousand Oaks, Calif.: Sage, 1999), p. 387.

12. World Bank, Latvia Welfare Reform Project, Project Appraisal document, April 16, 1997.

13. Adapted from Henry M. Levin and Patrick J. McEwan, *Cost-Effectiveness Analysis,* 2nd ed. (Thousand Oaks, Calif.: Sage, 2000), chap. 5 case study.

14. This type of analysis is reported in J. Gomez-Ibanez and G. Fauth, "Downtown Auto Restraint Policies," *Journal of Transport Economics and Policy* (May 1980): 221–241.

Chapter 14

1. Juliet Musso, Robert Biller, and Robert Myrtle, "Tradecraft: Professional Writing as Problem Solving," *Journal of Policy Analysis and Management* 19, no. 4 (2000): 635–646.

2. Ibid.

Appendix

1. Written by Raymond Struyk, Urban Institute, for the Policy Fellows course, 2001.

2. Written by Wayne G. Vroman, Urban Institute, for the Policy Fellows course, 2002.

3. At the regional level, local governments could be given a financial stake in identifying all enterprises operating within their borders. This could even extend to receiving a fee for discovering entities that are subject to national taxes (value added, income, and/or payroll).

4. Written by Kristin Morse, Urban Institute, for the Policy Fellows course, 2001.

5. Information on the prevalence of HIV/AIDS in Russia is from UNAIDS, "AIDS Epidemic Update, 2001."

6. Written by Raymond Struyk, Urban Institute, for the Policy Fellows course, 2001.

7. Written by Anastasia Alexandrova, Institute for Urban Economics, for the Federal Policy Fellows course, 2002.

8. The amount of the allowance increases by 50 percent for children of enlisted military personnel and for children whose parents evade alimony payments, and by 100 percent for children of single mothers.

9. Written by Shelli Rossman, Urban Institute, for the Policy Fellows course, 2002.

10. Once a person is arrested by the police on a drug charge, he or she may be held in a

detention facility/jail or released while awaiting trial—a determination that is made at an initial hearing. The district attorney makes a decision to (1) drop the charges (e.g., because of insufficient evidence), or (2) reach agreement with the person and his or her attorney to enter a pretrial diversion program (e.g., probation supervision) instead of going to court trial and risking a prison sentence, or (3) take the case to a court trial. If the case goes to trial and the person is found guilty, there are four possible outcomes: (1) receive little or no punishment and no supervision, (2) remain in the community under supervision of the probation department for a specified period of time, (3) go to jail (for sentences up to one year), or (4) go to prison (for sentences longer than one year).

11. After arrest, some accused individuals are permitted to remain in the community while they await trial. Others are detained in jail until trial, when the judge can hear the case and a finding of guilt or innocence can be determined. The Cook County Jail has an average daily population of 10,000 individuals who are being held awaiting trial.

12. *Relapse* refers to the resumption of drug use after a period of sobriety or nonuse. *Recidivism* refers to the commission of a new crime by an individual who has a history of criminal activity.

13. Initially, several times per week, then less frequently as the individual demonstrates progress in maintaining sobriety.

14. Written by Andrew Popelka, Urban Institute, for the Policy Fellows course, 2002.

15. Written by Alexander Puzanov, Institute for Urban Economics, for the Federal Policy Fellows course, 2002.

16. Written by Raymond Struyk, Urban Institute, for the Policy Fellows course, 2001.

17. If the cost per square meter is $700 and the apartment is 54 square meters (for a family of three), then the cost of the unit is $37,800. If the household makes a 40 percent downpayment, it would have a loan of $22,680. At a 12 percent interest rate, the monthly mortgage payment is $283. So the household would need an income of $600 per month, or 18,000 rubles, to afford the unit.

18. Written by Lynne Fender, Urban Institute, for the Policy Fellows course, 2001.

19. Written by Alexander Puzanov, Institute for Urban Economics, for the Federal Policy Fellows course, 2002.

20. Written by Kristin Morse, Urban Institute, for the Policy Fellows course, 2001. Based on World Bank, "Russian Federation: Municipal Water and Wastewater Project," project information document. March 2000.

Bibliography

Adolino, Jessica R., and Charles H. Blake. *Comparing Public Policies: Issues and Choices in Six Industrialized Countries.* Washington, D.C.: Congressional Quarterly Press, 2002.

Bardach, Eugene. *A Practical Guide for Policy Analysis: The Eightfold Path to More Effective Problem Solving.* New York: Seven Bridges Press, 2000.

Bell, Stephen H. "Review of Alternative Methodologies for Employment and Training Program Evaluation." Draft. Washington, D.C.: Urban Institute, 2003.

Black, Sandra E. "Do Better Schools Matter? Parental Valuation of Elementary Education." *Quarterly Journal of Economics* (May 1999): 577–599.

Brodkin, Evelyn Z. "Street-Level Research: Policy at the Front Lines." In M. C. Lennon and T. Corbett, eds., *Policy into Action: Implementation Research and Welfare Reform.* Washington, D.C.: Urban Institute, 2003, pp. 145–164.

Brown, Trevor, L., and Matthew Potoski. "Managing Contract Performance: A Transaction Costs Approach." *Journal of Policy Analysis and Management* 22, no. 2 (2003): 275–297.

———. "Managing the Public Service Market." *Public Administration Review* 64, no. 6 (2004): 656–668.

Center for Economic and Financial Research. *Monitoring the Administrative Barriers to Small Business Development in Russia: The Third Round.* Moscow: Center for Economic and Financial Research (CEFIR), November 2003. Available online at http://www.cefir.org.

Coady, David, Margaret Grosh, and John Hoddinott. *The Targeting of Transfers in Developing Countries: Review of Experience and Lessons.* Washington, D.C.: World Bank, April 16, 2002.

Conway, Francis J., Brian Desilets, Peter Epstein, and Juliana H. Pigey. *Sourcebook on Intergovernmental Fiscal Relations in Eastern Europe.* Washington, D.C.: Urban Institute, August 2001.

Cooper, Michael. "City Hall Gauges City Services, and Finds Them Not Bad." *New York Times,* September 18, 2003.

Corvington, Patrick A. *Monitoring Social Assistance and Social Services.* Washington, D.C.: Urban Institute, November 2002.

Coudel, Aline, Sheila Marnie, and John Micklewright. "Targeting Social Assistance in a

Transition Country: The Mahallas in Uzbekistan." United Nations Children's Fund, 1998.

Cove, Elizabeth, and Marty Abravanel. "Monitoring Financial Condition and Resident Satisfaction in Public Housing Developments in the United States." Washington, D.C.: Urban Institute, October 2002.

Cubbin, John, Simon Dornberger, and Shirley Meadowcroft. "Competitive Tendering and Refuse Collection: Identifying the Sources of Efficiency Gains." *Fiscal Studies* (August 1987).

de Rus, Gines, and Vincente Inglada. "Cost-Benefit Analysis of the High-Speed Train in Spain." *Annals of Regional Science* 31 (1997): 175–188.

deLeon, P., and T. A. Steelman. "Making Public Policy Programs Effective and Relevant: The Role of the Policy Sciences." *Journal of Policy Analysis and Management* 20, no. 1 (2001): 164.

Donahue, John D. *The Privatization Decision*. New York: Basic Books, 1989.

The Economist. "The Price of Prudence." January 24, 2004.

European Bank for Reconstruction and Development (EBRD). *Transition Impact Retrospective*. London: EBRD, 2001.

Fedida, Gaella. "Field Exchange March 2003: Disparate Responses to Need in Southern Africa." Emergency Nutrition Network, March 31, 2003, pp. 1–5.

Fox, Louise. "Safety Nets in Transition Economies: A Primer." Washington, D.C.: World Bank, March 2003. Available online at http://www.worldbank.org.

Gabor, Vivian, and C. Bsotko. "Changes in Client Service in the Food Stamp Program After Welfare Reform," report to the US Drug Administration, Food and Nutrition Service, Washington, DC: Health Systems Research 2001.

Gallagher, L. Jerome. *Implementation Assessment: Motovilikhinsky Targeting Pilot, Perm*. Moscow: Urban Institute/Institute for Urban Economics, 2001.

———. "Key Issues of Targeting in the CIS: Briefing Note." Paper presented at the international conference "Reform of Social Assistance in the Commonwealth of Independent States," Moscow, November 15–16, 2002.

———. "Means-Tested Targeting in Social Assistance Programs: An Overview of Benefit Calculation Issues." Moscow: Urban Institute Field Office, n.d.

Gallagher, L. Jerome, Raymond J. Struyk, and Ludmila Nikonova. "Savings from Integrating Administrative Systems for Social Assistance Programmes in Russia." *Public Administration and Development* no. 23 (2003): 177–195.

Gomez-Ibanez, J., and G. Fauth. "Downtown Auto Restraint Policies." *Journal of Transport Economics and Policy* (May 1980): 221–241.

Grossman, Jean Baldwin, and Joseph P. Tierney. "Does Mentoring Work? An Impact Study of the Big Brothers–Big Sisters Program." *Evaluation Review* 22, no. 3 (June 1998): 403–426.

Hanushek, Eric A. "Assessing the Effect of Schools Resources on Student Performance: An Update." *Education and Policy Analysis* 19, no. 2 (1997): 141–164.

Haskins, Ron, and Isabel V. Sawhill. "Work and Marriage: The Way to End Poverty and Welfare." Welfare Reform and Beyond Policy Brief no. 28. Washington, D.C.: Brookings Institution, September 2003.

Hatry, Harry P. *Performance Measurement: Getting Results*. Washington, D.C.: Urban Institute, 1999.

Hatry, Harry P., Louis H. Blair, Donald M. Fisk, John M. Greiner, John R. Hall Jr., and Philip S. Schaenman. *How Effective Are Your Community Services? Procedures for*

Measuring Their Quality. Washington, D.C.: Urban Institute and International City/County Management Association (IMCA), 1992.

Heckman, James. "Addendum to Sample Selection Bias as a Specification Error." In Ernst Stromsdorfer and George Farkas, eds., *Evaluation Studies Review Annual,* vol. 5. San Francisco: Sage, 1980, pp. 970–995.

———. "Sample Selection Bias as a Specification Error." *Econometrica* 47, no. 1 (1979): 153–161.

Jones, Elizabeth M., Gary D. Gottfredson, and Denice C. Gottfredson. "Success for Some: An Evaluation of a Success for All Program." *Evaluation Review* 21, no. 6 (1997): 643–670.

Kee, James Edwin. "Benefit-Cost Analysis in Program Evaluation." In Joseph S. Wholey, Harry P. Hatry, and Kathryn E. Newcomer, eds., *Handbook of Practical Program Evaluation.* San Francisco: Josey-Bass, 1994.

Kruger, Alan B. "Experimental Estimates of Education Production Functions." *Quarterly Journal of Economics* (May 1999): 497–531.

Kusek, Jody Zall, Ray C. Rist, and Elizabeth M. White. "How Will We Know the Millennium Development Goal Results When We See Them? Building a Results-Based Monitoring and Evaluation System to Give Us the Answers." Washington, D.C.: World Bank, 2003.

Levin, Henry M., and Patrick J. McEwan. *Cost-Effectiveness Analysis.* 2nd ed. Thousand Oaks, Calif.: Sage, 2000.

Lynn, Laurence E. "The Changing Public Policy Curriculum." *Journal of Policy Analysis and Management* 20, no. 1 (2001): 161–162.

Mark, Katharine. *Module on Performance Measurement.* Budapest: Central European University, Intergovernmental Fiscal Relations and Local Financial Management course, July 2000.

Mathematica Policy Research. "Evaluation of the Economic Impact of the Jobs Corps Program: Third Follow-Up Report." Washington, D.C.: Office of Policy and Evaluation and Research, Employment and Training Administration, US Department of Labor, 1982.

McDavid, James C. "The Canadian Experience with Privatizing Residential Solid Waste Collection Services." *Public Administration Review* 45 (1985).

McLure, Charles E., and Jorge Martinez-Vazquez. *The Assignment of Revenues and Expenditures in Intergovernmental Fiscal Relations.* Washington, D.C.: World Bank, n.d. Available online at http://www1.worldbank.org/wbiep/decentralization.

Moore, Mark A., Anthony Boardman, Aidan R. Vining, David L. Weimer, and David H. Greenberg. "'Just Give Me a Number!' Practical Values for a Social Discount Rate," *Journal of Policy Analysis and Management* 23, no. 4 (2004): 789–812.

Mroz, Tomas A., Laura Henderson, and Barry M. Popkin. "Monitoring Economic Conditions in the Russian Federation: The Russia Longitudinal Monitoring Survey, 1992–2000." Report submitted to the US Agency for International Development. Chapel Hill: Carolina Population Center, University of North Carolina at Chapel Hill, March 2001.

Musso, Juliet, Robert Biller, and Robert Myrtle. "Tradecraft: Professional Writing as Problem Solving." *Journal of Policy Analysis and Management* 19, no. 4 (2000): 635–646.

Nayyar-Stone, Ritu, Katharine Mark, Jacob Cowan, and Harry Hatry. "Developing a Performance Management System for Local Governments: An Operational Guideline."

Report prepared for UN Habitat and the World Bank. Washington, D.C.: Urban Institute, July 2002.

Norregaard, John. *Tax Assignment: Fiscal Federalism in Theory and Practice.* Edited by Teresa Ter-Minassian. Washington, D.C.: International Monetary Fund, 1997.

Office of Management and Budget. "Montgomery Measures Up!" Montgomery County, Md., 2003.

Osborne, David, and Ted Gaebler. *Reinventing Government: How the Entrepreneurial Spirit Is Transforming the Public Sector.* New York: Penguin Books, 1993.

O'Toole, Laurence J. "Policy Recommendations for Multi-Actor Implementation: An Assessment of the Field." *Journal of Public Policy* 6, no. 2 (1986): 181–210.

Patton, Carl V., and David S. Sawicki. *Basic Methods of Policy Analysis and Planning.* 2nd ed. Englewood Cliffs, N.J.: Prentice Hall, 1993.

Patton, Michael Quinn, *Utilization-Focused Evaluation.* 3rd ed. Thousand Oaks, Calif.: Sage, 1997.

Pickrell, Don H. "A Desire Named Streetcar: Fantasy and Fact in Rail Transit Planning." *Journal of the American Planning Association* 58, no. 2 (Spring 1992): 158–176.

Post, Johan, Jaap Broekema, and Nelson Obirih-Opareh. "Trial and Error in Privatisation: Experiences in Urban Solid Waste Collection in Accra (Ghana) and Hyderabad (India)." *Urban Studies* 40, no. 4 (2003): 835–852.

Rietbergen-McCracken, Jennifer, and Deepa Narayan. *Participation and Social Assessment: Tools and Techniques.* Washington, D.C.: International Bank for Reconstruction and Development/World Bank, 1998.

Rist, Ray, and Jody Kusek. "Designing and Building a Performance-Based Monitoring and Evaluation System: A Tool for Managing Projects, Programs, and Policies." Report prepared for the workshop "Government Officials and Their Development Partners." Washington D.C.: World Bank, 2000.

Romanik, Clare, and Raymond Struyk. "Assisting De-Mobilized Russian Officers Obtain Housing: The Housing Certificate Option." *Review of Urban and Regional Development Studies* 7 (1995): 97–118.

Romero, Francine S. "The Policy Analysis Course: Toward a Discipline Consensus." *Journal of Policy Analysis and Management* 20, no. 4 (2001): 771–779.

Rossi, Peter H., Howard E. Freeman, and Mark W. Lipsey. *Evaluation: A Systematic Approach.* 6th ed. Thousand Oaks, Calif.: Sage, 1999.

Roth, Gabriel. *The Private Provision of Public Services in Developing Countries.* Washington, D.C.: Oxford University Press/World Bank, 1987.

Salamon, Lester M., ed. *The Tools of Government: A Guide to the New Governance.* Oxford: Oxford University Press, 2002.

Sammartino, Frank J. "Designing Tax Cuts to Benefit Low-Income Families." *Tax Policy Issues and Options* no. 1 (June 2001). Available online at http://www.urban.org.

Savas, E. S. "Policy Analysis for Local Government: Public vs. Private Refuse Collection." *Policy Analysis* 3 (Winter 1977).

Shah, Anwar. "The Reform of Intergovernmental Fiscal Relations in Developing and Emerging Market Economies." Policy and Research Series no. 23. Washington, D.C.: World Bank, 1994.

Sivaev, Sergei, and Municipal Economics Division. "Analytical Overview: Practice of Reforms of the Housing and Communal Service Sector." Moscow: Institute for Urban Economics, 2003.

Small, Kenneth. "Project Evaluation." In Jose Gomez-Ibanez, William B. Tye, and Clifford

Winston, eds., *Essays in Transportation Economics and Policy.* Washington, D.C.: Brookings Institution, 1999, pp. 137–177.

Stevens, Barbara J. "Scale, Market Structure, and the Cost of Refuse Collection." *Review of Economics and Statistics* 60 (March 1977).

Stokey, Edith, and Richard Zeckhauser. *A Primer for Policy Analysis.* New York: Norton, 1978.

Struyk, Raymond J. "Flood Risk and Agricultural Land Values: A Test." *Water Resources Research* 7, no. 4 (1971): 789–797.

———, ed. "Restructuring Russia's Housing Sector: 1991–1997." Washington, D.C.: Urban Institute, 1997.

Struyk, Raymond J., Karen Angelici, and Marie Tikhomirova. "Private Maintenance for Moscow's Municipal Housing Stock: Does It Work?" *Journal of Housing Economics* 4 (March 1995): 50–70.

Struyk, Raymond J., and Marc Bendick Jr. *Housing Vouchers for the Poor: Lessons from a National Experiment.* Washington, D.C.: Urban Institute, 1981.

Struyk, Raymond J., Lisa Lee, and Alexander Puzanov. "Monitoring Russia's Experience with Housing Allowances." *Urban Studies* 34, no. 11 (November 1997): 1789–1818.

Tata Energy Research Institute. "Report on Regional Environmental Assessment and Social Assessment." Bangalore, India, March 2001.

Ter-Minassian, Teresa, ed. *Fiscal Federalism in Theory and Practice.* Washington, D.C.: International Monetary Fund, 1997.

Turnham, Jennifer, and Jill Khadduri. "Issues and Options for HUD's Tenant-Based Housing Assistance Programs." Report prepared for the Millennial Housing Commission. Cambridge, Mass.: Abt Associates, September 2001.

US Department of Housing and Urban Development. "Manufactured Housing: An Adequate and Affordable Alternative." Washington, D.C.: US Department of Housing and Urban Development, Office of Policy Development and Research, Fall 2002. Available online at http://www.huduser.org/periodicals/ushmc/fall02/summary_2.html (more recent versions of the report may be accessible).

Valadez, Joseph, and Michael Bamberger. *Monitoring and Evaluating Social Programs in Developing Countries: A Handbook for Policymakers, Managers, and Researchers.* Washington, D.C.: World Bank, 1994.

Vittori, Gail, John Ruston, Virginia Jones Smith, and Sally Lewis. *Reducing Houston's Solid Waste: A Plan for the City's Environment and Economy.* Austin, Tex.: Environmental Defense Fund, November 1993.

Weimer, David L., and Aidan R. Vining. *Policy Analysis: Concepts and Practice.* 3rd ed. Upper Saddle River, N.J.: Prentice Hall, 1999.

Weisstein, Eric W. "Bell Curve." Available online at http://mathworld.wolfram.com/bell-curve.html.

World Bank. "Improving Social Assistance in Armenia." Report no. 19385-AM. Washington, D.C.: World Bank, Human Development Unit, Country Department III, Europe and Central Asia Region, June 8, 1999.

———. "Kyrgyz Republic: Enhancing Pro-Poor Growth." Report no. 24638-KG. Washington, D.C.: World Bank, 2003.

———. *Toolkits for Private Sector Participation in Water and Sanitation.* Washington, D.C.: World Bank, 1997.

———. *Transition: The First Ten Years—Analysis and Lessons for Eastern Europe and the Former Soviet Union.* Washington, D.C.: World Bank, 2002.

Index